Consumer Behaviour

Srabanti Mukherjee
Indian Institute of Management Indore

CENGAGE

Andover • Melbourne • Mexico City • Stamford, CT • Toronto • Hong Kong • New Delhi • Seoul • Singapore • Tokyo

CENGAGE Learning

Consumer Behaviour

Srabanti Mukherjee

ISBN-13: 978-81-315-1622-5
ISBN-10: 81-315-1622-9

Registered Office:
Cengage Learning India Private Limited
T-303, 3rd Floor
DAV Complex, Plot 3
Mayur Vihar Phase 1
Delhi-110091
Email: asia.infoindia@cengage.com

Cengage Learning is a leading provider of customized learning solutions with office locations around the globe, including Andover, Melbourne, Mexico City, Stamford (CT), Toronto, Hong Kong, New Delhi, Seoul, Singapore, and Tokyo. Locate your local office at:

www.cengage.com/global

Cengage Learning products are represented in Canada by Nelson Education, Ltd.

For product information, visit **www.cengage.co.in**

Printed in India
Sixth Indian Reprint 2019

Dedicated
to my parents
Reba Mukherjee & Asim Kumar Mukherjee

Contents

Section III Environmental Determinants of Consumer Behaviour

Foreword

'All marketing decisions are based on assumptions and knowledge of consumer behavior'

(Hawkins and Mothersbaugh, 2007)

Marketers have long bickered that the 'marketing concept' is the most suitable philosophy for running a business. To be specific, the marketing concept suggests that for being more commercial, an organization must gratify consumer needs and wants. For marketing to be doing well, it is not enough to merely ascertain what customers require, but also to identify why it is required. Only by gaining a deep and all-inclusive comprehension of buyer behaviour, goals of marketing can be realized. Therefore, all stellar organizations on this earth pivot around the cliché quote of marketing—'The customer is the king'.

This book 'Consumer Behaviour' by Dr. Srabanti Mukherjee provides a thorough analytical insight on various facets of consumer behaviour with special reference to India as well as pan Asia.

Dr. Mukherjee, in the second chapter, has focused on the overall implications of the paradigm shift in demographic, technological, and public policy and the consequent momentous budge in marketing strategies in the present era. She believes that a swing will take place from product orientation to service orientation. All companies will try to put forward safety, quality, and chivalrous competence. Customization will carry on to be a tendency involving customers in the procedure. Expediency and time saving will persist to be a theme of production and consumption. Deliverance of services to the home and business will amplify. Focusing on social and emotional value in promotion will become an important marketing strategy.

In Chapter 3, she has articulated that 'consumerism' is likely to govern the world market in the coming decades, thanks to the liberalization and globalization measures across the globe. A bleak paradigm of this growing consumption results in the excessive exposure to promotional means. The special reference on child consumerism enhances the value of this piece of work. A proper analytical insight on the legal aspects of consumerism in context to India has also been nicely portrayed.

Chapters 4 through 9 in the book nicely reveal the individual determinants of consumer purchase decisions. The author has wonderfully portrayed Maslow's Need Hierarchy. Perhaps, the most interesting part is the depiction of different consumer emotions and needs of Murray and Dichter with suitable real world examples, and glimpses on how they effectually form marketing strategies.

The author, with close-to-real-life opening vignettes and closing cases and several exhibits, jubilantly moves on with the theories of perception, personality, self-concept, learning, attitude, values, and lifestyle.

In Chapters 10 through 12, the author portrays how the environmental determinants of consumer behaviour (culture, reference group, family) influence the buying decision of a consumer in today's competitive scenario. Especially the inclusion of the original research outcome on family buying behaviour of Professor Jagdish Sheth enhances the quality of the work.

Some very relevant real-life survey and observation-based cases have been used to describe the process of diffusion of innovation and the contemporary models of buyer behaviour. The integrated model using all three contemporary models developed by the author is worth mentioning.

The conclusion of the book is really intense with some dimensions on consumer research and some glimpses of the real-life research works across the globe.

Therefore, I trust the book is the 'view from behind the book'. Personally, I really like the way Srabanti Mukherjee illustrates various facets of consumer behaviour. She is conformist about brass tacks, but brave enough to challenge the common presumptions. I have enjoyed reading this book, and I hope you will, too.

Professor Debashis Chatterjee

Director

Indian Institute of Management Kozhikode,

Kerala, India

Preface

'Consumer is the king'—so runs the mantra of marketing in the 21st century. In keeping with this proclamation, it can be stated that since the era of consumer-centric marketing has emerged, the business houses are particularly interested to 'count their chickens' before they hatch. This first edition of 'Consumer Behaviour' is my humble attempt to unveil some of the crucial aspects of the widespread arena of the subject.

I have tried to group and present the various facets of consumer behaviour under four sections.

Section I: This section spans over Chapters 1 to 3 and gives an introduction to consumer behaviour. It encompasses the basic concepts, the changing trends, and the dimensions of consumer behaviour.

In Chapter 1, I have specifically tried to bring out the differences amongst the various buying roles. Emphasis has been laid on distinctive characteristics of Indian consumers. The chapter also portrays how the dynamics of the Indian rural market is changing sharply in terms of brand awareness, consciousness, and brand loyalty. The chapter ends with the elaboration of the simple five-stage consumer decision-making model.

In Chapter 2, I have attempted to showcase the worldwide trend and the implication of those trends in terms of three major consumer roles, namely, the buyer, the payer, and the user. Attention has been given to the post-liberalization changes in consumer behaviour.

The last decade of the 20th century and the dawn of the 21st century have been ushered with a new buzzword, which is expected to reign the entire 21st century, 'consumerism'. In Chapter 3, I have enumerated the roots and dimensions of consumerism. The provisions of Consumer Protection Act (1986) have also been thoroughly mentioned.

Section II: This section of the book is devoted to the individual factors that influence the consumer-decision-making process. Chapter 4 deals with the aspects of motivation. This chapter begins with the simple five-stage Maslow's Need Hierarchy and thereafter, analyzes various customer motives and their influences on consumer's product choice by means of Murray's psychogenic needs and Dichter's consumption needs.

Every information is not processed in consumer's black-box. If the extent, size, and shape of any marketer's provided or environment-generated stimulus falls within the perceptual threshold of the customer, then and only then the process of perception starts. This concept has been elaborated in Chapter 5 with suitable examples.

In Chapter 6, attempt has been made to foresee how personality and self-concepts shape the customer's product choice. Several personality traits and their implications to the marketers have been elaborated in the chapter with the aid of Fruedian and neo-Freudian theories of personality.

On the other hand, Chapter 7 typically focuses on the behavioural and cognitive theories of learning and their implications on the consumer attitude formation. The chapter also portrays how these theories influence the marketing mix strategies by the marketer's of the 21st century, in particular.

A special emphasis has been laid on the attitude formation and measurement in Chapter 8. I have portrayed how the Fishbein model can effectively be used to judge a consumer's choice given a pool of brands in the same product category.

As discussed in Chapter 1, with the opening up of the economy and a radical change in the social structure, lifestyle is perhaps one of the instrumental parameters behind the formation of consumer's perception and attitude. Apart from AIO classification, the original VALS^{TM} typology has been incorporated in Chapter 9. Furthermore, some of the recent researches on lifestyle segmentation of Indian men and women have also been included in the chapter. Even in the Cases section at the end of the book, a real-life study on lifestyle segmentation of Indian urban married women conducted by the Pathfinders has been incorporated.

Section III: In this section, attempt has been made to analyze how the environmental determinants shape consumer choice patterns. Amongst the numerous environmental variables, only three constructs have been addressed in the book, namely, culture, groups (with special emphasis on reference groups), and families. Attention has been paid in particular to identify and analyze the influence of family on the customer's choice process in Chapter 12, with special reference to the original Family-Decision Making Model of Professor Jagdish Sheth.

Section IV: In this section, all the individual and environmental constructs mentioned in the preceding two sections have been used to interpret the process of consumer decision-making. This section is comprised of five chapters: Diffusion of Innovations and Opinion Leadership, Consumer Decision-Making, Models of Consumer Behaviour, Organizational Buying Behaviour, and Dimensions of Consumer Research.

Chapter 13 showcases the steps involved in adopting a new product. Customers are grouped into various segments depending on their readiness to adopt any new product/brand.

In Chapter 14, Phillip Kotler's simple black-box model of consumer decision-making has been discussed with suitable examples. Special emphasis has been given to discuss the part of choice heuristics by customers. It has been shown how with the change of the heuristics method the preference of the customer does vary.

In Chapter 15, the well established and coveted models of consumer behaviour have been enumerated. These models have been categorized as traditional and contemporary models. The traditional models are essentially the economic models, be it the Marshallian microeconomic model based on the law of diminishing marginal utility or the macroeconomic models by Milton Friedman (Permanent Income Hypothesis) or James Duesenberry (Relative Income Hypothesis). On the other hand, five most coveted contemporary models (amongst a large pool of such models) are analyzed in the chapter along with their critical evaluation. These models are namely, Andreason model, Nicosia model, Howard–Sheth model, Engel–Kollat–Miniard model, and Sheth–Newman–Gross model. A real-world empirical research conducted by Sagnik Maitra, one of my students, to elucidate the assumptions of the Howard–Sheth model has also been incorporated in the chapter to make it comprehensible for the readers.

Classification, characteristics, and the pattern of demand of the industrial market have been illustrated in Chapter 16. Apart from that, the process of industrial buying has been presented in a simplified manner with the help of a flowchart.

Chapter 17 vividly illustrates the process of consumer research.

Each chapter in this book starts with a typical opening vignette to portray the relevance of the concepts discussed in the chapter. To reinforce the learning outcomes, each chapter ends with a closing case to provide food for thought on the concepts enumerated in the chapter. Apart from these, at the end of the book, there is a section on cases to address the entire gamut of consumer behaviour in general. These cases have been formulated by myself and other acclaimed academicians and corporate leaders. I have tried to provide a systematic insight into various facets of consumer behaviour with special reference to India as well as pan Asia.

I hope this book will serve its purpose and students in various universities and B-schools in India will find it useful. Please do share your feedback and/or suggestion. These will help me make amendments to the content and improvements in subsequent editions.

Srabanti Mukherjee

Acknowledgements

I consider myself extremely blessed as the Almighty has provided me the opportunity to pen down whatever little I know in the arena of consumer behaviour and has bestowed me with strength and willpower to successfully complete the book.

First and foremost, I am indebted to my parents who stood beside me in all evens and odds of life and provided consistent support and encouragement to develop this book.

I would like to convey my heartfelt regards and gratitude to my well-wisher Professor Debashis Chatterjee, Director IIM Kozhikode, for providing the foreword of the book.

I would also like to thank Ms. Carrie Hollenberg of Strategic Business Insights, USA, to permit me to use VALS™ typology to define several lifestyles mentioned in Chapter 9. I convey my deep regards to Professor Jagdish Sheth, Charles H. Kellstadt, Chair of Marketing in the Goizueta Business School at Emory University, for kindly allowing me to incorporate the original diagram of Family-Decision-Making in this book in Chapter 12. I am highly indebted to Mr. Sankara Pillai, Mentor QED Research (former Head Quantitative Research in Pathfinders), for providing the case 'Mrs. Urban India—A Business Opportunity Waiting' based on the original research findings of Pathfinders. My sincere thanks to Mr. Thamer I. al-Fassam, Academic Publishing Department, General Directorate for Academic Publishing and Press, King Saud University, for providing help in finding out the relevant data for Chapter 15.

I cordially thank my friend and ex-colleague Dr. Archana Sharma (Sr. Lecturer, IISWBM, Kolkata) for her consistent support throughout the project and for providing cases for the book. I express my heartfelt gratitude to my friends Dr. Ramendra Singh (Assistant Professor, IIM Calcutta), Dr. Jayashree Dubey (Assistant Professor, Indian Institute of Forest Management, Bhopal), and my ex-student Debanjan Guha (Manager Space, *The Indian Express*, Kolkata) for contributing cases for Section V provided at the end of the book. I would like to thank my ex-students Aritri Banerjee and Sagnik Maitra for incorporating their original research findings (under my supervision) in the book.

I sincerely acknowledge the initiatives and support from the entire editorial team of Cengage Learning India in the process of completion of this book.

Last but not the least, I thank all my students, friends, and relatives who provided me a convenient ambience to bring my project to its successful end.

Srabanti Mukherjee

Section I

Introduction to Consumer Behaviour

Chapter 1

Introduction

Chapter Goals

After completing this chapter, you will be able to understand

- the nature and scope of consumer behaviour
- application of consumer behaviour principles to strategic marketing
- characteristics of consumers worldwide
- special characteristics of Indian consumers
- distinctive characteristics of Indian rural customers
- four views of consumer decision making—economic man, cognitive man, emotional man, passive man
- simple five-stage consumer decision process

Opening Vignette

Discovering Fortune at the Bottom of the Pyramid—Project Shakti

The Indian rural market, with its vast size and demand base, offers enormous prospects to marketers today. Seventy-five percent of the country's populace resides in the rural expanses and almost half of the national income is generated from here. Hence it is imperative that rural markets constitute a significant part of the total market of India. Our nation spans around 640 districts and approximately 6,30,000 villages, which can be classified by different parameters such as literacy levels, accessibility, income levels, product penetration, distances from the nearest towns, etc. Nevertheless, the success of a brand in the Indian rural market is as capricious as the monsoon in Bengal. Many brands, which were tipped to be successful, failed miserably. Not surprisingly, many people attribute the success of a brand in the rural market to luck. However, marketers need to understand the social dynamics and attitude variations of the Indian villagers.

Nowadays, the socio-cultural and economic dynamics of rural India are changing. According to a corporate estimate, the disposable income spent on fast moving consumer goods (FMCG) by urban India was ₹49,500 crore as compared to ₹63,500 crore in rural India at the turn of this Century. The Indian rural market has been growing at 3–4% per annum, adding more than 1 million new consumers every year. It roughly constitutes about 50% of the volume consumption of FMCG in India. But, the rural market is scattered and the conventional hub-and-spoke distribution model, which is effective in urban and semi-urban markets, is not cost-effective in penetrating the smaller villages. Keeping this fact in consideration, FMCG giant Hindustan Unilever embarked on an ambitious venture called *Project Shakti* in 2003 to spur growth and penetration of its products in rural India while changing lives and boosting incomes.

Project Shakti, HUL

By means of blending micro-credit and training in venture management in this project, women from rural self-help groups (SHGs) were drafted as direct-to-home distributors of a lower price range products, such as soaps, shampoos, and detergents to help the company to penetrate hitherto untapped markets.

Outlining the business model, a senior company official explained that the company's objectives of *Project Shakti* were to form income-generating capabilities for underprivileged rural women by providing a sustainable micro-enterprise opportunity, to generate more income in the hands of rural families and perk up the purchase range of daily consumption products—from soaps to toothpastes. A woman from an SHG selected as a *Shakti* entrepreneur collects stocks at her doorway from the HUL rural distributor and sells door-to-door directly to the consumers as well as to the retailers in the village. Each *Shakti* entrepreneur serves 6–10 villages with a populace of 1,000–2,000 people. The *Shakti* entrepreneurs initially start with 4–5 budget brands from the company portfolio—*Lifebuoy*, *Wheel*, *Pepsodent*, *Annapurna* salt, and *Clinic Plus*. According to the company official, 'These are the core brands. Then we layer these with whatever else is in demand like talcum powder or vaseline during winters'. Normally, unit packs are small, mainly sachets. The company's intention here is to generate a rural-specific national brand so that the advertising media effort for the brands is dispelled.

By the end of 2009, there were more than 45,000 *Shakti* entrepreneurs covering 3 million homes in 100,000 villages in 15 states in India. According to Mart, a knowledge based consultancy organization on emerging markets, specially base of pyramid segments, 'the project has emerged as a win-win model for all—the company has penetrated deeper into smaller village markets generating hundreds of crores of rupees of additional sales revenue annually while the women earn a monthly profit of around ₹1,000 on a regular basis and are today more empowered.' The project has also enabled the government to provide more employment opportunities and banks are able to disburse more funds under priority sector lending.

'We are rolling out similar initiatives in Sri Lanka and Bangladesh,' a company report said. Buoyed by the success of *Project Shakti*, the company has engaged about 20,000 '*shaktimaans*' and equipped them with bicycles to distribute its products in 2,00,000 villages in the Indian hinterland. Acknowledging that good roads and geographical information systems (GIS), which enables them to keep track of the cycles, have helped them embark on this initiative, the company said it aims to employ 75,000 *Shakti* entrepreneurs by 2015.

Hence, knowing your consumers is extremely important!

Source: Kamath, Vinay, Where HLL's Shakti comes from, *The HinduBusinessline*, May 29, 2003, www.thehindubusinessline.com/catalyst/2003/05/29/stories/2003052900020100.htm; Women micro-entrepreneurs project takes on men to reach more villages, http://www.sustainable-living.unilever.com/news-resources/news/better-livelihoods/shakti-men/, accessed on September 6, 2011; HLL project Shakti, http://www.martrural.com/corporate_pilot_implementation.htm, accessed on September 6, 2011.

INTRODUCTION

The task of marketing is to identify consumers' needs and wants accurately and then develop products and services that will satisfy those needs and wants. Starting with the 1990s, more and more organizations have recognized that satisfying consumers with quality products and offering superior services are the foundations for success in highly competitive markets.

Marketers often argue that the concept of marketing is the appropriate philosophy for running a business. The marketing concept suggests that in order to be more profitable, an organization must satisfy its consumer's needs and wants. To implement the marketing concept, organizations must understand and stay close to their customers and provide them with products and services that suit their needs as well as budget. For marketing to be doing well, it is not sufficient to simply ascertain what customers require, but also to recognize why it is required. It has been said that by gaining a profound and all-embracing comprehension of buyer behaviour, the goals of marketing can be realized. Such an indulgent buyer behaviour works as the shared advantage of the consumer and the marketer, allowing the marketer to become better equipped to gratify the consumer's needs professionally and institute a loyal group of customers with positive attitudes towards the company's products.

Today many of the world's most booming companies have planned their entire organizations' effort to serve and stay in proximity to consumers. These companies are steadfast to develop quality products and services and sell them at a price that offers consumers value for money. In these booming companies, not only the marketing department, but also the design, engineering, production, human resources, finance, and other departments focus on doing their jobs in ways that augment the value of their products for consumers. Some firms perk up the product quality and trim down the costs at the same time. Other firms first determine what the consumers want and how much they are ready to pay and accordingly formulate their strategies.

But why are the firms so concerned to serve the consumers well? This is perhaps, because of the remarkable success of Japanese companies such as *Toyota* and *Sony*, which focus on providing value-driven products to their customers. The second reason for a shift to focus on the consumers is the boost in the quality of consumer and marketing research. Today, computer technology, scanner, and other data sources have made it possible for firms to know who their customers are and how their marketing strategy changes impinge on them. Both the manufacturers and retailers now have easier ways to track the consumer reactions to new products and services and to appraise their marketing strategies better than ever before.

In short, many successful companies understand the importance of consumers, and use different approaches and detailed data to build their organizational and marketing strategies. Thus, consumer behaviour has emerged as a new subject. Consumer behaviour refers to those acts of individuals that are directly involved in obtaining and using economic goods and services, including the decision processes that precede and determine these acts.

WHO IS A CONSUMER?

Researchers have borrowed ideas from diverse fields including economics, psychology, social psychology, sociology, and cultural anthropology to comprehend consumer behaviour. A fair insight into consumer behaviour is derived from hardcore field sales experience. Valuable information has been obtained from all the afore-mentioned areas, but no single approach is sufficient to explain a consumer purchase process. In many cases, ideas borrowed from different areas overlie and even race with each other as useful descriptions of consumers. Till date, no single approach is wholly accepted. A single, all-embracing definition of consumer behaviour that everyone accepts is unlikely to be devised. Even though an inclusive definition of consumer behaviour may not be possible, marketers need to have a somewhat generalised framework for studying and understanding consumers. A consumer is a person or an organizational unit playing the role of consumption in the process of transaction with the marketer or an entity. The term consumer refers to both the household and the business markets within this context.

The term consumer also has many variations that are used interchangeably. But this could create confusion. A common confusion in this respect is the difference between the terms consumer and buyer, which are very often substituted for each other.

A consumer is a person who actually consumes the product, i.e., the user of the product, whereas a buyer buys the product and the payer pays for the purchase.

The five main buying roles are as follows:

1. The initiator—the person who decides to start the buying process.
2. The influencer—the person who tries to convince others that they need the product.
3. The decider—the person who makes the final decision to purchase.
4. The buyer—the person who is going to write you the cheque.
5. The user—the person who ends up using your product, whether he had a say in the buying process or not.

Multiple roles can be performed by the same person or by different individuals. Let us be a bit specific. Suppose that Mr. Sharma pays his wife ₹250 to buy a school bag for their son Rahul who studies in the VI standard. Here, Mr. Sharma is the payer, his wife is the buyer, and Rahul is the consumer. On the contrary, if Mr. Sharma buys a packet of cigarette for his own consumption, he plays the roles of payer, buyer, and consumer alone.

THE RELEVANCE OF SEGMENTATION IN TERMS OF CONSUMER BEHAVIOUR

Market segmentation is one of the most significant concepts in consumer behaviour and marketing literature. A primary reason for studying consumer behaviour is to identify bases for effective segmentation. Hence, a large portion of consumer research is concerned with segmentation. Selecting a suitable target market is a prerequisite for developing an effective marketing strategy.

The need for segmentation results from disparity among people. If all humans were identical in their preferences and behaviours, market segmentation would not be needed. Because people differ so much in their motivations, needs, decision processes, and buying behaviours, the products ideally would be tailored to each user to give maximum contentment to them.

Earlier, many marketers focused on target markets in an all-purpose, non-personal way. But today enhanced methods of marketing research and efficient computers that can handle large databases give the marketers a detailed personal information on many members of their target market. This facilitates the firm to target appropriate and profitable segments to market its products. Thus, market segmentation can be defined as the process of dividing a market into groups of individuals with homogenous needs.

The first job involved in segmenting the markets is analyzing consumer/product relationships. This necessitates analysis of the affect and cognitions, behaviours and environments involved in the purchase/consumption process of a particular product. Managers have three general views regarding this task. They may come up with a product concept and consider what types of consumers are likely to buy and use the product and how they might vary from those less likely to buy.

The second task of the marketers is to decide the relevant bases for segmenting the markets. Figure 1.1 highlights the various bases used for market segmentations.

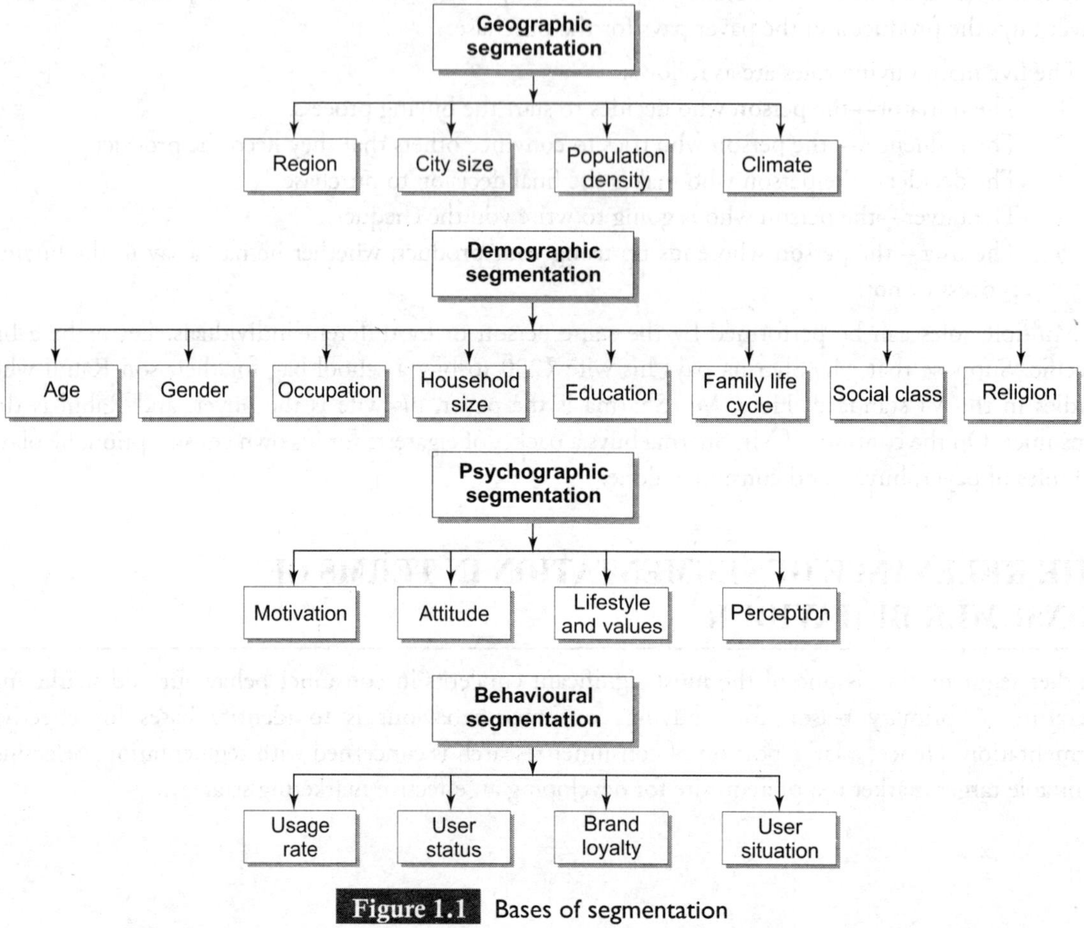

Figure 1.1 Bases of segmentation

The third task of the marketers is to choose a suitable segmentation strategy. Determining the magnetism of a market segment involves analyzing segments based on the following four criteria:

- *Measurability* It refers to the ability of the firm to obtain information about the size, nature, and behaviour of a market segment.
- *Accessibility* It is the degree to which the targeted segments can be reached.
- *Sustainability* It refers to the size of the market, i.e., whether the segment can generate adequate volume of sales for its feasibility or not.
- *Congruity* It refers to how similar the members within the segment are in terms of behaviours or characteristics that correlate with the behaviour.

In conclusion, segmentation methods and strategies continue to be fine-tuned by the marketers. Over a period, branded by increasing market diversity resulting in market fragmentation, segmentation strategy, based on data mining and customized manufacturing technology, allows firms to reach lesser but potentially more profitable segments.

DEFINING CONSUMER BEHAVIOUR

Consider a lady who regularly buys a particular fairness cream *Fair and Lovely*. To retain her as a potential customer, the marketer must understand why she uses a fairness cream: to retain fairness or to make her complexion fairer within two weeks (as advertised), which brand of fairness cream does she buy, why does she buy it (she probably thinks that it will give her the best results in terms of fairness as compared to other competing brands), when does she buy it (when she does the shopping for other items), from where does she buy it (the local grocery shop or a shopping mall), and how frequently does she procure it (once in two weeks).

Consumer behaviour has traditionally been thought of as the study of 'why people buy', with the premise that it becomes easier to develop strategies to influence consumers once a marketer knows why people buy certain products or brands.

Engel *et al.* defined consumer behaviour as 'those acts of individuals directly involved in obtaining, using, and disposing of economic goods and services including the decision process that precedes and determines those acts'.

Schiffman and Kanuk defined consumer behaviour as the behaviour that consumers display in searching for, purchasing, using, evaluating, and disposing of products, services, and ideas which they expect will satisfy their needs.

In short, the study of consumer behaviour provides an eye opening lesson regarding an individual's decision making to optimize utility from consumption with available resources (money, time, and effort). In other words, the study of consumer behaviour answers the following questions—*what they buy, why they buy it, how they buy it, when they buy it, where they buy it, and how often they buy it.*

NATURE AND SCOPE OF CONSUMER BEHAVIOUR

Consumer behaviour is a relatively new field of study developed in the mid-to-late 1960s. The study of consumer behaviour encompasses not only why consumers make decisions to buy goods and services, but also all the behaviours that consumers display in searching for, purchasing, using, evaluating, and disposing of products and services that they expect will satisfy their needs. Hence in short:

- Consumer behaviour may relate to the behaviour of an individual or a group (e.g., a classmate's influence on the choice of a mobile model) or an organization (say an MNC purchases 30 *Maruti Swift* cars for the official use of its executives).
- The implications of the study of consumer behaviour on society are worth mentioning. For example, aggressive marketing of junk foods resulting in obesity or by hook or crook type promotion of easy credit schemes, may have serious repercussions on national health and economy. In fact, the global economic crunch was triggered by the US home loan segment. Sometimes improper product disposal (e.g., using non-regulated oil for autos, garbage piling up on landfills, industrial effluents being drained into rivers creating water pollution) may pose serious environmental hazards. This is also an area of concern.
- The knowledge of consumer's needs, wants, attitude, and beliefs helps firms to improvise their marketing strategies by understanding issues such as how the consumers think, feel, comprehend, and select amongst various competing brands; how they are influenced by their environment (e.g., culture, family, signs, media); what is the pattern of shopping behaviour they are exposed to; what are their motivational parameters; and how their decision strategies vary across products that differ in their perceived level of importance. These understandings help the marketers to adapt and improve their marketing campaigns and strategies so as to more efficiently reach the consumer.

Consumer behaviour is all about understanding how consumers think, feel, comprehend, and select amongst various competitive brands

CHANGING CHARACTERISTICS OF CONSUMERS WORLDWIDE

The consumers of 21st century have evolved considerably from their counterparts of the 1960s.The joint family systems are breaking up, religious ethos have loosened their gallows and as a result of all these, consumers are becoming more pragmatic. Consumerism is at full throttle, and attention towards fitness and individual self is at its peak. The following trends emphasize these facets.

From Collectivism to Individualism

Apart from the jugglery of status needs, the consumers of these days have evolved in two directions—individuality and experience—from an era of affiliation to individualism. Consumption in conventional marketing scenario earlier implied family phenomenon taking care of husband/children/wife/family/friends/etc. Advertisements were accordingly focused upon. Conversely, present outlook has swerved towards individual consumption suggesting that consumers nowadays are more and more pragmatic and individualistic. The concepts of collective thinking and social or religious ideologies are gradually losing their relevance in today's marketing scenario.

Concomitant of Changing Demographics Trade Up and Trade Down

Another interesting fact is highly visible, in particular, in case of the Asian consumers. The same consumer exhibits extreme price sensitivity for the functional product (normally of low perceived differentiation such as soaps) on one hand, and an amazingly premium for the other (normally of high perceived differentiation such as white goods). Asian luxury products market is forecasted to become the leading one in the world in the forthcoming days.

Health and Wellness Consideration

Health products and supplements are some of the most publicized products all over the world. The prevalent diseases of these days viz. obesity, pulmonary problems, diabetes, blood pressure, etc. demand adequate exercise and fitness training. Health clubs and fitness centres have mushroomed across Asia and Europe.

Consumer Assertiveness

Customers nowadays are becoming more and more demanding. In Italy, a considerable part of the final consumption is represented by domestic consumption, which attained 76.2% of the total consumption basket in 1998. Within this category of consumption, rise is observed in sectors such as clothing and shoes (with figures of 9.9% and 9.7% in 1994 and 1998, respectively), transport (12.5% and 13.3% and expanding), furniture, household appliances, and house maintenance (9.5% and 9.6%), recreation and culture (7.4% and 7.6%), housing, water, electricity, gas and other fuels (19.6% and 19.2%).

A fitness club: Demand for exercise and fitness training has spawned health clubs across Asia and Europe.

Online Shopping

Online shopping is in boom. An online shop (e.g., e-shop, e-store, Internet shop, Web shop, Web store, online store, or virtual store) calls for the physical analogy of purchasing goods at a bricks-and-mortar retailer or in a shopping mall. Majority of big stores, nowadays, have retail Web sites, including those that do or do not have physical storefronts and paper catalogues. Online shopping is a type of electronic commerce which can be used for both business-to-business (B2B) and business-to-consumer (B2C) transactions. Some popular shopping sites are www.amazon.com, www.ebay.com, www.shopsland.org, etc.

Exhibit 1.1 Value Vaulters—A New Phenomenon

A new phenomenon of 'value vaulters' has come up with most of the FMCG companies as an effect of escalating their rigorous promotions on premium products. Value vaulters are consumers opting for novel

(Contd.)

Exhibit 1.1 *(Contd.)*

brands and products even at a premium price owing to the boom of variety and enticements like aggressive promotional offers. This may appear as an immense opportunity for the FMCG brands to upgrade their consumers to premium segments and as a consequence augment revenues. Nonetheless, many marketing experts opine that this upsurge can just be a temporary phenomenon among those consumers who may not bond to these premium-priced brands if their perceived value-for-money is not obtained.

The recent drift of value vaulting consumers can be measured from the flood of new brands in the market place, most of which are in the key premium categories like breakfast cereals, liquid utensil cleaner, liquid handwash, and skin creams. According to the acclaimed market research agency, *Nielsen*, in the year 2010 (data up to October), 137 brands were introduced in the breakfast cereals category which has increased from the last year's number 113. The situation is much alike in the skin cream segment too where the number of new brands was 562 compared to 420 in last year. Most interestingly, even in the category of liquid utensil cleaners, it was 59 as compared to the last year's figure of 43.

FMCGs flooding the market with premium brands to target value vaulting consumers

Basically, in the arena of consumer products three broad promotion strategies are emerging, namely the volume promotion, value promotion, and kind promotion. Volume promotion concept is quite similar to that of quantity discounts while the value promotion is parallel to the price discounts. On the other hand, the kind promotion refers to the offers of freebies or any other free gifts provided with a certain amount of purchase.

(Contd.)

Exhibit 1.1 *(Contd.)*

It is interesting to mention that in the year ending October 2010, there were 258 kind promotions for the skincare creams, which shows a consistent increase from the last year's figure of 140. On the contrary, volume promotions have become almost double as compared to the last year's figure.

These recent developments signify that consumers, though, elevate through the value chain but not essentially boost consumption till the penetration level is within their perceptual threshold.

This, as a result, emerges as the key driver of premiumization, especially among consumer segments who are enthusiastic to indulge into premium purchase and are not very conservative. For instance, *Marico*'s *Saffola*, the cholesterol-free edible oil, has digged out steady profit due to this upsurge of value vaulters. Looking at this Mr. Saugata Gupta, CEO (consumer products division), *Marico*, commented that 'The biggest trends in FMCG would be in personal care and value-added foods. Any category that drives wellness, convenience, and beauty will be ripe for premiumization.'

The spreading out of modern trade coupled with rigorous promotion and intensive distribution has given birth to the trend of specially the routine-response products (like ready-to-eat foods, soups, breakfast cereals, fruit juices, and dairy derivatives) owing to the inclination of the modern customers to flow with the fitness beacons.

Source: Singh, Namrata, Value vaulters emerge as companies push for premium products, TNN, *The Times of India*, April 23, 2011.

CHARACTERISTICS OF INDIAN CONSUMERS

India is a huge country with 28 states, over one billion population, and more than 120 dialect/languages.

From the market point of view, the country consists of diverse segments of consumers, depending on various social classes, place of inhabitancy, caste, race, and various other spectra. Among the total 164.8 million domestic units in India, 80.7 million constitutes the bottom of the pyramid (<US$ 581), followed by 50.4 million lower middle-income households (US$ 581–1162), 19.7 million middle-income group (US$ 1162–1190), 8.2 million upper middle-income group (US$ 1790–2465), and 5.8 million high-income group (>US$ 2465).*

Different Segments of Indian Consumers

The Indian market can be divided into four major segments to better understand the Indian consumers, according to a study on consumer behaviour in the country, done by MATRADE, the national trade promotion agency of Malaysia in 2005. The four segments are the socialites, conservatives, working ladies, and the Indian rich.

**Source*: Product market study: Consumer behaviour in India, MATRADE Chennai, 2005.

The Socialites

The Indian upper class has been analyzed in the said study under the nomenclature of the socialites. These groups, due to their affluence, are frequent visitors of shopping malls, departmental stores, multiplexes, and are usually more focused on purchasing luxury items. The highly brand-conscious socialites always look for exclusive items like boutiques.

Inox forum: Catering to the brand conscious socialites

The Conservatives

The Indian middle class, the beholders of true face of Indian culture and heritage are named as the conservatives. These traditionalists are relatively much more price sensitive than the socialites. They are more family-oriented and are cautious shoppers. Being risk averse, they focus more on savings than spending. They weigh the durability and functional attributes of the product more than the style and design. This turns them to slow diffusers to any kind of innovation in the market place. They are very sensitive about the social need and hence, are quite conscious about their self-image.

The Working Ladies

This group constitutes a large number of working women. This category had undergone a tremendous escalation in the late 1990s. The pressure of both office and household work puts them in tremendous time crunch. This has reduced their time for household activities and has raised the demand for crèches, washing machines, microwave ovens, cell phones, home deliveries, budget cars, etc.

Working women look for options to help them in the household activities

Indian Rich

India's rich can be further divided into five major categories as follows:

The rich According to the study, the Indian rich with an income more than US$ 11,000 per annum is very much upwardly mobile. The number of households in this category is nearly one crore. They squander more on leisure and entertainment items rather than on future looking nest eggs. Luxurious resorts or deluxe hotels in lonely places, like The *Radisson* in Raichak and the *Vedic Village Resorts*, mainly target these sort of customers.

© Indiatodayimages.com

Vedic Village Resorts and Spa in Rajarhat, Kolkata—targeting the Indian rich

The super rich The super rich have income greater than US$ 22,000 per annum. Total number of super rich families in India exceeds three lakh. They are mostly modern professionals with high inclination towards consumerism. They often buy a number of durables and are quite sensitive about their status.

The ultra rich Indians with earnings of more than US$ 44,000 per annum can be demarcated as ultra rich. The number of ultra rich families in India is quite meager (approximately a lakh some six years ago). Some middle-level managers or the first generation industrialists are the visible entities in this cluster. Some rich farmers of Punjab and Haryana also belong to this category.

The sheer rich Households crossing the income slab of US$ 110,000 per annum are known as sheer rich. However, in India hardly 20,000 families fall into this category. They do portray similar silhouettes as the ultra rich, although the extent varies. They look for possessing different brands of cars. They like to own houses and apartments in various posh locations of the country and abroad. They desire social status and power.

The obscenely rich In India, around 6000 households having an income of more than US$ 222,000 per annum constitute this cluster. They are mainly the first-generation entrepreneurs or technocrats. These people are equivalent to the moneyed class in the first world countries. They yearn for elitism in every purchase. Designer dresses, special diamond-studded watches, exclusive platinum jewelry are some of the products especially targeted towards them. The event management of marriage of the daughter of steel tycoon Lakshmi Mittal is one such service.

Mercedes Benz—Targeting the obscenely rich

Indian Rural Consumers of 21st Century

The vast hinterland of rural India allures interesting opportunities for marketers in 21st century. Given that the vast majority of the country's populace resides in villages, it is not at all surprising that almost half of the national income is generated from here. Therefore, the significance of rural consumers while analyzing Indian consumer behaviour is worth mentioning. Nonetheless, the accomplishment of a brand in the Indian rural market is quite uncertain, as understanding the motivational parameters of rural consumers has never been easy. Marketers need to understand the social dynamics and attitude variations within each village even though nationally it follows some common trait, as we saw in the opening vignette on HUL's *Project Shakti*.

The rural demand for consumer goods is often a derived one and is a function of agricultural inputs. Furthermore, as the agri-inputs largely depend on monsoons and other factors, the rural demand is often a fluctuating one. Nonetheless, there has been a perceptible change in the purchasing pattern of the Indian villager, which we will study in the following section.

Change in Purchasing Pattern

The rural consumers are evolving at a very fast rate not only in quantitative but also in qualitative terms. The rural consumption-basket these days is full of the so-called urban categories of products. Especially, the upper segments are buying some most contemporary range of products that were beyond the imagination of yesteryears villagers. Following a study by Rajesh Shukla, Director, National Council for Applied Economic Research (NCAER), it may be argued that the 'middle-income and above' households in the rural areas are supposed to experience a massive growth from 77 million in 2001 to 151 million in 2015. On the contrary, in urban India the projection for such rise is from 46 million to 87 million. Shukla's study is quite in line with the projection of a senior HUL official in the opening vignette. He had claimed that the disposable income spent on fast moving consumer goods (FMCG) by urban India is just ₹49,500 crore as compared to ₹63,500 crore in rural India.

A study on ownership of goods in rural India points to a similar trend. It categorizes all the consumer durable products generally opted by the rural customers into three distinct groups: (1) necessary products—cooking gas, bicycle/moped, etc.; (2) emerging products—cheaper mobile handsets; and (3) lifestyle products—CTV and refrigerators. Nonetheless, consumer durables continue to attribute just over 3% of the overall consumption basket in rural India. But with the rural–urban cultural mix due to frequent urban migration by the rural family members, the demand for durables is likely to be far more augmented in another five years down the line.

However, while talking about FMCG brands, it was quite clear that the extremely price-sensitive rural consumers prefer small consumption packages. Some companies have addressed this issue of price-sensitivity and affordability by introducing unitary packs or sachets. Hindustan Unilever was among the pioneering MNCs to capitalize the latent potential of India's rural market. They launched a variant of its largest selling soap brand, *Lifebuoy*, at ₹2 for 50 gm primarily targeted at the rural market and the bottom of the pyramid market as whole. *Coca-Cola* also responded to the price-sensitivity issue by launching '*Chhota Coke*' (200 ml) for ₹5. This effort of *Coca-Cola* paid so well that today, 80% of the new drinkers of '*Chhota Coke*' are from the rural network. Keeping this success in consideration, *Coca-Cola* has also introduced *Sunfill*, a powdered soft-drink concentrate. The instant and ready-to-mix *Sunfill* is available in a single-serve sachet of 25 gm priced at ₹2 and a multi-serve sachet of 200 gm priced at ₹15.

The instant and ready-to-mix *Sunfill* is available in single-serve and multi-surve sachets

Godrej also responded to this change in the rural market scenario with its recent launch of the three brands of *Cinthol*, *Fair Glow*, and *Godrej No. 1* in 50-gm packs, priced at ₹4–5 targeted towards the so-called 'Bimaru states' (viz. Bihar, Madhya Pradesh, Rajsthan and Uttar Pradesh).

Reasons Behind the Diversification of Rural Demand

An extensive and varied gamut of parameters determining the tastes and lifestyles of the rural market segment are responsible for the drastic change in the rural market scenario.

Increase in the agricultural output The growing emphasis on mechanized farming along with liberal government policies in the form of subsidies and supportive pricing strategies helped to augment the untaxed farm incomes. Furthermore, an estimated infusion of ₹140 billion and ₹300 billion in the rural sector through various government-run rural development schemes in the seventh and the eighth plans, respectively also made a significant impact on the rapid growth in rural demand for emerging and lifestyle products.

Growth in education The literacy rate in rural India is also on the rise. It may be recalled that just about a decade ago, the literacy rate in rural India was only 20%. However, the recent phenomenon is strikingly different with about eight million people getting added to the literacy bracket in rural India every year. With this decent growth, the knowledge about various products has increased among them. This, in turn, has resulted in amplified consumption habit of the rural middle class.

Exposure to mass media The persistent economic growth of 5.5% per year in the 1980s followed by the era of liberalization in the early 1990s exposed the rural upper and middle class consumers to the goods and quality they had been yearning for. Growth and spread of the cable network as well as the

DTH services, which are getting cheaper day-by-day, has contributed to enhanced awareness among rural consumers. The extensive reach of electronic media has made the job of the marketers to position their brand in rural India much easier. However, the traditional campaigning through fairs, festivals, *haats*, etc. is still used for brand communication. Sometimes, sticking posters in video parlours, cinema vans, shop walls, walls of houses, offices, community hand-pumps, walls of wells, trees around the ponds are very common contemporary practices to increase brand and pack visibility. Personal care items like *Lux*, *Lifebuoy*, and detergents like *Rin*, *Wheel*, have become quite popular with such campaigns.

© Indiatodayimages.com

Reach of electronic media in villages

Changes in pricing and the distribution channel In rural India, there are over 3.8 million estimated retail outlets (e.g. hut, a shack, a stall, or a store) across nearly 600,000 villages. Looking at the huge potentiality in the rural market, some of the FMCG marketers are coming up with innovative ideas for product distribution. One may recall the *e-choupal* (the agribusiness supply chain) of ITC Ltd. or the Project Shakti initiative (refer to the Opening Vignette) of Hindustan Unilever Limited in this context. While ITC focused on modernizing the agribusiness supply chain by extensive use of e-commerce, HUL has adopted the 'value co-creation' model by generating 'social entrepreneurship' as well as augmenting the distribution channels in rural India.

Growing interaction with urban consumers Owing to the boom in urban immigration of the educated youngsters of rural India in recent years, MNCs have realized that both the rural and urban markets are experiencing some sort of convergence in aspirations. Lot of people with rural backgrounds today work in urban banks and other government agencies in the cities. There they are exposed to their urban counterparts. Migration in search of jobs by the rural people is another crucial factor. While going back home, they generally carry some part of the urban lifestyle which they have picked up.

Even the farmers 'keep in touch' with the latest information to maximize profit from their produce at both ends. In this context, one may recall the *Kisan Mobile Sandesh* (KMS) effort by *Krishi Vigyan Kendra* (KVK), Madhya Pradesh. Through this system, the KVK provides updated agricultural information to farmers and other field workers to facilitate the farmers diffuse the technological interventions at a steady pace.

Marketers who feel the pulse of the rural consumer and fine-tune their strategy accordingly are sure to reap benefits in the coming years. In fact, leadership in any product or service is linked to the leadership in the rural India except for few lifestyle products, which depend mainly on the urban consumer.

THE APPLICATION OF CONSUMER BEHAVIOUR PRINCIPLES TO MARKETING

The ultimate aim of any business is to create and retain customers. This can be done by providing enhanced value to the customer as compared to its competitors. The study of consumer behaviour constantly appraises the target segments and focuses on customization of the products and services so as to provide better value to them ('competitive advantage'). The main problem with this process relates to the constantly changing 'environment' in which businesses operate. So a business must acclimatize to reflect changes in the environment and customize decisions about how to amend the marketing mix to adjust with the change. This course of adapting and decision-making is commonly referred to as marketing planning.

Consumer behaviour plays a pivotal role in strategic planning in terms of comprehending and managing the links between a business and its environment. However, well-organized marketing planning is required considering the challenge faced by marketing managers in multinational companies with hundreds of business units situated across the globe with a wide range of product offerings. The primary task of the marketing managers is to control and serve the consumers. The aim is to develop a steady marketing mix where all elements work together to serve the target market or markets which the company has chosen. Each of the marketing mix elements involves many decisions, and analysis of consumers which can help the marketers take the decisions more effectively for achieving company's objectives. Let us examine each of them separately.

Product

Marketing questions in this area include issues such as the following.

- What task does this product or service dish up for the consumers in a target market? And what does it signify to them?

- What attributes or features of the product are most significant to the target market?
- What types of packaging and labeling information would best attract consumers and persuade them to purchase the product?
- What brand name and trademark for the product would generate the appropriate image in the target market?
- What kinds of pre- or post sales services would gratify consumers in the target market?
- How many models, variations, or sizes of the product are needed to gratify various target markets?

While this list is not exhaustive, it shows that many product decisions depend on the comprehension of consumers in various target markets.

Price

Price is what consumers must give up to purchase a product. Marketing issues in this area are as follows.

- How much are the consumers in a target market ready to pay for a particular product?
- What price would consumers in this market judge this product is of worth?
- What do specific prices correspond to consumers about the quality of a particular product?
- If the price of a product were lowered in the short run, would consumers carry on to buy the product when it reverts to full price?
- Would consumers stop purchasing the product if the price were increased enduringly?
- How significant is price to consumers in an extremely price-sensitive target market?

Whether a company is introducing a new product or planning a short-term or long-term price-change, it needs to examine how the consumers will react to the price variable.

Promotion

Promotion refers to the variety of ways in which marketers communicate with consumers about products to sway their affect, cognitions, and behaviours. Marketing questions in this area include the following.

- What are the finest media for reaching a target market for a particular product?
- What image should advertising try to craft about a product?
- What types of sales promotions would be most effectual for getting customers to buy a product?
- What should be the salespeople's approach to match consumers' needs and wants with particular products?
- What task should publicity perform in communicating with customers about a product?

Decisions about these questions clearly depend on knowing a lot about consumers.

Place

Channels of distribution or place refers to the system by which products are directed from producers to consumers. Channels for consumer goods often comprise wholesalers and retailers. Consumers typically purchase from retail stores, but may also buy from mail-order houses, televised shopping, and other networks. Marketing questions from these areas include the following.

- Would consumers have a preference to purchase a product in stores or from different channels, such as mail-order catalogues or store sales people?
- What image does a store or chain have that might influence consumer preference and purchase behaviour for various products?
- Do various stores have particular environment that might influence consumer purchase of a product?

In this case, each marketing mix element fits with and reinforces the other elements to encourage a purchase. For example, the Mercedes Benz is clearly positioned as a top-quality product for serious purchasers, promoted only in selected media, and sold only by selected retailers. Thus, successful strategies for various elements of marketing mix are dependent on the consumer's affect, cognition, and behavioural changes.

IMPACT OF CHANGE IN CONSUMERS' PROFILE ON MARKETING DECISIONS

The changing profile and preferences of customers has given birth to some new and innovative trends in marketing to satisfy their needs and wants. Some of the efforts of marketers are elaborated in the subsequent paragraphs.

Online Marketing

With 100 million Internet users logging on an average 16 hours a week, Indian netizens are a segment no serious marketer would be willing to let go in the 21st century. Use of e-commerce, which primarily refers to buying, selling, marketing, and servicing of products or services over Internet and other computer networks, has taken off in India. Though not big enough currently compared to peer markets, e-commerce is expected to grow in the country in the near future.

In 2010, all of e-commerce was about US$5 billion in India. Industry estimate is that it will grow to US$40 billion by 2015. But Rajan Anandan, head of Internet giant Google's India operations, opines 'we think we will get to that much before that and by 2015, we will be much bigger. India crossed 100 million users last year (2010) despite poor Internet penetration and sluggish Internet speed. It is a big number because it makes India the third largest Internet market in the world by number of users', Anandan is reported to have said in an interview to an economic daily in August 2011, adding that 'More people are transacting business online and it's the right time to monetize the Internet.'

To tap this opportunity, the Internet giant's marketing plans for India include expanding the sales team, entering into partnerships with advertising agencies, increasing focus on mobile and display advertising, reaching out to small-and-medium businesses (SMBs) who at present don't advertise at all and lastly, its betting on cloud—software services available on the tap to companies big and small.

Globally, e-commerce growth has been led by the popularity of online shopping portals like amazon.com and ebay.com but in India it is mainly driven by the online travel industry and banking sector. According to Deep Kalra, founder CEO of makemytrip.com, online travel industry contributes about 50% of the revenue generated by e-commerce in India. 'In India e-commerce is being driven by the growing online travel industry and online travel bookings have increased substantially after the entry of low cost carriers. Currently, online travel industry is growing at 125% (compounded annual growth rate) annually. Generating revenues of around \$300–500 million, the size of the online travel industry was around 2% of the entire travel industry in 2006.'

Competitive air fares being offered online and convenience remain two most important motivations for booking tickets online rather than through a travel agent. Nonetheless, Anandan is upbeat about the prospects of non-travel e-commerce in the country. He points out that the world's largest online retailer amazon.com went public in 1997 when there were merely 50 million Internet users worldwide. Gradually though, Indian consumers have been making online purchases of greeting cards, clothes, CDs/DVDs/VCD/cassettes, books, magazines, medicines, and study notes. For online shopping, all a customer needs is a credit card. He/she chooses the product from the shopping Web sites and adds it to his buying cart. They make online payment through the credit card. The product is parceled by the company and reaches the customer's doorstep. Popular e-shops in India are www.amazon.com, www.ebay.in, www.shopping.rediff.com, etc.

Celebrity Influence

Celebrities have generally been roped in promotion activities by marketers to correlate personalities with their products. With the explosion of the electronic media, their role has been amplified. Indians

© Indiatodayimages.com

Celebrity endorsements: Aishwarya Rai Bachchan in *Lux* advertisement always love to imitate their heroes and heroines. In this context, it is not astonishing to see celebrities in advertisements as a common practice. Famous Bollywood and Sports celebrities like Amitabh Bachchan, Sachin Tendulkar, M.S. Dhoni, Shahrukh Khan, and Aishwarya Rai have great fan following and aid product recall simply by their presence in the advertisements. Celebrity endorsements usually help to break the clutter of advertisements and enhance recall rate.

Quality Oriented Outlets

In the absence of familiar brands in a particular product range, consumers are expected to take cue from well-established retail outlets with the hope of getting quality products. In such cases, the brand image of the retail portrays the product quality to the customers. For example, consumers feel the products of *Shopper's Stop*, *Wal Mart*, or *City Centre* might be costly but their quality has not been compromised.

Sales Promotion Offers

The buying behaviour of Indians is many a time predisposed by freebies. Freebies are consumer products provided free of cost with purchases of selected products at no extra price. Nowadays, it is common to see freebies along with purchases of TVs, washing machines, refrigerators, ready-made clothes, etc.

Eco-Friendly and Herbal Products

With the shrill against industrialization and its consequent pollution hazards getting sharper, organic, herbal and eco-friendly products are becoming a rage worldwide. Indians, who have been conventionally inclined towards herbs and home remedies are a veritable market for manufacturers of such products. Remember Shahnaz Husain, who pioneered the concept of herbal cosmetics and became famous the world over in the 1980s. More recently, the rising popularity of Yoga guru Ramdev and his brand of herbal medicines through the *Patanjali* chain can be attributed to the traditional affinity for environment-friendly and natural products among the Indians. In fact, India's Central Pollution Control Board even has an 'eco-mark' scheme, wherein 'eco-mark' certification is provided to manufacturers of organic and eco-friendly products. Like the ISI mark which is synonymous with quality of industrial products, the eco-mark logo (earthen pot) signifies that the product which carries it does the least damage to the environment.

Shahnaz Husain: Pioneered the concept of herbal cosmetics

Exhibit 1.2: The Changing Structure of Indian Market: From a Pyramid to a Sparkling Diamond

Tata Nano was introduced in the market to cater the needs of the neo-aspirars

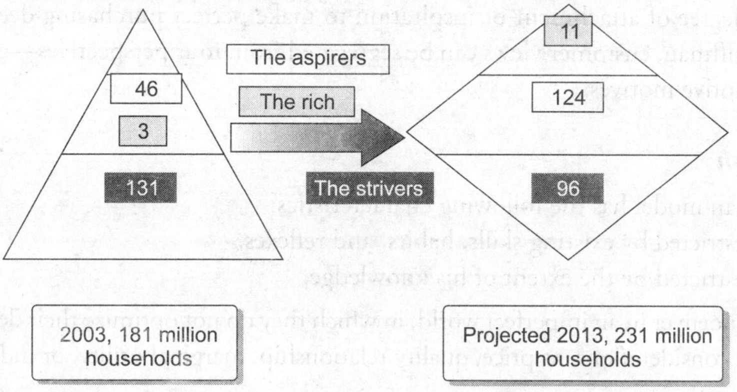

Figure 1.2 The transformation of Indian socio-economic structure—pyramid to diamond

Source: National Council of Applied Economic Research (NCAER)

The Indian market structure has been evolved from being merely a pyramid to a dazzling diamond. It is today one of the most enthralling markets in the world, probably, superseding China. A study by National Council for Applied Economic Research (NCAER) depicts a major amendment in the consumer class; while in 2003, India had 181 million domestic units of which only 3 million were in the rich bracket and 46 million as aspirers; by 2013 India is projected to have 231 million households of which 11 million would

(Contd.)

Exhibit 1.2 *(Contd.)*

be rich and 124 million aspirers! Thus the shape of Indian market is going to revolutionize within the next few years—a total transformation from being just a pyramid to a sparkling diamond. Now the people at the bottom the diamond structure can aspire to own a car. Figure 1.2 depicts the transformation of the Indian market structure.

To cater the changing needs of the neo-aspirers, *Tata Motors* introduced '*Nano*' in the market. *Nano* is supposed to be the cheapest car in the world. The word '*Nanos*' originated from Greece where it meant dwarf. In Gujarat, the foster house of '*Nano*', in local terms, the word *Nano* literally means small—exactly what the nanotechnology is supposed to be. Sitting in a gigantic fuel swigging behemoth is no longer neighbour's envy. On the contrary, priced just ₹100,000 ($1,979; £1,366), *Nano* began its journey across India with deliveries starting in July, 2009. It is the aim of *Tata Motors* Chairman Ratan Tata that the inexpensive 10-feet (3-metre) long, 5-seater car will encourage millions of Indians to trade up from their motorcycles.

Source: http://news.bbc.co.uk/2/hi/business/7957671.stm

CONSUMER DECISION MAKING

Four Views of Consumer Decision Making

The Indian consumer hardly ever has sufficient or adequately precise information about a product or even an enough degree of attachment or inspiration to make perfect purchasing decisions. According to Kanuk and Schiffman, customer views can be segregated from four perspectives—economic, passive, cognitive, and emotive motives.

Economic Man

The Economic man model has the following characteristics:

- Man is restricted by existing skills, habits, and reflexes.
- Man is restricted by the extent of his knowledge.

Consumers manoeuver in an imperfect world, in which they do not optimize their decisions in terms of rational economic considerations, as price, quality relationship, marginal utility, or indifference curves.

Passive Man

In this model, the consumers are basically subservient to the self-servicing interests and communication drives of marketers. Consumers are sometimes professed as impetuous and illogical buyers, ready to succumb to the charm and aims of marketers. These days salesmen often apply this formula, which can be condensed into the acronym AIDA (attention, interest, desire, and action). Psychology Professor E.K. Strong is credited with promoting this classical model in 1925 and it is still helpful because it effortlessly relates to the actions involved in the buyer decision process. According to it, there are four distinct stages to develop the sales process.

- The salesman must get the prospect's complete *attention*.
- This attention must be retained and enhanced in *interest*.
- This interest must be converted into *desire*.
- All existing doubts should be irradicated from the prospect's mind, and there must be firm resolution embossed to purchase *action*.

Figure 1.3 shows the AIDA steps leading to a purchase in the form of a sequential problem-solving process.

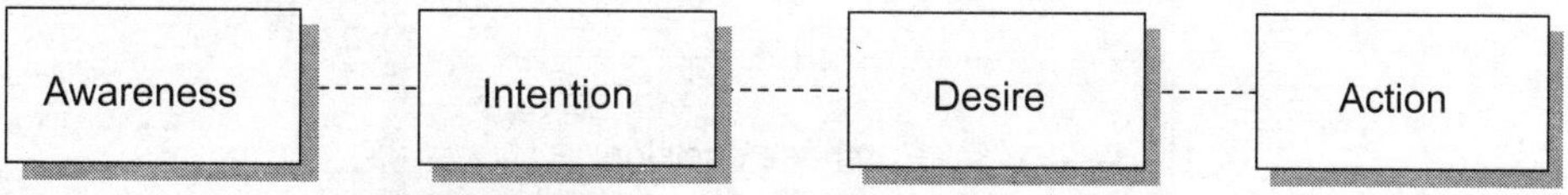

Figure 1.3 AIDA model of buying behaviour

Nevertheless, the most important drawback of this passive model is that it fails to recognize that the consumers play at least an equal, if not overriding, role in many buying situations looking for information about brand alternatives and choosing the brand that satisfies them the most.

Cognitive Man

A cognitive man or problem solving model positions a consumer somewhere between the edges of the economic and passive man. It models a consumer who does not have comprehensive product or brand knowledge and therefore, cannot make ideal decisions, but actively seeks information and tries to make reasonable decisions.

Emotional Man

When a consumer emphasizes less on searching for pre-purchase information, focuses on current mood and feelings, and makes an emotional purchase decision; he or she is referred as an emotional man. Nonetheless, an emotional man may make rational decision. Buying products rendering emotional satisfaction is absolutely a rational consumer decision. But sometimes, the preference of one brand over another has little to do with rationality, e.g., many consumers pay for tattoos because they feel they are coping with the recent trends and that makes them feel better. Advertisers are recognizing the magnitude of advertising with emotional appeals.

THE SIMPLE FIVE-STAGE CONSUMER DECISION PROCESS

The aim of various consumer behaviour models is to put together our understandings by presenting a series of conceptual frameworks that endeavour to explain the purchase decision process in relation to relevant variables. The most simplistic way of elucidating the buying behaviour is by resorting to the five-stage process. Figure 1.4 depicts the steps involved in the purchasing process.

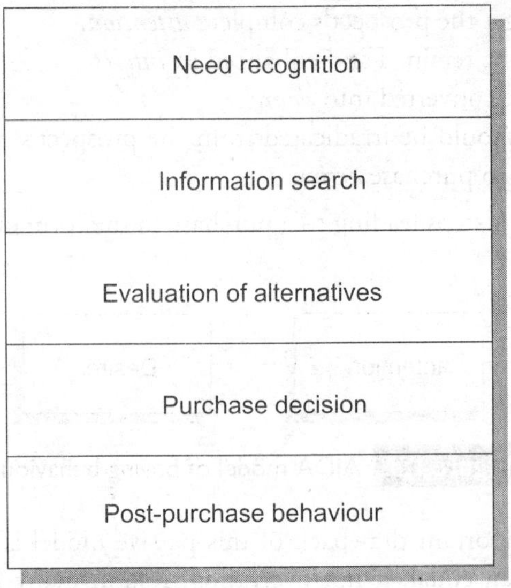

Figure 1.4 The buyer-decision model

The first step is recognition of need for a product or service. It is likely to occur when a consumer is faced with a 'problem'. This fact can be elaborated by the example of a washing machine purchase by Mrs. Chatterjee. Mrs. Chatterjee goes to her office every morning after completing her household chores, like cooking, washing clothes, etc. By the time she comes back late in the evening, she is exhausted and stressed. Once, she saw a washing machine in her friend's house. From that moment, she decided to buy a washing machine to ease some of her burden. To her, this was the immediate solution to her need.

Information search begins when a consumer perceives a need that might be satisfied by the purchase and consumption of a product. The recollection of past experiences (drawn from long-term memory storage) might provide the consumer with adequate information to make the present choice. On the other hand, when the consumer has had no prior experience, he or she might have to do an extensive market search for useful information on which to base a choice.

The consumer usually searches his or her memory before seeking external sources of information regarding a given consumption related need. Past experience is considered an internal source of information. Greater the relevant past experience, lesser external source information is likely to be needed to reach a decision. Many a time the consumer's information sources are a blend of memories and commercial or non-commercial peer sources. In the present example, Mrs. Chatterjee had very little information about washing machines. Hence, information was sought from a variety of sources including family and friends (called 'word of mouth'), advertisements, catalogues, visits to retail establishments, etc.

In this phase of information search, the role of the marketer is to make sure that the company's products get high revelation so that the unique selling points of their product are accentuated at the *evaluation of alternatives* phase .When evaluating potential alternatives, consumers tend to use two types of information:

- a 'list' of brands from which they plan to make their selection, alternatively named as evoked set; and
- the criteria they will use to evaluate each brand. Making a selection from a sample of all possible brands is a human characteristic that helps simplify the decision-making process.

This enables the company's product to be in the limelight prior to the *purchase decision*, because even then the consumer is vulnerable to additional influence in connection with making the right choice. Consumers make three types of purchases: trial purchases, repeat purchases, and the long-term commitment purchases. When a consumer purchases a product for the first time and buys a smaller quantity than usual, this purchase would be considered as trial. However, trial is appropriate mainly in case of fast moving consumer goods. Trial, of course, is not always practicable. For example, with most durable goods, as in the case of Mrs. Chatterjee's washing machine, a consumer usually moves directly from evaluation to a long-term commitment without the opportunity for an actual trial.

Marketers must also be aware of the *post-purchase behaviour* of consumers because this can have an effect on persisting business. Forward looking companies thus attach as much significance to after-sales service as they do to result while opening a sale. This trims down the degree of dissatisfaction (or cognitive dissonance) in the case of legitimate grievances. The most recent technique, these days, exercised for sales of major items, like new motor cars or water purifiers, is where companies follow up a sale by some form of communication, i.e., letter or telephone with their customers. The makers of consumer durables like washing machines and air conditioners have full fledged divisions to attend to repairs and faults. In most cases, they can be accessed by toll free numbers. This erects poise in the mind of the customer in having made the 'correct' purchasing decision. The term that has been attached to this kind of after-sales follow-up is called *customer care.*

The knowledge of how a buying/decision process works is critical to the success of any marketing strategy. For simple products, the task of marketing is to direct the purchase in favour of the company's products, perhaps through an effective mass media advertising campaign. For more complicated purchases, it is more important that the customers are helped in their problem-solving process and that reassurance is provided to show that their choice has been a wise one.

Closing Case

Project Shakti—Food for Thought for Base of Pyramid Marketing

A lot of consumer understanding and insights come from an exercise like *Project Shakti*, which in turn can lead to product innovation. This was a view expressed by Nikhil Vora, Sr. Vice President of market research group ASK Raymond James, in the early years of the project.

Company officials, who take pride in the project and briefly outline future aim for expanding reach in rural hinterland, said that this model generates a win-win partnership between HUL and its consumers, some of whom will also depend on the project for their livelihood, and it builds a self-sustaining virtuous cycle of growth for all. Almost ten years down the line, *Project Shakti* is cited as a case study for penetrating rural markets and a quintessential example of 'fortune at the bottom of the pyramid' by many management experts, including the late C.K. Prahlad. However, one of the most vocal critics of this business model has been Prof. Aneel Karnani, Ross School of Business, University of Michigan, who contended that although opportunities do exist, the market at the BOP is generally too small monetarily to be very profitable for most multinationals.

Until 2004, *Shakti* constituted 3.5% of the total revenue of HUL. No doubt, it was still profitable to continue growth trends. Perhaps because of the personal hygiene awareness (*Lifebuoy Swastha Chetana*), *Lifebuoy* provided a remarkable competitive advantage to HUL over its competitors. However by 2008, management experts found that *Project Shakti* 'had started to suffer from growing so big that its structure needed to be adjusted.' No doubt rural markets were alluring but not hassles free!

The success of HUL encouraged competitors to also penetrate into the rural market with existing HUL direct channels. Therefore, *Shakti* could initially meet the marketer's expectation of contributing 15–20% of total revenues, but with the entry of competitors in the market the assumption that Shakti would be able to continuously augment the usage rate of only HUL products by the current consumers might be questionable. So the threat of not achieving the market penetration of over 500 million rural population still prevails. This target implies that HUL would require to almost monopolize the rural market with 80% penetration rate; which sounds little difficult if competitors enter the market in similar fashion. Even at HUL's 2015 target of penetration, it seems a formidable task.

Moreover,with the fame of *Shakti* network, several other stakeholders, including government agencies and other private sector firms may feel motivated to opt for the same practice. It is known to us that *Shakti* has alliances with several NGOs and governmental agencies. In most cases, these alliances are formed based on the reputation of HUL and the mutual trust and benefit amongst the stakeholders. But, if other renowned and established MNCs enter the rural business and form a clout, the exclusivity of HUL in making rural alliances might be challenging. Without alliances with NGOs, the scalability of the programme is bound to face hassles in future.

The third problem, which *Shakti* might face in the long-run is the characteristics of the rural BOP market in general. As Karnani (2007) puts it, given the nature of opportunity present in the Indian bottom of the pyramid, it seems that the medium sized local enterprises would succeed more in this market. It needs to be noted that ensuring economies to scale by serving this bottom-end of the market is pretty difficult.

Moreover, as Karnani (2007) said, 'Markets of the rural poor are often geographically and culturally fragmented; this combined with weak infrastructure makes it hard to exploit scale economies. Products sold to the poor are also usually less marketing and brand intensive, further reducing scale economies.'

Needless to say that rural marketing itself has some inherent challenges. The first is to ensure wide availability of the product or service to the scattered rural populace. India's 627,000 villages are spread over 3.2 million sq km with a population of 700 million. Catching hold of them is not easy. Furthermore, given the existing precarious condition of roads, the challenge looks greater to regularly deliver products to the far-flung villages. But for the scalability of the business, the company must try hard to reach at least substantial number of villages with a populace of more than 5,000 so that they can trade off the distribution cost with incremental market penetration.

Second, given the low disposable incomes of the populace, price plays an important role to shape the purchasing decision in rural areas. It needs to be mentioned that a lot of spurious brands are widely available, which look quite similar as original ones and are providing low cost alternative choices to the rural customer. Due to ignorance and literacy, the rural poor cannot make out this issue. Moreover, the rural income is highly dominated by agriculture and hence, is quite seasonal in nature. This may result in fluctuation of sales, the company either has to accept or revisit its strategy to cope with.

Source: Kamath, Vinay, Where HLL's Shakti comes from, *The Hindubusinessline*, May 29, 2003, http://www.thehindubusinessline.com/catalyst/2003/05/29/stories/2003052900020100.htm, downloaded on July 10, 2009; Karnani, Aneel (2007), Fortune at the Bottom of the Pyramid: A Mirage, *California Management Review*, Summer 2007; http://thuyha-management.blogspot.com/2008/04/unilever-in-india-hindustan-levers.html, accessed on August 20, 2011; http://210.212.230.219/dde/downloads/markiv_rm.pdf, accessed on August 20, 2011.

Questions

1. Suggest appropriate marketing strategies for HUL to cater the needs of the rural Indian consumer.
2. What strategies can you suggest for *Project Shakti* to be sustainable in the long run?

Summary

This chapter serves as a prologue to the study of consumer behaviour. The chapter started with the study of nature and scope of consumer behaviour. It found that the knowledge of consumer's needs, wants, attitude, beliefs helps firms to improvise their marketing strategies. It provides a detailed understanding of issues such as how the consumers think, feel, comprehend, and select amongst various competing brands; how they are influenced by their environment (e.g., culture, family, signs, media); what is the pattern of shopping behaviour they are exposed to; what are their motivational parameters; and how their decision strategies and perception differ across the products. These understandings help the marketers to adapt and improve their marketing campaigns and strategies to more efficiently reach the consumer.

The next part focused on the application of consumer behaviour principles to strategic marketing. The most interesting part of the study is related to the features of the Indian customers and especially the changing profile of the Indian rural market. It showed how the rural consumers are evolving from simplistic purchase decisions to an era of brand consciousness.

Depending upon the varied nature of the customers, they have been categorized into four major groups namely—economic, cognitive, emotional, and passive. Thereafter the AIDA model proposed by E.K. Strong and the simplistic five stage decision-making model have been portrayed. AIDA model has four stages viz. awareness–intention–desire–action and the five stage model comprises five steps—problem recognition, information search, evaluation of alternatives, purchase decision, and post-purchase behaviour. Hence, the chapter provides an initial insight into the study of consumer behaviour and, therefore, serves as a gateway to the subject.

Key Terms

Consumer, buyer, payer The payer pays for the products, the buyer does the purchase, and the consumer uses it.

Consumer behaviour It is the consumer's response to the firm's offerings.

Post-purchase behaviour It is the satisfaction, dissatisfaction, or neutral state of the consumer after using the purchased product.

Cognitive dissonance State of disturbance in the mind of the consumer due to the difference between the expected performance of the product and its actual performance.

Customer care It is the proviso of service to customers before, during, and after a purchase, facilitating the customer's purchase process.

Emotional man These consumers stress less on looking for pre-purchase information, focus on present mood and feelings, and make an emotional purchase decision.

Passive man In this model the consumers act as basically submissive to the self-satisfying benefits and messages of marketers.

AIDA It is the attention–interest–desire–action theory of E.K. Strong. Now sales people use the acronym.

Cognitive man A cognitive man is someone who is at some place between the edges of the economic and passive man.

Economic man The economic man is restricted by existing skills, habits, reflexes, and the extent of his knowledge.

Consumer decision making It is a five-stage process by which the consumers take any purchase decision.

Aspirers A group of middle class people having a thrust to move to the next income group.

Sales promotion It is a short-term promotional step, like offering free gifts, coupons, etc. with the product to boost up sales.

Online marketing It is a term used for selling items and services on the Internet.

Strategic planning Strategic plan is to put down the roadmap of a business and to implement it in such a way that the products rendered by the company meet its overall business objectives.

Pricing It is the way of setting the selling price of any product.

Distribution channel It is the flow of finished products from manufacturer to the end user through different intermediaries.

Questions

1. 'Though face packs are manufactured combining various chemicals in the factory, yet the hope of fairness is initiated from the point-of-sale.'
   (a) Explain this proclamation of a marketer of a cosmetics industry.
   (b) In this context analyze the importance of studying consumer behaviour?
   (c) Is it possible to charge premium price from a repeat customer?
2. You want to buy a new mobile handset. Show through AIDA model and the five-stage decision model how your decision for purchase will be formed.
3. Explain the marketing manager's interface with strategic management process.
4. What considerations a marketer needs to keep in mind before launching a new brand of hair oil for the Indian rural market of 21st century.
5. You had bought a *Whirlpool* washing machine five years ago. This year you have replaced it with *Godrej* washing machine. Elucidate how the post-purchase outcomes of the consumption of *Whirlpool* washing machine influenced your next purchase decision.

Critical Assignment

1. *GlaxoSmithKline Consumer Health Care* asserts that its 135-year-old *Horlicks* brand makes kids taller, smarter, and sharper. Survey at least 10 mothers from your locality having children below 14 years and find out how this claim has influenced their purchase decision for health drinks.
2. *Ruf and Tuf* jeans are now the largest-selling brand in India, outshining *Levi's* and many other global brands. From the study of the profile of Indian consumers find out the reasons behind this.
3. ICICI bank wants to increase its penetration in rural areas. They have taken various measures for this purpose. Read related information available on their Web site and other sources, and comment on the appropriateness of the strategy.
4. *Brooke Bond Taaza* is HUL's mass-targeted tea brand, even targeting low-income consumers. For bottom of the pyramid customers, HUL has selected local tea retailers and provided them tea powder for a day on a 24-hour credit. Survey any slum of your locality and find out if this strategy will work in your town or not?

Chapter **2**

The Changing Patterns of Consumer Behaviour

Chapter Goals

After completing this chapter, you will be able to understand

- **the benefits of anticipating trends in customer behaviour**
- **worldwide trends of changing consumer dynamics**
- **implications of the changing trends on three consumer roles: user, payer, and buyer**
- **dynamics of change in Indian consumers**

Opening Vignette

The Agribusiness Supply Chain in India—Trends

The Indian rural market, although, characterized by a large number of buyers and sellers is highly scattered and not perfectly competitive. Too many undersized intermediaries, resulting in small size of businesses are the bane of agribusiness in the country. Their sum of investment and extent of procurement is considerably less. Moreover, the presence of too many small intermediaries increases the cost in the entire supply chain without adding value to it. Bulk procurement by government or any big agency directly from the farmers is one of the avenues to get rid of this problem. It is anticipated that the decrease in the number of intermediaries and bulk procurement will reduce the gap between the price we pay and the price paid to the farmers at the time of procurement. Concurrently, because of the existence of a large number of intermediaries, the margins of individual wholesalers and retailers are low as they transact to a very low extent. Above all, the rigid Indian Agricultural Produce Market Acts makes the assimilation of agricultural produce further difficult.

However, to understand the Indian agribusiness supply chain, a brief analysis of the prevalent systems is required. The following three methods in agribusiness supply chain are usually followed in India.

1. **Farm-gate purchases:** In this procedure there is a prior arrangement between the buyers and the farmers. Keeping in view the unpredictability of the process, the arrangement is usually made prior to harvest. Buyers in this issue are the marketing clusters, cooperatives, or the traders (contacted through a collection centre). This is a common process in the fruits market. The major benefit of this process is that it results in long-term relationship among the buyers and sellers. On occasions where the inspection of quality is costly, the reliance level and the standing (credentials) of the sellers are the only factors to judge the quality of the product. Further, this process reduces the number of intermediaries in the supply chain and thereby, reduces the gap between the supplier price and the consumer price. One of the flaws of this system, however, is that the farmers cannot go in for the best bid at the time of harvest. Another obstacle in the system is poor road conditions and transport facilities in rural India. Only the rural areas which are in the infringements of towns can avail this system. For instance, the orange farmers of Nagpur (Maharashtra) and the mango farmers of Malihabad (UP) are quite familiar with this system.

© Photos.com

Farm-gate purchases

2. **Local markets:** Alternatively known as *mandi*, this system is widespread in many Indian states, specially West Bengal. Here the farmers amass their produce and sell it in the rural *haats* organized in a central place in a village, a district centre, or adjacent to a village's access road on specific days. Generally, the small traders or the commission agents buy the agricultural produce from these farmers, sell it to the district level *mandi* and the district level traders and wholesalers, who in turn sell the produce to the large traders and wholesalers. In this system too, the existence of a large number of mediators pushes up the cost of the supply chain. This results in the further increase in consumer price. As the collection is made from various sources, the quality of the processed food product cannot be assured. All this bogs down the supply chain of Indian agribusiness into the vicious cycle of low demand, low capacity utilization, and high per unit cost.
3. **Assembly markets:** In certain areas of the hinterland, we come across assembly markets where agricultural produce are traded in bulk with external buyers, either by the producers themselves or by the traders. The buyers here are mostly the collection agents of the urban wholesalers. These markets function throughout the year (sometimes seasonal depending upon the nature of the farm produce) and are by and large in arrangement with the local market. These markets are located on the main highways, main roads, or ferry ghats (ferry stops in West Bengal).

Azadpur sabzi mandi, Asia's biggest fruit and vegetable market, serves as a National Distribution Centre for fruits and vegetables

4. **Direct sales to urban markets:** In this process, the farmers directly sell their products to urban market retailers or wholesalers. Nonetheless, due to deficiency in infrastructural facilities, poor road conditions, and unstable financial status of the poor marginal farmers, this method is seldom seen in the country.

However, the use of e-commerce can usher a big revolution in creating vertical coordination in the Indian agri-supply chain. Updated knowledge about weather forecast, crop cultivation practices, post-harvest technology, water management through satellite tracking, commercial information, market information for grains, fruits and vegetables, processed food, low cost technology, government schemes and policies on agriculture can augment the scope of agribusiness at rural places. For instance, Maharashtra Chamber of Commerce, Industries and Agriculture envisaged setting up Gramin Information Centres (GIC) for providing latest information on technology and market access to facilitate farmers and help rural food processing industries to plan their activities on commercial lines for realizing maximum value for their produce. For the sustainability of the food industry, it is imperative that it has sound backward linkages. Information technology can play a significant role in further intensification of these linkages, specially taking B2B customers into consideration.

Thus, there is growing awareness among Indian producers and consumers, especially B2B consumers, to integrate ICT (information and communication technologies) not only in their marketing strategies and the supply chain but also extend it to the producers by providing them market and weather-related information as mentioned earlier. A case in point is corporate giant ITC's *e-choupal* initiative that directly links with farmers through the Internet for procurement of agriculture and aquaculture products. Thus, the emergence of ICT based agribusiness market and its subsequent reach to the next level of customers may be considered as a sea change in terms of agri-customer's purchase pattern.

An ITC official explaining farmers the basics of e-trade in Thallarivu village near Kakinada in Andhra Pradesh

INTRODUCTION

The world is in the midst of a major demographic shift. The advances in science and technology have had a major impact on the human race in many ways. The quality of life has improved and pushed up longevity of human beings. Lifestyles have also improved with the availability of modern gadgets as the human race gets more materialistic and individualistic. Changes are also being witnessed in the social fabric of societies as modern definitions of development and progress have emerged. Academics studying these trends have made some interesting projections on how the world population will look like and behave in the years to come. For instance, Andy Hines, an academic futuristic in the University of Houston, has projected that the greying population is estimated to treble by 2050 while the 0–14 group will remain inert. Depending on indicators that rate a country's economic growth, social progress, and technological aptitude, Hines has divided the World of 2050 into World 1or W1, World 2 or W2, and World 3 or W3, whereby W1 comprises the most affluent nations, followed by the middle-income or W2 nations and then W3 or least developed and economically backward countries.

According to him, in 2050, W1 would comprise less than a billion people in affluent nations like the United States, Western Europe, Japan, South Korea, Australia, etc. W2 would comprise the huge chunk of 3 to 4 billion middle-income populace in countries that are characterised by somewhat balanced needs and resources, although they are not free from certain setbacks. However, a few W2 nations, such as India and China, are on a very rapid upgradation drive. But many other nations in W2, viz. countries in Latin America and Eastern Europe, are less so. W3 comprises 1 to 2 billion people who are in an ominous passage (most of Africa, Bangladesh, and Haiti). These trends are likely to be prominent with a relative economic stability over the forthcoming decades.

Such alteration in the size, structure, and distribution of the population will have far reaching implications on public policy as well as the industry. Thus, those at the helm of policy making in governments as well as business organizations can benefit immensely from tracking such futuristic trends. This precisely is the focus of our second chapter. In this Chapter, we will discuss the advantages of forseeing trends in consumer behaviour. We shall also study the impact of significant demographic changes on consumer behaviour observed on a global as well as national scale in the recent past and what they portend for the future.

The impact of technological trends and public policy on consumer behaviour are also discussed in detail in the chapter.

BENEFITS OF FORESEEING TRENDS IN CUSTOMER BEHAVIOUR

'It's not the strongest of the species that survives, nor the most intelligent; it is the one most adaptable to change.' This profound statement of Charles Darwin, one of the most celebrated evolutionary biologist, sums up the advantages that can accrue to any business organization if it keeps track of the changes in its external as well as internal environment. Consumers constitute an important element of this external environment. Thus, the key benefits of anticipating the trends in consumer behaviour are as follows:

- Anticipating trends can give companies a key premeditated gain.

- By forseeing a trend, a company can craft a market by tapping a dormant need.
- Tracking trends generate optimistic community views for the company as also the industry, thereby, enhancing their ability to promptly respond to change.

THE MAJOR WORLDWIDE CHANGING TRENDS

The changing patterns of consumer behaviour can be studied under the following heads.

- Demographic trends
- Technological trends and
- Public policy

Figure 2.1 depicts the conceptual framework for understanding the trends of client behaviour.

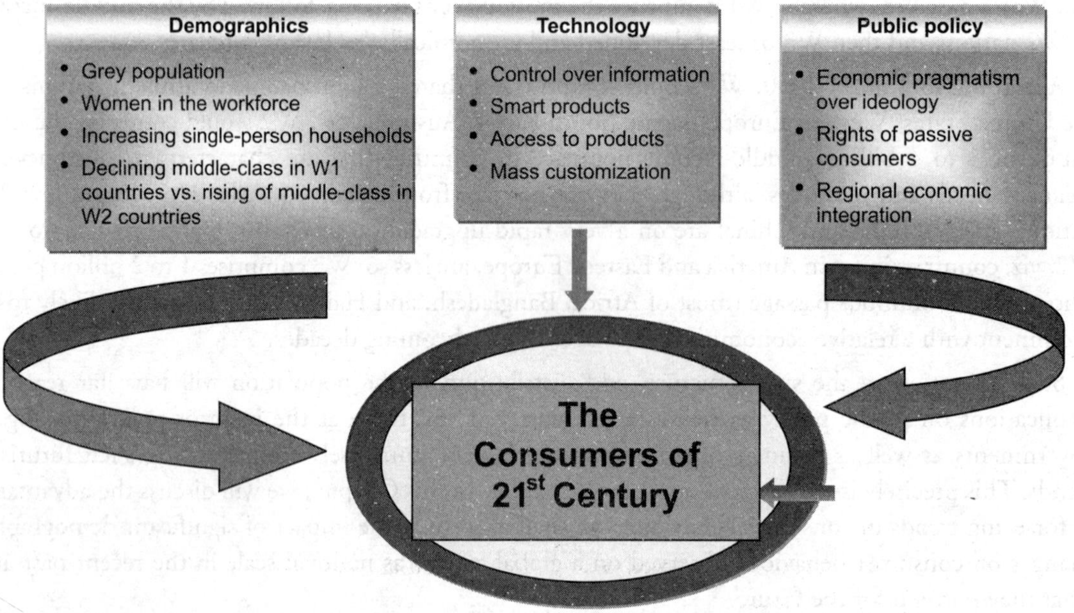

Figure 2.1 Conceptual framework for understanding the trends of consumer behaviour

Demographic Trends

Demography is the opening point for our trend analysis, because demographic indicators are reasonably predictable. While studying the demographic features of the world population, it has been observed that the exception is becoming the rule of late. The following are some significant demographic changes and consequent changing patterns in consumer behaviour that have triggered changes in marketing policies on a global scale.

Aging of the Population

The most developed portions of the world, W1, are skewing towards grey population. W2 is close behind.

According to Hines, the greying population in the world is expected to treble by 2050. India's population composition would then look very similar to that of nations like Russia and the UK. Their high aging index will designate that the 60 plus age group is bigger than the 0–14 group. While the aged people in the United States may harp on the 'broken' social security system, most of the silver-haired populace in W2 and W3 are not covered by any social security scheme. Nonetheless, new prospects are emerging for the financial services sector to address the needs of this growing segment in the society. A facet of the growing grey population in nations like the United States, and now India, is the mounting obsolescence of retirement. The US baby boomers are opting for post-work lifestyles that do not seem to be the typecast of the old-fashioned, relaxing senior citizens. In fact, the US today has nearly 12.6% of its population above the age of 65 years and the birth rates have been reduced drastically. In Asia, Japan has the highest greying population percentage (20%), followed by 12% in India.

The marketer may consider this as an emerging opportunity with a rising market for 60 plus years with considerable buying power. Their special and unique physical and emotional needs should be addressed by means of proper care in old age homes. Tours and travel companies may design special packages for them. Because of an increasing trend towards grey population, religious books, medicines, ambulatory care, super-specialty hospitals, spectacles, walking sticks, and many more items specified for the old are poised to register a boom in sales in the forthcoming years. Implications also exist on product design, formulations, packaging, special store and shelf design, and home delivery services for the old.

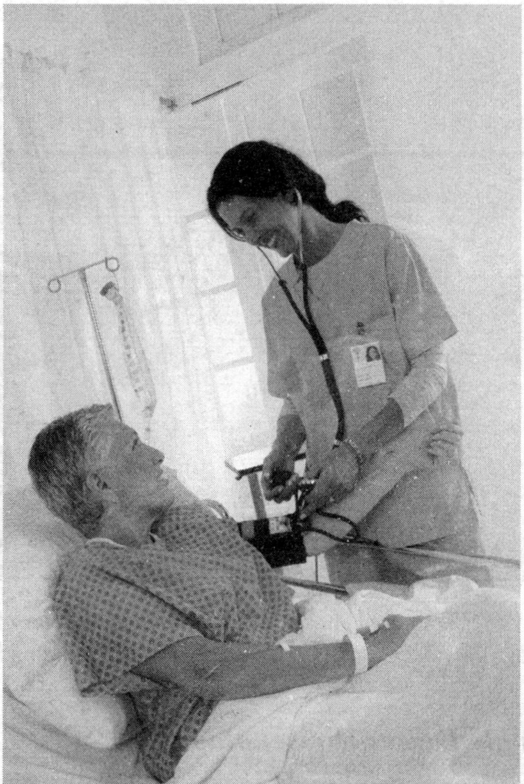

Because of the special physical and emotional needs of the grey population, there has been an increase in sales in the super-speciality hospitals

Fitness on the Rise

Health products and supplements are some of the most publicized products all over the world. Widely prevalent lifestyle diseases of these days such as obesity, cardiac and pulmonary problems, diabetes, etc. demand adequate exercise and fitness training. Health clubs and fitness centres have mushroomed across Asia and Europe. Not to be left behind, traditional health systems in India are being marketed with great zeal and have experienced a growing clientele including foreigners.

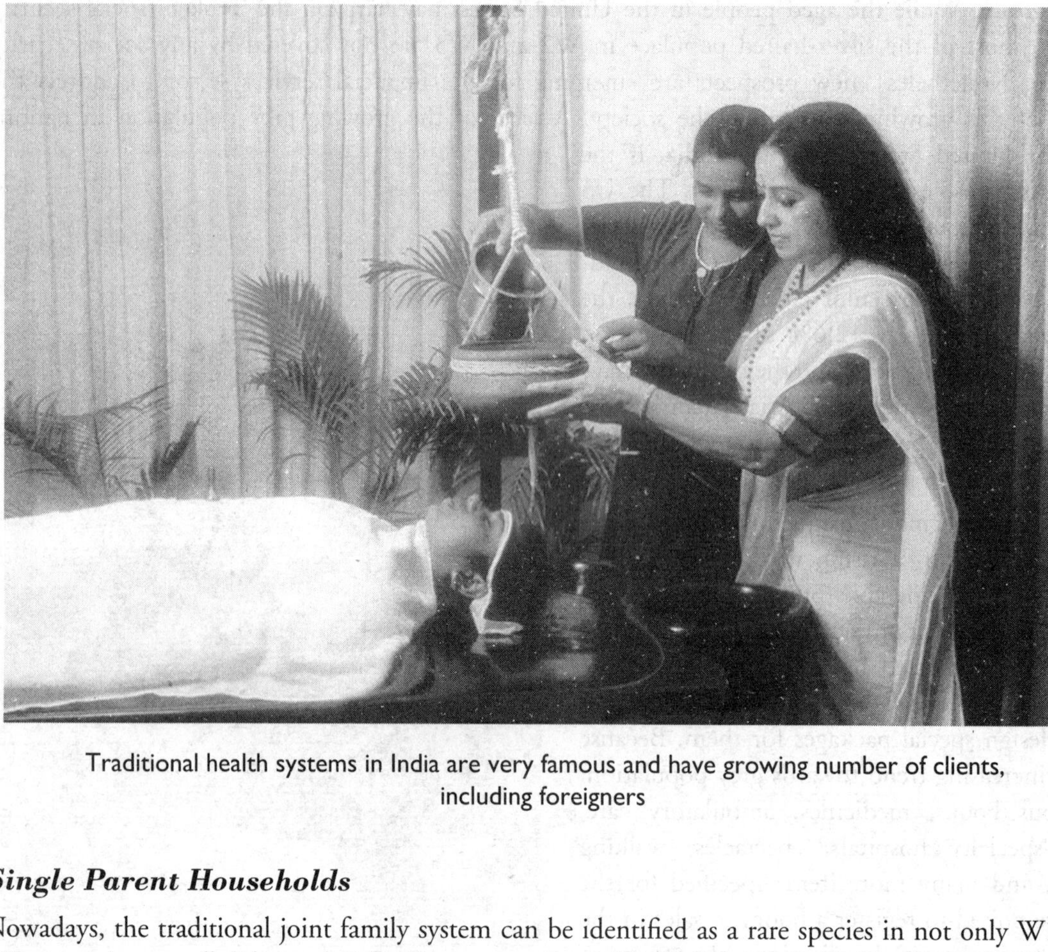

© Indiatodayimages.com

Traditional health systems in India are very famous and have growing number of clients, including foreigners

Single Parent Households

Nowadays, the traditional joint family system can be identified as a rare species in not only W1 but W2 countries as well. 'Alternative' family arrangements, that is the nuclear family that surfaced just a generation ago, is at the crossroads. The latest trend now is the emergence of single parent families and households. In the United States, 51% of women are now without a spouse and 37% of babies are born out of marriage. The percentage of divorced parents is also now very large across the world. In fact, single-person households are also the fastest-growing category of households in the W1 nations.

Add to this the rising cost of educating children in many W1 countries. Children now mature earlier than their counterparts a generation ago, and sarcastically, adults are 'growing up' at a snail's pace.

Early maturity among children is attributed to their exposure to adult messages from media. On the other hand, many adults are in a quest to evoke their lost childhoods. These youth-fanatic adults are named as 'rejuveniles' or 'kidults' in W1 nations.

© iStockphoto/Thinkstock

Kidults

These transformations in the structure of the 21st century family will force business organizations to reassess the family concept and decide how to communicate with each group, which is a veritable customer segment in itself. These transitions are already motivating the marketers, who hitherto relied upon customary age-based segmentations, to rethink their marketing strategies. Age is no more a dependable pointer of people's actions, interests, or opinions.

Women in the Workforce

At present roughly two-third of American families have women in the work force, a theatrical move from the 37% in 1960. With increasing number of women in the workforce, time is the most crucial factor in most households. Outsourcing of household chores and convenience has seen a significant rise. In Indian too, the share of women in labour force is 25.6 per cent. In 1981, it was 19.7% and rose to 22.7% in 1991, further rising to 25.7% in 2001. At present, in the IT sector, women account for nearly 36% of the total workforce. In Asia, China has the highest percentage of females in the workforce (75.8%) followed by 51.2% in Vietnam.

Women at work in India

As a result there has been a tremendous increase in the demand of time-saving consumer durables like microwave ovens, refrigerators, mixer grinders, and washing machines. The market for ready to eat food such as noodles and instant food preparations has grown manifold.

The Decline of Middle-Class in W1 vs. the Rise of Middle-Class in W2 and W3

In the wealthy countries, predominantly in the United States, the middle class is dwindling and the upper and lower classes are swelling. It needs to be mentioned that in the United States, in the last 27 years, the middle-income populace has shown a steady decline. Exasperation from poor financial state gives birth to discontented customers who demand more but are quite price-sensitive. They demand greater value for their money. On the other hand, as the consumers move from the middle-class to the upper-class, demand for more and more exclusive designer items increases and fashion products are tailored as per their standard of living. Nonetheless, the quality of life at the bottom of W1 is still higher than that of their counterparts in the W2 and W3 nations.

While the size of the growing W2 middle-class in countries like China is hard to nail down, it is charting a different course in countries like Europe, the United States. Asian economic giant, Japan, experienced this change a few generations ago, which created large numbers of 'first-time buyers' over there. In these markets the sales volume for middle-end consumer goods is increasing at a gradual and consistent pace. Given that in many affluent W1 nations with shrinking middle classes, the growth that many businesses have been accustomed with, will be reduced forcing those business houses to shift their attention to W2 and eventually W3 for burgeoning middle class.

The business implications of this fact are that in the bifurcating W1 markets, a pattern of prestige-conscious shopping is budding. Consumers are progressively more enthusiastic to expend huge money on 'identity-related' purchases. On the contrary, other less-important purchases are dependent exclusively on cost. Thus, we find people shopping at a local grocery for a pack of pickle on the one hand and at Wal-Mart for designer jewelry or Lexus showrooms for automobile on the other. This speaks of a need for innovative business models where manufacturers and retailers can earn profit by making petite quantity of bespoke products—particularly those identity-based products.

Back home, the Indian market structure has become one of the most enthralling markets in the world, probably superseding China. A study by the National Council for Applied Economic Research (NCAER) shows a major transformation in the consumer class. While in 2003, India had 181 million domestic units of which only 3 million were in the rich bracket, while 46 million were described as aspirers; by 2013 it is projected to have 231 million households of which 11 million would be rich and 124 million aspirers! The study covered 515 cities and 182,599 households in urban areas. Thus, the shape of Indian market is undergoing a silent revolution of sorts—a total transformation from being just a pyramid to a 'sparkling diamond' as we had read in Exhibit 1.2 in Chapter 1.

The government's most recent National Sample Survey claims that the number of households living below poverty line declined from 40% in 1988 to 25% in 1995. Also, the proportion of products owned by households in the lowest income level signifies a contrasting consumption pattern. Forty per cent of the Indian populace, as per the study, owns portable radios, mechanical wristwatches, and bicycles; 30–39 per cent has table fans; 20–29 per cent owns mono-cassette recorders, black and white TV sets, pressure cookers, electric irons, quartz wrist watches, ceiling fans, and sewing machines. The survey shows that nearly 10–19 per cent owns motorcycles, mopeds, colour TVs and mixer-grinders (refer Exhibit 2.1). Scooters and refrigerators are owned by 10 per cent. However, a very a small number of households are able to afford air conditioners. Even though India's climate is dusty and hot for a major part of the year, it is not very surprising with a small number of populace at the top of the 'diamond', just 230,000 units of ACs were sold nationally in 1995. Amongst them, about 90 per cent of the consumers were from the corporate sector.

Exhibit 2.1: The Refrigerator Market in India

One of the most basic durables introduced in India was refrigerator. Till mid-1985, the sales of such consumer durables grew at a very sluggish rate. There was not much differentiation amongst the sales of selected manufacturers like *Kelvinator*, *Godrej*, *Voltas*, etc. It is worth mentioning that in 1991–92, the sale of refrigerators stood at 1.04 million units. Nonetheless, the introduction of new advanced models and aggressive promotion strategy clubbed with the growing middle class has changed this scenario. The sales steadily grew 15% each in 1993 and 1994. Further, with huge expenditure in promotion and distribution channels, the output grew up to 9.5 million units in 2010 and is targeted at 12 million units for 2011.

Source: http://www.thehindubusinessline.com/features/brandline/article1773637.ece, accessed on February 14, 2011.

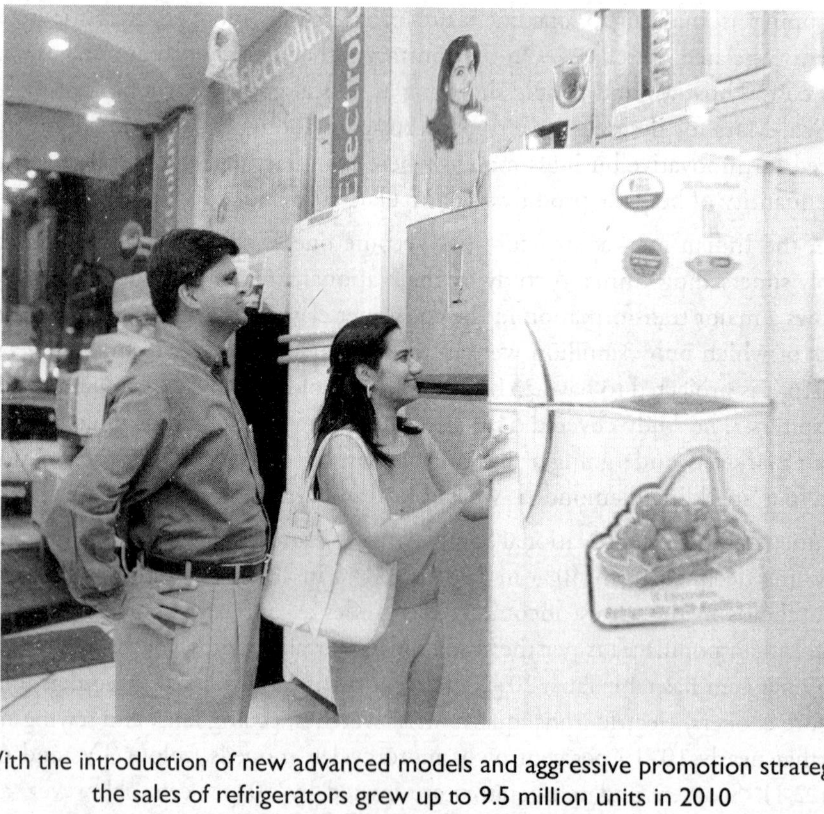

© Indiatodayimages.com

With the introduction of new advanced models and aggressive promotion strategy, the sales of refrigerators grew up to 9.5 million units in 2010

The Indian marketers, through aggressive promotion, have now inveigled many middle-income households to purchase air conditioners. Introduction of small models of 0.5 and 0.75 tonnes to fit the smaller Indian households is likely to be the key for the success. It is projected that in another 4 years, AC market in India will experience boom in sales. Annual sales then are projected to rise up to 900,000 units. It is, however, not easy to envisage the shock of this on the highly polluting and electricity-famished Indian economy.

Implications of Demographic Trends on Consumer Behaviour

The implications of the ongoing demographic changes has already influenced the needs and wants of the customers, and their response is likely to sway further in the forseeable future. The likely impact of such changes has been summarized in Table 2.1.

Table 2.1 *Impact of changing demographic trends on customers*

Change in demographics	*User*	*Payer*	*Buyer*
Increasing aging population	Augmented health and security needs. Need for pilgrim tours, religious books, spectacles, walking sticks, old age homes, etc.	Cost containment for health-care is an anxiety. Renewal of Mediclaim. Getting advantage of senior citizenship in railways, airlines tickets, and in many other projects	Home delivery and handiness in purchase becomes crucial. Keeping this into consideration, many old age projects are coming up to provide comfort and ease of purchase to the grey populace
Increasing working women	Emphasis on timesaving cooking, cleaning gadgets, creche for childcare, fast food for children	Affordability fairly improved. Many families are DINKS (double-income-no-kids). Their affordability is quite high	Male-female role specialization no longer exists. Females now take part in buying decisions which were till a decade ago strictly in male domain. Especially in case of investing in several financial schemes female participation is quite remarkable now
Increasing single-person households	Products of social and emotional values attain importance. Emphasis on timesaving cooking, cleaning gadgets, creche for childcare, fast food for children	High affordability	Tendency for more impulse buying and pragmatic decisions
Increasing middle class	Demand for medium priced goods	Ready to pay premium price for luxury goods but price sensitive in case of routine goods	Very cautious customers and first time buyers for many products

Technological Trends

The advancements in technology are also taking place exponentially. No sooner than a new product hits the market, innovations and improvisations follow suit such that the original product is rendered obsolete not within years but months. Such changes are most perceptible in electronic gadgets, especially models of mobile phones wherein manufacturers keep introducing additional features to stay ahead of rivals. The impact of such technologies has been tremendous on consumer behaviour. It is dealt with in detail in this section.

Impact of New Technologies

With the invasion of information technology, today's consumers have escalating command over the information available about the products and services of particular brands. Smart products (products that can be set, diagnosed, or attuned from an external driving force) will amend the usage pattern, maintenance, and adaptability of the products. Products are readily available to the customers anytime, anywhere. The stores are open round the clock, i.e., for 365 × 24 × 7, i.e., 365 days, 24 hours, 7 days a week.

Technology has facilitated mass production; however, its advancement has enabled customization of products on the other hand. Thus, there is an increasing demand for bespoke products and services to pamper the individual customer as per their required needs and whims. The Internet and Web related technologies have shown avenues to the marketers to reap the endowment of innovators working outside corporate boundaries, for example, online trade.

These days, with the advent of high-tech consumer products and services, the marketers regularly involve customers, suppliers, small specialist businesses, and independent contractors for developing and introducing new products across the line and mix. Also, the very structure and ambience of market place has changed with UPC scans and personal computers becoming an integral part of big retails and general stores in urban areas.

Information goods, such as software and editorial content, have matured for this sort of decentralized innovation. For instance, the Linux operating system was developed for this purpose. Physical goods can also be developed similarly. One may recall the experience of *Loncin*, a leading Chinese motorcycle manufacturer, in this context. They set wide specifications for their products. Thereafter, asked the suppliers to work collectively to design the components so that if everything is in desired shape, the cost can be optimized. Thus, it has become easier to co-create physical goods for more complex value chains in today's competitive markets.

Technology now permits companies to delegate assignments to various channel partners. This facilitates the process of 'value co-creation' with lot of innovative attempts in the value chain. With the flow of technology-led innovation through the value chain, companies may lessen their costs and steer new products to market more rapidly by getting rid of the inertia that comes with total control.

© Indiatodayimages.com

Modern gadgets

Almost a decade ago, ITC chose the most unexploited avenue of agribusiness in India. As per the annual report, 2004 of ITC, 'It articulated an inspiring vision; chose a challenging corporate strategy, and formulated a world-class execution plan with unmatched investments in technology, brands, people, and governance. The result: the ITC . . . has evolved from being a leading agri-commodity exporter to a major player across the agri-value chain'. But the most unique intervention is perhaps the concept of '*e-choupal*', which catalyzes the potential to address several issues confronting the competitiveness of the traditional Indian agricultural value chain, which have been discussed in the opening vignette and closing case. '*e-Choupal*' is till date the unparallel way to deliver real-time information and customized knowledge in local language to marginal farmers and small landholders to improve their decision-making ability. Thus, it is a drive to align the farm output with the market demand so as to bring a stable equilibrium is this arena.

Launched in June 2000, '*e-Choupal*', has already become the largest initiative among all Internet-based interventions in rural India. '*e-Choupal*' services today reach out to more than 3.1 million farmers growing a range of crops—soyabean, coffee, wheat, rice, pulses, shrimp—in over 31,000 villages through 5050 kiosks across six states (Madhya Pradesh, Karnataka, Andhra Pradesh, Uttar Pradesh, Maharashtra, and Rajasthan).

The concept of e-commerce (the virtual *mandis*) has already made forays in the rural market. So it can be forecast that virtual *mandis* would soon replace the rural intermediaries if state governments as well as leading players in agribusiness like ITC take proper initiative. It is expected that the Internet based e-commerce will increase the efficiency of the supply chain, which eventually will transform the Indian agribusiness into a new era of e-agribusiness in this millennium.

Implications of Technological Trends on Consumer Behaviour

Technological revolution these days has made consumer behaviour more unconventional and challenging. The implications of technological advancement in the changing pattern of consumer behaviour have been summarized in Table 2.2.

Table 2.2 *Impact of changing technological trends on customers*

Changes in technology	***User***	***Payer***	***Buyer***
Access to information	More tailored products	More information about the competing brands' prices	Shopping on the Web/virtual shopping malls. More product information on demand through emails
Smart products	A smart product with memory for user's likings	Updated methods of customers' and marketers' identity verification guarantee protection against deceptions	Automated purchase from virtual malls or buying direct from the factory by electronic data interchange system
Tech savvy buyers	Uses of hi-tech electronic gadgets are increasing	Customers are becoming more and more technology-savvy. In many cases payments are made online, for example, for railway booking, airlines booking, etc.	Buyers can purchase from virtual shopping centres like www.amazon.com, www.ebay.com, etc.

Trends in Public Policy

Public policy can be described as an endeavour by government to deal with a matter of public concern. Governments normally design public policy by formulating laws, regulations, decisions, and actions to deal with any public issue. At times, leaders of different religious and cultural institutions also craft public policy. However, the present focus of this chapter is on economic pragmatism vs. ideology, and global trends in public policy with respect to safeguarding the rights of consumers and crafting regulation for enhancing national wealth.

Economic Pragmatism Over Ideology

There is a worldwide progress from rigidity of government control to the liberalized open economy, i.e., to a laissez faire ideology. The spectacular socio-economic and cultural transformations that have taken place worldwide, especially in China, over a couple of decades have drawn the attention of one and all.

The old order sustained by stringent state control over the Chinese economy existed till the end of the 1970s, but thereafter, each day the market forces, step by step, conked it out. As a matter of fact, market forces were introduced as a therapy for the 'apparent letdown' of the Maoist democratic socialism. China is today cited as world economic power, thanks to a sound political structure that serves as a vital link between the prevailing blend of capitalism and socialism. Needless to say both are devoted to the same end of material progress or pragmatism, the buzzword these days. It is economic pragmatism that has overridden all kinds of ideology be it political or religious, or any other kind.

© Digital Vision/Photodisc/Thinkstock

New world shopping mall, Beijing, China—Opening up of market economy in China

Pragmatism over political ideology

In the post World War II era, many ex-communist nations have adopted the laissez faire system and are hospitable to Foreign Direct Investment. Hence, investment boom as well as a consumer-spending gush characterized the post-war renaissance of the market economy in many countries. While we have already seen the spectacular progress made by China as a result of pragmatism being given precedence over prevailing political ideology, the US experience in the post-war era is also worth mentioning. In current dollars, gross private domestic investment in the United States jumped from US$ 10.6 billion in 1945 to US$ 30.6 billion in 1946, US$ 34.0 billion in 1947, and US$ 46.0 billion in 1948. Moreover, thanks to an abridged tax burden—the Revenue Act of 1945, which lowered the top corporate income-tax rate and rescinded the excess-profit tax—the firms had the benefit of rising after-tax profits since 1946. The after-tax profits increased to US$ 15.5 billion in 1946, US$ 20.2 billion in 1947, and US$ 22.7 billion in 1948. The added retained earnings enabled higher business investment in the post-war era.

The corporate investment explosion of the post-war changeover years received its financing from a blend of the proceeds of sales of previously obtained government bonds, amplified current retained earnings (attributable in part to reduced corporate-tax liabilities), and the profits of corporate securities contributions. The then US President Harry S. Truman in his economic report of January 1948 commented, 'The extraordinary rate of business income in general allowed investment to proceed at record levels. Even greater expansion was prevented mainly by lack of material rather than by lack of intention to invest or lack of financial resources.'

Pragmatism over religious ideology

Religious ideology has been demonstrated to be an encumbrance to modernization and economic development. For example, for centuries together, poets have elegantly illustrated the rhythm of the Jewish Sabbath, which is a characteristic feature of Israeli culture. At Sabbath practically all traffic and business used to come to a standstill at sunset on Friday. Stores, restaurants, and bars were closed until Saturday night, while synagogues reverberated with prayers. But the tone and touch of the Jewish Sabbath is changing in the country. Globalization and other market pressures are pushing more and more Israelis to work even on Saturdays in new shopping malls and American-style outlets. The concept of 365×7×24 has been implemented in Israel Airlines superseding their religious ideology of Sabbath. Similarly, we find round the clock working culture seeping into other orthodox societies as well. A similar pattern can be observed in India too. Only a few years ago, we used to see business and commercial establishments completely closed on Independence day and Republic day. Nowadays, these are occasions for mega-discounts and sales in malls to raise footfalls.

Retailers or shopping malls offer heavy discounts during festive seasons

The Ideology of Central Planning

Government control in key societal infrastructures like airlines, railroads, banks across the world is being substituted by the introduction of liberalization and privatization.

In this respect China and the former Soviet Union experienced the most manifested and multifaceted shift from central planning to market economy. The United States had made a similar transition after World War II. The November 1993 resolution in China was a historical move as it symbolized a strategic shift in the path of country's reform. For the first time literally, it chose to put an end to the planning system as a whole and set the objective of reform to be the foundation of a contemporary market system. Sooner or later democratization was accepted as the 'best practice' to incorporate international institutions. The second phase of China's economic reforms started in 1994, a bit later than that in Eastern Europe after 1990 and in the former Soviet Union countries after 1992. In the initial five years of revolution since 1994, China undertook a lot of major reforms. The most important ones being unification of exchange rates and convertibility under the current account; the renovation of the tax and fiscal systems with the division of national and local tax administrations; and restructuring of the central bank, including establishing cross-province (i.e., regional) central bank branches.

Rights of Passive Consumers

Rights of consumers will continue to be a part of apprehension for governments. Governments shield consumers through latest laws, stricter enforcement, financial disincentives, and consumer edification. The Indian government too has espoused firm measures. For instance, on May 1, 2004, the Union Health Ministry affirmed that smoking in all public places would be a punishable offence. Clause 2(l) of The Cigarettes and other Tobacco Products (Prohibition of Advertisement and Regulation of Trade and Commerce, Production, Supply and Distribution) Bill 2001 has delineated 'public place' as any place to which the public have access, whether as of right or not. This includes auditoriums, hospital buildings, health institutions, amusement centres, restaurants, public offices, court buildings, educational institutions, libraries, public conveyances and the like, which are visited by common people. However, this does not take account of any open space. The most important intent of prohibition of smoking in public places is to shield non-smokers from the detrimental effects of passive smoking. Studies have revealed that cast-off smoke exposure causes pulmonary diseases among children and adults. It is totally unfair that people have to breathe in smoke against their will. This right of passive consumers is also exercised in countries like France, Jakarta, etc.

Smoking ban in public place

Regional Economic Integration

A fall out of the shift towards free market economy and globalization in the second half of the 20th century has been the emergence of trading blocs within and across continents. It was assumed that the seasonality of products will disappear with their worldwide circulation. Every product would be available anywhere and everywhere. Free trade permits quicker, cheaper, and enhanced supply of goods for companies. Consumers could contribute to globalization by purchasing products from around the world. This was the underlying idea when the World Trade Organization (WTO) was constituted following several rouneds of GATT talks between countries. However, much before WTO came into existence, the world had already seen the formation of regional trade blocs such as ASEAN, NAFTA, and SAFTA in which geographically close countries allowed free movement of goods and trade in a bid to achieve higher growth rates for its members. In this context it would be worthwhile to briefly discuss these trade blocs.

Association of Southeast Asian Nations—ASEAN

With an intention to develop a mutually caring society across Southeast Asia along with vibrant expansion in trade, five countries, viz., Indonesia, Malaysia, The Philippines, Singapore, and Thailand constituted the Association of Southeast Asian Nations (ASEAN) on August 8, 1967 in Bangkok. Later, Brunei Darussalam (January 8, 1984); Vietnam (July 28, 1995); Lao PDR and Myanmar (July 23, 1997); and Cambodia (April 30, 1999) joined the economic bloc.

According to the official statistics of ASEAN, till 2006, the region has a population of about 560 million, a total area of 4.5 million square kilometers, a collective gross domestic product of almost US$ 1,100 billion, and a total trade of about US$ 1,400 billion.

The ASEAN declaration claims that the aims and purposes of the association are as follows: (1) to hasten the economic growth, social progress, and cultural development in the region and (2) to endorse regional peace and stability through enduring admiration for justice and the rule of law in the relationship among countries in the region and obedience to the principles of the United Nations Charter.

North American Free Trade Agreement

North American Free Trade Agreement (NAFTA) started its operation on January 1, 1994. Under the NAFTA, all non-tariff barriers to agricultural trade between the United States and Mexico were eradicated. In addition, many tariffs were eliminated right away. Some tariffs, which could not be eliminated at that point of time, were phased out over periods of 5 to 15 years. This did a methodical adjustment to free trade between United States and Mexico, with full realization commencing from January 1, 2008. It is assumed that this agreement will take away nearly all blockades to trade and investment amongst the United States, Canada, and Mexico.

Mexico and Canada did a separate bilateral NAFTA agreement regarding the market admittance for agricultural yields. The Mexican—Canadian agreement abolished most tariffs either instantly or gradually over 5, 10, or 15 years. Tariffs between the two countries on trade in dairy, poultry, eggs, and sugar are, however, continued as before.

South Asian Free Trade Agreement

South Asian Free Trade Agreement (SAFTA) was signed on January 6, 2004 at the 12th SAARC summit held in Pakistan. The agreement envisaged the formation of a model of free trade zone among its seven member nations comprising nearly one-sixth of the world population. Member nations include India, Nepal, Pakistan, Bangladesh, Bhutan, Maldives, Sri Lanka.

The SAFTA agreement was initiated with a vision of imposing zero customs duty for deals of any product by the year 2012 within the trading bloc. The SAFTA agreement was put into practice only after corroboration of conformity by the governments of the seven member nations. The agreement aimed at bringing about economic steadiness in the member nations and smoothening the progress of healthy trade as well as investment relationship among the seven member countries. Nevertheless, there are certain impediments, which encumber trade across South Asian countries as a result of which trade across borders of the South Asian countries accounts for only 5% of the total trade.

Implications of Public Policy Trends on Consumer Behaviour

Public policy plays a great role in shaping the needs and wants of the customers of these days. The impact of such changes has been highlighted in Table 2.3

Table 2.3 *Impact of changing technological trends on the customers*

Public policy	***User***	***Payer***	***Buyer***
Economic Pragmatism	Superior products due to open-market economy	Reduced prices due to tough competition amongst the multinational corporate	Easy and fast movement of the products across the globe
Rights of Passive Consumers	Consumer's rights for information, the consumer forum, and the consumer court legally ensured protection against passive consumption	A financial penalty for consumption disturbing other's health or property	Difficult to use societal harmful products/services in public places
Regional Economic Integration	Seasonal products available for year-round consumption everywhere across the globe. World has become a global village	More cost-effectively created and more cheaply priced products and services	Easier to obtain products and services from varied consumption cultures
	Exposure to diverse consumption cultures resulting in cross-cultural consumers		Local accessibility of international products

OVERALL IMPLICATIONS OF CHANGING TRENDS OF CONSUMER BEHAVIOUR FOR THE MARKETERS

In this century, the speed of technological change and enhanced economic globalization will alter demographic profile of the world further, consequently leading to a change in consumer behaviour across the planet. These trends have multifaceted implications for the prospective workforce and workplace with respect to size, composition, and skills of the workforce; the nature of work and workplace arrangements; and worker payment. The appraisal of these fundamental structural forces can help all stakeholders—workers, employers, educators, marketers, consumers, and policymakers to make well-versed decisions. The overall implications of the changes in the trends in demographic, technological, and public policy to the marketers are as follows:

- Significant move in marketing strategies will take place in the forthcoming years.
- A sway will occur from product-oriented strategies to service-oriented ones.
- Most of the organizations will propose for more security, excellence, and enhanced capability.
- Marketers will need to tailor their products more and more in consultation with the customers.
- Smart and timesaving methods of production and distribution will emerge.
- Apart from just rampant promotion, more emphasis has to be laid on boosting up the emotive, cultural, and social values and ethos as a part of the marketing strategy in the 21st century.

Closing Case

Is e-Business Essential in the Paddy Zone of West Bengal?

Launched in June 2000, ITC's *e-Choupal* has already become the leading initiative of all Internet-based interventions in rural India. *e-Choupal* services today reach out to more than 3.1 million farmers growing a variety of crops—soyabean, coffee, wheat, rice, pulses, shrimp—in over 31,000 villages through 5050 kiosks across 6 states (Madhya Pradesh, Karnataka, Andhra Pradesh, Uttar Pradesh, Maharashtra, and Rajasthan). *e-Choupal* has become so popular today that it has almost become a generic brand in the agribusiness market.

However, the agri-market in West Bengal is still scrappy and subjugated by a number of intermediaries. As a result, the consumers pay higher price for agricultural products, and the farmers also do not get a standard price for their produce. The following factors afflict the West Bengal paddy farmers:

1. **Absence of relevant and real-time information** The farmers are too dependent on grapevine information (especially regarding price) within the village, and commission agents of the traders, or at best from the local *mandis*. Quite often this information is imperfect or conflicting.

2. **Absence of proper information regarding commodity prices, local weather, news** The weather report on television or radio mostly focuses on state wise information, which is of little use to farmers who are in need of localized weather information.
3. **Absence of customized knowledge** The farmers produce different types of paddy. The traders then assort the entire produce and the farmers obtain average price for the product. Furthermore, the farmers do not have expertise to improve and produce special quality products. The storage and other logistics facilities are not owned by the farmers and only possessed by *mahajan*—the village moneylender. Therefore, to produce and store high quality farm products and to preserve their identity from the 'farm-gate to dinner plate' by developing a proper supply chain is a real challenge for them.

This situation calls for connectivity between the farmers and the exporter/trader/grower/industry of national and international associations in order to provide online information with regard to commodity entrance, current prices, most recent research in agricultural marketing, export related credentials, etc.

Hence, there is a need to set up an agricultural marketing information service at the national level. It should be an integrated service incorporating the farmer consultative service with decision support system (DSS). The system should be broad based to provide information related to storage, transport, weather forecast, export potential, etc. A brief business profile of all agricultural commodities would help the buyer in making relative analysis of costs and margins. These profiles would be conveyed to the international markets through Web pages. This would help the traders in preparing commercial profiles of exportable cargo and to give them spotlight in the international markets. All regulated markets, along with their details like infrastructure facilities available, quantum transacted, area and population served, outflow and inflow of various commodities, etc. need to be plotted.

Not that it is impossible. The *e-Choupal* proves that. In *e-Choupal* system, the first option is to bring the entire produce to the ITC warehouse and get reimbursed for the logistics cost. The other alternative is selling the entire produce to the *sanchalak* who runs the *Choupal* or to the ITC collection centre set up for a group of villages. This trims down the gap between the farmer's price and the consumer's price because of the total absence of any intermediaries and the *mandi* system.

But, in an attempt to understand, whether e-business would be viable for West Bengal paddy cultivation, it is imperative to ascertain that they are economically sound. The market's impact has to be quantified by calculating costs and benefits in order to see whether the capital and running costs are likely to be covered by the projected revenues. This depends on two aspects: expenditure levels and the market's skill to catch the attention of the traders willing to rent or lease space. The costs must cover so that such projects can be replicated and scaled up throughout the country and should not depend too much on government subventions. In order to achieve this, investments in physical infrastructure must be kept to a bare minimum by using low-cost construction process. The market must also be appraised in social and qualitative terms. An estimate of the market's operational and maintenance costs can be made as follows:

Farmer cost	**₹ per metric ton**
Trolley freight to *mandi*	100
Labour (filling and weighing)	70–75
Labour cost in *kacchha adat* (small traders)	50
Handling loss	50
Total cost to farmer	*270–275*
Processor cost	
Commission to agent	100
Cost of gunny bags (net)	75–80
Labour cost (stiching gunny bags and loading)	35–40
Labour cost at factory (for unloading)	35–40
Freight to factory	250
Handling at *haat*	10–15
Total cost to processor	*505–520*
Total chain cost	775–800

Source: http://planningcommission.nic.in/reports/sereport/ser/stdy_ict/4_e-choupal%20.pdf and the micro level discussion with the farmers of paddy belt in West Bengal to get their consensus on the applicability of the data obtained from these two sources.

The farmers of the locality claimed that it might cost them around ₹150 (per MT) if they needed to transport the produce within 25 km distance. Going by the calculations of S. Sivakumar, the chief executive of the agribusinesses division of ITC Limited, India, the processor cost of ITC *e-Choupal* would be around ₹215 per metric ton.

There is no doubt that with the implementation of e-commerce, the logistics cost of marketing agricultural produce is bound to go down. However, before trying to implement the concept of e-commerce in paddy business in West Bengal, some facts should not be overlooked. A business house, which wants to expand its agribusiness division by implementing e-commerce in this zone will be subjected to several tribulations, like intermediary strife, illiteracy, outmoded telephone exchanges, irregular electricity supply, and some other hindrances. These are elaborated below:

(a) *Outdated telephone facility* The telephone connectivity is bad due to the deficiency of suitable telephone lines. Especially, in rainy season, some of the underground cables get affected and the telephones are out of order for a number of days.

(b) *Sporadic electricity* Rural West Bengal is often stagnant with frequent power-cuts for long hours. This can pose hindrance in uninterrupted use of the computers in the critical hours.
(c) *Government regulation* Agricultural Produce Marketing Committees Act (APMC Act) forbids any company from acquisition of certain commodities from any source other than the government nominated *mandis*. These items include soyabean, coffee, wheat, and many other products. It is essential to take license for processed rice meant for trading by non-farmers in areas other than the notified market yard or regulated market. In fact, after 2007, private trade has been restained from buying wheat and rice directly from farmers.
(d) *Low education level* The prevailing illiteracy and semi-literacy of the farmers, particularly with almost no knowledge on the usage of computer may pose barriers to convince them about the use of technology per se.
(d) *Probable resistance from the intermediaries* The intermediaries like the *mahajans* or the village traders are supposed to be losing their work in course of abolition of intermediaries. Therefore, in this context, their repercussions can be well predicted. Moreover, the farmers often take loans from them for the purpose of farming. Often these loans are conditional (for example, the farmers need to sell their final produce to them). Moreover, there are several kinds of labour and transporters, small traders involved in the process of *mandi*. With the influx of e-commerce based trading system of agriculture, lots of protests are expected from them too.

Question

1. Given this context, would you, as a marketer, like to implement e-commerce in West Bengal paddy zone? Explain with reasons.

Sources: www.itcportal.com; Sivakumar, S., ITC e-Choupal, Experience sharing: workshop on scaling up ICT for poverty alleviation in India; Indian Institute of Management, Ahmedabad, February 26–27, 2004; Sharma, Devinder, Putting India's Food Security at Stake, http://www.countercurrents.org/dsharma210111.htm, accessed on March 12, 2011.

Summary

We read in this chapter that the world is undergoing a significant change in its population profile as a result of the scientific revolution unleashed in the 20th century. Advancements in science and technology have not only increased the longevity of human race, but vastly increased its adaptability to survive challenging conditions with a host of appliances such as air conditioners and refrigerators that have altered lifestyles across the world. Studies by academic futurists such as Andy Hines have projected that the greying population in the world will treble by 2050. India's population composition then would be very much similar to the developed nations of today. In fact India's census projections for 2026 estimate that the grey population will then be 12 per cent, and size of children's age group (5–14 years) will come down from 19 per cent in 2011 to 16 per cent in 2026. Such demographic changes have wide implications for not only governments, but the industry as well, which has to cater to the consequently changing consumer profiles and behaviour. In this chapter we studied the significance of understanding and tracking the demographic trends and the industry response thereof.

Significant move in marketing strategies will take place in the forthcoming years. A sway will occur from product oriented strategies to the service oriented ones. Most of the organizations will opt for more security, excellence, and enhanced capability. Marketers will need to tailor their products more and more in consultation with customers. Smart and timesaving methods of production and distribution will emerge. Apart from just rampant promotion, more emphasis has to be laid on boosting up the emotive, cultural and social values and ethos as a part of their marketing strategy in the 21st century.

Key Terms

Agribusiness supply chain The agribusiness supply chain integrates the business transactions in all steps of agricultural produce distribution—from the farm, past the farm-gate right to serving the final consumer.

Grey population The section of population which is above 60 years of age.

Single-parent households A single-parent household is one in which either the mother or the father takes care of children without the assistance of the spouse.

Smart products These products are generated by the recent innovations in mobile and sensor technologies. With the help of these technologies, a digital representation of almost any physical entity and its parameters, in other words smart products, can be made available over time at any place.

Mass customization The procedure of delivering goods and services across a wide-market that is tailored to meet a particular need of a customer.

Pragmatism It is the dogma of accepting the facts of life and favouring material realism and literal truth.

Passive consumers This is a term used for indirect consumers.

Central planning It is the system where a big part of economic activity of a nation is under government management.

Regional economic integration Agreements among countries in a particular geographic bloc to relax trade barriers and allow free flow of goods, services, and factors of production.

NAFTA It is an agreement to create free trade zone amongst Canada, Mexico, and the United States.

SAFTA It is an agreement to create free trade zone in the South Asian region comprising India, Pakistan, Nepal, Sri Lanka, Bangladesh, Bhutan, and Maldives

ASEAN It was formed in 1967 between Thailand, Indonesia, Malaysia, the Philippines, Singapore, and Brunei in an effort to develop a free trade area in South East Asia.

Questions

1. Which demographic factors help marketers to identify the target market for the following products?
   - Spectacles
   - Old age homes
   - Broadband connection
   - ICCU of any corporate hospital
   - Day care centre for children
2. What is the importance of anticipating demographic transition in society to develop appropriate marketing communication strategy?
3. What impact does the changing family structure have on children's purchase behaviour?
4. What trends characterize the age distribution of Asian population?
5. What are the purpose and aims of the following organizations:
   - NAFTA
   - SAFTA
   - ASEAN
6. Explain how in various nations economic pragmatism supersedes religious and political ideology?

Critical Assignment

1. With the demographic shift, if any, do you feel that there will be a perceptible impact on the markets for the following products in India?
   (a) Expensive car
   (b) Magazine readership
   (c) Dishwasher
   (d) Crèche
   (e) Pilgrim tour
2. Go through newspapers, magazines, and Internet and find out the impact of shift from central planning to market economy in Russia. Compare and contrast the background and impacts of Russian liberalization with that of China.

Chapter **3**

Dimensions of Consumerism

Chapter Goals

After completing this chapter, you will be able to understand

- **the roots of consumerism in various nations across the globe**
- **marketers responses to consumer issues**
- **the dimensions of consumerism and its implications worldwide**
- **the threats of child consumerism and its implication particularly in India**
- **the types of information a consumer is entitled to in any nation**
- **the Consumer Protection Act, India, 1986**

Opening Vignette

Impact of Celebrity Endorsement on the Choice of Health Drinks—An Opportunity for Marketers to hook Child Consumers

Alluring punch lines such as 'collect them all' or '*taste bhi health bhi*,' motivate young television spectators to exercise their pester power over their parents to get them all. It is amazing to see children emerge as the biggest consumers in this millennium. Nowadays, there are lots and lots of advertisements on innumerable television channels promoting toys, health drinks, soaps, stationery, confectionery, biscuits, and anything that a child could use. It's simply a never-ending list. Many celebrities, specially from sports and Bollywood, are roped in for endorsing these products specially targeted at the kids

Some popular health drinks

Recently, a survey was conducted by the author on 100 children from different towns like Serampore, Chuchura, Seoraphuli, Konnagar, and Uttarpara in Hooghly district of West Bengal, India to find out the impact of celebrity endorsement on the choice of health drinks. Four brands *Horlicks*, *Bournvita*, *Complan*, and *Boost* were selected for the purpose. *Horlicks* and *Boost* were endorsed by celebrities (*Horlicks* by child actor Darsheel Safari and *Boost* by cricket icons Sachin Tendulkar and Virender Sehwag) while *Bournvita* and *Complan* did not opt for celebrity endorsement. The objectives of the study were to find out the following:

- children's most preferred brand of health drinks
- the reasons for selecting a particular brand
- the association between the celebrity endorsement and the choice of brands

From the responses of the survey, it was identified that *Horlicks* was the most preferred brand with 42% of share in the sample, followed by *Boost* (28%), and *Complan* (26%) (refer Chart 3.1).

In the quest to identify the reasons for selecting a particular brand, the following results were obtained.

- Amongst the kids who selected *Horlicks* as their most preferred brand, 53% acknowledged the impact of the Safari's endorsement as the most important parameter behind their choice (refer Chart 3.2).
- Amongst the kids who selected *Boost* as their most preferred brand, 76% admitted to the impact of the endorsement of Tendulkar and Sehwag as the most important parameter influencing their choice (refer Chart 3.3).

- Amongst the kids who selected *Complan* as their most preferred brand, 56% identified the impact of their parent's choice as the most important parameter behind their brand preference (refer Chart 3.4). The other influencing parameters behind the selection of *Complan* were availability and packaging.
- However in case of choice of *Bournvita*, the important parameters were packaging and availability (refer Chart 3.5).

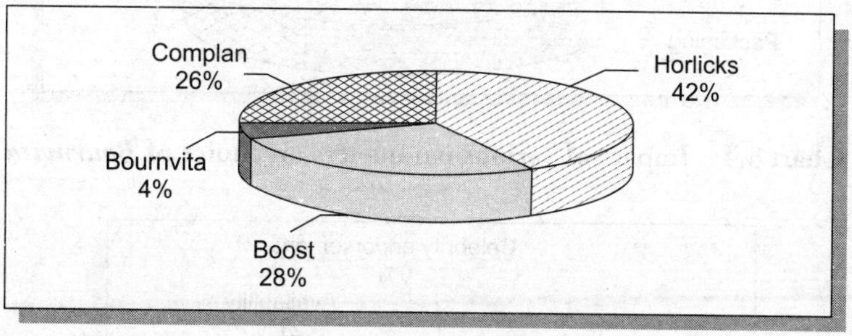

Chart 3.1 Brand preference of health drinks by kids

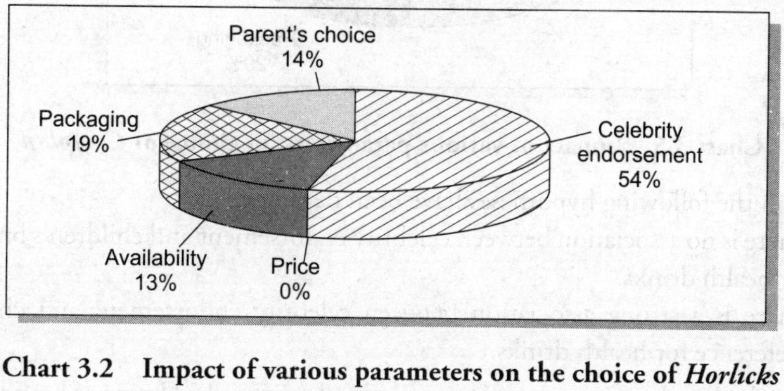

Chart 3.2 Impact of various parameters on the choice of *Horlicks*

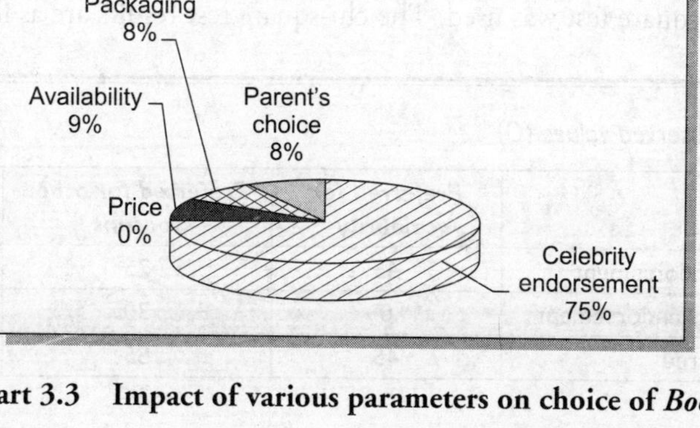

Chart 3.3 Impact of various parameters on choice of *Boost*

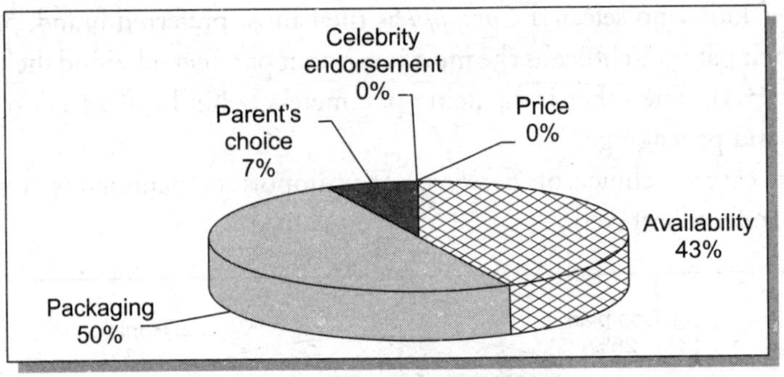

Chart 3.4 Impact of various parameters on choice of *Bournvita*

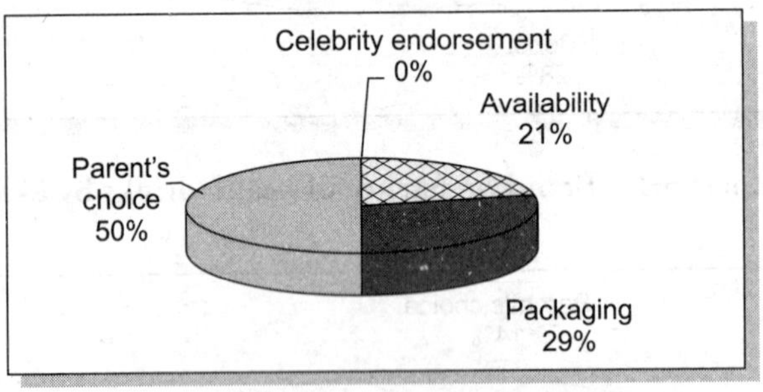

Chart 3.5 Impact of various parameters on choice of *Complan*

In this situation the following hypotheses have been developed:

H_0 There is no association between celebrity endorsement and children's brand preference for health drinks.

H_1 There is a strong association between celebrity endorsement and children's brand preference for health drinks.

To identify whether there is any strong association between the choice of brands and celebrity endorsements, i.e., which of the two hypotheses to accept, the null hypothesis (H_0) or the alternative hypothesis (H_1), chi-square test was used. The chi-square test results are as follows:

Table 3.1 *Table of observed values (O)*

	Preferred for celebrity	*Preferred for other reasons*	*Total customers preferred*
Brand with celebrity endorsement	45	25	70
Brand without celebrity endorsement	0	30	30
Total customers preferred	45	55	100

Table 3.2 *Table of expected values (E)*

	Preferred for celebrity	Preferred for other reasons	Total customers preferred
Brand with celebrity endorsement	31.5	38.5	70
Brand without celebrity endorsement	13.5	16.5	30
Total customers preferred	45	55	100

$O_i - E_i$	$(O - E)^2$	$(O - E)^2/E$
13.5	182.25	5.79
–13.5	182.25	4.73
–13.5	182.25	13.5
13.5	182.25	11.04

where $I = 1, 2, 3, \ldots$

Therefore, $\lambda^2 = \Sigma (O - E)^2/E = 35.06$

Now, the degree of freedom = (no. of rows – 1) (no. of columns – 1)

Here, the degree of freedom = (2 – 1) (2 – 1) = 1

The table value of λ^2 at 95% level of confidence, i.e., $\lambda^2_{0.05} = 3.84$ at degree of freedom = 1

From the calculated value of λ^2, i.e., 35.06 > 3.84, we can conclude that the null hypothesis is rejected and the alternative hypothesis is accepted.

Therefore, it can be concluded with 95% level of significance that there is a strong association between celebrity endorsement and children's brand preference for health drinks.

The survey puts forward the reason, why the marketer does rampant advertising, targeting the children. Darsheel Safari was a celebrity after the superhit Hindi movie *Tare Zameen Par. Horlicks* has successfully pushed up the children's motivation towards the brand by roping him.

Not just health drinks, marketers are increasingly opting for advertisements targeting children, which in turn boost child consumerism.

INTRODUCTION

Consumerism is the fastest growing environmental power affecting the vital business decisions. Humans use an array of wherewithal not only for their basic needs but also to indulge in luxury items and technological innovations to enhance their standards of living. Such consumption is not always detrimental. From time immemorial man has always sought to make life effortless and luxurious. An economic order that is based on the creation and nurturing of desires for increasing consumption of goods and services is termed as consumerism. In the Oxford dictionary, consumerism is 'emphasis on or preoccupation with the acquisition of consumer goods.'

In economics, consumerism refers to economic policies placing emphasis on consumption. In an abstract sense, it is the belief that the free choice of consumers should dictate the economic structure of a society. Thus, in contemporary usage, the term consumerism is often associated with the criticism of increasing human consumption, starting with 19th century American economist Thorstein Veblen. However, consumerism is also associated with the movement that seeks to ensure consumer protection and rights of consumers by seeking honest and fair trade and marketing practices. Nowadays consumers are confronted with some common and relevant questions regarding consumerism.

(a) How the products and wealth they devour are really created?
(b) Was there any negative impact of that process of production on the environment, society, or individual?
(c) Do their forms of consumption pose any threat to the environment, society, or individuals?
(d) Which are the driving forces behind their picking of consumption bits and pieces?
(e) Was their purchase a necessity or simply lavishness?
(f) How does their change in lifestyle influence the societal change?
(g) To what extent is their consumption basket influenced by advertising strategies of the marketers?
(h) How does pragmatism influence their societal relationships, culture, and value system?

In the course of seeking answers to the afore-mentioned questions, we can see consumerism as a movement or a set of policies aimed at regulating the products, services, methods, and standards of manufacturers, sellers, and advertisers in the interests of the buyer.

Thus, we come across two aspects of consumerism: one in which it is seen as an economic order that sustains 'conspicuous consumption' as Veblen called it, and second; consumer activism. As a result we come across a range of definitions of consumerism by several stalwarts of marketing some of which are as follows.

- Consumerism is 'a social movement seeking to augment the rights and powers of buyers in relation to sellers': Kotler (1972)
- Consumerism is 'the voicing of consumer discontent and the furtherance of corrective actions': Maynes (1990)
- It is defined as 'a citizens' movement which will make broad-reaching social, ecological, and political demands on suppliers of goods and services': McIlhenny (1990)
- From the W2 and W3 angle, consumerism has been delineated as 'the efforts made either by the consumer himself, the government, and/or independent organizations to protect the consumer from the unscrupulous practices of businesses in their quest for profit': Onah (1979).

No doubt, the impacts of consumerism, positive and negative, are noteworthy to all facets of our lives.

In this chapter, we shall discuss both these aspects of consumerism.

A vignette of consumerism

MARKETERS RESPONSE TO CONSUMERISM

The ultimate objective of any marketing strategy is to accomplish better sales figures and market performance by ensuring enhanced customer satisfaction. Prior to the emergence of the consumer-centric epoch, marketing activities were developed only to promote a product, shore up an impressive sales figure, and manipulate market shares. But times have evolved and new business approaches are put into practice. Today, consumer-oriented marketing is an emerging trend.

From the Indian perspective, D.P.S. Verma and Shashi Nanda (2007) found from a survey of 65 consumer durable companies, located in Delhi and the surrounding National Capital Region (NCR), that firms are inclined to be more consumer-oriented rather than product-oriented. Attributing this shift towards the customer-centric approach to 'rapid escalation in consumerism,' they observed that consumerism is a prospect for those corporate managers who are able to spot and foresee the consumer's needs and wants.

Certainly, these days the consumers revolve around the business and drive it either towards accomplishment or dismiss it as failure. To penetrate your target market accurately, it is always better to first consider who really your consumers are. There are three points to ponder in determining whether the target segment is profitable or not. These are size, congestion, and purchase ability. In fact, the ability of people within the group to buy or avail a product determines the actual profitability of the business. Explicitly, the corporate needs to identify those groups of people who really need, use, and purchase their products directly. And once they have identified the main market movers of their products, they can judge their needs, aspirations, and wants more precisely. And to achieve that, an in-depth marketing research is essential. Doing so allows a business to generate exact mechanisms to precisely comprehend the consumer's behaviour.

Consumer-oriented marketing also calls for checking of pricing strategies by the companies and finding out their relevance and appropriateness to general consumers. Doing so averts companies from overpricing or underpricing their offerings, and at the same time offering the best value to the customers.

It also involves the process of scrutinizing the effectiveness of the existing distribution channel. These tests are performed to assess a particular store's aptness to carry a product title. In this era of 'customer is the king', all distribution strategies are pinpointed towards the lone goal of selling multiple assortments from multiple touch points to intensify the business.

In W2 and W3 countries, to make the marketing strategies more and more customer-centric, an assessment of customer feedback and opinions for the product should be given the highest priority. Marketers have to make sure that they are doing well in providing perfect solutions to the customers. For this purpose, primary research on customer's views, feelings, and thoughts needs to be conducted. If the research outcomes are not favourable to the company, it needs to reorganize its existing system. The targeting, positioning, and marketing mix strategies should be redesigned in the best possible way to be in sync with the needs of the customer. Developing a proper customer-oriented marketing strategy is a step towards customizing the marketer's offer to the end user. While gratifying the explicit requirements of the underscored consumers, the marketers also need to inculcate best value to them. And perhaps, delivering supreme value to the customers might result in long-term relationships. These steps will certainly open up marvelous prospects for the company.

CHILD CONSUMERISM: A VERITABLE THREAT

In an era of cable TV and media blitzkrieg, the progressively escalating impact of gorgeous and swaying TV commercials has unleashed unprecedented consumerism among children by targeting them through 'hard-sell'.

Children, exposed to hundreds of ads everyday by watching nearly 80 million TV sets, are evolving today in a different way. They not only spend several hours watching television, but also feature in endorsements of banks, water purifiers, soaps, toothpastes, airlines, etc. Thanks to unregulated advertising on private TV channels, children many a time exercise pester power on their parents to get them certain expensive brands. According to child psychiatrist Dr. S.M. Manohari 'Parents use TV as an electronic babysitter and bribe them by toys or chips seen in ads to get children to behave properly, eat, or cooperate. Children get into a rut of wanting things all the time.' The enduring consequence of advertising on small children is for all to see. Says Manohari,: 'They learn what they see. Advertisements also encourage children to be fickle in their loyalties. They do not develop long-lasting values and children mature in skewed patterns.' A rather shocking finding in this regard is the extent of the social impact of this unfettered child consumerism being promoted by the corporate in India (refer Exhibit 3.1).

The story is not very different in other nations. What is different, however, is the developed world has woken up to this threat and has initiated steps to counter the adverse impact of child consumerism. While USA woke up to the waves of advertising on children long back in 1970s, UK has sternly controlled the TV commercials that target children. Countenanced with obesity endemic in children, it has banned commercials targeting children, especially in case of advertisements of food items. In many other nations like Sweden, commercials targeting children below 12 have been prohibited.

Sweden, in contrast to any other nations, endows the school children with media education. On the contrary, USA and UK are struggling with evils of child obesity, school shoot-outs, disenchanted teenagers, broken families, and rising child consumerism. With almost the similar properties arising out of the rapid societal change in this century, the most pertinent question for the Indian children is: how does the rising trend of consumerism shape their destiny?

Exhibit 3.1: Child Consumerism: A Cartoon Network Survey

In a survey carried out by *Cartoon Network* in alliance with *Synovate India*, it was observed that kids these days are playing the roles of both direct and indirect consumers in the Indian market. They apply 'pester power' on their parents even in buying classy items like cars. They splurge around ₹291 crores simply as pocket money. The findings of the survey carried out in 14 Indian cities covering 4,043 children by *Cartoon Network* are as follows:

- *In 84% of the families surveyed, children accompanied their parents to shopping. In these cases, parents divulge that the kids were subjective in big purchases such as television sets, cars, and mobile phones.*
- *71%, 70%, 67%, and 66% of the surveyed parents admitted that their child manipulated the brand choice while buying TV sets, computers, mobile phones, and car, respectively.*

To excerpt the quote of Mr. Duncan Morris, the Vice President Research and Marketing, Turner International, it may be concluded that the Indian kids are becoming more and more tech savvy and technology oriented. Nowadays, mobile phone and camera are included in their list of desire. Mobile, although, is considered as the principal means of communication, is nonetheless, used by them for text messaging and playing games.

(Contd.)

Exhibit 9.1 *(Contd.)*

© Indiatodayimages.com

Indian kids are becoming more and more tech savvy and technology oriented

DIMENSIONS OF CONSUMERISM

During the last three decades, consumerism has received an impetus in business and academia. Hence, it is imperative to scrutinize the scope of consumerism and to find out the level to which consumer protection, education, and information are available to several customer groups. Simply by appraising the present shape of these consumer issues with special focus on consumerism (consumption), any country can embark on exposing its populace to unfettered play of market forces.

In this context, the study of Thorelli (1990) on attitudes toward consumerism in four developing countries—Singapore, India, Nigeria, and Kenya—is worth mentioning. This study scans the present extent of consumerism in these countries and judges them against the underlying dimensions of marketing strategies. These countries symbolize two different continents (Africa and Asia). Hence, the study provides an interesting facet to the evaluation of dimensions of consumerism in two different continents.

According to this study, consumerism in developing countries is starkly different from that of developed countries in several ways. The divergence stems from the following three aspects: (a) insufficiency of passable quality control of locally manufactured products, (b) derisory logistics services, and (c) perceived low significance placed on consumer contentment by vendors who willingly trade adulterated products. Apart from these factors there are some peripheral influences ensuing from developed nations exporting goods. In most of the W3 countries, there are stringent government policies to control consumerism. India is also not an exception. Consequently, consumerism in most W3 countries is a subject of government policy and legislation. In particular, it is the proficient enactment of such policies rather than an issue of affianced public support system.

CONSUMER PROTECTION ACT, 1986

The Consumer Protection Act, 1986 (Act no. 68 of 1986) is a signpost in the history of socio-economic legislation in the nation. The key object of this latest law is to endow the consumers with better safety and security by offering uncomplicated, prompt, and economical remedy to aggrieved consumer.

A complaint, either handwritten or typed on a plain paper, can be filed by a consumer, a registered consumer organization, central or state government, and more than one consumers identified by common concern. Stamp or court fee is not required in this processing.

However, the fields of consumer complaints are specified. They are as follows:

- Any unfair trade practice or restrictive trade practice adopted by the trader
- Defective goods
- Deficiency in service
- Excess price charged by the trader
- Unlawful goods sale, which is hazardous to life and safety when used

The three tier forums enact the Consumer Protection Act. These are usually referred as 'Consumer Courts'. The tiers are as follows:

- District Forum: For claims up to ₹20 lakh
- State Commission: For claims above ₹20 lakh but less than ₹1 crore
- National Commission: For claims above ₹1 crore

The nature of complaint and the relief sought by the consumer must be evidently cited. It has to be filed in quadruplicate in district forum or state commission (as the case may be) if it is against only one opposite party. In case of multiple parties, additional copies are to be filed simultaneously. By and large complaint should resolute within 90 days from the date of notice issued to the opposite party. In case a sample testing of any product is needed, a complaint is to be disposed off within 150 days.

© Indiatodayimages.com

Consumer court in Delhi, India

Consumer courts may grant the petitioner the following reliefs:

i. Repair of defective goods.
ii. Replacement of defective goods.
iii. Refund of price paid for the defective goods or service.
iv. Removal of deficiency in service.
v. Refund of extra money charged.

However, Verma and Nanda (2007) claimed in their paper that even though comprehensive statutory measures have been provided for restricting the business practices encouraging consumerism, the Indian corporate is yet to go a long way to furnish that goal.

Closing Case

Targeting Kids through Advertising—A Chat in Office Bus

Nirmal was on his way to office. Ujjwal was waiting for the office bus to come. It will take another hour for him to reach his office even if he gets the bus right now. Ujjwal looked at his watch. Meanwhile, the bus arrived. Ujjwal boarded it and found a vacant seat beside Nirmal. Both of them work in a reputed ad agency in the city and have known each other for the last seven years.

Nirmal looked at him and the conversation started.

Nirmal: My 15-year-old daughter had demanded a cell phone as she completed her high school. I had to buy one for my 12-year-old son too; otherwise, he would have got a complex. It is difficult for me to manage a household, but parents, you know Ujjwal, are helpless. Our children are constantly comparing us with our neighbours.

Ujjwal: It is not only your problem Nirmal, but children these days constitute an important target market and merit attention from a marketing perspective. The children play major role in making purchase decisions concerning the entire family.

Nirmal: I agree, consumerism per se is fantastic for the industry. Nearly all the consumer good sectors have experienced tremendous growth due to this. Consequently, there has been an exponential growth in sales and ad budgets of various companies. Nevertheless, tell me, do the hefty ad budgets ensure ethical advertising?

At this moment, another colleague Anant intervened.

Anant: Correct, Nirmal. It is definitely the social responsibility of the companies as well as the ad agencies to pass the correct information to young and impressionable minds. Children's interest is more important than the profit. Kids are not mature enough and are easily trapped every time they buy a new toy or gizmo. But are the parents always aware of the bad effects of this rampant consumerism? The moment we succumb to the pressure of demands of a hysterical child, we welcome materialistic forces in our society. We are ourselves giving rise to an acquisitive generation.

Ujjwal: Come on. What is the harm in it? After all, we are marketers. Sales and profit are our prime targets. It is not a new phenomenon. Even when we were kids, many a times we had exerted pressure on our parents by irresistible power of child-like nagging to persuade them to buy whatever we wanted.

Anant: These days, the preteens are having a tremendous voice in the process of family buying decision-making.

Ujjwal: In many cases the borders of consumption are no longer age-restricted. So the preteens are intervening in the process of family purchase decisions. You may be aware that the average ad expenditure is around ₹38,000 million. Ad expenditure per year on products meant for children and bought by them, like chocolates, is only around 7–8%. Recent buzzword of innovative marketing strategies is 'target the kids', directly or indirectly. Just recall the *Maruti* ad with the little Sikh boy, the *Hutch* ad with the boy and the dog, the spectacled boy in the LG TV ad, and of course the *Pepsodent* ads.

Nirmal: But do you know the result of pester power these days? Last time, I was going through an article and found by 2030, in India 6 out of 10 children would pester an average of 9 times even after their parents refusal to buy a particular product for them. The study also predicted that children in the age group of 9–14 would control 80% of all brand purchases by parents. The article was published as a book titled *Brand Child*.

Ujjwal: I think you have heard the name of Prasoon Joshi of *McCann Erickson*, the man behind the '*Thanda matlab Coca-Cola*' campaign. He said kids are one of the major factors behind the success or failure of an ad. If a kid likes an ad, he remembers it and repeatedly views it. Soon enough the parents are found to hum the tune too. See Nirmal, we have to catch the market. If the product sells well for these ads targeting the kids, I do not mind.

Nirmal: Pester power is the new buzzword in marketing circles and the country's business houses have realized that the child is the key to loosen his parents' purse strings. Have you thought of its social consequences?

Anant: I do agree. Last year in our neighbourhood slum, a poor lady could not provide her 14-year-old son with a motorbike and the boy committed suicide. The son used to watch TV in our nearby TV shop and used to ask the shopkeepers regularly about the price of such a bike. This is really tragic.

Nirmal: This is not an isolated incident. A number of such cases have been reported.

Economically weak parents are also burdened with these expenses. Sometimes they feel guilty when they cannot provide their children with such amenities and they get depressed.

Anant: Moreover, kids today are demanding things, which are not at all meant for their consumption. Advertisers should not make kids the puppets of their hand. After all Ujjwal, business has some responsibility towards the society too.

Ujjwal: See, the foremost responsibility of the business is to earn a steady profit. Again, why always you people are thinking in a negative direction? Exposure to mass media and discussions with parents ensure that children are not only aware of the new brands available, but also know how to evaluate them on various parameters. It's true that the kids clearly influence the family purchasing behaviour in several cases but they are not puppets in the hands of the marketers. Today's adolescents have full cognitive development. I believe that most of them have a clear comprehension of the financial aspects required for processing information and selection of products and brands. In fact an analysis of children as consumers will definitely help in the formulation of marketing strategies. Two years back, *Coca-Cola* conducted a research called 'Teen Machine' by identifying the motivations, interests, and attitudes of teens. The results show the greatest involvement in purchase decision-making.

Roma, who was a silent listener until now, intervened.

Roma: In many cases, the children act as purchasing agents for the family. Sometimes the teens are delegated the task of purchasing products meant for their parents.

Ujjwal: Yes Roma. In fact, the products for which children are the purchasing agents are also a golden goose for the marketers. What all they need here is to understand the mindset of these little purchasing agents and to communicate direct appropriate messages towards them. The kids in India are of course the pivotal point of the Indian family system.

They can drag their parents to visit a particular shopping mall repeatedly. What I precisely mean is that they are emerging as the most important medium for relationship building in India. You cannot deny that they are not only the influencers of family purchase decisions, but are also the future consumers.

Nirmal: But Ujjwal, what's the use of targeting future consumers? An advertisement that endangers the safety of children or creates interest in unhealthy practices shall not be accepted. In any case, there is no competent monitoring system in our country, which could be entrusted in this regard. Targeting the kids through advertising in the absence of a steady policy framework and wider awareness could really be detrimental to the kids. However, a consolation for parents like us is that there is of late a realization for a comprehensive policy on Indian Broadcasting System.

Ujjwal: See, because of today's dual career world and nuclear family, TV has become the 'foster mother' of the children. They become brand conscious and of course what you say as consumerism is there. You cannot help it.

Roma: Yes. Sometimes, I feel guilty of not spending enough time with my kids and try to satisfy them with whatever they ask for. I know sometimes, I am wrong but I want to see them happy.

Anant: According to a study conducted by the Centre for Media Studies (CMS) in Tamil Nadu and West Bengal, parents consider the increasing television viewing habits of their children as a threat. Some days before, the teachers in Kolkata publicly demonstrated against television. Although the situation is not that grave in the northern states but the teachers in the South are more concerned about the effects of television on their pupils. However, a new thought of disciplining child viewers has emerged recently. In a slow and steady manner, it has started spreading in various families.

Roma: Yes, I have heard that they are talking of some methods to regulate the children.

Nirmal: Like?

Roma: Like not allowing the children to handle the television set and restrict their viewership in only some selected programmes. The study suggested allowing children to watch TV only after completing schoolwork and set a fixed time for their viewership.

Nirmal: Do you think TV is the only medium to provoke the children? It is true that the children are more influenced by audiovisual means but do not forget about the posters, banners, magazines, and newspapers. How would you restrict the viewership of these?

Anant: All that we require is to demonstrate the ad in a positive manner.

Nirmal: Meaning?

Anant: Nirmal do not forget the social ad on literacy drive. It is showed how a poor boy gets the light of education. Even if we agree that as advertisers we have to target the kids, yet isn't there a better way to encourage the children to help the society? Can you recollect the ad of *Dettol* soap where the children are on a cleanliness drive?

Roma: Moreover, we have to explain to the children that all the images and ads they view on TV or other media, and make them understand the difference between the reality and fantasy. Moreover, we are the people who should help them build their sense of reasoning.

Nirmal: But my question is still unanswered. Suppose a poor child is exposed to an ad of expensive mobile and demands it from his parents. Later, if he commits suicide on not getting it, would you still say that this ad should be continued?

Anant: It is really a debatable issue and of course a management dilemma. However, let us stop here. See, we have already reached our office.

Ujjwal: Yes! Let us plan for the project that came up last night.

They all got down from the bus and entered the office.

(This is a fictitious case to stimulate classroom discussion. Any resemblance with any character or incidence is totally unintentional.)

Questions

1. What steps can be taken to make children logically comprehend the images and advertisements they view on television or in any other public media?
2. As a marketer, if your rampant promotion gives rise to child consumerism how would you balance between your marketing objective and social responsibility of business?

Summary

'Consumerism' is likely to govern the world market in the coming decades, thanks to liberalization and globalization across the globe. A bleak paradigm of this growing consumption pattern and its allied implications is the excessive exposure of children to the promotional means of a profit-hungry corporate. Children's markets are vast and there are a lot of products and fast foods aimed at them. Parents now are hard-pressed raising child as the latter are more and more predisposed to commercialism.

As conspicuous consumption threatens the social fabric and, in the words of Veblen, breeds 'economic waste', there is a big shift in the marketing strategies from becoming product-centric to consumer-centric. More and more companies are focusing on consumer needs and desires and altering their promotional strategies to captivate their target segment for raking in sales.

This has raised the pitch for regulation of market policies specially in the W2 and W3 countries, where protection of consumer rights leaves a lot to be desired. Thus, consumerism may also be defined as the fundamental practice of recognizing the rights of the consumer as envisioned in the Consumer Protection Act (1986) and guaranteeing correct standards for the procured goods and services. This objective can be accomplished in a reasonable time frame only when all the parties concerned act in a harmonious manner. The parties include consumers, governments, regulatory authorities like consumer courts, trade, industry and service providers' organizations, and those in charge of execution of the laws and orders in the market place.

Key Terms

Consumerism Consumerism is a social movement in quest of boosting the rights and powers of buyers in relation to sellers.

Pester power It is the children's coercive power to influence the parents.

Consumer Protection Act (1986) It is the act to protect the rights of the consumers against any frauds by the marketer.

Consumer court It is the forum where consumers seek relief for the frauds by the marketer.

District forum For claims up to ₹20 lakhs the consumer can lodge a complaint in this forum.

State commission For claims above ₹20 lakhs but less than ₹1 crore, the consumer can lodge a complaint in this commission.

National commission For claims above ₹1 crore, the consumer can lodge a complaint in this commission.

Consumer-oriented marketing In this system, all marketing mix policies are directed towards the satisfaction of the ultimate customers.

Questions

1. Compare and contrast the pattern of consumerism in developing and developed countries.
2. Today consumer-oriented marketing is an emerging trend—Elucidate the statement with respect to a company of your choice.

Critical Assignment

1. Dr. S.M. Manohari articulated that 'Parents use TV as an electronic babysitter and bribe them using TV, toys or chips seen in ads to get children to behave, eat or cooperate. Children get into a rut of wanting things all the time.' In this context, identify one double income and one single income nuclear family in your locality and compare the impact of child consumerism in both the families.
2. Find out some examples from the real life where Consumer Protection Act (1986) has successfully solved the customer grievances.

Section II

Individual Determinants of Consumer Behaviour

Chapter **4**

Motivation and Involvement of the Consumers

Chapter Goals

After completing this chapter, you will be able to understand

- **the importance of understanding customer motives**
- **the process of motivation**
- **Maslow's need hierarchy**
- **Murray's psychogenic needs**
- **Dichter's consumption needs**
- **the needs identified by marketing scholars**
- **how do motives interact with each other to affect consumer's behaviour**
- **the nature of involvement and its influence on consumers**

Opening Vignette

Taste and Convenience, Not Health, Driving Factors in Bottled Water Consumption—A Study at the University of Birmingham Campus

There has been a steady increase in bottled water consumption over the last decade or so. A qualitative study by means of semi-structured interviews of 23 users of the Munrow Sports Centre in the University of Birmingham campus was done by Lorna A. Ward *et al.* The idea behind this study was to perk up the comprehension about the public's health values relating to the bottled mineral water, and to the degree to which these ideas influence their drinking habits.

A qualitative content analysis using fundamentals of the grounded theory was used to scrutinize the responses. The inductive method of classifying themes from the composed data, rather than applying *priori* classes in a top-down mode, was suitable given the dearth of earlier research exploring public insights and beliefs about bottled water. *The results were indeed amazing!!!!!!*

It was pragmatic that most of the respondents considered that bottled water was healthier than the normal tap water. Nonetheless, they were ignorant of the exact advantages of consuming packaged water. The research found some interesting results. It projected that the convenience and taste parameters were the core motivating factors for choosing bottled water. Only for a minority of the respondents, as the study shows, the beliefs about the health benefits of bottled water emerged as a motivating factor for choosing to drink bottled water. Some customers chose to drink bottled water because of apprehensions about the safety of tap water. However, the majority of people were of the belief that tap water was quite healthy and safe for drinking purpose. As a whole, convenience, taste, and cost considerations were almost universally significant for the selection of drinking water.

Other factors behind the fondness of bottled water over other soft drinks were the persuasion of the media, positioning of mineral water as a class symbol by the manufacturers, and re-use of the bottle as a pot for reserving tap water. So the first and foremost job of the marketer, in this context, was to understand the motivational cues or motives behind any purchase decision of a consumer.

IMPORTANCE OF UNDERSTANDING CUSTOMER MOTIVES

Marketers are fascinated by the motivation of customers normally when it is related to purchase behaviour. This behaviour recounts to the intention for the aspiration to possess the particular goods or services, and it can also be expressed as 'goal-related behaviour'. Behind every motive there lies an analogous need. Some motives are physiological in nature. These are basic human needs like hunger, thirst, warmth, shelter, etc. Some motives, such as desire for approval, success, and prestige are psychological. Most often, buying decisions are a blend of motives. In the alternative evaluation stage, in choice heuristics, some motives might seem to be stronger than others, and the final choice might be a negotiable solution. For example, price might be the deciding parameter, where more evidently financial restrictions dominate the motive. It can, therefore, be seen that a number of motives might play significant roles while taking a purchasing decision.

As a result of increasing globalization, economies in W1 countries have developed a large scale of differentiated and value-added customer-friendly products. Besides, consumers now have not only the option to differentiate amongst various alternatives of goods and services to fulfill their needs but also multiplicities of companies that offer different brands of similar products. In fact, to become the market leader within its industry, a marketer needs to understand the market properly and comprehend the latent needs of its customers very well. Undoubtedly, well-developed commercial tactics add a part of this success too. Nevertheless, in saturated markets in which products demonstrate tiny variation in their values, it is of the essence for companies to engender bizarre motivational stimuli in their offered marketing mix, in order to grab an elevated level of attention and attraction from the consumers. But what stimulates people to prefer a certain brand? Is it, at all, possible for marketers to manipulate the consumer decision-making process to develop their positive attitude for their brands? The consumer decision process is not superficial; it rather portrays the internal psychological process, for example, what happens in the mind of a customer at the time of the evaluation of alternatives.

Let us consider the example of buying a car in several stages of family life cycle. The question is what motivates a person to purchase a car? Is it because a 30-year-old bachelor wants to perk up his standard of living or is it for the reason that a man of the same age wants to have a well guarded and strongly fortified car for his family given the accident prone city traffic? Therefore, purchase of a product may be a resultant of various motives. Every individual has needs; some needs are innate, others are acquired. Innate needs are physiological; they include the needs for food, water, air, clothing, shelter, and sex. Because they are needed to sustain biological life, the biogenic needs may be thought as the primary needs or motives.

Acquired needs are those needs that we develop in response to our culture or environment. These may include needs for self-esteem, prestige, affection, power, and learning. Because acquired needs are generally psychological or psychogenic, these are known as secondary needs or motives.

Several psychologists have nurtured the concept of motivation. In many decision-process-models such as Dubois (2000); Engel, Kollat, Blackwell model (1978); the Nicosia model (1966); the Howard and Sheth model (1969); and the Howard–Ostlund model (1973), the root of 'motivation' can be traced to the words 'motive' or 'motives'. But then what does 'motivation' exactly mean? Are all our purchase decisions allied to some motives to a certain degree?

MOTIVATION—DEFINED

Motivation is the defined state of drive or arousal that propels behaviour toward a goal object. Motivation is comprised of two components: drive or arousal and goal object. In other words, motivation may be referred as the state of mind that energizes and directs goal-oriented behaviour. Eminent psychologists state that motivation might be entrenched from the basic need to quench thirst or satisfy hunger to less-apparent reasons like satisfying hedonism, altruism, morality, or avoiding mortality.

Fonvielle (1997) advocated that if a company's marketing section needs to figure out how to stimulate a target group to persuade in favour of their brands, they first have to identify what their target group actually needs. Here the central question of consumer behaviour is rooted: how the purchase motives are spawned.

PROCESS OF MOTIVATION

Motivation refers to the process that causes people to act the way they do. It follows sequential steps.

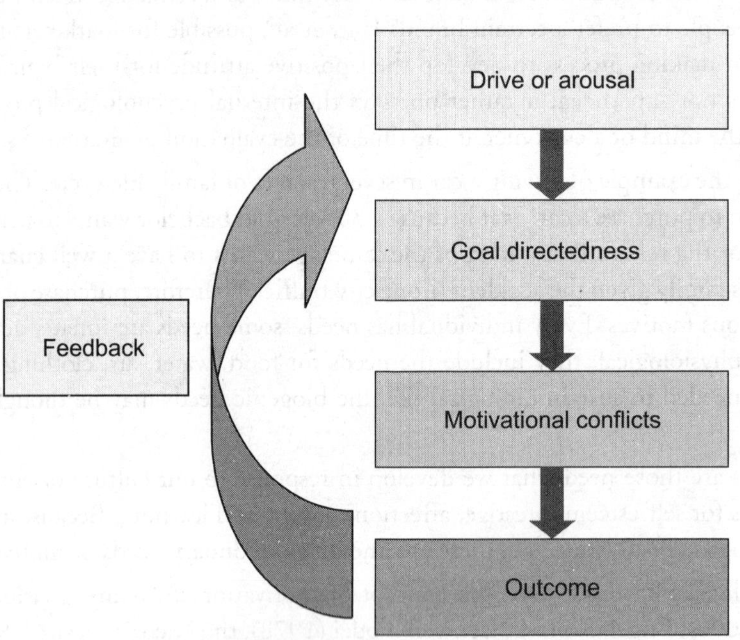

Figure 4.1 Process of motivation

Drive or Arousal

When a person feels a difference between the present state and the ideal state, an inner force directs him towards attainment of the ideal state. This inner force is called the drive. It can be explained in terms of the degree to which an individual is eager to spend energy to achieve one goal ahead of their many other goals. Drive theory is centered at biological needs that create disturbed states or arousal, for example, hunger, thirst, etc. Victor H. Vroom, whose primary research area was on the expectancy theory of motivation, is a business school professor at the Yale School of Management. He was born on August 9, 1932 in Montreal, Canada and holds a Ph.D. from The University of Michigan. Some of his phenomenal books are *Work and Motivation, Leadership and Decision-Making*, and *The New Leadership*. Vroom's expectancy theory states that actions are mostly drawn by expectations of derived outcomes, for example, some positive incentives, rather than pushed from within. Drive may also result from hedonic needs, i.e., to utilise products and services that confer pleasure through senses that generate fantasies and that provide emotional arousal, sensory pleasure, aesthetic pleasure, emotional experience, fun, and enjoyment.

Goal Directedness

Motivation is directed towards the attainment of one's goal. Marketers try to produce goods and services that will endow the customers with desired benefits and allow them to trim down the state of tension.

Motivational Conflicts

Kurt Lewin (September 9, 1890–February 12, 1947), a distinguished German-born psychologist and the founder of social psychology, shaped the conflict theories about individual's experience as: approach–avoidance, approach–approach, and avoidance–avoidance.

1. *Approach–approach conflict*: An individual must opt between two enviable alternatives. In fact, the theory of cognitive dissonance is based on the hypothesis that people normally want regulation and stability in their lives and a state of tension is created only when beliefs, values, or actions conflict with one another.
2. *Approach–avoidance conflict*: An approach–avoidance conflict occurs when one goal contains both positive and negative characteristics. This means, an individual is also apprehensive about the negative consequences from his desired product. When the goal is far away, both positive and negative feelings about the goal are less strong. However, as the person approaches the goal, the feelings about the negative characteristics arise, and the person backs down, avoiding getting too close to achieving the goal. Many products or services we desire have negative consequences attached to them. For example, when a father chooses a good school for his child, the long distance of the school from his residence might be the negative consequence of his selection.
3. *Avoidance–avoidance conflict*: When an individual needs to make a choice between two undesirable alternatives, avoidance–avoidance conflict occurs. For example, whether to repair a damaged car or travel to office by cab everyday both have financial consequences to the customer and, therefore, are undesirable. This situation may result in avoidance–avoidance conflict. In this case, the closer the customer towards his goal, stronger is his desire to avoid it.

Outcome

Outcome relates to motivation generated out of this process. It can be of two types—intrinsic and extrinsic. Intrinsic motivation comes from rewards inherent in a task or action itself, like the pleasure of solving a puzzle or the passion for playing chess. Extrinsic motivation comes from external factors. Money is the most palpable motivator, but coercion and the threat of chastisement are also common extrinsic motivations. Demonstration effect is often extrinsic because it encourages the performer to satisfy esteem needs over others, rather than having only the benefit of the intrinsic incentive of the action. In fact, Lewin's social psychological research pointed that extrinsic satisfactions can well lead over to rationalization and a subsequent diminution in intrinsic motivation. Extrinsic incentives at times can wane the motivation as well. D. Greene and M.R. Lepper, in 1974, had written a classic article titled 'How to turn play into Work' while focusing on the intrinsic behavioural pattern of the kids when they played with toys. In their study, it was observed that children who were sumptuously rewarded for sketching with felt-tip pens later showed little interest in playing with the pens again.

Feedback

The experience in the motivational process results in increased drive or internal force to attain the goal.

THEORIES OF MOTIVATION

To explicate how human beings generate motives, a prologue to a few theories of motivation will follow in this section. Furthermore, some realistic instances in regard to these theories will be revealed while elucidation.

Looking back at the literature and theories of motivation of different era, a huge diversity is well noted. Firstly, there are the monothematic theories, which assume that human behaviour is directed towards only a single and specific motive. The second prominent theory of motivation relates to the motive theory pioneered by Freud (1927). Freud called this innate motive 'libido'. Other behavioural scientists claim that motivation is not an outcome of a single need, rather it is a resultant factor of many diverse needs. Consequently, Adler (1927) explicates that existing needs are subjective to experiences in early childhood. Horney (1945) found the association between motivation and anxiety. However, the most conversed and latest theories in the gamut of motivation are Maslow's need hierarchy, Murray's psychogenic needs, and Dichter's consumption motives. In the subsequent sections, these theories are discussed in details.

Maslow's Hierarchy of Needs

In 1954, the great psychologist Abraham Maslow put forward his classic 'hierarchy of needs', as is shown in Fig. 4.2. This hierarchy is now central to many theories in buyer behaviour.

Physiological needs

Physiological needs literally mean the necessities for human endurance. Physiological needs are need for water, sleep, food, sex, clothing, shelter, etc.

Sprite, a *Coca-Cola* brand, initiated its burlesque finishing with the tagline '*Seedhi Baat, No Bakwaas*' campaign with Shiv Pandit–the *Sprite* boy. This advertisement was later replaced by the '*Sprite bujhaye only pyaas, baki all bakwaas*' campaign. However, both the taglines direct towards quenching thirst—the physiological need. Some of the edible products such as flour, rice, etc. often resort to these kinds of motives while designing their advertisements.

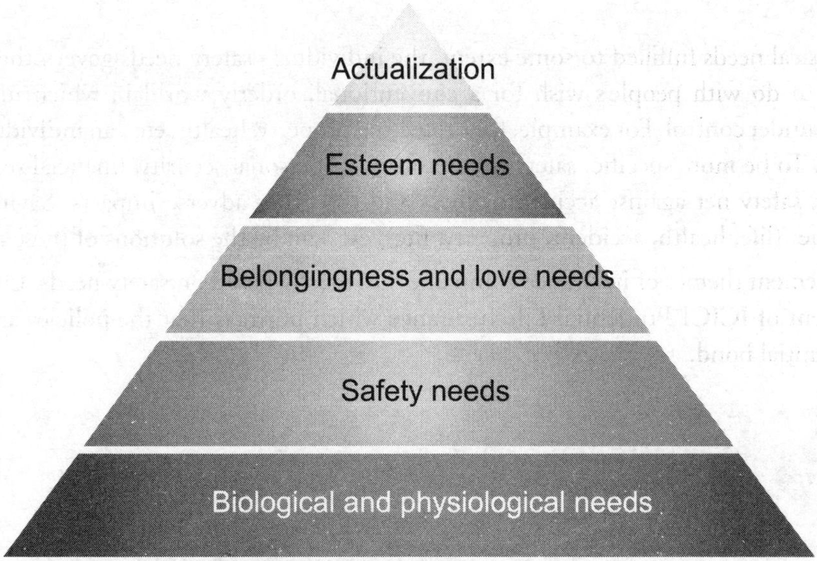

© Hemera/Thinkstock

Figure 4.2 Maslow's hierarchy of needs

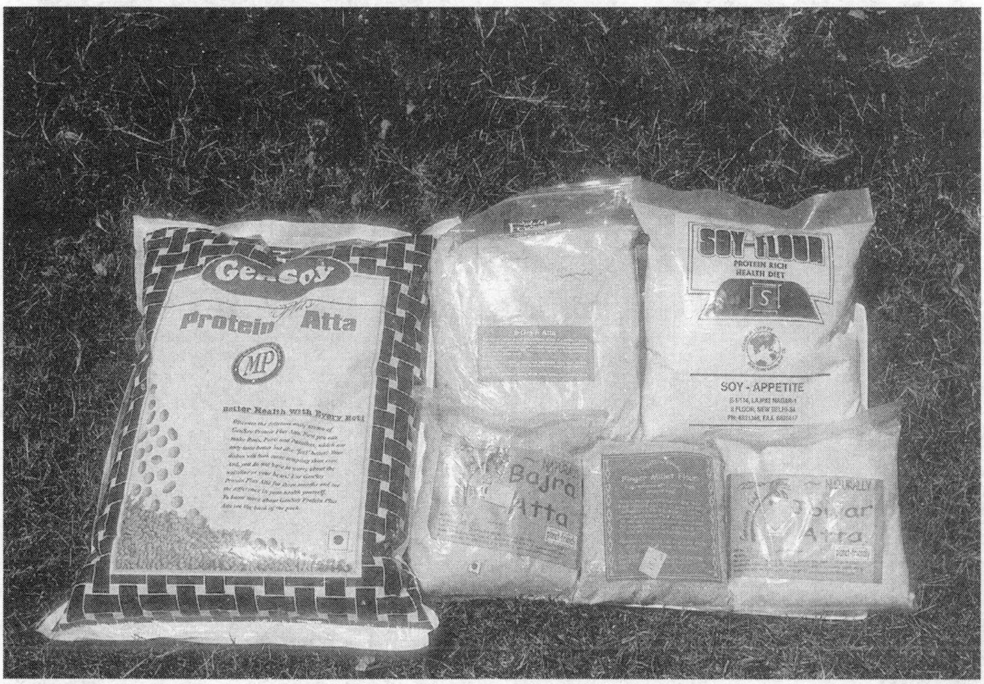

© Indiatodayimages.com

Flour products for satisfying hunger needs

Safety needs

With their physical needs fulfilled to some extent, the individual's safety needs govern their behaviour. This need has to do with people's wish for a conventional, orderly world in which unfairness and discrepancy are under control. For example, for protecting property, health, etc., an individual prioritises the safety need. To be more specific, safety needs consist of personal security, financial security, health and well being, safety net against accidents/illness and the other adverse impacts. Savings accounts, insurance policies (life, health, accident, property, fire), etc. can be the solutions of these needs.

The advertisement themes of insurance companies are mostly based on safety needs. One may recall the advertisement of ICICI Prudential Life Insurance which portrays that the policies are as safe and strong as the nuptial bond.

Insurance products based on safety consideration

Social needs

After the physiological and safety needs are satisfied, the individual looks for satisfying the third layer of human needs, that is, the social and belongingness needs. This psychological facet of Maslow's hierarchy entails emotion-based needs, for example, friendship, intimacy, family bondage, etc. Individuals also need to feel a sense of belonging and recognition, need of conformity to large social networks, such as clubs, office culture, religious groups, professional organizations, sports teams, or small social connections (family members, intimate partners, mentors, close colleagues, confidants). They need to be loved and recognized by others.

© Pixland/Thinkstock

Presenting gifts is a manifestation of social and belongingness need

Esteem needs

Everyone feels the need to be appreciated, to have self-esteem and self-respect. Esteem need represents the common human yearning to be acknowledged and admired by others. People need to employ themselves to gain appreciation and have an action that gives the person eagerness to be involved, to be accepted and self-valued, either in a professional or in an informal circle.

© Indiatodayimages.com

Satisfying esteem needs

Self-actualization

The motivation to comprehend one's own highest potential and possibilities is considered to be the only key and genuine motive, all other motives being just its diverse forms. In Maslow's hierarchy of needs, the need for self-actualization is the ultimate need that is apparent when lower level needs have been fulfilled.

© Indiatodayimages.com

Sachin Tendulkar, campaign ambassador of Support My School, a campaign and movement for healthy, active and happy school, during a programme organized by *Coca-Cola* and NDTV

Murray's List of Psychogenic Needs

Henry Murray (1893–1988), an eminent American psychologist, initiated a neo-theory of motivation. In this regard, he has pointed out that humans normally have two types of needs, namely, primary needs and secondary needs. While the primary needs indicate the needs for biological demands, such as oxygen, food, and water; the secondary needs relate to the psychological needs, such as nurturing, independence, and achievement.

Murray and his other group members have recognized 24 such psychological needs. These 24 needs can be distributed under five heads—ambition needs, materialistic needs, power needs, affection needs, and information needs. These needs, therefore, may be referred as psychogenic needs. A partial list of such needs is provided in Table 4.1.

The ambition needs are divided into three subcomponents—need for achievement, need for exhibition, and the need for social recognition. Under the leadership of Mr. Adi Godrej, Godrej Consumer Products showed that in spite of the slowdown in the FMCG sector, the ₹490-crore Godrej Consumer Products Ltd (GCPL) managed to buck the trend. This achievement of *Godrej* can also be considered as the success of Adi Godrej as a Chairman and Managing Director and significant social recognition for the Godrej Consumer Products.

The subcomponents of materialistic needs are the needs for acquisition (obtaining things), retention (keeping things), order (making things neat and organized), and construction (creating things). These needs are quite common in people who run after materialistic needs, e.g., branded suits, in order to look organized. In other ways, when a person wants to own a house in a posh area of the city, or wants to maintain his ancestral luxurious bungalows, he is basically trying to satisfy his materialistic needs in terms of the acquisition of a house or retaining their property.

The power needs are divided into subcomponents such as abasement (confessing and apologizing), autonomy (independence and resistance), aggression (attacking or ridiculing others), blame avoidance (following the rules and avoiding blame), deference (obeying and cooperating with others), and dominance (controlling others). Several advertisements in India, especially those of the fairness creams, soaps, and detergents ridicule the people for not using some particular brand. The *Tide* detergent advertisement claims that it provides such superior quality of cleanliness in a boy's shirt that the other boys in the school get punished because their detergents do not provide such cleanliness. Many of the corporate houses resort to comparative advertisements to catch hold of the competitor's revenue curve and get lead in the market. The advertisement of *Bharti Axa General Insurance* focuses on the exclusion of several major diseases by other insurance companies. It, therefore, draws attention of the customers towards their USP, i.e., the almost exhaustive list of diseases under the umbrella of coverage.

On the contrary, the affection need encompasses need for affiliation (spending time with other people), nurturance (taking care of another person), play (having fun with others), rejection (rejecting other people), and succorance (being helped or protected by others).

Next broad need identified by Murray is information need (specially the need for cognizance and exposition). Customers, worldwide, are now dependent on knowledge process outsourcing centres and business process outsourcing centres for getting information about several products and even for maintaining them.

Table 4.1 *List of Murray's psychogenic needs*

Broader needs	Specifications of needs	Examples
Ambition needs	*Achievement*: Success, accomplishment, and overcoming obstacles	 © Indiatodayimages.com Adi Godrej, Chairman and Managing Director In spite of the slowdown in the FMCG sector, the 490-crore Godrej Consumer Products Ltd (GCPL) managed to buck the trend under his leadership
	Exhibition: Shocking or thrilling other people	
	Recognition: Displaying achievements and gaining social status	
Materialistic needs	*Acquisition*: Obtaining things	 © Jupiterimages/Photos.com/Thinkstock Looking for materialistic needs
	Construction: Creating things	
	Order: Making things neat and organized	
	Retention: Keeping things	

Power needs	*Abasement*: Confessing and apologizing *Autonomy*: Independence and resistance *Aggression*: Attacking or ridiculing others *Blame avoidance*: Following the rules and avoiding blame *Deference*: Obeying and cooperating with others *Dominance*: Controlling others	 © Jupiterimages/Photos.com/Thinkstock Dominance and move towards globalization
Affection needs	*Affiliation*: Spending time with other people *Nurturance*: Taking care of another person *Play*: Having fun with others *Rejection*: Rejecting other people *Succorance*: Being helped or protected by others *Affiliation*: Spending time with other people	 © Jupiterimages/Goodshoot/Thinkstock Looking for protection and affection
Information needs	*Cognizance*: Seeking knowledge and asking questions *Exposition*: Educating others	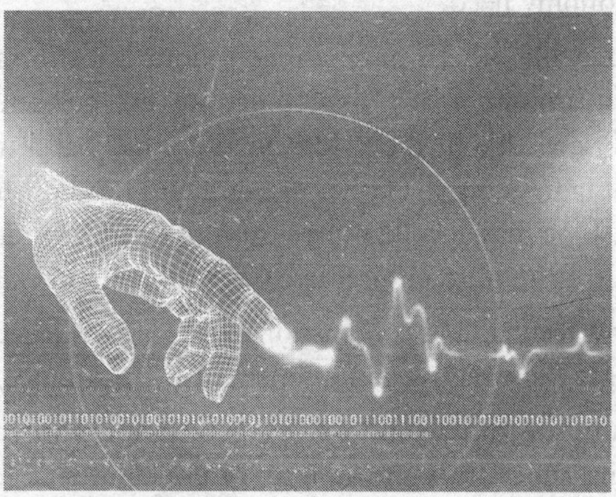 © Jupiterimages/Creatas/Thinkstock World communication montage

Research on Psychogenic Needs

Other psychologists have claimed that Murray's psychogenic needs should be subjected to substantial research. For instance, studies on the need for achievement have exposed that people with a lofty want for achievement are inclined to opt for more exigent tasks. Research on the need for affiliation has established that people who stress more on affiliation needs tend to have bigger social groups, fritter more time in social interfaces, and are prone to endure with solitude when the social contacts are somehow reduced. Murray's list, however, is too explicit in spotting the latent motives lying beneath customers' particular marketplace actions.

Ernest Dichter's Consumption Motives

In the early to mid 1900s, Ernest Dichter, the famous Viennese psychoanalyst, emerged as a profounder in the arena of qualitative marketing research. He recommended that consumer motives were time and again elicited by concealed comatose needs. The marketing promotions that are based on Dichter's theories on buyer motives in case of selling cars, furs, cell phones, and even paper towels have demonstrated accomplishment by augmented sales. Dichter himself happened to be a 'brand' in 1950s in the US, where he recommended the strategies for corporations on the usage of psychoanalysis in order to explore the 'hidden' motivations of their consumers.

The needs identified by Dichter can be classified into six categories—autonomy, dominance, nurturance, exhibition, cognizance, exposition.

Independent and impulsive decisions come under the autonomy needs. In many cases, these may be irrational, irresponsible, and unconventional. Wearing a dress or buying some edibles without any prior planning can be an example of this kind of motive. A child suddenly asking for an ice-cream just by seeing the point-of-purchase stimulus also demonstrates autonomous motive. Purchase of a dress without any prior planning by a working lady can be an independent and impulsive decision satisfying her autonomy need.

Influencing other's purchase behaviour leads to satisfying the dominance need. The floor manager of a tourism company may motivate his customers towards a specific package because of her better knowledge in the field. On the other hand, in a family decision to purchase a music system, Mr. Ramani, being the father of Sonu and head of the family, may dominate Sonu's choice of a music system. One may recollect the vision of Dr. Govindappa Venkataswamy while he pioneered 'Aravind Eye Care System' to ensure 'Eye Care for all' and eradicate the curse of blindness from the country.

Fellow feelings and compassion for underprivileged or distressed leads to satisfying nurturance needs. Helping others many a times satisfies the nurturance need.

To impress others and be recognized and appreciated by others, i.e., to excite, amaze, fascinate, entertain, shock, intrigue, amuse, or entice others, forms the exhibition needs. For example, wearing high fashion dresses, buying a luxurious car, etc. can be considered as the items to impress others. Shifting into a newly constructed luxurious 27-storied house on his wife's birthday by industrialist Mukesh Ambani is sheer satisfaction by fascinating his wife.

Cognizance needs lead a consumer to explore, be inquisitive, and be knowledge seeking. One might visit an information kiosk to satisfy their need for information about various products. These days, call centres or the KPOs also serve this purpose.

Exposition needs mean information sharing, elucidating, or interpreting something to the customers, shareholders, or anybody linked to the business. Businesses give press briefs about their company policies/performance and their products regularly.

A list of Dichter's needs is given in Table 4.2.

Table 4.2 *Dichter's needs*

Needs	Definition	Examples
Autonomy	Independent and impulsive decisions. In many cases irrational, irresponsible, and unconventional. For example, buying a dress	 © Hemera/Thinkstock Impulse purchase
Dominance	Influencing other's purchase behaviour	 © BananaStock/Thinkstock Influencing other's choice

Nurturance	Fellow feelings and protectiveness for poor or distressed	 © Indiatodayimages.com Rohini Nilekani, wife of Nandan Nilekani, with some of the poor targeted by microfinance initiative Sanghamitra in Bangalore, India.
Exhibition	To impress others and be recognized and appreciated by others, i.e., to excite, amaze, fascinate, entertain, shock, intrigue, amuse or entice others. For example, wearing high fashion dresses, buying a luxurious car, etc.	 © iStockphoto/Thinkstock Fashion wear
Cognizance	To explore, be inquisitive, and knowledge seeking	 © Indiatodayimages.com Information kiosk

Exposition	Information sharing, elucidating or interpreting something	 © Indiatodayimages.com Nitin Paranjpe, CEO and Managing Director, Hindustan Unilever Ltd sharing information about different FMCG brands of Hindustan Unilever Ltd

Needs Identified by Marketing Scholars

Through ages, psychologists have devised several hypotheses for consumer behaviour. Apart from the needs identified by the eminent traditional psychoanalysts, some neo-age psychologists, for example, Holbrook, Ahtola, Hirchman, advocate for two other consumption motives. These are utilitarian and hedonic motives underlying consumption decisions. These motives shape the facets of attitudes enroute for buyer behaviour. The utilitarian aspect recounts to utility, worth, and wisdom motives that direct consumer's purchase behaviour. On the contrary, the hedonic aspect relays about pleasure derived or estimated from the purchase. Hedonic aspect falls out from the aesthetic/emotional feelings listed by Holbrook and Hirschman (1982). Michael R. Solomon, Professor of Marketing and Director of Center for Consumer Research in the Haub School of Business at Saint Joseph's University in Philadelphia, in 1984 categorically stated that these motives are love, hate, fear, joy, boredom, etc. Both the utilitarian and hedonic features are bipolar and diverge in degree. The hedonic aspect is comprised of agonizing, unlikable, or pleasing stances. The utilitarian aspect, on the contrary, contains illogicality as well as wisdom and rationality.

Fennell (1978), on the other hand, recognized motives based on aversive (to avert an adverse situation) or positive (to gain recompense or incentive) arousal. Sheth, Newman, and Gross (1991) claimed that the individual choice behaviours root in functional, social, emotional, epistemic, and situational aspects. Hanna, another eminent psychologist, jotted down seven consumer needs–- physical safety, material security, material comfort, acceptance by others, recognition from others, influence over others, and personal growth.

HOW MOTIVES INTERACT WITH EACH OTHER TO AFFECT CONSUMER'S BEHAVIOUR

Abraham Maslow added an enormous deal to contemporary social welfare. His concept of self-actualization revolutionized the prevailing opinions about human nature in the social sciences and popular culture. In concert with other humanistic works, a more positive paradigm of human development was created in the American culture. While the theory may be limited in some ways, it continues to provide a valuable framework for social work research, policy, and practice. Maslow's concept of self-actualization could be useful in working toward a better performing society populated by more highly functioning individuals.

Every need is significant by itself. However, Murray also believed that every need could be consistent, could sustain with other needs, and also conflict with other needs. For example, the need for dominance may clash with that for affiliation and thereby may drive away friends, family, and partners. Murray also assumed that environmental aspects play a part in the ways these psychogenic needs are manifested in actions. Murray termed these environmental forces as 'presses'.

Ditcher made a study on persons of diverse age groups or demographics and found that each demographic segment was concerned about varied things, and had various comatose motives and needs. In a study on the US car market, accomplished in 1939, Dichter revealed that teens and post teens want 'new beginnings and liberation' while taking any car purchase decision. This is to cherish their need to flee from life, or simply become proactive in the matters of their pleasure (Ziems, 2004). People aged above 35 prefer the 'practicality and safety' characteristics while procuring a new car as they have families to be concerned about and sense the need to proceed maturely. Although this looks like commonsensical, Dichter also revealed some obscure consumer motives at the time of buying cars. Dichter also stated that men at the age of 35+ years who bought a moderate-ranged product were in fact repressing the craving to have a mistress (Ziems, 2004). The implication of this conclusion of Zeims on Dichter's consumption motives leads to a conclusion that in spite of several attempts to frame a set of generalized motives, the obscure instances often contradict the assumptions behind such generalizations.

INVOLVEMENT

Consumer involvement theory is one of the most dependable approaches to comprehend the psychology of the prospective customers. It refers to the extent of time, thought, energy, and other resources people apply to the purchase process.

Depending upon the purchase situation, involvement can be of four kinds—high involvement in rational purchase, high involvement in emotional purchase, low involvement in rational purchase, and low involvement in emotional purchase.

High Involvement in Rational Purchase

This class involves pricey industrial procurement of something related to the hi-tech infrastructure, the office setting, or the employee's benefit insurance plans. At the consumer's end, high involvement in rational purchases also refers to pricey decisions. Nonetheless, the purchase items in industry and household are not identical. On consumer's side, this category is related to the purchase of financial services such as mutual funds, bonds, shares, home, car, expensive jewelry, major household electronic appliances, furniture, etc.

High involvement consumer purchases might diverge considerably on the basis of rational or emotional scale wise deviation from person to person. For example, Mr. Grover wants a mobile phone which is highly durable and therefore has chosen *Nokia 1100.* His son Andy wants a very stylish and cheap set and has chosen *Simocco* set. It is the task of the marketer to find out how an average customer reacts to the firm's offerings. For consumer and business markets, promotion for these kinds of purchases is more conventional, with emphasis to merge the features and benefits of the products the consumers look for with their selling propositions

High Involvement in Emotional Purchase

High involvement in emotional purchases of any individual normally includes expensive diamond jewelry, wedding dresses, and vacation tours. It can also be the purchase of a home, a car, or even choosing a mobile service provider.

In B2B world, this type of purchase might include things such as office decors, spending on advertising, or hiring of certain top-level employees.

For the consumer market, the companies often resort to emotional appeals to promote their products. Some examples are the advertisements of *Titan* watches, *De Beers*, or *Vodafone* network connection.

Low Involvement in Rational Purchase

This type of purchase relates to our routine response behaviour. These purchases are functionally made out of habit, without much thought and involvement. Recollect the five-stage behaviour of consumer's purchase decision making in Chapter 1. In this low involvement purchase, the information search stage is hardly found. Normally, after recognizing the need, customers decide to purchase. So the time taken in this decision-making is quite less as compared to the extensive problem-solving behaviour resulting in high involvement and visibility of all five stages of buying decision-making. This category includes most of the fast-moving consumer goods in the daily consumption basket of consumers.

Here the role of the marketers is to ensure the availability of products at stores so that customers do not switch to competing brands. To break the automatic habit of spending their money on the competitor, the marketer may think of continuous advertisement to ensure the top of the mind recall by consumers. The marketers might also think of strategic product differentiation, for example, *Horlicks: Horlicks Lite, Women's Horlicks, Junior Horlicks*, etc. *Sunsilk* of Hindustan Unilever Ltd has also adopted this strategy by differentiating into seven possible combinations of shampoos, which may be used for different types of hair conditions. Hindustan Unilever Ltd used seven different hair experts to endorse each of these variants of *Sunsilk* shampoos.

Low Involvement in Emotional Purchase

These kinds of purchases are not functional, rather the purchase drive is emotional or sensual. But these drives are ephemeral. So the customers do not spend a lot of time in deciding about the purchase. Normally, movies, candies, magazines, greeting cards, treating a friend at a particular restaurant are some examples of this kind of purchase. The advertising challenge here is to flicker the assurance of happiness and fulfillment. In the spur of globalization and highly competitive market strong positioning can be the only resort for marketers looking to target the benefit segments.

Closing Case

Health Beliefs about Bottled Water: Results of a Survey in Users of the Birmingham University's Sports Center

The study of Lorna A. Ward established that a good number of populace agreed that the packaged mineral water has some health benefits but this factor was not strong enough to motivate them to purchase the bottles. Other aspects such as convenience, cost, and taste were far more significant motives for the predilection for bottled mineral water in England. Moreover, most participants considered that there was not a noteworthy health benefit in consuming bottled water while judged against the tap water. This was because they felt that the tap water was pretty good and safe for drinking. From the results of this study, it was doubtful that the recent drive in bottled water use was because of the idea about health gains derived from the bottled mineral water.

These study outcomes are significant, as till date, no qualitative research has been carried out to search for a general opinion about bottled water and the issues governing the people's intention to buy it. These results harmonize with earlier quantitative researches on the topic.

However, the study unveiled many facts that have not been covered in previous quantitative studies. Surprisingly, convenience was identified as the main motivating factor for buying bottled water. It seems apparent that people who usually favour drinking normal tap water would only agree to pay money for bottled water if the tap water was unavailable. During outings, visit to shopping malls, or movie theaters where they did not get tap water, they opted for bottled mineral water. 'Convenience' as a motivating factor was dogged by the circumstances rather than the beliefs about bottled water.

Interestingly, a greater part of partakers articulated the belief that bottled water has some health benefits. But strangely enough, these same people also affirmed that these health benefits are insignificant. This possibly mirrors the perplexity in the mind of respondents that they do not have belief on the marketing measures regarding the health benefits of bottled water.

Lorna A. Ward *et al.* referred to a far-reaching study carried out in the US by Azoulay *et al.* That research revealed that some brands of mineral water do certainly have a greater content of calcium and magnesium than the tap water, which was supposed to be low in minerals. Conversely, in the same study, however, some brands of mineral waters were in fact found to contain much less mineral content in contrast to the tap water.

Lorna A. Ward *et al.* claimed that although Azoulay's study was based on the responses obtained in the US, the condition was not unlikely in the UK too. Moreover, even as this study identified that some bottled waters endow with a considerable quantity of minerals such as magnesium and calcium, nevertheless, none of these brands were in line to the brands that the Birmingham participants used. Of these, the favoured brands of bottled water articulated low mineral content categorizations than the water with so-called moderate mineral content.

It is also imperative to remember that these minerals can also be acquired from dietary supplements, so the health benefits of the minerals contained in bottled water are not limited only to this source. Besides, research shows that drinking water with low mineral content does not always result in mineral deficiency in human bodies.

Some respondents had typical beliefs, which in many cases are illogical and impractical. For example, a participant thought that bottled water was particularly useful for babies. Conversely, another contemporary study suggested that choosing a mineral water with low sodium content might be handier in preparing baby food because a hyperosmolar diet has been associated to hypertension and fatness afterwards. So, there was no harm found in using tap water for this purpose.

Moreover, as per the UK law, in 1985, natural mineral water could not be untainted or otherwise treated to obliterate microorganisms. Therefore, the bottled water was not free of microorganisms, as some might believe.

From another study by Doria in Sydney (1998), it was found that there was an epidemic attributable to tap water. This augmented the bottled water sales. But the bottled water was also not free from these epidemic causing elements. The familiar brand *Perrier* was tainted with benzene in 1990 and in 2004 *Coca-Cola* also pulled out *Dasani* due to apprehension about the levels of carcinogen in the water.

A number of participants articulated apprehensions about cancer, which they felt could be generated from the plastic container of bottled water. In fact, a carcinogenic material di-ethylhexladipate was actually used in the production of polyethylene terephthalate (PET), a plastic commonly used to manufacture most water containers.

Approximately one-third of the participants expressed disquiet over the ecological impact of bottled water. These apprehensions included explanation about the 'carbon footprint' shaped by the transport of imported bottled mineral water. Furthermore, a 2006 Earth Policy Institute study identified that the British bottled water industry produced about 30,000 tonnes of carbon dioxide per year, which was equivalent to the energy consumption of 6,000 homes per year.

Source: Ward Lorna A., Cain Owen L., Mullally Ryan A., Holliday Kathryn S., Wernham Aaron G.H., Baillie Paul D. and Greenfield Sheila M., Health beliefs about bottled water: A qualitative study, *BMC Public Health* 2009, 9:196. Refer Web site: http://www.biomedcentral.com/1471-2458/9/196

Questions

1. Identify the appropriate motivational strategies for bottled water to increase their role in creating health beliefs in the general public.
2. If you were a marketer of bottled mineral water in this context, what issues would you consider for designing a positioning strategy for your company's product?

Summary

The mission of marketing is to understand the consumers' needs and wants correctly and then to develop products and services that will gratify them. For marketing to be successful, it is not enough to simply discern what the customers need, rather to find out why it is required is precisely more important. Marketers are more concerned in motivation when it relates to consumer's buying behaviour. This behaviour relates to the motive of acquiring the desired goods or services in question, and it has been phrased as 'goal-related behaviour'. According to Maslow, for a motive to exist there are five types of a corresponding need. Motives such as hunger, thirst, warmth, and shelter are physiological. Others, such as approval, success, and prestige are psychological. Some theories like Ernest Dichter's consumption motives or Murray's psychogenic needs have also been discussed in this text. However, most purchasing decisions are a combination of such motives; pretty often the choice factor might be price where an economic restriction dominates the motive. It can, therefore, be concluded that a number of motives might be at play when taking a purchasing decision and the final decision is a compromised result.

High involvement refers to a delicate state of consciousness that stimulates consumers to vehemently search for, attend to, and assume about product information preceding to purchase with increased attention. In this process, the memory is improved. Highly involved consumers tend to put larger weight on information sources such as newspapers and advertising.

Key Terms

Motivation The state of drive or arousal that propels behaviour toward a goal object.

Drive An inner force that directs towards attainment of ideal state.

Involvement Sense of concern and curiosity about someone or something.

Physiological needs A person's most basic needs: food, shelter, and clothing.

Safety need A person's need to be safe from harm.

Social need Need for love and belongingness.

Esteem needs Normal human desire to be accepted and valued by others.

Self-actualization needs The motivation to realize one's own maximum potential and possibilities is considered to be the master motive or the only real motive, all other motives being its various forms.

Ambition needs Need for success, accomplishment, etc.

Materialistic needs Acquisition, order, construction needs, etc.

Power needs Need for dominance.

Affection needs Same as social needs.

Information needs Cognizance or exposition needs.

Questions

1. What is the relevance of studying motivation for the marketers?
2. Identify at least five advertising themes targeting towards five needs specified by Maslow.
3. Critically evaluate the relevance of Dichter's consumption motives.
4. Write a note on the level of involvement in routine response behaviour, limited problem solving behaviour, and extensive problem solving behaviour.
5. Compare and contrast amongst Dichter's consumption motives and Murray's psychogenic needs.

Critical Assignment

1. Identify all the purchases made by you in a week and compare the buying motives in terms of Maslow, Dichter, and Murray's need hierarchies.
2. Survey 10 customers and find out the products leading to high emotional or rational involvement to them and compare the behavioural traits related to both involvement situations. What implications do these two situations have on the marketers?

Chapter **5**

Perception of Consumers

Chapter Goals

After completing this chapter, you will be able to understand

- **the basic concept of perception**
- **levels of perceptual thresholds**
- **process of perception formation**
- **interrelation between perception and consumer imagery**

Opening Vignette

Tanishq—A Fast Growing Brand in the Indian Jewelry Market

The Indian jewelry market is the second largest in the world sprawling behind the USA. From the time immemorial Indians have unquenchable thirst for the yellow metal. The total gold jewelry demand in India experienced an immense growth in the first half of 2010. 'The volume of growth increased by 67%, to 272.5 tonne from 163 tonne in H1 2009. In INR value terms, demand increased to ₹45,700 crore, an increase of 94%.'

Although Indian gold market has a huge potential, but it's largely fragmented and unbranded. Branded jewelry accounts for less than 2% by value. The rest of the market is in the hands of about 300,000 unorganized jewelers. These unorganized jewelers are mostly the individual family jewelers and the local goldsmiths with whom the Indian middle class has been associated for centuries together.

Titan considered that in the absence of branded players in the Indian jewelry market, there exists a window of opportunity for them to penetrate into this segment. *Tanishq*, launched in 1994, has grown to a ₹3000 crore brand even outdoing *Titan* watches in terms of the annual turnover. Established basically as a retail brand, *Tanishq* is a chain of jewelry shops set up by *Titan* across the length and breadth of the country. According to *Titan*'s Web site, *Tanishq* has over 118 stores across 76 Indian cities. The chain is working in a franchise system.

Tanishq initiated the process of selling lightweight 18 carat gold ornaments in India. The brand resorted to the positioning as 'jewelry for daily wear'. But it landed into trouble since the Indians usually considered 22 carat gold as the real one. The featherweight jewelry was yet to be accepted by the consumers.

Tanishq relied on the design ranges and the goodwill and dependability factors of the *Tata* brand. One of the main obstacles in the success of the brand was the recognition problem in its early days. Since gold ornaments are high value–high involvement products, consumers tended to be apprehensive in trying out a new format shop. The consumers were also less receptive to the premium that *Tanishq* jewelry claimed.

It was a herculean task to change the consumer perception. It was even harder as this behaviour had been there from time immemorial. The goldsmiths in many families worked across generations. Since the pricing of gold jewelry was very complicated, consumers were more inclined to rely on their customary stores rather than try the new ones.

Along the way, *Tanishq* also had to combat with the perception of being a premium brand. To overcome this issue, *Tanishq* came out with comparatively lower priced collections which somewhat rectified the bias in perception. Now, as the company claims, *Tanishq* had a turnover of over ₹3000 crore in the last fiscal year. This is perhaps because the younger generation is now accepting the concept of collection of daily wear light jewelry. The escalating gold prices also acted as a golden opportunity for *Tanishq* to rejuvenate such a line of jewelry. Now, *Tanishq* has reached a position from where it can plan to scale up the business to the next level. However for that the brand needs to be more localized in terms of promotion, designing, and pricing. Therefore, understanding consumer perception is extremely important for the marketers.

Source: http://www.indiainfoline.com/Markets/News/Indias-gold-demand-soars-94-percent-in-H1-2010/4914698481, accessed on October 14, 2011; http://www.lbma.org.uk/assets/3d_c_bhat_lbmaconf2004.pdf, accessed on October 14, 2011.

PERCEPTION: BASIC CONCEPTS

Perception is the sensory understanding of the world around us. It basically means how we receive environmental stimuli and react to them. In other words, perception consists of a set of actions by which an individual receives a stimulus and comprehends it. Therefore, the first step of the perceptual process is the exposure to a message. Exposure happens when our sensory receptors are exposed to certain colour, texture, or sound associated with certain products or brands (e.g. the red waves of *Coca-Cola* or the puppy and jingle of *Vodafone*). Thereafter, the consumers selectively attend to those stimuli that catch their attention and rest are simply received by the sensory receptors, but are not processed. For example, consider a person aspires to buy a *Mercedes Benz* car but does not have the financial capability to buy the same. Naturally, he might attend to the pictorial projections of the said car in commercials, however, there is a low chance that he would resort to a mental processing of the information received from the commercials given his low financial status. Usually, once attended, the consumer processes the information based on his own judgmental norms and forms his perception about the product/brand. In short, this is the gamut of perception.

In short, *perception* can be defined as *the active process of selecting, organizing, and interpreting the information brought to the brain by the senses* (Solomon, 2006).

Although the consumer perception process is significant in all facets of marketing, the strategic implications of the same to the brand builders and advertisers are worth mentioning.

LEVELS OF PERCEPTUAL THRESHOLDS

The exposure methods of active search and passive reception generate a lot more stimuli than the normal consumer's processing capability. The gate keeping devices that trim down this blooming confusion about the attention of stimuli involve consumers' physiological precincts viz. awareness thresholds. It means that any given stimulus can be either too small or weak to notice, or too huge that it gets above from the awareness levels. The second question related to this concept is how the level of awareness can be changed. There are four such thresholds – absolute, terminal, differential, and subliminal – to classify the consumers' zones of stimulus awareness (stimulus refers to something that causes a change in an organism).

Absolute Threshold

Absolute threshold is the minimum value of a stimulus, which can be consciously noticed. In other words, absolute threshold is the lowest level at which an individual can experience a sensation. It is that end at which a person can distinguish between 'something' and 'nothing'.

Marketers must try to boost the sensory input in order to be noticed through the daily clutter of advertising messages individuals are exposed to. Packaging should be attractive enough to catch the attention of the consumers. For example, without a colourful glossy package, kids' attention cannot be grabbed. Point of purchase displays often play the role of stimulus for the children to notice the chocolates.

Terminal Threshold

Terminal threshold is the maximum value of a stimulus that can be noticed. For example, an average person passes by a billboard within 20 seconds. The part of the billboard that cannot be read in 20 seconds is left unnoticed. So the readable and viewable information in 20 seconds is the terminal threshold for that customer.

Differential Threshold

The minimal noticeable difference between two comparable stimuli is called the differential threshold or the just noticeable difference (JND). The JND between two stimuli is not merely an absolute value of the stimulus but the difference between the awareness generated by the two levels of stimuli.

The famous German psychologist of 19th century, Ernst Weber, revealed that the just noticeable difference between two stimuli was not an absolute amount, but an amount relative to the magnitude of the initial stimulus. It was the first thought on JND.

Weber's law states that stronger the first stimulus, bigger is the added intensity required for the next stimulus to be perceived as different, and there is a fixed proportion by which with the change of the stimuli the level of response is changed.

Weber's law can be expressed as:

$$\frac{\Delta R}{\Delta S} = K$$

where R is the response, S is the stimulus and K is a constant.

Subliminal Perception

Subliminal perception refers to the level where the stimulus provided to the customers goes completely unnoticed. When the stimulus level is much below the absolute threshold, it develops subliminal perception. For example, display of a very light coloured saree will never catch the attention of a lady who likes to wear darker shades. Psychological concept applied to consumers' buying patterns holds that the consumers are more prone to buy products based on the perceived divergence between the traits of the products.

PERCEPTION PROCESS

Perceptual process is a chain of events that starts with our exposure to stimuli and leads successively, by our own comprehension mechanism, to interpret them. Perception is formed in three stages: selection, organization, and interpretation.

Selection

Selection is the first stage in the perception process. Selection rests on the verity that the consumers opt for a small portion of the stimulus to which they are exposed for conscious processing; it is alternatively termed as focal attention. To obtain the consumer's focal interest, an intensification of the sensory impulses is necessary.

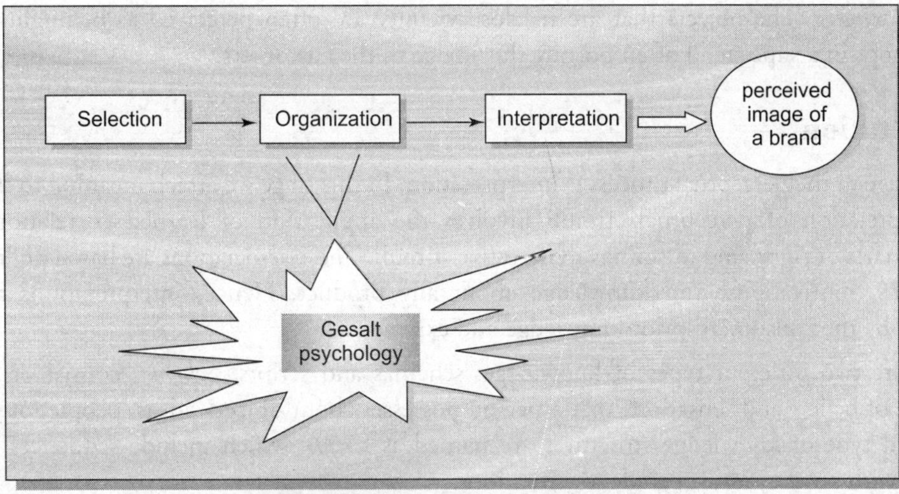

Figure 5.1 Process of perception

Organization

The second stage in the perceptual process is perceptual organization. Consumers categorize the stimuli into groups to make sense out of them. Basically, categorization process refers to the contrast between a perceived target and the categorical knowledge. It is a basic awareness activity that includes all forms of stimulus situations. One fundamental theory attached to this process is Gestalt psychology.

Gestalt Psychology

Gestalt is a German word that means pattern or configuration. Gestalt psychology is a school of psychology that was initially developed on the fundamental principles of perceptual organization. It relates to our understanding of how and why we perceive things. One of the most distinguished Gestalt principles is the phi phenomenon. It is the optical illusion that allows us to perceive constant movement instead of a sequence of images. For example, when one is exposed to running Christmas lights, he sees this non-existent movement just because of this principle. Some principles of Gestalt psychology of perceptual organization are as follows:

1. *Figure-ground*: This is the elementary way by which we organize visual perceptions. When an object is seen, both the object (figure) and the background (ground) are noticed. For example, when one sees the advertisement of Raymonds, the model Rajat Kapoor with his dress and peripherals displays the image of a complete man.
2. *Simplicity/prägnanz (good form)*: Normally, in this process, the stimuli are grouped to shape a 'good form'. Nevertheless, the idea of 'good form' is a little confusing and biased one. A 'good form' is whatever is easiest or most simple.

3. *Proximity*: The objects that are in close vicinity are often perceived as belonging together. Shops in a super mall often portray this image to the customers.

Interpretation

The last stage in the perceptual process is interpretation. In this stage we attach meaning to the stimuli. The interpretation of perceptual stimuli involves the application of learned correlation between perceptual cues or signs, and meanings to narrative stimuli. These associations are based on individual's expectations, motivations, and knowledge about any product. Hence, interpretations are largely influenced by the consumers' prior knowledge and experiences.

There are two different types of knowledge: schemas and scripts. *Schemas* consist of structured collections of beliefs and sensations that a person possesses about objects, ideas, people, or situations. The second type of knowledge structures are named as *scripts*, which include sequences of actions associated with objects, ideas, people, or situations.

PERCEPTUAL DISTORTION

Human brain stores information in schemas. These are constructed from experience, and help in comprehending and recalling various situations. For example, just from the physical gigantic structure of the Taj group of hotels, it can be easily predicted that they fall under deluxe category. This is because people know that deluxe hotels have certain kind of state-of-art infrastructures. Nevertheless, the schemas also form errors, in particular erroneous recalls of usual events and omission of unusual ones, or improper association of the attributes. For example, Ravi bought a *Voltas* refrigerator and has been using it for the last two years with certain complaints about its performance. Shyam, his friend, knows about this matter. Therefore, Shyam perceives that the brand *Voltas* always supplies erroneous products, which in reality is not true. This distorted perception is alternatively known as *halo effect*, which means one trait of a product/brand shapes the perception about the product/brand as a whole. Understanding an advertising message often results in perceptual distortion, where the message from the marketer and the understanding by the customer do not match.

However, perceptual distortion can be rectified through effective marketing strategies. For example, in India, more than 600,000 children aged below 5 years are subjected to annual morbidity due to diarrhoea. Diarrheal death causes at least one-third of the death cases across the globe in infectious disease category. Researches revealed that the diarrheal morbidity rate can be cut down to at least 50% by simply resorting to safe hygiene practices, like drinking safe water and washing hands with soap before eating.

Keeping this notion into consideration, the FMCG giant Hindustan Unilever, in partnership with the local government bodies, designed a campaign named '*Lifebuoy Swasthya Chetna Programme*' to spread awareness about the significance of washing hands with soap. *Swasthya Chetna*, which literally means 'health awakening,' is however, a multi-stage campaign that targets to change the consumer's perception to 'visibly clean is not really clean'. Together, the famous advertising agency *Ogilvy & Mather* and FMCG major HUL coined the word 'Active-B' to highlight the soap's anti-bacterial characteristics as its unique selling proposition. The result of this campaign was phenomenal.

ISSUES IN CONSUMER IMAGERY

Imagery is an association of attributes a brand gets coupled with over a period of time. It has an influence on how customers perceive a brand and how they react to it over a considerable time horizon. For instance, *Horlicks* had a 'patient's drink' sort of image just two decades ago which has been subsequently changed to a 'tasty and nutritious health drink'. In fact, a brand metaphor plays a significant role in determining the association in the consumer's mind. Several brands, today, are putting lots of efforts to develop an image in different aspects. Imagery is significant, as a brand has to acclimatize itself to the varying atmosphere. To elucidate, *Vicco*'s facial skin cream, over the period, has been positioned amidst the events of a wedding. *Fair & Lovely*, a brand that entered to the Indian market much later, had adopted a different kind of imagery by capitalizing on the average Indian's perception that 'fair is beautiful'. Earlier HMT had been positioned as a value-based Indian brand of watches. It was later outshined by *Titan*, which created a unique and unforgettable emotional imagery.

Considering price as an indicator of product quality (i.e., higher the price, greater is the perceived quality of the product) is our common perception from time immemorial. Nevertheless, some studies have revealed that consumers often consider price to evaluate the esteem of the brand but not when evaluating the product's actual performance. *Dove* was launched in India in 1995 and was advertised as the 'mildest soap' in the premium soap category. However, in India, the brand did not get much momentum as its global counterpart. The small size of the premium market and higher price could have been a few hindrances in the formation of positive perception. In addition to the high quality promise, *Dove's* original price was around ₹50 that pushed away many premium customers too. Although the 'Campaign for Real Beauty' and mildness were excellent USPs, the brand could not fascinate the Indian consumers. Now, with the present pricing at ₹28, the brand has somewhat become affordable and the price quality cue is working rationally

The strategic implication of analyzing consumer imagery to the marketers is to segment their markets on the basis of relevant consumer self images and position their products accordingly. Sometimes, for penetrating in a new market, formation of perception is extremely relevant. For example, the 'iodine' campaign of HUL *Annapurna* salt made the rural semi-literate customers feel for the need of iodized salt. By effectively understanding the nitty-gritty of the consumer perception about financial services, it was possible for ICICI bank to extend its services to the so far untapped rural hinterland of India. In case of product designing implementation, frugal engineering may help to shape the consumer's imagery and formulate positive perception about certain products. The prosthesis attempt by Jaipur foot shows how perception and lifestyle can be altered.

Keeping the increasing popularity of *Apple* iPad into consideration, *Amazon* has planned to launch its low priced 'Kindle Fire' (to catch hold of the middle class customer's imagery). However, as sources state, though *Amazon* is offering the Kindle Fire for just $199 while the simple models of iPad sell for $499 and the higher-featured ones for $829, still 'competing with the iPads will not be as easy as swiping a finger.'* Hence a detailed understanding of consumer imagery is always necessary from the marketers' point of view, particularly because these days most of the marketing strategies are skewed towards a hitherto untapped complicated market, named 'bottom of the pyramid.'

Closing Case

Ganga Soap—Where was the Problem?

If the western media's perceptions about the social and cultural values of India were not prejudiced, then *Ganga* soap would have been the best seller brand in the world. For the entire western media, it was an astonishing fact that *Ganga*—the name associated with the holy river—failed to create any significant impact in India, the land perceived to be characterized by crores of pilgrims and saints.

In 1993, Godrej Group of Industries, launched their new brand of toilet soap, named *Ganga*, in the Indian market. The brand was supposed to harness the religious psyche of the Indian consumers as it was claimed to be made of water from the holy river Ganges.

Ganga soap was promoted heavily and was endorsed by the popular Bollywood star Govinda with the famous tagline '*Now bath in Ganga*'. Although the initial sales figures were encouraging, the initial fads were soon wiped away with the breakup of *Procter & Gamble* and *Godrej*.

Ganga was revitalized and relaunched in 1997 under the name '*Doodh Ganga*'. But even this effort of *Godrej* did not get any encouraging results.

This was indeed a paradox because 80.5% of the Indian population is comprised of Hindus who by nature are very religious and respect their tradition. But as discussed in Chapter 2, for the 21st century consumers, pragmatism often overrules the religious ideology. While choosing their daily consumables, the Indians resort to rational rather than emotional or impulse buying. They are often guided by Maslow's need hierarchy or Murray or Dichter's needs but not by their religious needs.

The Indian consumers may feel sanitized by getting dipped in the holy Ganges, but are discerning when it comes to buying products. While buying a soap, their considerations would be cleanliness, quality, ingredients, price, foaming, etc. Sometimes they even consider brand name, celebrity endorsement, and the freebies associated with the products, but not really the religion.

*http://www.buffalonews.com/business/article575000.ece, accessed on October 14, 2011.

Moreover, this concept was too old dated for the young consumers as they are more concerned about the match of ingredients of the soap with their skin conditions.

Hindus have a high regard for the holy Ganges, but they are equally aware that the river is highly polluted. Hence, the fact that the soap was manufactured from Ganges water puts the health sensitive customers in double mind. *Godrej* realized this problem and claimed that the water for manufacturing this soap was taken from *Gangotri* (the origin of *Ganga*) and hence was safe to use. But this made the consumers further confused.

Source: http://marketingpractice.blogspot.com/2006/11/ganga-soap-rip.html, http://nt.walletwatch.com/ascerc/History.asp?CompanyCode=12520018&companyname=Godrej+Industries+Ltd.Mouthshut.com. This case has been incorporated in this book to purely stimulate the classroom discussion.

Questions

1. Can you cite any other reasons behind the failure of *Ganga*?
2. Suggest how consumer's perception can be rebuilt in favour of *Ganga*.

Summary

Perception is the understanding of the environment by organizing and interpreting the information. Products are not merely physical entities, but also a bundle of benefits to the consumers. The marketers are paying attention on how the buyers perceive and act in response to the products in relation to quality, artistic sense, price, and image. The feature of the product itself exaggerates this perception by the buyer. It is, no doubt, essential that the product or service (i.e., the stimulus) grabs the attention of the prospective buyer. There are many stimuli contending for the buyers' attention, hence the marketers must make their design, the advertising stimuli, in such a way that it becomes as interesting and attractive as possible. It is not essential that perception of the customers about a product or service is always the same as the marketer intended. Many rational as well as irrational motives offered by the marketers might sway the consumers favourably towards the brand. There might be certain positive or negative preconceptions from personal familiarity, peer group, family advice, or from other emotional motives, all merging to modify and form the final perception and the ultimate buying decision.

Key Terms

Perception Perception can be defined as the active process of selecting, organizing, and interpreting the information brought to the brain by the senses.

Absolute threshold It is the minimum value of a stimulus capable of being consciously noticed.

Terminal threshold It is the maximum value of a stimulus capable of being consciously noticed.

Differential threshold The minimal difference that can be detected between two similar stimuli is called the differential threshold.

Weber's law According to this law, stronger the initial stimulus, greater is the additional intensity needed for the second stimulus to be perceived as different.

JND Just noticeable difference (JND) is the minimal apparent difference between two products as observed by the consumer.

Subliminal perception Subliminal perception occurs when stimulus is presented below the threshold and thereby does not generate thoughts, feelings, or actions.

Gestalt psychology It is the school of psychology that first developed the basic principles of perceptual organization. Much of our understanding of how and why we perceive things comes from Gestalt psychology.

Halo effect It is the distorted perception where one characteristic of a product/brand affects the perception about all the other characteristics of that product/brand.

Perceptual distortion It is the lack of correspondence between the way a stimulus is commonly perceived and the way an individual perceives it under a given condition.

Consumer imagery Consumers often attempt to preserve or develop their self-images. They select the products or the distribution points and interpret the marketing communication messages in such a way that these consent with their perceived self-image. This is known as consumer imagery.

Questions

1. What is meant by consumer perception? Explain the process of perception of a consumer about *Pepsi* soft drinks after witnessing a cricket tournament sponsored by *PepsiCo. Ltd.*
2. Explain the correlation between consumer's imagery and perception.

Chapter **6**

Theories of Personality and Self-Concept

Chapter Goals

After completing this chapter, you will be able to understand

- theories of personality (Freud and neo-Freud)
- how the theories of self-concept and extended self shape consumer's choice and imagery

Opening Vignette

Bond with the Best Persona—Great Positioning Strategy by Reid & Taylor

Friedman (1979) once stated that quite often high psychological or social risk is involved with the purchase of the products reflecting one's self or social image. The images of these brands usually have a high correlation with those of the celebrity endorsers promoting the brand. These spokespersons commune the value of the products with customers and thereby augment the brand value of the products (e.g, Shahrukh Khan for ICICI Bank and Aishwarya Rai for *Loreal*).

The esteem brand *Reid & Taylor* offered a wonderful exemplar of celebrity endorsement when it first launched its advertising campaign featuring Mr. Pierce Brosnan, playing James Bond in Hollywood movies at that time. The advertisement came out along with the famous tagline 'BOND WITH THE BEST'. However, the James Bond idea did not carry in the Indian apparels market properly as the prospective customers could not find a slice of life in it. Keeping in view the catastrophe of the first campaign, the company launched an ad where the children were celebrating their parents' silver wedding anniversary and they were out with their father to buy a suit for him. Although this advertisement portrayed the slice of life, still it was not in line with the targeted Indian consumers' psychology. So the commercial did not work and it was taken off air within a short span. Ultimately, the company introduced Mr. Amitabh Bachchan as the *Reid & Taylor* man. He was portrayed in this advertisement as a man who proliferated the brand for special occasions and for very special people in life. The initial recall effect of the advertisement was pretty good. Gradually, people started identifying the brand's face with Mr. Bachchan's charisma, and the brand succeeded as an executive brand in the elite and upper-middle-class market and jubilantly excelled in the Indian market. For the masses, *Reid & Taylor* was perceived as a brand for an ideal Indian elite family man, a star, and a superior person who has excelled in his career. Therefore, the brand was positioned as a highly priced one for very special people in special events.

© Indiatodayimages.com

Amitabh Bachchan replaced 'James Bond' Pierce Brosnan as the brand ambassador for the premier clothing and fashion company *Reid & Taylor*

In fact, here, we found a complete congruency and compatibility among the celebrity endorser, the product, the message, and the advertisement campaign as a whole, and, as a result, the commercials generated an elevated recall effect.

INTRODUCTION

Consumers can be classified depending on whether they have introvert/extrovert and stable/unstable personality traits. These traits, as marketers believe, can lead to classification of a number of personality types. Consumers diverge in terms of their personality or the way they retort to a particular situation. For example, while listening to a sales pitch one consumer may listen graciously and when pressed to buy, even if the consumer finds the product interesting, he/she still may not be certain about purchasing it. Another customer might act more aggressively, interrupting the salesperson halfway through the pitch to indicate that he/she has no interest in the product at all. Thus, a study of personality helps marketers to appreciate why people behave differently in different situations. The present chapter explores this sphere.

Personality encompasses those comparatively long-lasting personal qualities that allow consumers to respond to the world around them. A person can effortlessly (although perhaps not always accurately) describe his or her personality or the personality of a friend. Personality is an individual's typical response tendency across parallel situations.

For example, one might say that one of your friends is fairly aggressive, very prejudiced, spirited, sociable, and witty. What you have described are the behaviours your friend has exhibited over time across various situations. These characteristic ways of responding to a wide range of situations also reflect the ways a consumer may retort to the marketing strategies.

There exists immense controversy about the definition of personality, worth of studying it, and the problems associated with its measurement. Nonetheless, the personality characteristics help us to describe and differentiate amongst individuals. For marketers, personality characteristics can also be used to help formulate the marketing strategies.

PERSONALITY DEFINED

The personality of a consumer guides and directs his/her behaviour to realize goals in diverse situations. Personality is a relatively long-term personal quality that allows us to respond to the world around us. Personalities, therefore, are meaningful to consumers and thus of enormous significance in marketing strategy formulations. Thus, we can say that while motivation is an emerging and directing force for consumer behaviour, it is the personality of the consumer which guides and directs the chosen behaviour to achieve goals in different situations.

Personality can be defined as a steady pattern of responses to the world over time and across situations. This consistency of response allows us to classify people as aggressive or submissive, fascinating, or loathsome. A person's reaction to an internal environmental state or to a new stimulus depends upon his/her perception on the event. The perception, in turn, depends upon the person's usual mode of coping with the environment, since individuals generally react in a consistent or stable fashion in a variety of environmental situations. For example, a cautious, careful, and methodical type of person will usually react cautiously, carefully, and methodically to a new stimulus. Personality characteristics help a marketer describe and differentiate among individuals and accordingly structure the marketing strategies.

According to Schiffman (2008), personality is defined as the unique dynamic organization of physical and psychological characteristics of a person, which influence his/her behaviour and responses to the social and physical environment.

CHARACTERISTICS OF PERSONALITY

Personality is the summation of an individual's psychological traits, characteristics, motives, habits, attitudes, beliefs, and outlook. It is an internalized system which includes all those aspects of a person that are inherited as well as those that are learned. Therefore, the characteristics of personality can be noted down as follows:

- Personality reflects individual differences.
- It is a distinctive combination of inner characteristics.
- No two individuals are exactly alike.
- Personality allows marketers to divide people into different groups based on their traits.
- Personality is steady and permanent in short run. Nonetheless, it might change in the longer run owing to the change in the person's social status and stage in family life cycle. It can be altered by major life events—marriage, birth of a child, significant career promotion, and personal tragedies—accident, health problems, divorce, death of a loved one, etc.
- Marketers cannot alter consumer's personalities to convene their products.
- Marketers strive to understand the personality traits of consumers. Therefore, they use a variety of ploys and tactics to get at their target consumers.
- Women's personality in general has been shifting faster. Today, women splurge on their new-found freedom, which can best be seen in *Indica V2* ad.

THEORIES OF PERSONALITY

The marketers of the 21st century often feel that the consumer purchases are always influenced by their personalities. Therefore, many marketers make use of personality traits in the commercials of brands. However, some connoisseurs highlighted that sometimes the personality is related to the inheritance and the experience of early childhood. Meanwhile, other experts stressed that personality may also change as a result of the various environmental influences in different phases of life. In fact, some parts of personality are unique to a certain person while some parts of it can be common amongst a number of individuals (Chaudhuri, 2006). More often, we depend on three basic features to understand the concept of personality per se (Schiffman *et al.*, 2008).

To begin with, it may be said that personality differentiates amongst individuals. Personality is usually a steady trait in humans and for that they behave consistently over time. However, personality can alter due to sudden unpredicted incidents in life like accident, death, etc. It is also possible that a person might demonstrate various patterns of personality at different stages of family life cycle.

Personality theories can be classified as either individual personality theories or social learning theories. Understanding of these two general approaches of personality will provide an appraisal to the marketers to potentially use the personality traits while formulating marketing decisions.

Several personality theories have been developed over time—from Freud's psychoanalytic theory of personality to trait theory and self-concept theory. Freud's theory proposes that an individual's personality results from the interaction between the desire to satisfy his or her needs and perceived societal values.

Individual Theories of Personality

All individual personality theories have the following two common assumptions:

1. All individuals have internal characteristics or traits.
2. For these characteristics, there are consistent and measurable differences amongst the individuals.

The external environment or events around us (situations) are not considered in these theories. Most of these theories state that the traits or characteristics formed at a very premature age are relatively static over the years. However, the differences between individuals' theories centre on mainly the personality traits or characteristics.

Single-trait theories

Single-trait theories underline one personality trait as being particularly relevant to understand a specific set of behaviours. They do not suggest that other traits do not exist or are not significant enough; rather, they study a single trait for its relevance to a set of behaviours; for example, consumption-related behaviours. Some examples of single-trait theories are those that deal with intransigence, conviviality, neuroticism, conformity, narcissism, totalitarianism, and need for cognition.

Multi-trait theories

In contrast, multi-trait theories specify several traits in combination that capture a considerable part of an individual's personality. Cattell's theory illustrates this view of personality. According to Cattell, traits are acquired at an early age through learning or are innate.

A distinctive aspect of his approach is the demarcation of surface traits, or observable behaviours, which can be grouped together on the basis of their resemblance and source traits that stand for the causes of these behaviours.

Cattell suggested that if we could identify the surface traits that correlate highly with one another, we would be able to identify an underlying source trait. For example, a source trait of insolence could account for the surface traits of aggressiveness, competitiveness, and obstinacy. Table 6.1 shows some of Cattell's major source traits and the corresponding surface traits.

Table 6.1 *Cattell's major source traits and the corresponding surface traits*

Source trait: surface trait	VERSUS	***Source trait: surface trait***
Reserved: detached, critical, aloof, stiff		Outgoing: warm-hearted, easygoing, participating
Affected by feeling: emotionally less stable		Emotionally stable: mature, faces reality, calm
Humble: stable, mild, easily led, docile, accommodating		Assertive: aggressive, competitive, stubborn
Sober: taciturn, serious		Happy-go-lucky: enthusiastic
Expedient: disregard rules		Conscientious: persistent, moralistic, staid

Shy: timid, threat-sensitive	V	Venturesome: uninhibited, socially bold
Tough-minded: self-reliant, realistic		Tender-minded: sensitive, clinging, overprotected
Practical: down-to-earth	E	Imaginative: bohemian, absent-minded
Forthright: unpretentious, genuine, but socially clumsy		Astute: polished, socially aware
Self-assured: placid, secure, complacent, serene	R	Apprehensive: self-approaching, insecure, worrying, troubled
Conservative: respecting traditional ideas, conservatism of temperament	S	Experimenting: liberal, freethinking, radical
Group dependent: a joiner and sound follower	U	Self-sufficient: resourceful, prefers own decisions
Undisciplined: lax, follows own surges, careless of social rules	S	Controlled: exacting willpower, socially precise, compulsive, following self image
Relaxed: tranquil, torpid, unfrustrated, composed		Tense: frustrated, driven, overwrought

Source: Cattell, R.B., Eber H.W. and Tasuaka, M.M., *Handbook of the Sixteen Personality Factors Questionnaire*, Institute for Personality and Ability Testing, Champaign, IL, 1970, pp.16–17.

Exhibit 6.1: Some Popular Celebrity Endorsements

India has only two major obsessions, cricket and Bollywood. Both guarantee excitement and eyeballs. Not surprisingly, advertisers, forever searching for the magic to hold audiences, have been frantically (even blindly) using celebrities to prop up their brands. But there is nothing like an endorsement from a Bollywood matinee idol. Deepika Padukone pilots the youth brigade as brand ambassador for *Kingfisher* and watchmaker *Tissot*, along with *Levi Strauss India*. Bipasha Basu endorses *Kinetic's Sym Flyte* and Real Estate Developer, *Emgee*. Sushmita Sen has been spotted in a wide array of brands such as *Olay*, *Tag Heuer*, *Kiah Diamonds*, *Pantene* and others. Hrithik Roshan remains excelling as ever with *Acer*, *John Players*, *Parle*, *Tata Sky*, *Sony Ericson*, and *Radico Khaitan*. Saif Ali Khan for *Taj Mahal Tea*, *Royal Stag*, *Newport*, *Lenovo*, and *Aveo* is also doing well. Akshay Kumar too has rushed headfirst into everything from *Grassim Suitings* and *Thums Up* to *Microsoft's X-Box 360*. Finally, there are, of course Amitabh Bachchan, Shahrukh Khan, and M.S. Dhoni, the reigning emperors of Indian endorsement world.

However, the reason behind the impact of personality on consumers' behaviour can be found from the Sigmund Freud's psychoanalytic theory of personality (Schiffman *et al.*, 2008). The precondition of Freudian theory claimed that unconscious needs were the key reasons for certain human behaviour and personality. In recent years, there has been increased interest in the brand personality construct as its strategic importance has become more apparent. Brand personality is defined as 'the set of human characteristics associated with a brand' (Aaker, 1997, p. 347). A distinctive brand personality can help to create a set of unique and positive associations in consumer memory and thus construct and boost up brand equity (Keller, 1993; Johnson *et al.*, 2000; Phau and Lau, 2000). As a result, brand personality is considered to be an imperative aspect for the success of a brand in terms of preference and choice (Batra *et al.*, 1993; Biel, 1993). Indeed, a well-established brand persona can result in stronger emotional knots with the customers and thereby, higher mutual trust and loyalty (Siguaw *et al.*, 1999; Johnson *et al.*, 2000), thus providing an enduring basis for differentiation (Aaker and Fournier, 1995; Halliday, 1996; Haigood, 1999), which is hard to imitate (Aaker, 1996). A recent survey conducted jointly by IMRB and i-Pan of over 2000 respondents across 12 cities (small and big metros) found that 86% of those interviewed divulged that the commercial with higher recall effect had a celebrity, nonetheless, only 3% said it influenced their buying decision. The IMRB study found that 'more than the celeb pull, factors like quality, price, and experience ultimately drove consumers' purchasing pattern.' Furthermore, 'only 22% of this sample believes that the celebs really use the products endorsed', the IMRB report claimed. So, should celebs be discarded? 'Not really' said IMRB's Sanjay Pal. He continued, 'at a primary level, celeb endorsements help to break the clutter but beyond that it is doubtful whether they add any real value.' In fact, the survey found that Amitabh Bachchan and Shahrukh Khan have so many commercials across the product categories. Nonetheless, the report also states that in recent past, there occurred several cases of mismatch between product/brand persona and celebrity persona. The study revealed that such mis-associations occurred in 15% of the cases for Amitabh Bachchan and in 9% cases for Sharukh Khan. Exhibit 6.2 portrays more of such examples.

Exhibit 6.2: Failure of Judgment May Create Adverse Effect

The celebrity-based campaigns not only are basking with the glory of success stories, but also are characterized with a considerable number of failures. Assuming that a person just has to be famous to represent a successful brand, however, would be incorrect and may turn out to be a very dangerous preposition resulting into a big calamity for the entire advertising campaign or the brand. Very well accepted and attractive superstars Abhishek Bachchan and Amitabh Bachchan failed in turning their endorsements into success in case of *Maruti Versa*. Similarly, Virendra Sehwag also failed to deliver *Reliance Telecommunication* with the master stroke of his cricketing genius.

Freudian Theory of Personality

Sigmund Freud (1856–1939), a Vienna-based neurologist, developed his psychoanalytic theory while working with mental patients. He claimed that there are basically three components that elaborately explain the human behaviour—id, ego, and superego. The following sub-sections explain the three structures identified by Freud.

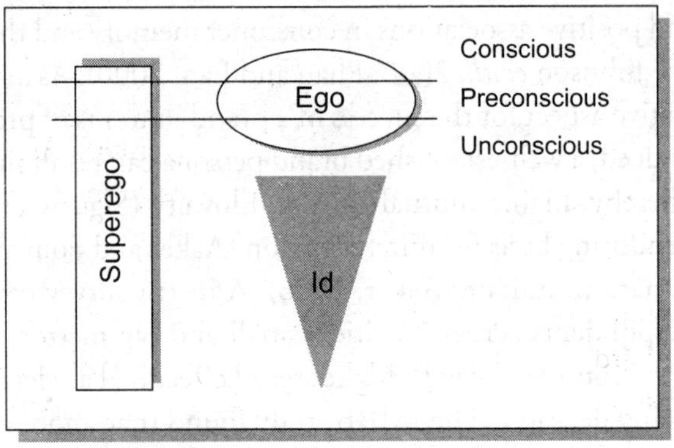

Figure 6.1 Freudian theory of personality

Id

Freud considered id as the root of all psychic energy, and thus the only inheriting constituent of personality. This facet of personality is completely below the conscious line and demonstrates mostly some kind of the innate and elemental behaviours.

The driving force of id is mostly the pleasure principle, which calls for instantaneous realization of all desires, wants, and needs. The unfulfilled desires give birth to a state of anxiety or tension. For example, thirst calls for some water or drinks instantly. In childhood, the features of id are pretty well visible (sometimes even in the form of pester power) as it ensures the fulfillment of the kid's desire instantly.

Nonetheless, it is not always a pragmatic consideration to assume that all needs would be readily satisfied. If pleasure principle rules the universe, then we might find ourselves snatching things we want out of other people's hands to gratify our own desires. This type of behaviour will definitely create a mess in the society. According to Freud, the id tries to resolve the tension created by the pleasure principle through the primary process, which in future emerges as a psychological image of the desired object as a way of satisfying the need.

Ego

The ego is that constituent of personality which balances the primal desires of id with reality. Rather, as Frued put it, ego is the next step of id, i.e., confronting with the reality while fulfilling primitive desires. In that way, the ego acts in all the conscious, preconscious, and unconscious conditions of mind.

Unlike the pleasure-seeking principle of id, ego is governed by the reality principle. This means ego state attempts to satisfy the id's desires in realistic and socially apposite ways. The reality principle makes a trade-off between the costs and benefits of an action prior to embarking on to react upon or cast off impulses. Sometimes, the id's impulses can be contented through a course of deferred gratification—the ego will ultimately permit the behaviour, but only in suitable time and place. The ego also releases the tension generated out of unfulfilled impulses through the tertiary process, in which it tries to find an object in the real world that matches the psychic image formed by the id's prime process.

Superego

The last component of personality is the superego. The superego is that aspect of personality that caters to all of our inherent moral standards and ideals that we obtain from both family and society as a whole. In other words, superego is governed by our conventional sense of morality.

It provides a person the ability to judge while fulfilling desires. According to Freud, the superego begins to show up at around the age of five.

There are two parts of the superego—the ego ideal and the conscience.

1. The ego ideal encompasses the norms and benchmarks to behave in appropriate societal way. These behaviours are those that are acceptable by parental and other authority figures. Compliance with these norms leads to feelings of self-satisfaction, value, and triumph.
2. The conscience comprises information about behaviours that are considered as unacceptable by elders and society. These behaviours are normally forbidden and any violations lead to penalty, reprimand, or feelings of guilt and lament.

The superego acts as ideology to refine our behaviour. It works to repress all deplorable urges of the id and puts effort to make the ego perform on idealistic standards rather than upon pragmatic principles. As ego, the superego too is present in the conscious, preconscious, and unconscious stages.

Interaction between Id, Ego, and Superego

Nonetheless, with so many diverse forces, it is quite easy to understand that conflict might arise between the id, ego, and superego. Freud coined the term 'ego strength' to elucidate the ego's ability to function in spite of these conflicting multi-directional forces. An individual who is powerful in his ego strength is usually capable to proficiently handle these pressures, while those with too much or too little ego strength would appear to be too adamant or wearisome. According to Freud, the essentials to a strong personality are to harmonize the conflicts in all these three stages of personality formation in preconscious, unconscious, and conscious stages.

SELF-CONCEPT

These concepts are linked with two key concepts of psychoanalytic theory, the ego and the superego. In fact, ego is similar to one's objective reality, so it can be treated similar to the actual self. On the other hand, superego is defined by the way things should be and hence can be seen as a reflection of the ideal self.

Another school of thought states that there is no single actual self. Consumers have various role identities—mother, wife, working woman, volunteer, etc. One of these roles is dominant in specific situations. Any specific role affects the behaviour (dressing style, conduct, talking, etc.) in specific ways. The combination of individual roles makes up the individual self. Studies have confirmed that consumers buy products related to their self-concept. Dolich studied the buying pattern of beer, cigarettes, soaps, and toothpaste and found the respondents to be inclined to prefer brands they rate similar to their perceived personalities. The same is in the case of automobiles. Nonetheless, the concept of 'actual self', which is relevant for the marketers, is that image consumers have about themselves which is reflected in their product choice heuristics. As a matter of fact, they attain 'self consistency' by buying products they perceive as similar to their self-concept.

For example, *NIIT* adopted a very elegant strategy by roping in Vishwanathan Anand, a worldwide chess wizard, for their advertising campaign. Chess, in India, is considered to be a game full of strategies and is meant for elegant people; so when one of the greats of the game asked people to join *NIIT*, it was supposed to have an affirmative persuasion effect on the people and in pragmatic note it was successful.

Compatibility of the celebrity's persona with the overall brand image is very important, as a celebrity passes on the credibility and motivating value to a brand and his or her image should flawlessly match the brand's image. A good brand campaign idea and an essential association between the celebrity and the message are must for a successful campaign.

The above points can be put to view by using two examples, first Kapil Dev's *Palmolive ka jawaab nahin* and second *Nakshatra's* brand recall due to its endorser, the beautiful Aishwarya Rai Bachchan. Both brands had edged out and carved their niche in consumer's mind due to the reflection and trustworthiness of their endorsers. These were the cases of perfect match between the brand image and the image or persona of the celebrity endorser.

SELF-CONCEPT AND BRAND IMAGE

In diverse contexts, consumer's behaviour might be steered by different self-concepts. The marketer needs a proper perceptive of this. For example, daily use items including the purchase of consumer durables will be more guided by actual self-concept. However, socially noticeable products or status products will be guided by social self-image. Fantasy products, cosmetics, fashion items, or accessories will be guided by ideal self-image or ideal social self-image. In this sense, ideal self-concept can be considered synonymous with one's self-esteem. The greater the difference between the actual and the ideal self, the lower is the individual's self-esteem. Dissatisfaction with actual self will end up in purchases of such products that they think will enhance their 'self-esteem'. A woman who wants to be more up-to-date, competent, and creative will use different perfumes, deodorants, etc. or will shop at different stores than a woman who wants to be friendly or good-looking. Advertisements that feature gorgeous models and deluxe lifestyles leave a sense of insufficiency based on a comparison of their real self with idealized self. For example, an average fashion model is 5′9″ tall and weighs 55 kg. But an average Indian woman is 5′2″ tall and weighs 65 kg. Sometimes, the desire for both self-consistency and self-esteem can be contradictory. Generally, consumers buy products that conform to their actual self-image. But if they are lower in their self-esteem they are more likely to be won over by appeals to flight of imagination characterized by idealized self (the alluring woman, the lone biker on *Bajaj Discover*, or the well-groomed male in *Vimal* suiting).

A craving to attain an unrealizable self-image can lead to obsessive purchasing behaviour (frequent buying to overcome the discrepancy between the real and the ideal self).

Well-known brands have distinctive personality which is generally consistent and may be implied. Brand personality enables to establish relationship between brands and consumers with emotional substance. The degree of closeness between brands and consumer personality influences the purchase intension and brand loyalty. Brands need to keep informed of contemporary and relevant personality, as target audience personality may change over a period of time due to changes in cultural, economic, and media exposure. Brand personality should not be confused to the target audience character. Personality may be existing or aspirational. Projective techniques can be used to represent brands. Consumers can be asked to correlate the brand with adjectives (word association, sentence completion, etc.) and also about user imagery.

Personality of the brand and celebrity should complement each other. Reliable celebrity ensures instantaneous consciousness, appropriateness, and positive approach towards the brand, which is a prerequisite for buying a product. The use of celebrities like Chiranjeevi, Amitabh Bachchan, and Shahrukh Khan in published ads to revive and/or strengthen the brand image of brands (*Thums Up*, *Pepsi*, *CDM*) after setbacks is a brilliant way to cash on the celebrity credibility. This provides the much-needed assurance to the consumers and also supports the brand image and values. The element of creativity is very important in celebrity endorsements. If creativity element is missing, then the celebrity may overshadow and outperform the brand (vampire effect). Boost advertisement featuring Sachin is an archetypical example of effective celebrity endorsement.

The use of film stars for *Lux* beauty soap and highly successful sportspersons for *Nike* is rational and focuses on the suitability of the brand rather than just the name of the celebrity. Sachin Tendulkar, Shahrukh Khan, and Amitabh Bachchan endorse many brands in India. Fitness of the celebrity persona with brand persona is important; otherwise, celebrity endorsement may end up as a pointless exercise resulting in the wastage of money. Sachin symbolizes style, power play, technique, excellence, and performance which carry very nicely with the positioning strategy of *Boost*. *Exide* has roped in captain M.S. Dhoni as its brand ambassador because of his power play and talent. On the other hand, John Abraham, the famous model and actor, is the endorser for brands such as *Yamaha*, *Garnier Skin Care*, etc., because of his rugged and manly looks, good physique, and youthfulness.

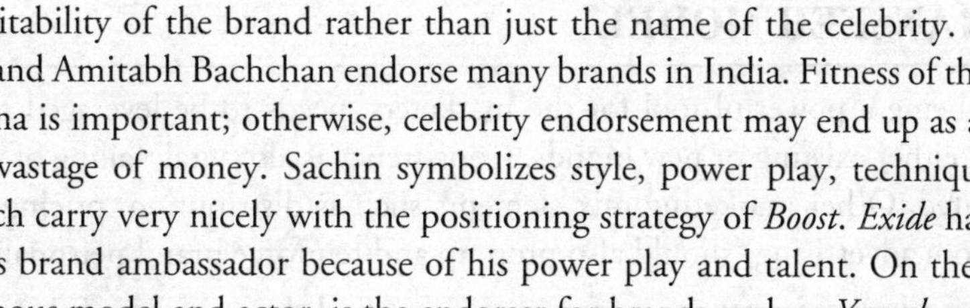

© Indiatodayimages.com

Celebrity persona in conformity with brand persona: Aishwarya Rai endorsing *Lux*

Indian celebrities can connect foreign brands with Indian consumers with great effect. S. Kumar's has roped in Amitabh Bachchan as the brand ambassador for *Reid & Taylor*, and it has effortlessly facilitated them to Indianize their global brand, a kind of looking back from global to local perspective.

User imagery also communicates about the lifestyle of the user. User imagery results in user-driven image which is transmitted to the brand. Brand personality needs to be rationalized with alteration in user imagery and information so that the brand remains up-to-date and pertinent.

Products like *Thums Up* and *Marlboro* are good exemplars of using 'user imagery' contributing to brand personality and thereby succeeding. In fact, some of the brands have become cult brands—for the promotion of these brands, it is important that the product should match up with endorser's personality. *Kingfisher* has associated their brands with personalities symbolizing fun, frolic, and sparkling charisma.

Many a times, the elements such as layout, colour (in print ads), visual appeal, music, etc. (in broadcast advertisement) also get associated with the brand. For example, Mozart symphony is well blended with the *Titan* ad which typecast the sophistication and elegance of *Titan*'s image, the way *Titan* wanted to position itself.

MEANING TRANSFER MODEL

Brand personality, being a powerful tool for the marketers, needs to be leveraged to accomplish the principal mottos of either existing or new brands. Consistency is also vital, failing of which the brand's image may get diluted. Other marketing mix elements such as distribution, pricing, promotion, and packaging (apart from advertising) should also prop up and reinforce brand personality.

After watching an advertisement, consumers may try to find the meaning of the advertisement if it has drawn their attention. If any celebrity endorser is attached to it, then there would be a tendency to associate the same with the endorser and eventually transfer to the interpretation process of the brand attributes. To understand this phenomenon, McCracken (1989) suggested a comprehensive model commonly referred as 'meaning transfer model'. This three-stage model shows how meanings attributed to the celebrity get associated with the brand and project a certain image in the consumer's mind. In the consumption process, customers comprehend the brand's meaning. The third stage of the model states the significance of the consumer's role in the process of endorsing brands with famed persons.

In contrast to unidentified endorsers, celebrities can add value to the image transfer process by offering meanings to the message behind the commercial, what is complemented by their lifestyle and personalities. Therefore, to transfer the correct meaning to the consumer the company should select a celebrity in such a way that produces the fitting set of characteristics, and the public should be able to visualize and comprehend the same. The company should consider the consumer's needs while formulating their communication strategy and selecting an appropriate celebrity to convey the same. For example, *Kurkure* used actress Juhi Chawala with the punch line *Masti Bole To Kurkure*. Juhi's onscreen and offscreen effervescent presence personifies jubilance, and this endorsement, thereby, helps the brand in communicating the same in a spontaneous manner.

Certain essential factors that engender a perfect match or compatibility between the celebrity and brand image are as follows:

- Celebrity fits with the brand image along with celebrity–target audience match
- Celebrity associated values and celebrity–product match
- Costs to obtain the celebrity and his or her popularity along with the controversy risks associated with the celebrity
- Credibility, availability, and physical charisma of the celebrity.

Advertisements work on image resemblance and try to sway consumer attitudes, preferences, and brand evaluations.

The problem arises when brand's self-image is not in sync with that of the consumer and vice versa. The need arises to settle on the brand personality (existing) and change it so as to match with that of the consumer's self-image. For example, brand which is understood for elders cannot be targeted to young audience. In case of non-resemblance, advertising needs to underline functional facets and highlight brand image in case of image congruence. Thus, brand image may become a leading aspect influencing the buyer behaviour. It also helps to invalidate the limitation of the brand contributing to poor discernment.

Closing Case

Accenture Confiscates Tiger Woods—An Effort to Revamp Brand Image

'It's what you do next that counts', says the commercial of *Accenture* featuring bemused Tiger Woods, the demigod golfer, looking down into a water body for his ball. But finding his lost ball at this present moment seems to be the least of Tiger's concern and so is of *Accenture*.

Accenture is a global management consulting, technology services, and outsourcing company. Combining unmatched experience, comprehensive capabilities across all industries and business functions, and all-embracing research on the world's most successful companies, *Accenture* collaborates with clients to help them become high-performance businesses and governments. With around 2,36,000 people serving clients in more than 120 countries, the company engendered net revenues of US$25.5 billion for the fiscal year that ended on August 31, 2011.

For the past six years, *Accenture* and Tiger Woods have had a very successful sponsorship arrangement and his achievements on the golf course have been a powerful allegory for the business success in *Accenture*'s advertising. As a matter of fact, *Accenture* made the brand building of Tiger Woods an equal part of their own brand building. The New York-based firm in 2006 crediting its *Go on, be a Tiger* campaign boosted its image significantly. *Accenture* has used Woods to personify its claimed attributes of integrity and high performance.

Nevertheless, some time back Tiger Woods, the so-called demigod of golf, was mired into several kinds of controversies ranging from car accident to sex scandals. *Accenture* spent millions of dollars to develop its superior brand equity based on the credence of Tiger. These scandals not only brought down the image of Tiger Woods from demigod to most common individual with all his frailties, they also raised the eyebrows of *Accenture*'s spiky heads in Chicago.

As a result, *Accenture* finally decided to call off their long-term association with Tiger on December 13, 2009. However, the marketing head of *Accenture* was determined to continue with their same positioning strategy 'high performance delivered'. For the purpose, in the later 2010 they resorted to a new advertising campaign. Nonetheless, the task was quite difficult. Actually, *Accenture's* continuous attachment with Woods had created a kind of joint branding. The situations were almost like two boats joined by ropes floating in the ocean. As the adage goes, if one sinks the other too faces the consequence. Further, *Accenture* failed to see how Woods's brand image is extended over a range of other products such as *Nike*, *Gatorade*, *Gillette*, and *Accenture*.

© Indiatodayimages.com

Accenture, upholding its image and integrity

The question was not exactly whether Tiger was a God of golf or just a human being. The challenge for *Accenture* was furthermore critical. After a long attachment with Woods, it became a real problem for *Accenture* to come out of joint branding effort and establish itself as a 'high-performance brand' on its own.

Accenture's problem raised another critical issue; whether tying up with a living personality would be risky? Or it is better to use the long-deceased icons like Donald Bradman as brand identifiers as no one is likely to dig up any new dirt on these legends. Moreover, as they are no more on this earth, there is no scope for the dead celebrities to do anything further questionable. Some animated characters or animal characters can also be a solution.

Whatever alternative be suggested, it is difficult to refrain today's marketer's from the most alluring option of celebrity endorsement to break the clutter of innumerous advertisements the customers are exposed to. But, no doubt tying a company's brand to a celebrity is always chancy.

For example, one day, they might highlight a celebrity having long straight hair on their products. Simultaneously, another ad might showcase the same celebrity photographed with short curly hairs. Celebrities are humans and are not free from the frailties that we all have. They too get addicted to sex, gambling, food, drugs, etc. They may be parents. They get snapped in compromising poses, places, etc. Therefore, celebrity endorsements are seasoned for mess and only a small number of celebrity endorsements can last for a long time. Moreover, *Accenture* has perhaps hanged around its joint branding with Tiger. This gives birth to a question 'when does the risk (and cost) start to outweigh the benefit of continuing such relationship?' It's time for *Accenture* to wean itself off its Tiger Woods fixation.

Source: The case is based on the articles published in several newspapers such as *The Times of India*, *The Telegraph*, *The Hindustan Times*; television coverage on channels such as NDTV and BBC news; and some Web sites such as http://golf.about.com/b/2009/12/13/accenture-fires-tiger-woods.htm, http://www.msnbc.msn.com/id/34406263/, accessed on November 6, 2010; http://newsroom.accenture.com/article_display.cfm?article_id=4915, accessed on November 6, 2010.

Questions:

1. Do you really think that *Accenture* needs to rebrand in order to come out from Tiger's handicap?
2. If yes, how is that rebranding possible?

Summary

To summarize the key points of the chapter it may be concluded that personality can be described as the psychological characteristics that both determine and reflect how a person responds to his or her environment. Although personality tends to be consistent and enduring, it may change unexpectedly in response to major life events as well as gradually over time.

Freud's psychoanalytic theory provides a strong base for the study of motivational research, which operates on the idea that human drives are mostly conscious in nature and serve to motivate several consumer actions.

A brief assessment of the current market situation indicates that under the right conditions celebrity endorsement advertising strategy can indeed justify the high costs coupled with this form of advertising. The use of celebrity for endorsements creates a very positive impact on consumers and creates links which force a consumer to purchase a product. However, as several failures show, it is necessary for advertisers to be conscious of the complex processes underlying celebrity endorsement.

No doubt celebrity endorsement is a dominant tool that magnifies the effect of a campaign but the word of caution also has to be followed seriously. Neither the celebrities nor the great advertising campaigns or the best possible products can pledge success on their own. It is the blend of several factors and elements that work together for the success of a brand and its acceptance in the minds of consumers as well as for its market offering.

Modern day consumers are well informed and smart, they know celebrities are being paid for these endorsements and this awareness makes consumers rather more pessimistic about the product and celebrity endorsements. A majority of the consuming population also know what is advertising and how it actually works and this knowledge of consumer makes the task of celebrity endorsement all the more difficult and challenging. Indian companies, both in terms of advertising and product offerings, have to make an attempt to overcome this ever-mounting challenge.

Key Terms

Personality A combination of traits of an individual.

Superego The superego is the aspect of personality that holds all of our internalized moral standards and ideals that we acquire from both parents and society—our sense of right and wrong.

Ego The ego is the component of personality that is responsible for dealing with reality.

Id The id is driven by the pleasure principle, which strives for immediate gratification of all desires, wants, and needs.

Self-concept Self-concept can be defined as the totality of individuals' thoughts.

Questions

1. Describe personality trait theories. Explain with appropriate example. Show how advertisers can use personality traits to design their commercials.
2. Find some TV advertorials reflecting the use of Freudian concepts id, ego, and superego.
3. A marketer of breakfast cereal is attempting to segment its market on the basis of self-image of consumers. Discuss how the marketer can proceed.
4. Exemplify the cases of brand failure due to association with unmatched celebrity persona in your own country.

Critical Assignment

1. How do your preferences for soft drink differ from those of your friends? What personality differences might explain why your preferences are different from those of other people?
2. Identify ten shampoo brands, five with non-celebrity endorsements and five with celebrity endorsements. Conduct a pilot survey and find how much celebrity endorsements matter to the customer's brand choice.

Chapter 7

Theories of Learning

Chapter Goals

After completing this chapter, you will be able to understand

- **the basic concepts of learning**
- **behavioural theories of learning (classical, operant, and instrumental conditioning)**
- **cognitive theories of learning**

Opening Vignette

Nicorette: An Initiation to Learn Anti-Smoking

Nicorette, recently launched in India by *Johnson & Johnson*, is a brand one of its kind. It has been introduced as a chewing gum in India with a unique anti-smoking feature. It is considered to be the world's bestselling brand for smoking cessation.

Nicorette was first launched in Sweden in 1967. The context of launch of such a brand was interesting enough. During 1960s and 70s, there was an immense aggravation by the crew working in submarines under Swedish Royal Navy. There was a strict ban on consuming tobacco inside the submarine wherein this crew had to stay for days together. The crew was very much irritated on this issue and the Royal Navy was in search of some alternative to reduce nicotine addiction. After a long search, the scientists discovered *Nicorette*—a therapeutic nicotine-based chewing gum which reduced the cravings for nicotine among the smokers. The gum when chewed discharges nicotine in minute extent and thereby dispiriting smokers' cravings for cigarettes. Thus, it helps to quit smoking. The brand started positioning it as a new system of nicotine replacement therapy.

With a huge size of tobacco consumers in India (more than 275 million), the country appears to be an alluring market for this brand as well as the product.

Nicorette frames a painless support system for those who wish for give up smoking. Painless, because, the chewing of the gum discharges a small amount nicotine to gratify the passion and over a period of time the addict can reduce the intake of the amount of gum also.

In India, *Nicorette* has appeared in two packs. The 4-gm pack was designed as a prescription drug targeted towards the heavy smokers. However, the 2-gm packs were sold over-the-counter.

Nicorette has espoused the tagline 'Doubles Your Chances of Quitting Smoking' both in television commercials and digital promos. The tele-commercial portraying a smoker wishing to quit smoking but the cigarette pack sticking to his hands (symbolic cue of nicotine addiction) with the pain on his face to give it up has already become very popular. As a matter of fact people learned to believe that it is truly useful for a person who genuinely wants to refrain from smoking.

Nicorrette was in use in most of the European countries, US, Canada, Mexico, etc., for many years but the marketers felt that Indian market was yet to adapt such new products. Nonetheless, with the opening up of the economy in the post liberalization (1991) phase, the global players were becoming more confident of bringing their inventive out-of-the-box products to India and slowly but surely making the consumers learn to use these products by effective communication and positioning strategy.

Source: Nicorette: For Every Cigarette, There is Nicorette, http://marketingpractice.blogspot.com/2011/01/nicorette-for-every-cigarette-there-is.html

DEFINITION OF LEARNING

Learning may be defined as the changing pattern of responses of consumers arising out of experience. The contemporary schools of thought have defined learning in innumerous ways; nonetheless, the basic concept was never altered. Domjan and Burkhard (1986) opined that learning is the process of 'enduring change in the mechanism of behaviour that results from expertise with environmental events'.

As per the studies of Hoch and Deighton (1989) in the contemporary market, the process of learning occurs when consumers implement their beliefs to interpret a new set of data. They have viewed learning as a psychological attribute. It includes the learning of attitudes of consumers.

According to Hoyloak, Koh, and Nibsett (1987) learning is a process of adaptation whereby an individual alters the goal-directed behaviour in reaction to the changing environmental situations. Combining these definitions, one may reach to a general definition of learning from marketing viewpoint. Consumer learning is the process by which individuals acquire the purchase and consumption knowledge, experience and form a predisposition which they apply to future-directed behaviour.

From this generalized definition, the following points come into sight:

- consumer learning is a process.

- consumer accumulates knowledge and experience through the process of learning.
- the knowledge and experience thus accumulated forms predisposition in the consumer's mind and, thereby, shapes the foundation of his future behaviour.

The process, through which consumers acquire knowledge and experience, is of enormous significance to the marketers. It is because marketers always have to follow the nature of products and services used and preferred by the customers and also the attributes, qualities, and benefits of using them. They also edify the customers how a product should be used, maintained, and disposed off when they do not remain usable for new products.

Marketing strategies pose a great emphasis on learning theory. The advertisement, packaging pamphlets, stores, and distribution channels all are based on the consumers' evaluation and formation of predisposition of the brands. It is important for marketers that their carefully and expensively designed integrated marketing communications should not only be noticed but also be believed, remembered, and recalled while buying the product. Nevertheless, till date there is no single concrete and universally accepted theory which interprets all facets of consumers' learning process.

Exhibit 7.1: The Introduction of Noodles in India The Case of *Maggi*

Indian social structure experienced a boom of working ladies in the 1980s. Immediately after returning back from their whole day's work at office, they had to prepare tiffin for their children who also had come back from school and were very hungry. The tired ladies aspired for an alternative. To capitalize on this change in the social structure, *Nestle* India Ltd. (NIL), the Indian subsidiary of the global FMCG major *Nestle* SA, launched *Maggi* 2 Minute Noodles, an instant food product, in 1982. No doubt, *Maggi* noodles called for a shift from the age-old tiffin items like roti, paratha, idli, dosa, etc. It actually introduced a new tiffin food category—instant noodles—in the Indian market. Nevertheless, within a short span, *Maggi* realized that the sales figure was not getting the required momentum and it called for repositioning. They understood when the kids were the largest consumers of the brand, it's better to shift their target from working women to children. Therefore, they repositioned the brand towards the kids effectively utilizing its integrated marketing communications. For the purpose, they used interesting taglines such as 'Fast to cook', '*Mummy Bhook Lagi*', '*Bas 2 Minute*', and 'good to eat' and provided with various free samples, gifts on return of empty packs, etc. This increased the wide acceptance of *Maggi* across the country and especially the urban consumers heartily liked it. The popularity of *Maggi* reached to that extent gradually that the brand introduced many other products like sauces, ketchups, etc., under the umbrella brand of *Maggi*. Since 2005, *Nestle* started offering a variety of new 'healthy' product mix under the same umbrella of *Maggi*, especially to attract health-conscious consumers.

(Contd.)

Exhibit 7.1 *(Contd.)*

Nestle's 2-Minute noodles introduced a new tiffin food category

TYPES OF LEARNED BEHAVIOUR

Learning is a human behaviour and it is quite natural. Learning comes from experience and knowledge. The process of learning has always remained a matter of interest to a marketer. The marketers advertise their products through different media, like print media (newspaper, magazines, and journals), audio and audio-visual media (radio, television), and the consumers come to know about the product characteristics, brand labeling, packaging, etc. through such effective communications. Types of learned behaviour have been discussed in the following sections.

Physical Behaviour

We learn the physical behaviour in our day to day life and in a variety of situations. As consumers we learn the methods of responding to various purchase situations. These may take the forms of learning to read closely the fine print in purchase contracts. Consumers may also learn certain physical activity through the process termed modeling, in which they mimic the behaviour of other individuals, such as actors. Therefore, the learned physical behaviour is an important constituent of consumer's psyche.

Symbolic Learning

Much of the learning is also acquired by effective use of symbols. Thus, symbols allow marketers to communicate with the consumers through vehicles such as labeling, slogan, caption of a brand of product or services. For example, when we see the slogan 'Great people to fly with', we understand what Pakistan International Airlines is offering.

Problem-Solving Learning

One can also engage in problem-solving learning by employing the processes of thinking and insight. Thinking involves the mental manipulation of symbols representing the real world to form various combinations of meanings. The jingles of *Titan* or the red colour of *Airtel* is such kind of symbolic cue. *Cadbury's Dairy Milk* is associated with the violet colour.

© Indiatodayimages.com

Dairy Milk: A Cadbury product

Affective Learning

Affective learning is alternatively referred as environmental learning. Humans learn to value certain elements of their environment and dislike others. In fact, the consumers learn most of the things from the surroundings and environment. For example, a consumer buys a product when he feels that the product suits him well and is capable of satisfying his needs and wants.

PRINCIPAL ELEMENTS OF LEARNING

Learning occurs in various phases of life cycle of consumers in various ways. But for the learning process to take place, there should be four major factors playing their roles effectively. These elements are motives, cues, response, and reinforcement. These elements precisely determine on what, how, and at what diffusion rate something is learned from the environment or consistent efforts of the marketers. The next sections focus on these four key elements of learning.

Motives

The most important factor for effective learning is motive, motivation, or drive as it may be referred in various marketing issues. Motives trigger the individual's readiness in initiating the learning process. They also stimulate the positive energy needed to do so. However, motives are also determined by the extent of involvement by the consumers. Motives are quite important from the marketer's point of view, as they need to decide on their unique selling propositions based on these. For example, showing advertisements for winter goods just before winter and cotton products just before summer are some common strategies in India.

Cues

Although motives initiate the process of learning, but cues give it a momentum. These are not as strong as motives to initiate the learning, but they can persuade the consumers to respond to a motive in a certain fashion. For example, in the market place, price, styling, packaging, point-of-purchase display all a dish up as cues to help consumers decide on a particular product from a group. Price, quite often acts as a 'significant' cue. Marketers use this cue well in the form of off-season discounts, buy-one-get-one-free, etc.

Response

Response is how the consumers respond to the motives or cues and demonstrate certain behaviour in the market place. Learning takes place irrespective of the response being overt (open, physical, or visible) or covert (hidden or mental). Gradually, over a time period in life cycle, the responses over certain motives and cues become consistent. Therefore, it is possible that in spite of resorting to a proper marketing mix, the marketers may not succeed in driving a positive response from the customers instantly. But over a period of time they may succeed in shaping a favourable positioning of a particular product/brand in the consumer's mind.

Reinforcement

Reinforcement is also an important constituent of learning. Given a particular set of motives or cues, reinforcement amplifies the possibility or likelihood of a specific response to occur in specific situations in future. Therefore, the reinforced behaviour often has a tendency to be repetitive and consistent. This facilitates the consumers to learn to imbibe the effective ways to respond to their needs or changing conditions.

CLASSIFYING LEARNING THEORIES

The concept of learning has been evolved around various theories. Nonetheless, the most recognized ones of them are based on stimulus–response theory. These theories presume that the noticeable response of the customer to a particular external stimulus implies that the process of learning has occurred. More often, if a consumer responds to a known stimulus in a consistent fashion and demonstrates a particular kind of behaviour over a period of time, he is said to have 'learned'. So, in the stimulus-response models, the inputs and outcomes of learning are considered to be more important than the process of learning. These stimulus–response concepts pivot around some well-known theories, namely, the classical (or respondent) conditioning and instrumental (or operant) conditioning. They are discussed in the following sections.

Classical Conditioning

Classical conditioning theory, developed by the famous Russian Psychologist Ivan Pavlov, is based on the principle of 'repetition' responses. Pavlov called it 'conditioning'. As Pavlov pioneered this concept of stimulus–response pattern of learning, this theory is alternatively known as 'Pavlovian learning theory'.

The basic assumption of classical conditioning theory is over a repetitive exposure to a certain stimulus, the individual starts responding to the same in a similar and consistent way. Classical conditioning or respondent conditioning pairs or connects one stimulus with another known stimulus that has demonstrated a certain kind of response consistently over time. Over repeated trials of exposure, the new stimulus will also generate similar response pattern.

Ivan Petrovich Pavlov postulated the above theory based on his experimentation on a dog. He offered a hungry (motive) dog a piece of meat (unconditioned stimulus). Then he rang a bell, and instantaneously after it, offered some more meat to the dog. He found the dog was salivating (unconditioned response). Over a period of time, the dog understood that meat could satisfy its hunger. Therefore, when it was driven by the motive of hunger, meat appeared as an unconditional stimulus to it. Then, Pavlov continued ringing the bell while offering meat for some days thereafter. After ample exposure of this procedure, he rang the bell (conditioned stimulus) without offering the meat. He still observed the dog salivating. This means over a period of time and over repetitive exposures, learning (conditioning) had occurred and the dog began to bracket the bell sound (conditioned stimulus) and the meat (unconditioned stimulus) together and responded (salivating) in the similar way to both of them. This process of associating conditioned and unconditioned stimulus is referred as 'classical conditioning theory of learning' in consumer psychology.

In context of consumer behaviour, a recognized brand may be considered as an unconditioned stimulus. For example, *Dettol* antiseptic lotion of Reckitt & Colman India Ltd. is well known in the Indian market for its hygiene attributes. This previously acquired perception of *Dettol* may be called the 'unconditioned response'. The company offered a new product (*Dettol* bathing soap) having the same brand name '*Dettol*' (the unconditioned stimulus). The soap may be considered here as the 'conditioned stimuli' as it was expected to initiate similar kind of perception of hygiene quality as that of the antiseptic lotion. The consumers readily responded in the same way as was expected and tried the product (conditioned response). Thereby, an association of the 'conditioned and unconditioned stimuli' was successfully done by many marketers of this century by effective use of 'umbrella branding'.

In a similar way the brand-stimuli association (e.g., the red colour of *Coca-Cola*, the dog of *Vodafone*, the jingles of *Titan*) also generates quite similar pattern of responses observed in the classical conditioning theory. For example, the jingle of *Titan* also reminds about the *Titan* watches only. Figure 7.1 portrays an idea about the conditioned learning process.

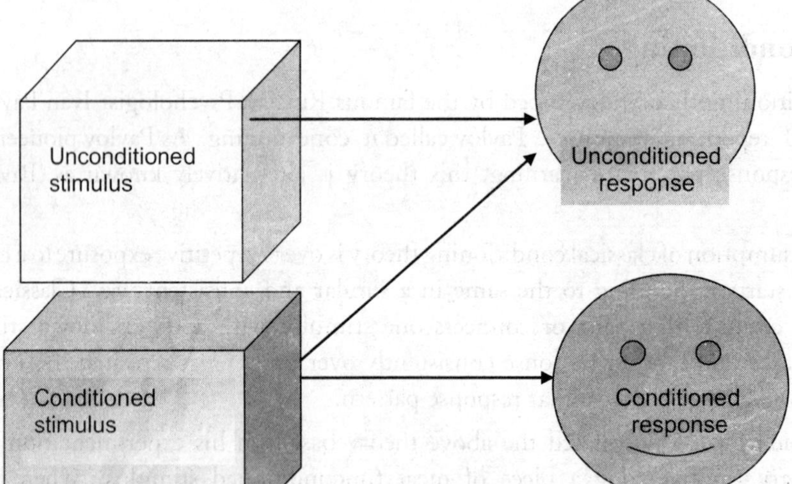

Figure 7.1 Classical conditioning process

Instrumental Conditioning

B.F. Skinner, an American psychologist pioneered the theory of instrumental conditioning in learning. The instrumental conditioning theory of learning depends on the principle of trial-and-error. This theory stresses on identifying the particular stimulus generating the most favourable response. Gradually, the association between the stimulus and response is learned with the rewards received for reinforcement from certain response behaviour time and again.

Skinner was of the opinion that majority of the individual learning situation occurs in controlled environment. He suggested that in this process the individuals are rewarded for choosing the appropriate response pattern given a particular set of stimulus and cues. To prove the theory, Skinner also resorted to the experimentation method. As he deliberately used instruments/levers for the purpose, his theory is known as 'instrumental conditioning theory'.

Skinner made a box fitted with several levers and kept a few pigeons in it. This instrumented box was, therefore, named as 'Skinner Box'. The idea was if the birds pressed the right lever, they would get food as reward. This reward reinforced the birds to keep on pressing the levers at random. In the process, they finally pressed the right lever and got rewarded with grains. This experimentation led to identifying a reward-reinforcement method of learning. In context of consumer behaviour, this theory is often referred as operant conditioning.

Today's FMCG market is characterized with immense competition. To grab the attention of the customer and facilitate them to adopt the right choice, marketers often resort to trial pack offers. This provides the opportunity to the customers to test the acceptability of various brands and thereafter diffuse the most suitable one for them. Not only FMCGs, even car companies quite often allow a test ride to their customers.

So, the major task of the marketer to shape the operant learning process is to first ensure the trial, followed by developing purchase intention, and finally diffusion by means of rewards and reinforcement. To ensure the initial trial, *Reader's Digest* opts for direct mailing to the customers. Reinforcement plays a much larger task in operant conditioning than in classical conditioning. The reinforcement sometimes reaches to the customers in the form of discounts, allowances, free gifts, contests, etc. To ensure continuous purchase, marketers sometimes provide discounts for repeat purchase. Airlines often use the technique by frequent flier advantages and redemption of miles.

Sometimes, famous jewelry houses offer special *Dhanteras* offers to existing customers to reinforce repeat purchase. Discount coupons or a free dinner with a star offered to the lucky winners of contests are also used by several tele-soaps to increase the TRP rates. Recently, *Tata Nano* has increased its warranty period up to 4 years as a part of such reinforcement.

Discount coupons

Cognitive Learning Theory

Another out-of-the-box learning theory is based on using the individual's psychic ability to notice, form perception, and develop knowledge about them. In this process, the individual resorts to either extensive information search or sudden impulse learning to gratify his motives. As this process of learning focuses on the mental activity, it is often referred as 'cognitive learning'. Given the fact that the *Homo sapiens* are blessed with the power of rational thinking, reflection, and problem solving ability, the cognitive theories involve a complex mental route for information processing. It further underlines the role of motivation and other mental processes to turn out the desired response.

Cognitive theory is perhaps best understood looking at the experiment of Wolfgang Kohler with a chimpanzee. The animal was put in a cage containing a wooden box. Some bananas were hung from the roof of the cage in such a way that the chimpanzee could not reach them. Within a short span, the animal started jumping to catch hold of those bananas. But as they were kept out of its reach, it was not able to do so. Out of the blue, the chimpanzee placed a box just beneath the place where the bananas were hanging. Now, it jumped on to the box to get to the bananas and succeeded. This behaviour of the animal clearly portrays that it did learn to reach its objectives by a spontaneous insight into the problem-solving process. Although the bananas in this experiment do not reinforce any rewards, nonetheless, motives still play a crucial role for developing such cognitive ability for rational/impulsive problem-solving techniques.

In context of consumer behaviour, the individuals are considered to show problem-solving behaviour and have active understanding of situations confronting them. This view is therefore most important in understanding how consumers learn which stores, methods of shopping, or products will best meet their needs.

Various forms of cognitive learning could be as follows:

(i) *Iconic Rote Learning*: This encompasses the association between two or more concepts in the absence of conditioning. An ad slogan which says, '*Dove* is a moisturizing soap' or 'Johnson baby soap is too mild and gentle for baby skin' can be some examples of iconic rote learning.

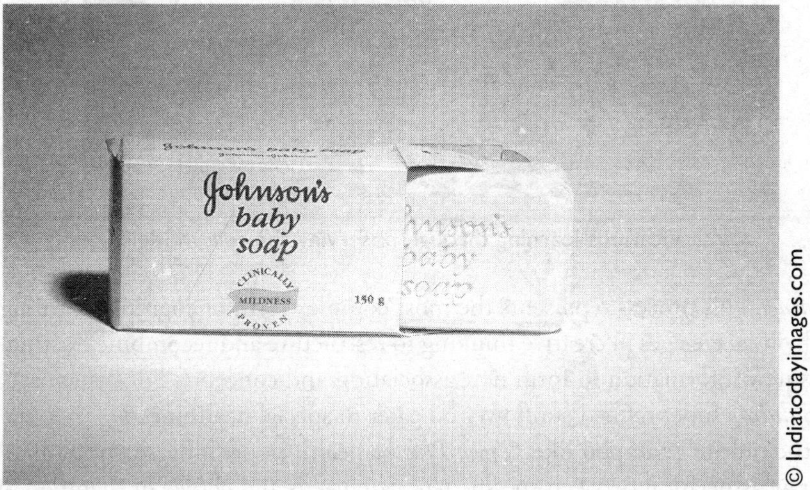

Johnson baby soap: its promotional ad slogan is an iconic rote learning

A substantial amount of low-involvement trial purchase involves iconic rote learning. Numerous repetitions of a simple message invariably results in the essence of the message being learned.

Through iconic rote learning, consumers may form beliefs about the characteristics or attributes of products without being aware of the source of information. When the need arises, a purchase may be made based on those beliefs.

(ii) *Vicarious learning*: This is another important way in which consumer learning takes place. It is not necessary for consumers to directly experience a reward to learn. Instead, a consumer can observe the behaviour of others and adjust that of his accordingly. Likewise, he may also use imagery to anticipate the outcome of various courses of action. This type of learning is common in both low- and high-involvement situations. In a high-involvement situation (such as purchasing a mobile phone or an ipod which are costly and reflective to one's personality), a consumer may deliberately observe the styles in vogue at that point of time, or that are worn by the role models from other environments, including advertisements.

Vicarious learning through observing the role models

(iii) *Reasoning:* This process represents the most complex form of cognitive learning. In reasoning, an individual engages in creative thinking to restructure and recombine existing information as well as new information to form new association and concepts. For instance, *Saffola*, *Horlicks Lite*, *Sundrop* super refined sunflower oil cater to special health needs.

Anti-dandruff shampoo like *Clinic Plus* or health nourishing shampoo like *Pantene Pro V* also draw association between specific hair care needs and choice of shampoo brands.

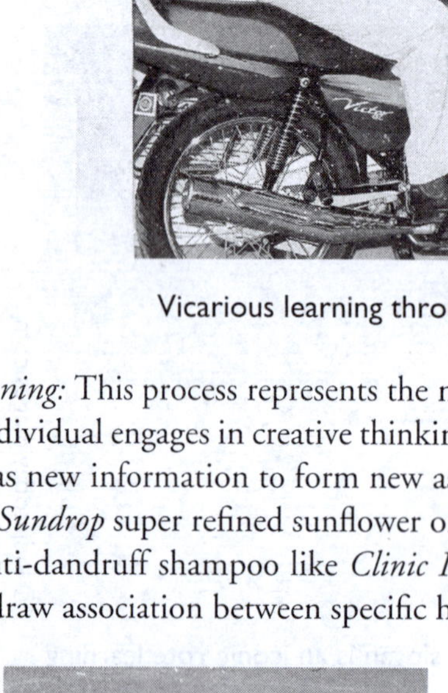

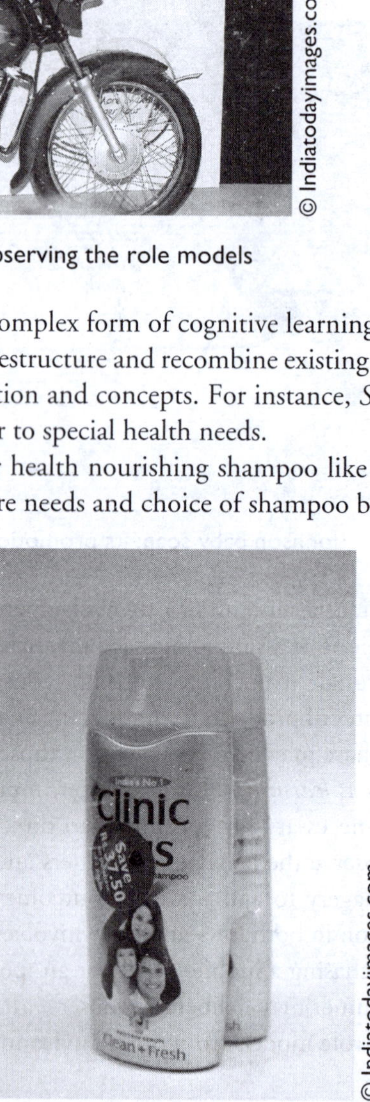

Reasoning: Products catering to specific hair care needs

MARKETING IMPLICATIONS OF LEARNING

To be precise, consumer learning is a process by which individuals acquire knowledge and experience from different sources which they apply in future events. Marketers, however, are principally concerned with:

- how consumers possibly learn
- what are the barriers of their learning process
- how certain cues such as brand, corporate names, packaging, and advertising meet consumer's expectations in specific product-buying situations
- how consumers process information regarding what, when, and where to buy in terms of different products and services
- elements of positive and negative reinforcement
- how to develop associations among different brand extensions and 'umbrella brands'.
- how consumers across different segments decide to buy new products or dispose of the old ones

Thus learning can facilitate a marketer to build demand for a product by associating with strong drives using motivating cues and providing positive reinforcement. In general, marketers try to make a typical consumer learn about their brand names, specific features or attributes, spectrum of consumer benefits, etc. However, consumer learning is continually evolving and changing as a result of newly acquired knowledge through extensive media exposure and social networking. To conclude, it may be said, it is really difficult to generalize a set of rules universally applicable to explain today's consumers' learning process.

Closing Case

24×7 Cooking Gas Booking System through SMS—A Flop Initiative by South Gas

In one wonderful morning of February 2010, Mr. Mayank Vimani, Vice President, Customer Care of South Gas, was in a tensed mood. His Secretary, Naina, informed him that he had been bombarded with thousands of complaint letters regarding the customer handlings of majority of its distributors. South Gas is one of the oldest cooking gas providers in the country distributing cooking gas across the country for years together.

It was not a very pleasant state for them, so Mr. Vimani, along with his secretary, carefully read all the letters and found some common threads in them. From majority of the letters, only a few common problems emerged. His secretary listed the following problems:

- In houses where both partners are working, it was not possible to go to the agency and book for refill of the gas cylinder during the office hours. All the agencies were usually open during 10.30 am to 5.30 pm. As this timing coincided with their office hours, it was difficult for them to personally go to the agency for booking.

- There were telephonic booking numbers, but most of the times the numbers were busy. Each of the agencies had a staff of 4–5 and 2–3 van-boys, and served a huge number of customers.
- It was difficult to estimate the date the cylinder would be supplied as the time gap between the booking and supply often fluctuated. It was not possible for someone to stay at home 24×7. But, once the gas van returned seeing the concerned house locked, it was too difficult to arrange for getting back that booked cylinder.
- The phone operator in the distributor's office used to cut the phone before the queries were answered properly and called the docket number so fast that it was difficult to note down. Before asking for repeating the number, the operators used to disconnect the phone.
- In case of discrepancies with the distributor, it was too difficult to communicate the issue to the head office. First of all, whom to address in the head office was not clear to many customers. Even if they knew whom to report (e.g., managers, customer care), it was too difficult to contact them and the letters sent to them were seldom answered.

© iStockphoto/Thinkstock

Mobile booking facility

Mr. Vimani was in a fix and called a meeting with all his major distributors. He also arranged a meeting with the managers (customer care) of all the sales districts. They all raised one point that due to the large number of enquiries from existing prospective customers, it was not possible to pay proper attention to them.

Understanding the deadlock situation, Mr. Vimani, in September 2010, in alliance with two leading mobile service providers, launched 24×7 refill booking and leakage complaint logging system for customers under the municipalities and municipal corporations. For this the customers could utilize a unique single-point number. First-time consumers were needed to dial the toll-free single-point number from their mobile (from those two service providers only), select the language option, enter the telephone number of their South Gas distributor, dial the seven-digit consumer number, and then pick the option for booking in that order. The auto-generated system would instantly provide the refill booking number for future reference and ask the user to register his/her mobile number. The SMS booking facility was also available on a single-point number 678665. Once the customer's phone number was registered, the expected date of delivery of cylinders was also communicated to them through SMS. Nonetheless, the customers had to make advance payments for the gas through credit/debit card by using their mobile, if booked through SMS. If they asked for amendment for delivery date (any date after the expected date of delivery) through SMS, then some additional payment had to be done through credit/debit card.

By February, 2011, Mr. Vimani was again showered with the almost similar complaints as he faced last year. He was astonished to see that the mobile-commerce was not properly utilized by the customers even after six months of its launch. Mr. Vimani now appointed a market research consultant to find out the reasons behind the unpopularity of the implemented mobile commerce system.

The consultant Mr. Jogesh Verma conducted a survey with his research team. The survey results showed that the awareness level profusely varied across the respondents. On an average, 33% of the respondents were aware of the m-commerce and amongst them 70% were below 35 years of age. However, it was observed from the survey, that the average age range of the customers booking or logging complaint was 40–50 years.

Secondly, 70% of the respondents in the age-group of 40–50 years were in a dilemma, whether their local gas agency will at all access to the booking orders sent through mobile or not.

Thirdly, 60% of the respondents in the age-group of 40–50 years claimed that they were not very conversant in such technical procedure (linking mobile technology and gas booking). Many a times they made mistakes in operations and the purpose was not solved.

Fourthly, 40% of the respondents were not in a habit of checking SMS regularly, and hence possibly overlooked any SMS from the gas agency. They also claimed that many a times their inboxes were full with promotional junk SMSs from different companies and the new SMS regarding the estimated date of gas delivery might be bounced.

Mr. Verma submitted his key findings to Mr. Vimani. Now, Mr. Vimani was really in trouble. He had made a huge expenditure to initiate this process. Within another month, that was end of March, he had to be present in the meeting with board members and was quite likely to be held accountable for the failure of the project.

(This is a fictitious case prepared to stimulate classroom discussion. Any resemblance with any character, company, or incident is purely coincidental.)

Questions

1. Can you think of some more blockades for adopting m-commerce in India?
2. Design an appropriate integrated marketing communications strategy to facilitate the learning of the consumer about mobile commerce in order to increase its adaptability?
3. If you were in the position of Mr. Vimani, what learning techniques for the customers would you have initiated to facilitate the use of the m-commerce service?

Summary

This chapter provided an overview of two of the fundamental methods by which consumers are able to adapt to their environment. Classical conditioning is a process by which a neutral stimulus becomes capable of eliciting a response when repeatedly paired with a stimulus that naturally causes the response. Marketers use classical conditioning to create favourable affect for products and stores and increase the chances that consumers will perform desired behaviours. Operant conditioning deals with influencing behaviour with both antecedents and consequences. On the flip side, cognitive learning theory is based on mental activity and learning happens on mental information processing or in response to problem solving. Here information processing is related to both the consumer's cognitive ability and the complexity of information.

Nowadays, consumers are attracted to companies that offer some scope of learning experience. The crux of the problem lies in positioning the product that makes a linkage with experiences in the customer's life. Apart from typical features and benefits that a product has to offer, a company has to constantly focus its marketing strategy to have a stronger appeal to attract customers. If companies can stimulate the senses, touch the hearts, and excite the minds of the customers, their appeals will be more effective and offer long-lasting connections. This is what an experienced marketer does and it is the solution to today's fast changing consumer needs.

Key Terms

Learning Learning is a process of adaptation whereby an individual alters goal directed behaviour in reaction to changing environmental situations.

Classical learning Classical conditioning is a process by which a neutral stimulus becomes capable of eliciting a response when repeatedly paired with a stimulus that naturally causes the response.

Operant conditioning It deals with influencing behaviour with both antecedents and consequences.

Cognitive learning theory It is based on mental activity and learning happens on mental information processing or in response to problem solving.

Iconic rote learning This encompasses the association between two or more concepts in the absence of conditioning.

Vicarious learning The consumer can observe the behaviour of others and adjust that of his accordingly. Likewise, he may also use imagery to anticipate the outcome of various courses of action.

Reasoning An individual engages in creative thinking to restructure and recombine existing information as well as new information to form new association and concepts.

Questions

1. Describe classical conditioning and identify three responses in your behaviours that are the result of classical conditioning.
2. Under what conditions would the use of classical conditioning be likely to produce positive results as part of marketing strategy?
3. What are the major differences between classical and operant conditioning?
4. Review each of the four types of manipulations of consequences that can be used to change the behaviours under operant conditioning.
5. How is cognitive learning process used by marketers of modern days? Elaborate with real life examples.

Critical Assignment

1. Select a product and develop three advertising, product introduction, or trial scenarios that would make use of learning or memory principles discussed in the chapter. Be specific in discussing how the particular principles are being applied.
2. Select three willing participants and choose a brand that is familiar to all three. Use observation method and checklist attempt to discover the semantic network for this brand.

Chapter **8**

Attitude Formation and Change

Chapter Goals

After completing this chapter, you will be able to understand

- **the concepts of attitude**
- **how attitude is formed**
- **models and theories of attitude formation**
- **how attitude can be altered**

Opening Vignette

Love in the Air—Valentine's Day Special Offers Flooded the Market

It was a cold morning of February 16, 2011. The Valentine's day fever had just been over. Romi Irani, the Managing Director of Holimyth Jewelry Chain in Delhi was very upset. Their jewelries were very famous in Delhi market, especially in the elite class. Therefore, the company expected a good sale during the week of Valentine's day. However, the floor statistics did not fulfill her expectations. Romi discussed the issue with the sales managers Hitesh, Rajiv, and Ambrish. Hitesh was very clear in his points. He said, 'Valentine's day market is specifically targeted to the youth. The craze of buying gifts, as we often see, is more amongst the teenagers.' 'Well I know that. We had many new designs specially for them,' Romi countered. Rajiv opposed, 'Yes madam, but our price was very high and designs remained bulky. Most of the teenagers cannot afford to buy expensive gifts, given their limited pocket money. Even rich class teenagers can manage upto ₹4000–5000 out of their pocket money for the purpose.' Ambrish took out a newspaper cutting from his file and said, 'Madam, look at this *The Times of India*, Kolkata edition report, printed on 12th February.'

She went through the article and found that Anjali Jewelers in Kolkata had a special Valentine day gold chain priced at ₹2950.

Other items of cosmetic jewelry ranged from ₹300 to 1000, which even the middle class teens could afford out of their savings. *Nnoni*, a famous costume jewelry brand, offered a range of Valentine's collection starting from ₹750. *Senco Gold*, another eminent West Bengal based jewelry house, offered gold and diamond pendant collections at ₹999 onwards. The Valentine collection from *Diya* started from ₹3000. *D'damas* and *Asmi*, also offered their 'Valentine collection' crafted in diamond and gold in affordable price. *Gaja Heritage* came out with an affordable and exclusive collection of diamond and pokri rings, earpieces, and neckpieces.

© Photos.com

Markets are flooded with gift items during V-day

After going through the article, Romi and all her marketing managers came to the conclusion that they made the following mistakes in understanding the consumer's attitude about special purchase on V-day.

- Teenagers, the more involved customers in V-day purchases, were price sensitive.
- Teenagers were restrained by their budget, but wished to buy exclusive and branded items.
- There was a need to offer light weight, sleek, and attractive jewelry sets at affordable price.

Therefore, understanding consumer's attitude is extremely important.

(All the characters and the company Holimyth Jewelry Chain are imaginary. However, information related to Valentine's day special price list of different jewelry brands has been obtained from the published report by Asabari Chakrabarti, 'More or Less', *The Times of India*, February 12, 2011.)

ATTITUDE DEFINED

The notions of attitude are multi-faceted and perhaps constitute the most important dimensions to explicate, comprehend, and foresee possible changes in human behaviour. The spirit of the psychological aspect of attitude is articulated by Baron, Branscombe, and Byrne (2008). In their opinion, attitude refers to 'people's evaluation of virtually any aspect of their social world.' In their process of constant evaluation of people, objects, and situations, Dennis and Wartella (1996), concluded that we have a natural propensity to evaluate stimuli (provided by the marketer or marketing environment) as favourable and unfavourable. These evaluations, or beliefs, form our attitude for any product and, thereafter, are reflected in our purchase actions.

Of late, a new definition of attitude is gradually emerging. This definition illustrates that a person's overall attitude towards an object is explained as a function of (a) strength of each belief that a person holds about various products/brands and (b) what is an individual's evaluation towards each belief associated with the particular tangible or intangible object. In short, attitude may be defined as a 'learnt predisposition to behave in a consistently favourable or unfavourable manner towards a given object'. The term 'object,' in marketing purview, refers to products, brands, services, usage, promotional measures, price, point of purchases, etc.

The latter definition, however, seems to be more appealing as it is quite conclusive about the consumer's evaluative criteria and how they form attitude towards a brand depending on these criteria. For example, when a middle-class consumer wants to buy a small car, the evaluative criteria are generally price, fuel efficiency, purchase schemes, available bank loans, comfort, etc. *Tata Nano* car scores high in the minds of the middle-class consumers in terms of all these criteria, and hence could be chosen easily.

Therefore, it may be stated that

- An attitude is a resultant factor of learned predisposition.
- Attitudes are targeted at specific objects, individuals, groups, or situations.
- The motivational-affective feature of attitude distinguishes it from simply being the predisposition or habit.

Attitudes, hence, can be strongly positive, undecided, to strongly negative, and can either be unambiguous/explicit or implicit/hidden. An attitude can also be intense, as in the case of prejudice, which can lead to perceptual bias and vice versa.

FUNCTIONS OF ATTITUDE

Attitudes serve the following four major functions.

Utilitarian function Consumers form a particular attitude about an object primarily based on its utility. If the consumer has a favourable prior experience with any brand or product, or has been exposed to some positive word of mouth by formal or informal sources, the consumer's attitude towards it may tend to be favourable. Normally, to highlight the brand's positive aspects, the marketing communication is directed at evaluative attributes, like reliability, safety, cost-effectiveness, and definite need fulfillment. *Women's Horlicks* depicts in its advertisements the importance of consuming iron and calcium especially for Indian women. Similarly low calorie *Horlicks Lite* focuses on middle-aged customers (for maintaining calorie level) and *Mother's Horlicks* (supporting the nutritional requirement) on the lactating mothers.

Mother's Horlicks for pregnant and lactating mothers

Ego-defensive function Consumers develop attitudes to attain personal goals and defend their self-images. For example, most of the commercials on cosmetics and personal care products stress on the sense of personal confidence and at sometimes on the fear of embarrassment. Indian skin care market is dominated by enormous traditional beauty care products like *besan, multani mitti, talcs, creams,* etc. Indians have a tendency to believe that fairness and beauty are synonymous. *Fair & Lovely* encashed this prejudice and generated a revolution in the market. Specifically focusing on the fairness benefit, *Fair & Lovely* was launched in 1975 in India by the Hindustan Unilever. The brand crossed the national borders in 1988. Today, with a successful positioning, *Fair & Lovely* leads the ₹1000 crore Indian fairness cream market with a share of over 70%. *Krack* cream was also a big hit in the Indian market because it addressed to the issues of winter scratches and crack marks by the '*fati ediah*' advertisement.

Knowledge function Consumers strongly insist on more information about the products they use or want to use, often to assure their right selection. This inclination helps the marketers to make the customers recall about the advertising messages or themes and in resorting subsequent positioning/repositioning decisions. This facilitates the consumer's evaluation of alternatives and, thereby, assists their decision-making process. For example, *Dell*, *Apple*, or *Sony* laptops always advertise about their performance superiority and dependability features, and form the consumers' presumption about certain configuration of the systems. This trims down uncertainty and perceived risk of buying the product from consumer's view point. For majority of the hi-tech products'/brands' advertising message is primarily designed to inform the consumers about the key features or appeals of the product and, thereby, help the customers to understand why the brand would fit with their requirements.

Sachin Taparia, MD of Aviall India, launching Sony VAIO X—World's lightest laptop, in Chennai, Tamil Nadu

Value-expressive function Attitudes are shaped to exhibit consumer's own values, lifestyle, and outlook. Sometimes, advertisers appeal to self upgradation, accomplishment, or liberty. For stylish or noticeable consumption objects, most of the products/brands take an attempt to highlight their value-expressive functions or advanced lifestyle. The distribution outlets of *Allen Solly*, *Louis Philippe*, *Peter England*, provide a portrayal of their lifestyle positioning while targeting towards the urban elites.

ATTITUDE FORMATION

For a marketer, one of the vital concerns is to understand how human attitudes are formed. In fact, the marketers can control consumer's preference by understanding the process of attitude formation. The following three models explain the process of attitude formation depending on the various threshold assumptions about essential parameters.

Exhibit 8.1: Tamarind Candies Fly up and up

Maujgarh, a small village in the Ferozpur district of Punjab, with a population of about 2500, is the principal supplier of the popular sweets and tangy tamarind candies in domestic flights. Commonly, they are known as *Mili*. Sandeep Jakhar, the man behind the venture, claims that it was not easy to enter the domestic airlines market. Originally, developed by the recipe of Madalsa Shastri, this tamarind product was selected by the Jet Airways after a lot of quality checks. Jet approved this product based on the following assumptions about their customer's satisfaction.

- Hygiene aspects were taken care of at the time of production. In fact, Sandeep had ensured that the ladies working in the project washed their hands before they started work. Working with *mehendi* in hands was never allowed.
- Tamarind was considered to be good for digestion and contained vitamin C. It was also used as a remedy to heat stroke and cured several mouth and throat infections.
- Tamarind was believed to reduce air-sickness, which was one of the most important reasons of its selection as a during-fly product.

The product gradually became so popular that it is now found in the stores of South Africa, France (as Bon Bon), and Canada. Sandeep got the order for Canada after a buyer tasted the product while traveling in Jet Airways. Interesting enough!

Source: Chhabra, Shruti Seth, Candies Take off, *The Times of India*, February 22, 2011.

Tri-Component Attitude Model

The hierarchy of effects model was developed by Robert J. Lavidge and Gary A. Steiner in 1961. This theory is comprised of some sequences by which consumers collect and use information to arrive at a final decision on the probable actions (for example, whether to buy or not to buy a certain product/brand), through a consecutive sequence of seven stages:

- Unawareness: The assumption behind this step is that there exists a considerable set of potential customers fully unaware about the existence of the product.
- Awareness: At this step, the prospects are aware about the existence of the product.
- Knowledge: At this stage, the consumers become well informed about the attributes and substitutes of a product.
- Liking: On developing knowledge about the product, the consumers form a favourable attitude towards it.
- Preference: After a detailed comprehension and liking about the product, the consumers develop preference for a particular brand.
- Conviction: When the customer forms the desire to buy a product, he reaches the stage of conviction.

- Purchase: At this stage, the consumer is ready to purchase and actually procures the product. In India, *Hyundai Motors* resorted to this model effectively while introducing its model '*Santro*' in the small car category.

Leon G. Schiffman in 2006 further condensed these seven stages into three distinct categories and named it as the tri-component attitude model. These stages are explained below.

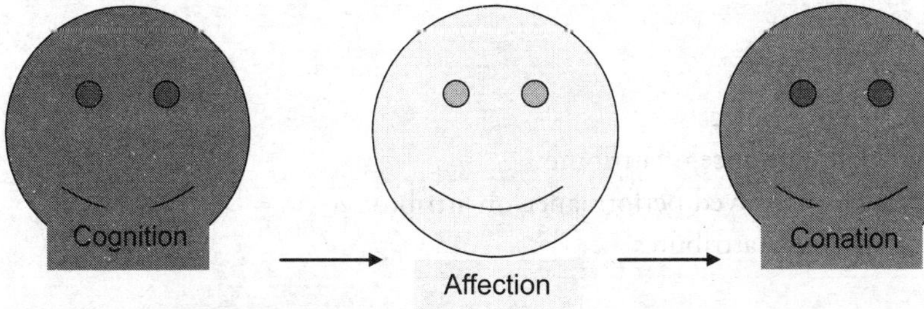

Figure 8.1 The tri-component attitude model

Cognition (Thinking) Congnition is the awareness about a particular object. Here, awareness includes its traits and benefits based on the customer's own knowledge and the information about the product collected from the marketers and other formal/informal sources. In Lavidge and Steiner's hierarchy, this phase encompasses the sequences of unawareness, awareness, and knowledge.

Affection (Feeling) This phase, according to Schiffman, encompasses the customer's outlook or sentiments about an object. Alternatively, this step refers to the evaluation of products or brands. This phase actually matches to the sequences of liking and preference as mentioned in the Lavidge and Steiner's hierarchy.

Connation (Doing) In the connation stage, an individual forms either predisposition about the product or a purchase intention to buy it. Lavidge and Steiner divided this step into phases of conviction and purchase in their hierarchical theory.

The Multi-Attribute Model

The multi-attribute model, developed by Martin Fishbein, is an attempt to reveal consumer attitudes with respect to an object (for example, a product, a service, or even the other three Ps of marketing). Fishbein projected attitude towards a product as a function of consumer's perception and evaluation of the major characteristics or beliefs held about it. There are two types of multi-attribute models: *the attitude toward objects (ATO) model* and *the ideal point multi-attribute model.*

The Attitude Toward Objects (ATO) Model

Consumer research has many ATO models developed during the course of the 20th century. Nonetheless, majority of these models primarily look at the relative importance posed by the customers on the salient brand attributes. Secondly, they search the consumer's beliefs about the degree of presence of those attributes in the available brand alternatives. These two sets of information have a combined effect on the alternative evaluation. Fishbein's model (1972) was the pioneer of this genus of models. Fishbein presented the model with a set of equation. The ATO equation is as follows:

$$\text{ATO} = \sum_{n}^{i=1} b_i e_i$$

where

ATO = attitude towards object

b_i = the relative importance of attribute i

e_i = the product's perceived performance on attribute i

n = number of salient attributes

Exhibit 8.2: Selecting a Car

Mr. Umesh Nair wanted to buy a car for himself and his family. Umesh is a middle-income salaried professional. He thought a small car would serve his purpose. He also wanted the car to be moderately priced, fuel efficient, and comfortable. Moreover, his wife should like it. Also, there had to be a dealer of the car near to his office or house. He thought warranty period and extra offers (e.g., car insurance, etc.) were also quite important criteria and had to be considered.

Availability of easy bank loan was also an important criterion to him. Umesh called his friend Satish, a market research executive by profession. Satish asked him to jot down the criteria and put relative importance to them.

The list of six most important criteria with their weights looked as follows:

Criteria	*Weights*
Price of the car (C_1)	$W_1 = .32$
Fuel efficiency	$W_2 = .28$
Warranty period	$W_3 = .18$
Dealer's proximity	$W_4 = .12$
Bank loan	$W_5 = .06$
Wife's choice	$W_6 = .04$

Satish calculated the summation of $W_i = 1$

Then Satish told him to select five cars which more or less matched his preferences.

Umesh selected five such brands—*Maruti* 800 Std BSIII, *Tata Nano* Std BSIII, *Maruti Alto* Std, *Tata Indica* V2 Xeta GL, *Hyundai Santro* Xing (non-AC).

© Indiatodayimages.com

Tata Nano car

(Contd.)

Exhibit 8.2 *(Contd.)*

Satish drew a table and asked him to fill up each cell in a five point scale where 5 meant the most preferred and 1 the least. When Umesh filled up the table, Satish started calculating the ATO scores for each brand and put the scores in the table. The table finally looked as follows.

Table 8.1 *The evaluation table*

Criteria	*Weights of criteria*	*Maruti 800 Std BSIII*	*Tata Nano Std BSIII*	*Maruti Alto Std*	*Tata Indica V2 Xeta GL*	*Hyundai Santro Xing (non-AC)*
Price of the car (C_1)	.32	4	5	3	2	2
Fuel efficiency	.28	3	4	3	4	3
Warranty period	.18	3	4	3	3	3
Dealer's Proximity	.12	5	2	5	4	3
Bank loan	.06	4	4	4	5	5
Wife's choice	.04	1	2	3	3	5
Preference for brands (ATO scores)		*3.54*	*4*	*3.26*	*3.20*	*2.88*

From the table, it was quite evident that the ATO score for *Tata Nano* was the highest. Satish handed over the scores to Umesh. Finally, Umesh decided to buy a *Tata Nano* car.

(All the characters in this case study are fictitious.)

The Ideal Point Multi-Attribute Model

In this model, Fishbein depicted the consumers' attitudes with regard to an ideal object. For example, a product, service, or any other marketing P is evaluated by consumers with respect to the key attributes or beliefs held with regard to a particular attitude object.

In line with this assumption, the consumer's attitude towards a product or specific brand of a product, can be projected as a function of the presence (or absence) and assessment of particular product-specific beliefs and/or attributes. The ideal point multi-attribute attitude model, therefore, can be represented by the following equation:

$$A_{\text{p}} = \sum_{i=1}^{n} W_i \left[I_i - X_i \right]$$

where A_{p} = attitude towards a product

W_i = relative importance of attribute i

I_i = ideal performance of the product on attribute i

X_i = belief about product's actual performance on attribute i

n = number of salient attributes

Consumers point out where they consider a product can be placed in an attitude scale (five point likert scale, seven point scale, or staple scale) in terms of the most significant evaluative criteria. This model adds up the perceived relative performance of a product on all significant criteria with respect to the perceived ideal product. Consumers, at first, have to state where an ideal product falls in terms of all probable criteria on the selected attitude scales. Next, these ratings are compared with a parallel survey on the perceived performance of the product on same evaluative criteria and scales. The attitude will be favourable or unfavourable depending on the proximity of the ideal and actual evaluative scores of the product.

The multi-attribute models, however, suffer from some major drawbacks. They fall short to judge that many a times consumer attitude does not comply with resultant behaviour. Thus a prospective buyer, despite having the most affirmative attitude towards any product in reality, may not buy it. This occurs as several parallel forces, like reference groups and opinion leaders, play their own roles in the alternative evaluation stage. Sometimes, some situational influences may also put the customer off from involving in a purchase action. The theory of reasoned action (TRA) model attempts to overcome this drawback in alternative evaluation. This model is discussed in the next sub-section.

Theory of Reasoned Action (TRA)

Adhering to the social psychology framework, the theory of reasoned action was developed by Martin Fishbein and Icek Ajzen in 1975 and 1980, respectively. TRA not only focuses on the steps of attitude formation but also appraises social and marketing parameters. TRA can be analyzed based on three broad constructs. They are as follows:

(i) Behavioural intention (BI)
(ii) Attitude toward behaviour (AB)
(iii) Subjective norm related to behaviour (SN)

As per TRA, a person's behavioural intention is a function of his attitude towards the behaviour related to the product and subjective norms. As a matter of fact, the behavioural intention calculates the consumer's extent of intention to reveal certain behavioural actions. Attitude comprises of beliefs about the underlying impact of the behaviour multiplied by a person's assessment of these effects. Subjective norm, on the other hand, can be viewed as a blend of perceptions and predispositions of pertinent reference groups and opinion leaders, and the person's inclination to behave in compliance to their expectations and perceptions. Hence, TRA model can be expressed by the following equation:

$$BI = W1\ (AB) + W2\ (SN)$$

where B = behaviour, BI = Behaviour intention, AB = attitude toward performing the behaviour, SN = the subjective norm, W1 and W2 are empirically determined weights through regression analysis.

AB and SN can be derived straight from the survey of consumers. Hence, TRA can be presented diagrammatically based on the Fishbein's theory (1980) as shown in Fig. 8.2.

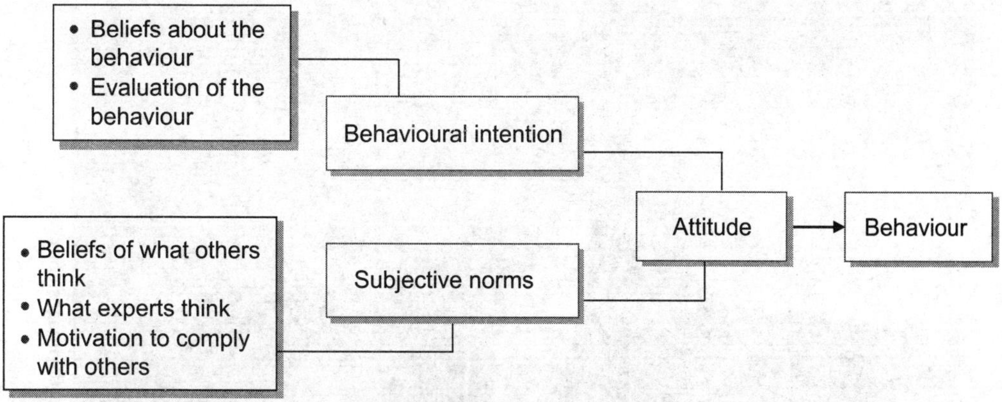

Figure 8.2 TRA model

Source: Figure drawn on the basis of assumptions of TRA developed by Martin Fishbein, 1980

Here attitude refers to the summation of various probable beliefs about certain behaviour multiplied by weights of these beliefs to the customer. Subjective norms are mostly the social and environmental pressures that the consumers come across as restraining or forming parameters for developing behavioural intentions. The beliefs of customers, weighted by the importance one attributes to each of these opinions, influence one's behavioural intentions. Hence, behavioural intention is a function of both attitudes towards a behaviour and subjective norms towards that behaviour.

ALTERING CONSUMERS' ATTITUDE

From the earlier sections, especially the multi-attribute attitude model of Fishbein, it may be concluded that there can be eight major ways to alter the consumer's attitude.

By altering the consumer's beliefs Consumer beliefs can be altered by several ways. Marketers normally believe that shifting beliefs about products will in effect derive more positive attitudes and persuade the consumers in favour of their products. Government, sometimes, deliberately looks to alter many myths, false beliefs, and irrelevant predispositions. The advertisements of pulse polio vaccination by superstar Amitabh Bachchan or the widespread HIV awareness campaign are some of the recent examples. The Government of India and the Bill Clinton Foundation HIV/AIDS Initiative have agreed to collaborate on the development and implementation of the Government's plan to scale up HIV care and treatment. Bill Clinton on May 26, 2005 addressed a meeting of the Clinton Foundation HIV/AIDS Initiative assisting India's National AIDS Control Organization (NACO) in New Delhi.

The support of the Clinton Foundation to NACO has proved to be a milestone in India's effort to fight AIDS

By developing new beliefs Apart from altering the existing beliefs, new beliefs can be formed by means of non-personal endorsements and genuine source messages. For example, to make consumers believe that the *Women's Horlicks* has a special nutritional value suitable for busy ladies, the concerned company roped in Konkona Sen Sharma, who is one of the celebrity movie stars of this time.

By changing attribute importance Changing attribute's importance is far more intricate than altering beliefs about a brand. Nonetheless, various marketers have productively used their own strategies to contradict this. In general, it is a time-taking procedure where marketers try to communicate to the consumers (by means of understated commercials, teaser campaigns, and other promotion stuffs) that the most significant attributes are nothing but the unique selling propositions of their own brand. In a recent example, *Dove* soap came out with their USP '3/4 moisturizing substance' and *Britannia* milk biscuits or *Horlicks* biscuits used the 'strength of a glass-full of milk' as their USP.

By changing ideal points Many new products/brands are coming up with completely innovative traits. The marketers of the existing products are also putting their effort to incorporate some innovative traits in their products. In this case, the marketers opt for changing consumers' perception about the ideal product attributes. This, undoubtedly, is not an easy job. Nonetheless, in the present era of information snowed under, some level of innovation, proper planning, and foreseeing the changing trend of perception of the customers can get the purpose served.

Changing the relative evaluation of attributes When too many brands clutter in the same product category, brands try to emphasize on some distinct features or attributes. Sometimes, this can be done with product differentiation. For example, *Garnier* is advertised as a root-nourishing shampoo, while *Clinic All Clear* as an anti-dandruff shampoo. *Sunsilk* has differentiated their product into seven different colours and claims that all these products cater to different needs of the customer.

Changing brand beliefs This is done by changing the attitudes of the consumers by altering beliefs or predispositions about a brand in the already established product category. Sometimes, there may be disputes in terms of brand perception. For example, in 2009, there was an allegation that the bottles of certain soft drinks had fungal growth. The sales of *Coke* and *Pepsi* were hampered for quite some time. Thereafter, *Coke* used Amir Khan as a finicky Bengali man in their advertisements and tried to depict the safety aspects of the product. Similarly, *Pepsi* portrayed that their product was safe and used the Bollywood '*Badshah*' Shahrukh Khan for this purpose.

Adding new attribute A new attribute can be identified by the marketers about a product. They may also add an attribute for improvisation of the product. For instance, *Colgate*, an almost hereditary brand in India, had added the content 'active salt', as salt helps the gums and teeth to be stronger. *Close-up* toothpaste had also made a number of renovations like 'micro granules' and so on.

Shifting general brand rating This implies to changing the consumer's overall assessment of a brand depending on the changed notion about the product and brand attributes. For example, due to rapid escalation of trendy designs and value-added services of the mobile handsets, the product's positioning has evolved from being just a 'communication medium' to a 'style statement'.

MARKETING IMPLICATIONS OF ATTITUDE

After analyzing the concept, importance, and models of attitude and its formation, the two most pertinent questions may crop up in the reader's mind. What are the marketing implications of the aforesaid theories and by what actions do the marketers manage them?

Table 8.2 outlines the areas in which such inferences and actions can be mulled over.

Table 8.2 *Areas of marketing inference and actions*

Area(s)	*Inference(s)*	*Action(s)*
Market segmentation	Divide the market into suitable clusters on the basis of product/brand beliefs, relative importance of attributes to different segments of customers, identifying the right segment to target, etc.	Select the appropriate marketing strategy based on lifestyle and benefit segmentation
Competitive analysis	Possibility of benefit, beliefs, and promoting the USP of the company's brand as compared to the competitors	Alter the product's positioning, if required. Company may go for product differentiation or brand line extension

Designing marketing mix	Developing ideas about new products, communication mix, developing proper distribution channel, and pricing strategy	Setting price in line with the consumers' perception, developing proper distribution channel, and identifying the most impact-making promotional message, media and brand ambassadors
Marketing opportunity analysis	Constant monitoring of attitudinal change due to demographic or psychographic change	Cater new markets based on the newly found upward or downward marketing opportunities
Altering the consumer's attitude	Proper understanding of consumer's changing perceptions about the product and the brand due to the change in their demographics and external marketing environment	Develop positioning and particularly the repositioning strategy by the company

In particular, marketers may prefer one or a mixture of marketing strategies to draw the consumers' evaluation of brand alternatives in their favour. Moreover, the marketers may attempt to amend consumer beliefs about various brands in a particular product category by means of smart promotion and distribution planning. Nevertheless, during the process of competitive assessment, marketers also try to change consumer beliefs regarding rival brands with reference to theirs. Ideally, this can either be done by diminution of the perceived-to-be-important product attributes, based on which rival brands are generally rated; or by disparaging their acts. Another, better way is to develop fresh brand attributes or give attention on some of the so far ignored potential brand attributes. This can also be done by trying to change the perception about an ideal-product so that it is perceived closer to the marketers' offerings. Nonetheless, the effectiveness of marketing strategy for forming or altering an attitude can be analyzed depending on consumers' actual purchase decision. The response, in either way, will articulate verdict on the competence of marketing reactions.

Closing Case

Expanding the Customer Base for DTH Service in North Bihar—Challenges to Convert Non-Users to Users

In the morning of the December 15, 2010, Mr. Rohit Kumar, Area Sales Manager (North Bihar, India) of Global TV Limited was quite upset. He was anxious about the Annual Sales Meeting that he had to attend in the coming week in New Delhi.

Rohit had left his previous organization, Vishal Network Ltd., three months back after working there in direct sales for about seven years. He had an excellent sales record. He had been appointed as the Area Sales Manager of Global TV Limited and was held responsible for the complete North Bihar region. North Bihar sales area covered the northern part of Bihar, comprising of primarily Muzaffarpur, Motihari, and Sitamahri districts. The company had huge expectations from him.

The interview panel had explicitly pointed out that he was being selected because of his in-depth understanding about the industry and his accomplishment rate at Vishal Network Ltd.

Rohit was, therefore, feeling concerned and was trying to devise some concrete plans which would facilitate him in escalating Global TV Limited's market share in north Bihar, thereby moving towards fulfilling the company's expectations.

A great opportunity in the form of the forthcoming ICC World Cup 2011 was knocking at the door and Rohit recognized that with the cricket fans of north Bihar, it was a make or break opportunity which he required to tap with the prearranged organizational resources.

Rohit appointed some of his sales people to conduct micro-level attitudinal survey on the prospective customers of north Bihar. The results highlighted the important factors hindering the increase in the customer base. Rohit prepared a list of these factors.

Factor 1 – Satisfactory present relationship with local cable operators: Customers had a positive and favourable attitude towards the cable operators because of their familiarity and long-term relationships with them. The customers felt that the cable operator was known to them personally and attended to all technical complaints as early as possible. Therefore, they did not feel the need to change over to the DTH system.

Factor 2 – DTH perceived as a richman's service: There was a perception amongst the customers that the DTH service was for the rich people, and not for the middle class.

Factor 3 – Higher installation and rental charge of DTH: For a package of about 125 channels that included the major channel categories and most watched channels, cable providers charged a rental of ₹180 per month in the suburban areas. They even kept the installation charges very low. In cities, the cable providers usually took deposits to the tune of ₹500 which was reimbursable at the time of discontinuance of the services by the customer. DTH, on the other hand, had high set-up costs, including the installation charges and monthly subscription charges. The initial set-up for DTH required a price as high as ₹1000 and the channel package offers were priced over and above this. The rental charged was perceived to be quite high by the consumers. This resulted in lower switching of consumers from cable to DTH. The price per channel ratio was also very high in case of DTH providers, and cable was stealing the march in this area over them. It was thus important for DTH to improve its distribution and customer services rapidly to meet with the increasing customer participation in the process of value realization. Also, DTH had to closely monitor its costs to be able to challenge cable's supremacy.

Factor 4 – Cumbersome payment procedure: It was found that the prospective customers considered the payment procedure of DTH service very cumbersome. In case of cheque payments, normally the drop box method was being used. But the number of drop boxes was highly inadequate in small towns. Furthermore, only the cheques above ₹1500 could be deposited. Another payment option was e-charging, but customers of rural areas and suburbs due to low penetration of Internet in the said places were unable to use this option. For paying by mobile option, handsets required to support JAVA MIDP 2.1 and telecom connection was needed to be GPRS activated. Connection error in GPRS, no network, incorrect PIN, incorrect Global Sky subscriber id, wrong card details, etc. led to transaction failure. On the other hand, the cable operator was normally a local person, and collected the rentals from home at a convenient time of the customer.

Factor 5 – No differentiation between DTH brands: This factor highlighted the fact that there were a growing number of DTH service providers creating a clutter. There was not much differentiation between them which confused the customers in their purchase decisions. Thus, the DTH brands needed to differentiate themselves from each other in the market to capture more continued attention of the consumers.

Moreover, just last week, one of Rohit's friends had said that all DTH services were very expensive and therefore did not target the middle class population of India. This made him think that if the mobile market could appeal to mass market, why not DTH? Till now, the company had concentrated their marketing efforts towards the urban high-middle class and upper class niche. Now it was time to concentrate on changing the middle income customers' attitude and perception towards the DTH services as well as the Global TV brand.

With these thoughts in mind, Rohit finally sat down to prepare a comprehensive marketing plan to address all the challenges and thereby come up with a strategy to augment the market share.

(This survey based case has been prepared by Dr. Srabanti Mukherjee, IIM, Indore and Dr. Archana Sharma, IISWBM, Kolkata. All the companies and characters are fictitious. Any resemblance would be highly coincidental.)

Questions

Considering you to be Rohit,

1. Prepare a marketing strategy to develop the evaluative criteria of the customers.
2. Design an action plan for converting the non-users to users of DTH in north Bihar.
3. How would you enhance your brand's credibility in the given market?

Summary

In this chapter, the basic concepts, functions, and characteristics of psychographic component of marketing 'attitude' has been explained with illustrations from real marketing world. Thereafter, the chapter proceeds with several theories and models. Specifically the belief-based models of Fishbein have been discussed in detail wherein focus has been given to the concepts of attitude – towards objects, subjective norms, and ideal point multi-attributes concept. The chapter has projected how Fishbein's multi-attribute model has given impetus to newer ways of conceptualization of behavioural intentions, in which consumers' attitude towards behaviour has been portrayed as a function of attitude towards objects and subjective norms. The end of chapter depicts the peripheral routes to form and alter customer attitudes. It has been identified that there are several possible ways to alter customer's attitude towards a product/brand. These are mainly altering the consumer's beliefs, developing new beliefs, shifting general brand rating, changing attribute importance, changing ideal points, changing the relative evaluation of attributes, changing brand beliefs, and adding new attributes. The chapter concludes with analyzing the importance and use of all the above mentioned concepts and theories to the contemporary marketing world.

Key Terms

Product-attribute It is the trait of a product.

Brand attribute It is the trait of a brand.

Unique selling proposition (USP) It refers to the distinctive feature of a brand as compared to its rivals.

Belief It is the behavioural notion people have about the relation amongst attributes, benefits, and objects.

Hierarchy of effect Various models elucidate the order in which beliefs, feelings, and behaviours occur. This hierarchical process comprises of three stages: cognition, conation, and affect.

Multi-attribute models The models that recognize how consumers merge their beliefs about product attributes and make choices among various brand alternatives are the multi-attribute models.

Ideal point It is the degree of presence of certain attributes in an ideal product.

Questions

1. What do you understand by consumer attitude? Do you feel it is really required to study the theories of attitudes when they may sometime fail to predict purchase behaviour accurately? Elucidate your answer with suitable examples.
2. Explain the TRA model with suitable example.
4. Hindustan Unilever Limited is moving towards the yet untapped market in rural areas by *Project Shakti* Initiative. What will you suggest for modification of rural consumers' attitude towards the branded FMCG goods and their brand evaluation pattern?

Critical Assignment

1. Devise an attitude questionnaire on five point scale to find out the consumer attitude toward any of the following: (a) *Apple ipads*, (b) *Turtle* shirts, (c) *Mother's Horlicks*, (d) *Loreal* hair colour.
2. You are a very busy corporate head in Navi Mumbai and wish to purchase a luxury car for yourself and your family. List the possible evaluative criteria and possible subjective norms which may shape your behavioural intentions.

Chapter **9**

Values and Lifestyle

Chapter Goals

After completing this chapter, you will be able to understand

- the concept of value
- lifestyle defined
- AIO classification of lifestyle
- VALS I and VALS™ classification
- the changing values and lifestyle of Indian consumers
- impact of values and lifestyle on consumer buying decisions

Opening Vignette

Impact of Fast Changing Lifestyle on the Youth—A Vignette on Nostalgia

In the days of yore, it was by and large the old fashioned traditionalists who endured with their fond old memories, alternatively known as nostalgia. The energetic youths often scoffed at them for it. The youths used to feel that it was the natural inclination of their grandparents to reminisce and moan about the days when the young honoured the old; women followed particular dress codes. Sometimes, they even felt like listening to stories when the aged people claimed that they added up endless numbers without the help of calculators, a kilo of rice was purchased at even less than a rupee, and people often required cycling 12–15 km to go to work at the crack of dawn. It is a common phenomenon that every generation muses over the 'better and simpler' days left behind. Nonetheless, a very surprising trend was noticed of late.

In fact, it is astonishing to find that people even in their 20s and 30s are in retrospection. In the era of 'Hinglish' culture or boom of night clubs, discos, and shopping malls, the young people are turning back to their sweet old memories of childhood days to probably find 'whom you left behind ... oh my mind' as Tagore said.

According to the eminent psychologist, Jitendra Nagpal, nostalgia is more popular than ever before and is no longer the prerogative for the old only. In the modern era, even the youngsters dream about the times when things were better. Nagpal referred to a most recent study which portrayed that the early ending of the sweet childhood, almost at an age of twelve, is perhaps the key motivating force for this present day's 'new nostalgia' phenomenon. After that the grind starts at every stage of life. Children are always under stress to perform in class and make a career. Teenagers are working as interns at multinational firms and call centres to gather some work experience to combat with the rat race. More serious thing is the rampant change in lifestyle; the just-adults are facing tussles in relationship, and having mounting bills of their credit cards, mobiles, etc. Due to this immense instability in life, they try to reminisce the past, when life was much stable and search some sort of control and comfort from those nice memories. To be more specific, they are reacting to the qualms and harshness of life by holding on to things that were a situation of stability and belief.

Internet marketing expert Amit Nair puts it in a different way. He says that the jet speed of technology is changing the lives of the youngsters very fast and that probably is the reason for their turning to old times. Just a decade ago, people sent letters and hand-made cards to each other. People used to think twice before calling in the odd hours of the day. Emails, mobile phones, social networking Web sites, and digital camera have changed the dynamics of communication. People who grew up in the end of the last century were always in a psychological pressure to communicate. It's like what the others would think if they did not frequently update their status message on Facebook. No doubt technology has made life faster but in no way simpler.

This erratic change in lifestyle resulted in threefold effect. Although, these day's consumers cannot renounce their cell phones or online access for a long span, but Nair has observed a very recent phenomenon of people trying to re-erect their past through technology. Lately, more than a million have downloaded the memorable '*Ek Chidiya*' animation (a part of growing up with *Doordarshan* in the 80s) from www.youtube.com. *Ramayan* and *Mahabharat* soaps had to be re-telecasted due to their immense popularity in those days. Yesteryears soaps like *Buniyaad* and *Intezaar* are downloaded and watched by enormous number of Internet users and retro ring tones (old movie songs of Kishore Kumar and so on) are at zenith of the popularity index.

In fact, it may be stated that the Internet today as a part of futuristic aura has stepped into nostalgia. A yearning to develop a community of friends or people of similar taste and profession is probably the driving force for most of the online activity. Mr. Amit Nair claims that the expansion in social networking sites is one of the results of the desire to recreate the past, no matter even through a virtual platform of social bonds. The social networking Web sites like classmates.com or facebook.com are good platforms for rejuvenating the school-college friendships.

The cravings for the 'nuggets of wisdom', the rise in the number of 'Ask your Grandma' sites are a sign of the youth's longing for the past.

Technology in use to re-erect past

That may be the placate precinct of the new youth, but there is nothing as awkward as untimely greying of the hairs—a condition for which there is no peroxides as yet.

(This case study was developed from the information based on the article 'Nostalgia on Speed' by Agarwala Vishant V, published in *The Times of India* on February 8, 2011 and the author's own views. It is intended to be used to stimulate class discussion at postgraduate level. It is not meant for illustrating effective or ineffective handling of a management situation.)

VALUES DEFINED

Values are intensely held visions about good, pleasing, precious, and important. Values are central points of people's existence (Rokeach, 1973). Many behaviours are acted out to realize values. Values control the shaping of attitude and the way in which information is processed; for example, most of the Indian female smokers feel hesitant to buy cigars from shops directly. Students do not consume cigarette in front of their teachers and elders in most of the suburban towns in India. Recent marketing research has shown that values have a noteworthy influence on, among other things, television watching habits, activity preference, selection of a store, shaping the consumer decision-making factors, selection of products and brands, and cigarette smoking (Becker and Conner, 1981; Kahle, 1985; McQuarrie and Langmeyer, 1985; Pitts and Woodside, 1984).

Values provide indications about how a particular culture functions when all the social functions rotate around the core cultural values of the society. Some researchers analyze values as the individual's depiction of a society's aspiration. If culture has to be understood, exploration of the values of people in that culture shows the most potential preparatory point. Even for cross-cultural research, value is the key issue. One may recollect the recent study by Kahle (1986), which has recognized that values diverge among geographic sections in the US. Nonetheless, the comparative value varying internationally has also been an area of interest by many scholars (Berrien, 1966; Zavaloni, 1980).

CORE VALUES

Every culture is defined by its own set of values those are imbibed by its affiliates. Some cultures may focus towards individualism and some towards attainment of social goals. According to the researches by Wirthlin Worldwide, hard work, respect for learning, and honesty are the primary values considered by the Asian executives. On the contrary, the business people of US or Europe lay more emphasis on the values of sovereignty, independence, and freedom of expression.

This diversity in values plays a categorical role behind the success and failure of marketing efforts across the cultures and countries. There was an incident some days back. A hugely successful commercial in Japan promoted breast cancer consciousness by showing a gorgeous woman in a sundress attracting gazes from men passing by her. The ad ends with a narration stating, 'If only women paid as much attention to their breasts as men do.' The same advertisement drooped in France as the French were very affronted by the use of hilarity to mention severe ailments.

In many cases certainly the cultural values are general; for example, the values of health, freedom, wisdom, etc. Nevertheless, several sets of values are undeniably being accumulated from the cultural heritage, religion, tradition, and overall beliefs and principles of life in any country. Especially, in a country like India, the cultural value varies like its vast geography. People speak in diverse languages, dress in different ways, pursue different religions, have totally different food habits across the states; nonetheless they pursue some common values like respecting the elders, honesty, hardwork, and deep-rooted philosophy of harmony. So whether it is a festive juncture or a minute of sorrow, people partake with all their heart, experiencing the bliss or curse together. A festival or a celebration in India is by no means constrained to a family. The entire society or environs take part to celebrate the occasion. Let us consider an Indian wedding case. May it be a Hindu, a Parsi, or a Christian wedding; it is considered not just the union of two souls, rather it is taken as the unification of two families.

Native Indian man hand-painting a cotton cloth

The worldwide reflection of India is that of an upcoming and progressive nation. India, these days, has really surpassed numerous precincts in almost all sectors—commerce, sports, technology, development, etc., without losing control over her other creative genius and of course own heritage. One small example may be the alternative science that has been continuously practised in India since times immemorial. *Ayurveda* is a distinctive type of medication made solely of basils and natural weeds. *Ayurveda* has also been talked about in the primordial Indian epics like *Ramayana*. Even today, when the western concept of medicine has reached its zenith, there are people looking for alternative methods of treatment for its multifarious qualities. The Government, looking at this issue, had to incorporate the *Ayurvedic* and *Unani* practitioners into mainstream government-run hospitals and health centres as integral part of the National Rural Health Mission (NRHM). With growing complications in lives these days, people are continually looking for some means to get some peace of mind, the '*Shanti*'. Meditation and spirituality are some attempts to attain peace of mind. Meditation and yoga are identical with Indian mysticism.

Another extensively pursued phenomenon in India is the *Doctrine of Karma* which states that one should only focus on his work and not on its outcome and behave impartially as every act returns in full circle with the re-birth of an individual.

Nonetheless, the most significant aspect of India in the recent past is the emergence of the new age woman. Women in India were primarily homemakers till 1980s. This myth is breaking now. Today, especially in metros and other cities, women are often the bread earners of the house or are at par with their male counterparts. Even in rural India, with the *Swanirvaar* projects women are getting self dependent in terms of economy and are, in many cases, the principal contributor in their household expenses. The augmentation in the cost of living and inflation rate are also some parameters behind the upsurge of women economic empowerment. The splendour of the Indian people lies in their strength of tolerance while maintaining their own entity and rich cultural heritage.

IMPACT OF VALUES IN CONSUMER BEHAVIOUR

Despite its immense importance, understanding of the concept of values alone does not have much bearing on marketing strategy formulation. This is perhaps because the broad-based concepts such as autonomy, safety, or intenseness may impinge on product purchase situations, but do not really differentiate between brands within a product category. In a recent study, the product-specific values had been analyzed thoroughly based on the behaviour of a group of Australians who engage in games like surfing, snowboarding, and skateboarding. The researchers identified four central values that drove brand choice for them, namely, freedom, belongingness, excellence, and connection. As the example projects, one female surfer in the study held close to the 'belongingness'. She articulated her inclination towards 'belongingness' by wearing popular brands of clothes. Some facets of brand reflections such as style and class tend to be common across cultures, but others like religious practices or sub-cultural myths are more likely to be pertinent in particular places. The Japanese emphasize more on serenity, while Spaniards stress on fervour, and the US people have an inclination towards rugged appeals.

A special case may be referred here. Processed and tinned food marketers have a typical challenge with respect to the Indian market. *Tropicana* experienced this problem in their fruit juice in tetra pack. The processed food market in India is purely an urban phenomenon. Conventional food practices are still prevalent and western style items have limited appeal. People still prefer to cook food in traditional ways for their family. Normally housewives take pride and get satisfied if they can cook something their family members like. *Roti*, *parathas*, *idli*, *utthapam*, etc., are always more adored by the housewives. The consumption expenditure of such food is low and these homemade foods are healthy too. Processed food are tried out by some urban families normally when there is time constraint to cook or when people want some change in taste. Hence, the manufacturers of processed food are yet to create any major value proposition for the consumers of all segments to buy. The products that are difficult to replicate or to make at home, like noodles, have gained quick acceptance but the western style products and semi cooked curries or processed fruit juice have not been accepted so far. Brand marketers are struggling to make that happen.

Conventional food practices—a challenge to the processed food market in India

LIFESTYLE DEFINED

Demographic variables facilitate the marketers to trace their target market and psychographic variables provide the marketers with more insight about the characteristics of the segment. But lifestyle, which is a psychographic variable, is the way of living of individuals, families (households), and societies, which they manifest in coping with their physical, psychological, social, and economic environments on a routine basis. Lifestyle is articulated in both work and leisure behaviour patterns and (on an individual basis) in actions, attitudes, values, and distribution of expenditure. It also reveals people's self image or self concept; the way they perceive themselves and trust the way they are comprehended by others. In other words, lifestyle is a combination of motivations, needs, and wants and is subjective as per different environmental dynamics such as culture, family, reference groups, and social class. Hence, the study of lifestyles (called psychographics) is a significant factor in shaping purchase decisions of the contemporary consumers—rural or urban.

The demographic and psychographic lifestyle approaches are highly complementary and work best in concert. People hailing from the same sub-culture, social class, and even occupation follow quite different lifestyles. Lifestyle study perhaps leads to more comprehensive ways to analyze how consumers think and act.

Feldman and Theilbar describe lifestyle by the following characteristics:

1. *Lifestyle is a group phenomenon*
   A person's lifestyle bears the control of his/her involvement in social groups and of his/her interaction with others. Two doctors in the same hospital may exhibit different lifestyles.
2. *Lifestyle pervades various aspects of life*
   An individual's lifestyle may result in certain kind of stability of behaviour. Knowing a person's demeanour in one facet of life may facilitate us to foresee how he/she may act in other situations.

3. *Lifestyle implies a central life interest*
   For every individual, there are many central life interests like family, work, leisure, sexual exploits, religion, politics, etc., governing their interactions with the environment.
4. *Lifestyles vary according to sociologically relevant variables*
   The rate of social change poses a great influence on the variations in lifestyles. Similarly, the other demographic parameters also influence the age, sex, religion, ethnicity, and social class. The augmentation in the number of double income families and that of working women has resulted in completely different lifestyles since 1980s in India.

Changing lifestyle in Kolkata

AIO CLASSIFICATION OF LIFESTYLE

There are many researches directing towards the various means to study lifestyle classification of customers. One of the ways is to study the lifestyle variables with the help of AIO inventories to segment the market, target the appropriate segment, and thereafter formulate the appropriate positioning strategies.

AIO studies comprise of a wide variety of variables and measures, the major dimensions of consumer lifestyles.

AIO Inventories

Activities	*Interests*	*Opinions*
• work	• family	• themselves
• hobbies	• home	• social issues
• social events	• job	• politics
• vacation	• community	• business
• entertainment	• recreation	• economics
• community	• fashion	• education
• shopping	• food	• products
• sports	• media	• future
• club membership	• achievement	• culture

Some researches on the lifestyle by the AIO inventory of heavy/medium/light users of a product turn out incalculably constructive for marketers. Ideally, identifying the heavy users facilitates the selection of a target audience. William Wells and Douglas Tigert used an AIO inventory to explore the heavy user of eye cosmetics. Demographic data exposed that the heavy users of eye cosmetics were normally the young, well educated, and metropolitan women. Further, the survey revealed that these respondents were also inclined towards heavy smoking and habituated in long distance telephone calls. From the survey, they appeared to be aspirers for trips around the world, and as ones who wanted a very fashionable home with all modern and classy furniture. In a study that Plummer applied to bank credit card users, he described the males who used bank credit cards heavily as debonair and dynamic with a high profile background with respect to income, occupation, and education. The heavy card user placed a huge importance on individual manifestation consistent with his career and lifestyle. Normally, these types of customers bought at least three new suits a year. They belonged to several organizations and clubs and demonstrated a tendency to reveal modern and fashionable opinions.

Female Lifestyle Types by AIO Classification

Using the AIO inventory, the Chicago-based advertising agency of Needham, Harper and Steers, have recognized five female lifestyle groups and five male lifestyle groups. However, we also have the Indian parallels of these types. These are as follows:

Cathy—The Contented Housewife

Cathy symbolizes simplicity. She is faithful to her family and loyally serves them as mother, housewife, and cook. She likes a tranquil pace of life and stays away from anything which might upset her stability. In some of the advertisements like *Horlicks Lite*, *Sundrop* super refined sunflower oil, *Saffola* edible oil, we find the replicas of Cathy.

© Photos.com

Cathy—the contended housewife

© Indiatodayimages.com

Kareena Kapoor depicting the chic suburbanite in *Vivel* shampoo ad

Candice—The Chic Suburbanite

Candice is a metropolitan woman. She is sophisticated and courteous. Socializing is a significant part of her life. She is an active person, fascinated by sports, outings, movies, politics, and current affairs. Her life is quite hectic and she lives at a speedy clip. She is an insatiable reader but there are few magazines she may not like to read. Kareena Kapoor in *Vivel* shampoo advertisement portrays such personality.

Eleanor—The Elegant Socialite

Eleanor is a woman typified with style. She is a city-dweller. She likes the socio-economic sides of the city in terms of her profession and spare time actions. She is a style conscious and well-dressed lady.

She is economically secure and a graceful shopper. She shops for esteem and social needs, and hence is not so price conscious. She is a cosmopolitan woman who has toured across the world and is willing to do so more.

© Indiatodayimages.com

Simi Garewal, the elegant socialite

Mildred—The Militant Mother

Mildred is a woman who had a very early marriage and had children before she was ready to raise a family. Now she is discontented. She is perturbed and expels her frustration by rebelling against the system. She may be called as anxious rebel too. Sometimes, young ladies who disposed of their marital life by unavoidable circumstances (death of spouse at very early age, divorce, separation, etc.) also accumulate such characteristics. Television provides an ideal medium for her to live out her fantasies.

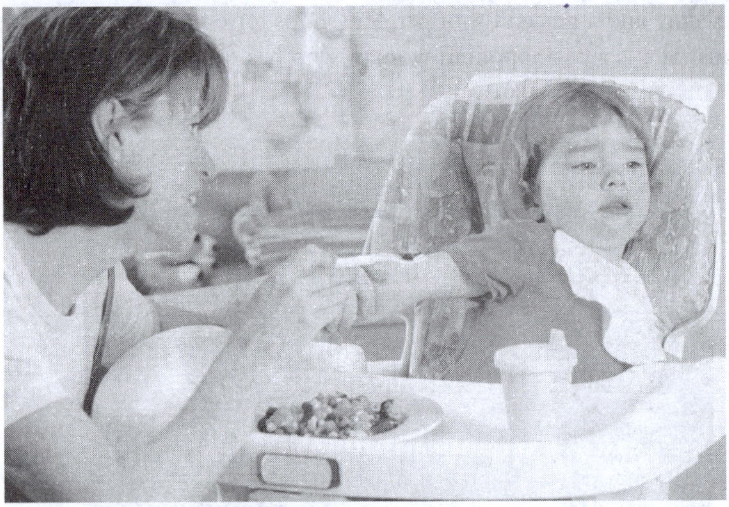

© Photos.com

The militant mother

Thelma—The Old Fashioned Traditionalist

Thelma is a lady who has lived a peaceful life. She has been a dedicated wife, an affectionate mother, and a diligent housewife. Even now, when her daughters are married and sons have left home for job, etc., her life is centred around the kitchen. She is not very highly qualified and has little interest on arts or cultural activities. Her spare time is spent watching TV, chatting with neighbours, or spending time with grandchildren.

© Yamini Chao/Digital Vision/Thinkstock

Thelma—the old fashioned traditionalist, middle-aged Indian housewife

Relevant Marketing Strategy for This Classification

To make this categorization even more functional for segmenting markets for specific products designed for women, the contemporary researchers have projected these segments in terms of an indicator of product usage. To exemplify, we can infer that Thelma—the traditionalist—is more probable to use hair dye, but least likely to use make-up. On the contrary, a marketer of a leading line of cosmetics, for example, *Lakme*, in India will principally target the Eleanors. Such women are inclined to using perfumes, body spray, lipsticks, hairspray, nailpolish, and various other forms of expensive make-up.

VALS CLASSIFICATION OF LIFESTYLE

VALS™ is a system for understanding different kinds of consumers and their distinctive products, services, and media preferences. The original VALS typology, developed by SRI International in 1978, segmented people based on their social values—hence the name, Values and Lifestyles. Since then, SRI research has found that psychological characteristics combined with several key demographics were better predictors of consumer preferences than social values. The VALS typology that has been in use for over 20 years is based on psychological differences. A person's VALS type is determined by the way he responds to a short questionnaire. The VALS questionnaire is often integrated into custom surveys of client interests, such as car preferences, attitudes about climate change, or fashion. The VALS questionnaire has also been integrated into GFK MRI's Survey of American Consumers for 10 years. VALS, therefore, provides a comprehensive framework for characterizing different American lifestyles. The system is at present functional in many areas of business and is inducing importance in circles as varied as marketing, sociology, politics, and even health. VALS is now owned and operated by Strategic Business Insights (SBI), an SRI spin-out.

VALS ™ Typology*

VALS™ segments US adults into eight distinct types—or mindsets—using a specific set of psychological traits and key demographics that drive consumer behaviour. The US Framework, a graphic representation of VALS, illustrates the eight types and two critical concepts for understanding consumers: primary motivation and resources. The combination of motivations and resources determines how a person expresses himself or herself in the marketplace as a consumer. While VALS research in other countries shows that basic psychological motivations such as self-expression and achievement are common across cultures, the way they are expressed in day-to-day life varies. For example, status symbols, expressions of achievement, often vary with countries. Other VALS frameworks include Japan VALS™, Venezuela VALS™, Nigeria VALS™.

**Source:* http://www.strategicbusinessinsights.com/vals/academics/permission.shtml, published with permission.

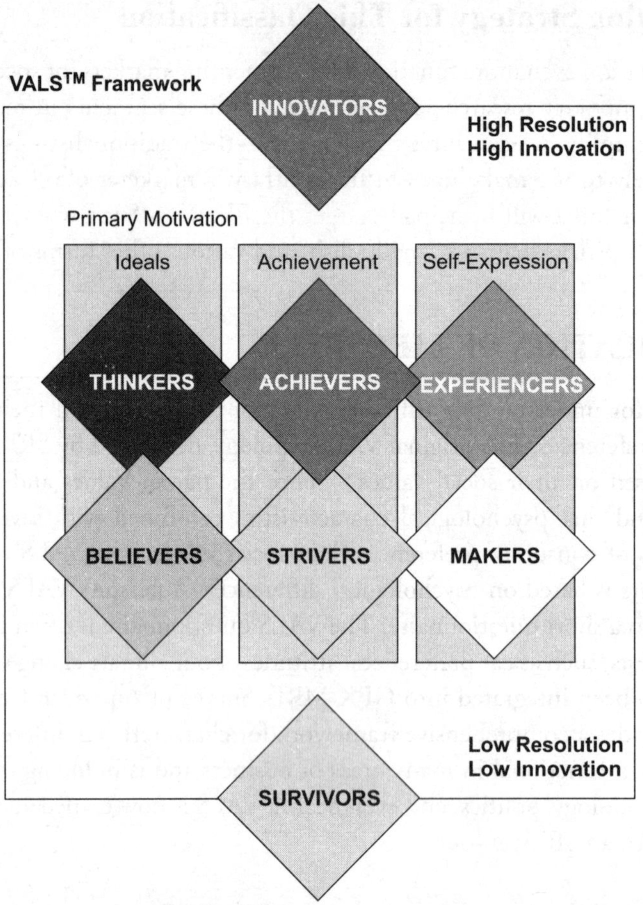

Figure 9.1 VALS™ typology

Source: Strategic Business Insights (SBI); http://www.strategicbusinessinsights.com/vals/academics/permission.shtml, published with permission.

Innovators

Innovators are successful, sophisticated, charge-taking people with high self-esteem. Because they have such abundant resources, they exhibit all three primary motivations in varying degrees. They are change leaders and are most receptive to new ideas and technologies. Innovators are very active consumers and their purchases reflect cultivated tastes for upscale, niche products, and services.

Image is important to innovators, not as an evidence of status or power but as an expression of their taste, independence, and personality. Innovators are among the established and emerging leaders in business and government, yet they continue to seek challenges. Their lives are characterized by variety. Their possessions and recreations reflect a cultivated taste for the finer things in life.

Thinkers

Thinkers are motivated by ideals. They are mature, satisfied, comfortable, and reflective people who value order, knowledge, and responsibility. They tend to be well educated and actively seek out information in the decision-making process. They are well-informed about world and national events and are alert to opportunities to broaden their knowledge.

Thinkers have a moderate respect for institutions of authority and social decorum but are open to consider new ideas. Although their incomes allow them many choices, thinkers are conservative, practical consumers; they look for durability, functionality, and value in the products they buy.

Believers

Like thinkers, believers are motivated by ideals. They are conservative and conventional people with concrete beliefs based on traditionally established codes: family, religion, community, and the nation. Many believers express moral codes that have deep roots and literal interpretation. They follow established routines, organized in large part around home, family, community, and social or religious organizations to which they belong.

As consumers, believers are predictable; they choose familiar products and established brands. They favour US products and are generally loyal customers.

Achievers

Motivated by the desire for achievement, achievers have goal-oriented lifestyles and a deep commitment to career and family. Their social lives reflect this focus and are structured around family, their place of worship, and work. Achievers live conventional lives, are politically conservative, and respect authority and the status quo. They value consensus, predictability, and stability over risk, intimacy, and self-discovery.

With many wants and needs, achievers are active in the consumer marketplace. Image is important to achievers; they favour established, prestige products and services that demonstrate success to their peers. Because of their busy lives, they are often interested in a variety of time-saving devices.

Strivers

Strivers are trendy and fun loving. Because they are motivated by achievement, strivers are concerned about the opinions and approval of others. Money defines success for strivers, who do not have enough of it to meet their desires. They favour stylish products that emulate the purchases of people with greater material wealth. Many strivers see themselves as having a job rather than a career, and a lack of skills and focus often prevents them from moving ahead.

Strivers are active consumers because shopping is both a social activity and an opportunity to demonstrate to peers their ability to buy. As consumers, they are as impulsive as their financial circumstances will allow.

Experiencers

Experiencers quickly become enthusiastic about new possibilities but are equally quick to cool. They seek variety and excitement, savouring the new, the offbeat, and the risky. Their energy finds an outlet in exercise, sports, outdoor recreation, and social activities.

Experiencers are avid consumers and spend a comparatively high proportion of their incomes on fashion, entertainment, and socializing. Their purchases reflect the emphasis that they place on looking good and having 'cool' stuff.

Makers

Like experiencers, makers are motivated by self-expression. They express themselves and experience the world by working on it—building a house, raising children, fixing a car, or canning vegetables—and have enough skill and energy to carry out their projects successfully. Makers are practical people who have constructive skills and value self-sufficiency. They live within a traditional context of family, practical work, and physical recreation and have little interest in what lies outside that context.

Makers are suspicious of new ideas and large institutions such as big business. They are respectful of government authority and organized labour but resentful of government intrusion on individual rights. They are unimpressed by material possessions other than those with a practical or functional purpose. Because they prefer value to luxury, they buy basic products.

*Survivors**

Survivors live narrowly focused lives. Because they have few resources with which to cope, they often believe that the world is changing too quickly. They are comfortable with the familiar products and are primarily concerned with safety and security. Because they must focus on meeting needs rather than fulfilling desires, survivors do not show a strong primary motivation.

Survivors are cautious consumers. They represent a very modest market for most products and services. They are loyal to favourite brands, especially if they can purchase them at a discount.

VALS I Typology

The original VALS typology designed by SRI in 1978 was divided into four major categories, with a total of nine lifestyles. This typology has not been used for over 20 years. However, for those interested in the history, the original VALS system is presented here. The original nine lifestyles were as follows:

- Need-Driven
  - Survivor lifestyle
  - Sustainer lifestyle

**Source:* Strategic Business Insights (SBI); http://www.strategicbusinessinsights.com/vals/academics/permission.shtml, published with permission.

- Outer-Directed
  - o Belonger lifestyle
  - o Emulator lifestyle
  - o Achiever lifestyle
- Inner-Directed
  - o I-Am-Me lifestyle
  - o Experiential lifestyle
  - o Societally Conscious lifestyle
- Combined Outer- and Inner-Directed
  - o Integrated lifestyle

In the paragraphs that follow, an attempt has been made to elucidate the psychosomatic essence of each segment of the typology and thereby, to offer an understanding of widening concerns and multiplying values of individuals as they move up along the typology.

Need-Driven

The need-driven are people so inadequate in terms of mainly economic resources that their lives are driven more by need than by choice. Many demonstrate the features to withdraw from the social and cultural mainstream. Values of the need-driven people normally evolve around the concerns of survival, safety, and security. They have a common tendency to be distrustful, dependent, and unplanned. Need-driven category is sub-divided into two lifestyles:

Survivors Survivors (4% of the population aged 18) are the most underprivileged in American society because of their acute poverty, low education, old age, and narrow access to the channels of upward mobility. Often they are oriented to customs and rituals but characterized by anguish and misery.

Sustainer Sustainers (7% of population) are a group besieged in the boundary of poverty. However, they are better off and younger than survivors, and many have not lost all their aspirations. Their values are quite diverse from those of survivors. Actually the sustainers have passed off the stage of acute despair and hopelessness typical of survivors to express anger at the system. But they see as repressing them, and they have developed a shrewd determination to get ahead. Many of them even work in the underground economy.

Outer-Directed

The outer-directeds conduct their lives in response to cues symbolic or significative from the external environment. Psychologically, outer-direction is one-step advanced stage from the need-driven state in that the viewpoint of inclusion of other people, a host of institutions, common goals, and an array of personal values and options are far more multifaceted than those presented to the need-driven. In general, the outer-directed are the most contended of Americans, thoroughly adjusted to the mainstream culture and also impacting influence on it. The VALS typology defines three major types of outer-directed people:

Belongers Belongers (39% of population) comprise of the mass and much steady, middle-class group of Americans who are the most important balancing entities of society. They are also the preservers and protectors of the ethical status quo. Ideally, this category inclines to be conventional, conformist, evocative, and maudlin. The main drive is to fit in the requirements of the society and not to be the odd-man-out. Family, church, and tradition impend to a large extent. It is evident that the belongers, in terms of psychological maturity, are to the fore of the need-drivens in having a much wider range of associations (both personal and institutional), a steady long-term planning for future, and a less opportunistic pattern of behaviour. These are comparatively well integrated with their external environment.

Emulators Emulators (8% of population) live in a totally diverse world from that of belongers. Emulators try to embark on the upper levels of the socio-economic hierarchy. The purpose of their emulation is to adapt the achiever lifestyle. They are go-getting, upwardly mobile, esteem-oriented, chauvinist, and aggressive. Many perceive themselves as coming from the other side of the tracks. They are deeply suspicious, are irritated with the way things are, and hardly have any faith that 'the system' will give them an even chance.

Achievers Achievers (20% of population) comprise the selected few in business, the professions, and government. Proficient, self-sufficient, competent achievers tend to be acquisitive, meticulous, oriented to recognition and accomplishment, and comfort loving. These are mostly the well-heeled people who have shaped the economic system in response to the American dream. As such, they are the protectors of the financial status quo. Achievers are amongst the best attuned of Americans, being well contented with their position in the system. Nonetheless, only 5% of achievers come from minority backgrounds.

Achievers, though, are psychologically more advanced than emulators in terms of prolonged array of values like liberalness and trust for others, improvement of technology, nonetheless they resist radical change.

Inner-Directed

Inner-directed people tend to be self-reliant, individualistic, person-centred, passionate, and versatile. However, it is beyond any doubt that one can hardly be intensely inner-directed without having internalized outer-directedness through far-reaching and profound revelation as a child, adolescent, or adult. This does not mean that the happiness of the outer world fades away (for the VALS typology is a nested model) when one is inner-directed, rather the inner needs become more crucial than the outer ones. VALS has identified three stages of inner-directedness: I-Am-Me, Experiential, and Societally conscious.

I-Am-Me The I-Am-Me person (3% of population) is youthful and intensely individualistic to the point of being egotistic and showy. These groups of consumers are often full of confusions and emotions and tend to be dramatic and impulsive. Much of their inner-direction shows up in great creativity and an eagerness to try a new thing.

Experientials Experientials (6% of population) are those types of beings who prefer direct experience and energetic participation. Life seems to be casual to them at one moment and a passionate, often mystical, inner experience the next. They are fascinated to the foreign (such as Oriental religions), to the outlandish (such as parapsychology), and to the normal (such as 'organic' gardening and home baking). These people also are probably the most creative, imaginative, and most zealously involved with others than any other groups of VALS.

The Societally Conscious The societally conscious (11% of population) seek to live careful lives that preserve, guard, and make well. Inner growth remains a vital part of life. As a result, many societally conscious people believe in a high degree of independence, which extends to holistic health and a sense that they are in touch with internal forces that direct their activities.

Combined Outer- and Inner-Directed: The Integrated

At the apex of the VALS typology is a tiny group named as the integrated (2% of population). These atypical people meld the power of outer-direction with the sensitivity of inner-direction. They are completely in their prime in a psychological sagacity—able to make out many sides of a subject, capable to direct if necessary and ready to take even a secondary role if that is suitable. They generally own a profound sense of the appropriateness of certain aspects of actions and reactions. They tend to be self-confident, self-actualizing, self-expressive, and intensely conscious of social and emotional issues. They try to view things from world's point of view. These extraordinary people are the Lincolns, Jeffersons, Einsteins, Schweitzers, Huxleys, Hammarskjolds, Mahatma Gandhi, and Swami Vivekananda.

Exhibit 9.1: The Memory Market for Gramophones

The Market of Believers

The old artifacts are, these days, no more only the collector's item. Instead, they have dripped down to mass markets, tiptoeing into the lounges of art aficionado middle-class not just as a peculiar show-piece, but as a quality product that talks about a certain time, perchance even the lost epoch.

A street seller in Janpath, Delhi, as per a *The Times of India* report (The Memory Market, February 8, 2011), claimed gramophones sell a lot. He confidently asserted that he has sold a large amount of such rare objects to even strangers who are eager to pay handsome price for them. Pricing anywhere between ₹3000–10,000 a piece, based on the size and rarity, in flea markets such as those of Janpath in New Delhi, these oddballs are no longer the cartel of selected vendors.

(Contd.)

Exhibit 9.1 *(Contd.)*

© Photos.com

© Indiatodayimages.com

A gramophone—an artefact of the bygone-era. Old disc records too have made a great return. From Naushad to Manna Dey and Asha Bhonsle duets to Bade Ghulam Ali Khan, the list is quite long. The price is often quoted depending on the scarcity of the album

So, one thing is certain, looking back to the past certainly makes for a great business strategy.

APPLICATIONS OF LIFESTYLE MARKETING

Lifestyle concept has been most effectively used in positioning of new products, repositioning of existing products, developing new product concepts, and creating new product opportunities in specific fields. In analogy to the product concept preferred, lifestyle research is utilized for choosing a media and also formulate integrated marketing communication strategies in order to facilitate the point of purchase sales and improvement in retail performance. Lifestyle concept is also employed as a skeleton for formulating the marketing decisions articulated in the subsequent paragraphs.

Positioning of New Products

A marketer needs to identify the most cost-effective and profitable segment for selling a new product. Lifestyle research, for example, an AIO portrait or VALS classification, for any given consumer product provides the information regarding the age, place of residence, social class, interests and opinions, actions, and of course value system. This provides rich database for use in marketing decisions related to the positioning of a new product. Decisions pertaining to positioning of a product encompasses the designing of product image, media planning, and developing proper integrated marketing communication mix so that the complete product package is in conformity with particular lifestyle(s).

Exhibit 9.2: *Domino's*: An Attempt to match to the Indian Tastes

At the time of its launch in India, *Domino's Pizza* just carried with it all the western offerings in the Indian market. Nonetheless, the company in due course realized that it had to bend over to local tastes. Moreover, they have also shifted their focus from only metropolitan areas to the expanses of 'mini metros' and B-category towns across the country in the last two years. But it was really difficult to penetrate those markets with solely western tastes and flavours. So they also tried out with Indian taste and flavour options, especially for smaller towns. Consequently, *Domino's* came up with local toppings such as '*Peppy Paneer*' and '*Chicken Chettinad*'. This, however, is not a unique attempt. *Domino's* main Indian competitor, US Pizza, was the pioneer to offer local toppings by any western food court. In fact, long ago in 1995, they offered *tandoori chicken* and *paneer* toppings. Wahid Berenjian, the Managing Director of US Pizza told *The Hindu* newspaper Business Line that US brands such as *Domino's* oversighted the preference for local taste by thinking that US tastes are universal. 'You cannot change the taste buds that were developed more than a thousand years ago,' he claimed.

Dominos came up with local toppings such as '*Peppy Paneer*' and '*Chicken Chettinad*' to match the Indian taste

Repositioning an Old/Existing Product

Sometimes existing products may not assume the targeted sales volume. Repositioning is often an eventuality designed in the new product development process itself, mainly as a corrective measure. Usually in markets where the cut-throat competition is high, proper positioning is needed to get a foothold in the market. In case of existing products, where the physical attributes are difficult to change completely, repositioning becomes a saviour. Lifestyle repositioning would gradually move the product closer to the psychographic profile of the core market segment, by changing the consumer's perception about it or some of its attributes so as to go well with the lifestyle of the core segment.

Tanishq—Repositioning from Western to Indian culture

A recent example of repositioning is that of *Tanishq*, the jewelry brand from Tata group, which initiated their business with western style of jewelry and outlets. They initially tried to sell 18 carat gold ornaments. The strategy failed and *Tanishq* had to reposition their brand with 22 carat gold and change the style and design as per the Indian market. They also sponsored the jewelry of the historical movie *Jodha Akbar*, as Jodha Bai (Akbar's wife and sister of Maharana Mansingha of Jaipur) symbolized Indian rich cultural heritage.

Johnson & Johnson Ltd. moved from their baby shampoos and lotions to the adult market by altering the promotional and packaging strategy of the product to appeal to the emergent 'natural healthy look' lifestyle.

Mahindra & Mahindra are currently repositioning their jeep, by aiming at the lifestyle of the triumphant professionals who fancy a rugged lifestyle instead of a chic one. These people are more outer-directed and value their comfort.

Developing New Product Concepts

Study of existing market segments and examination of their needs have typically been used to conceptualize the new products. Conventionally, demographic segmentation or standard consumer categorization of major groups like the sophisticated youth, the youthful collegiate, the metropolitan homemaker, etc., have been used to describe and study the segments. Lifestyle studies conversely can be used to harmonize the demographic studies in terms of market needs, customer and non-customer outlooks, the attitudes related to product usage, and the awareness of the target customers, in order to understand which product features may be amiable to certain lifestyles. While *roti*, *paratha*, and *idli* may be considered as staple breakfast items in suburbs, in metros cornflakes, noodles, cakes, and bread–butter are quite palatable breakfasts. While developing the concept of a new product, a complete inventory of attitudes, interests, and opinions of the consumers helps in defining the attributes of the final product. Further, the marketers may also identify the diverse lifestyle segments and accordingly decide in which segment they intend their product to target.

Creating Promotional Strategies

Lifestyle information is useful in formulating promotional strategies in numerous ways. It provides the decision maker an all-inclusive report of the type of consumer who will be at the receiving end of the advertising communication. Lifestyle data can even identify which language, accent, appeal, and ambience of advertisement should be used for a particular kind of consumer. Further, lifestyle information also provides clues for the benefit segmentation of the market.

The Indian marketing scenario, particularly for consumer durables, is characterized by fierce competition. Hence companies are realizing that merely stressing upon the attributes of their product or of the company in terms of demographic or geographic dimensions is not enough to be successful in the market place. Marketers must understand that buying behaviour is largely influenced by the consumer's lifestyle. Companies dealing in cosmetics, apparel, packaged food, etc. are seeking opportunities in lifestyle segmentation.

The apparel stores, these days, are also visualizing their merchandise matching with the target customer's lifestyle. For example, *Bata North Star* advertisement aims at the 'Young, western oriented, fun loving crowd'. In pursuant with this proclamation, *Bata Ltd.* has expanded its product range to a full range of active sports shoes named '*Power*'. This is no doubt planned lifestyle marketing. Moreover, the emergent westernization of youth in our country and the consequential alteration in lifestyle is accountable for the growing demand for jeans. Denim as a lifestyle-fabric is fast gaining acceptance in the country, going beyond just demographic segments, and marketers are nicely utilizing this phenomenon. Nonetheless the Indian market is quite unpredictable.

While in Exhibit 9.1, it has been stated that there is a memory market for the believers; on the other hand the Indian youth did not show any interest as such with the coloured revival of the classic Hindi film '*Hum Dono*' by Dev Anand, the Indian movies' evergreen legend. Despite the media hype surrounding its re-release, the movie viewers gave a cold shoulder to it (*The Times of India*, February 10, 2011).

Therefore, the strategy formulation keeping pace with the ever-changing Indian lifestyle is really a challenge for the marketers.

Closing Case

Lessons from Kellogg's Cereal Company

'Our only rivals are traditional Indian foods like idlis and vadas.'

—Denis Avronsart, Managing Director, *Kellogg's* India

Kellogg's is, certainly, an immensely powerful and worldwide recognized brand. It is the highest selling breakfast cereal across the globe. Majority of the sub-brands of *Kellogg's*, such as *Corn Flakes, Frosties*, and *Rice Krispies*, are considered as the most palatable breakfast by millions.

© Photos.com

Corn Flakes—the breakfast cereals

In the late 1980s, the company surpassed all its sales records and reached an all-time peak, imposing an astounding 40% of the US ready-to-eat market from its cereal products alone. In 1980s, *Kellogg's* were proud owners of over 20 plants in 18 countries worldwide, with a staggering sales figure of almost above US$ 6 billion/year. No doubt, the picture was amazing in context of breakfast cereals.

In 1994, three years after globalization and liberalization took place in India, with the inclusion of New Economic Policy (1991), *Kellogg's* resolute to put in US$ 65 million into debut its number one brand, *Corn Flakes*, in Indian market. By that time, *Kellogg's* was the world's most important producer of cereals and convenience foods, including cookies, crackers, cereal bars, frozen waffles, meat preparations, piecrusts, and even ice cream cones.

However, the Indian sub-continent found the entire concept of eating breakfast cereal as an alien. It is known to all of us that Indians have a practice to have a bowl of hot vegetables with *roti*, *paratha*, and even hot *idli* or *dosas*. So in one way, *Kellogg's*, at that time, had few direct competitors, and in the other way, it was clear that the company now had to promote not only its product, but also the very idea of replacing the traditional food habit with breakfast cereal.

Initially, there was an attempt by many urban 'innovators' to embrace the alien food. This gave rise to the first year's sales figures, and gave a false impression that breakfast cereal consumption was on the surge. Nonetheless, in no time it became visible that many people had bought *Corn Flakes* just as a curiosity or novelty sake. Even if they liked the taste, they thought the product to be very costly. A 500-gm box of *Corn Flakes* cost three times more than its nearest competitor *roti–sabji* or *idli-vadaa*.

However, *Kellogg's* did not want to lower the skimming price and instead decided to launch some more products in India without carrying out any further analysis of the market. Over the next few years, Indian market was flooded with *Kellogg's Wheat Flakes*, *Frosties*, *Rice Flakes*, *Honey Crunch*, *All Bran*, *Special K*, and *Chocos Chocolate Puffs*. But similar to the cornflakes, none of these products have managed to reproduce the success they have come across in the West.

Thereafter, the company started to 'Indianite' its range without any proper analysis and hence, the attempt became catastrophic. Its *Mazza-branded* series of flavoured cereals (mango, coconut, and rose flavour) failed to make any long-lasting inkling. As expected, in April 1995, *Kellogg's* India Ltd. received worrying reports of a steady drop in sales from its distributors in Mumbai. In fact, the reports showed that there was a 25% decline in countrywide sales since March 1995, the month *Kellogg's* products had been made available all over the country. *Kellogg's* India Ltd. was the wholly-owned Indian ancillary of the *Kellogg's* company based in Battle Creek, Michigan.

Kellogg's, actually, rode on the globalization horse confidently hoping for a smooth growth and revenue in the Indian economy. The company left no stones unturned except realizing that they were about to enter a rising economy with deep-rooted culture and lifestyle. They did not consider the importance of a very low-priced (moreover universally embraced) breakfast industry competition which included hot milk, *idli*, *dosa*, *vadaa*, *bread* and *spread*, etc., depending on the tastes of various regions.

Moreover, *Kellogg's* thought that its brand equity which has been carried forward from the West would echo its success in India. So it initiated positioning its brand by promoting its quality aspect of crunchy flakes for which it was famous throughout the western countries. But what was supposed to be a safe and sound strategy in the West, turned out to be radically reverse for the company in India.

Firstly, Indians normally preferred hot milk. When the *Kellogg's* crispy flakes are mixed with hot milk, they became mushy and were not liked by the consumers. For this *Kellogg's* modified their products later on to suit hot milk but the perceptual damage had already been done.

Secondly, the cost of a 500-gm package of *Kellogg's* was itself much higher than its traditional rivals that time. *Kellogg's* brand was designed to target the middle-class consumer but the high price-differential with traditional breakfast items resulted in the consumers buying their products as occasional purchase just for a change and not as a regular nutritionally rich breakfast.

Furthermore, *Kellogg's* possibly overlooked the cultural dimensions of India. This is quite similar situation which has been observed in case of *Pizza Point* too when they entered India. Apart from the high pricing, it bears out to be an unattainable task of pursuing consumers about the rich dietary ingredients of the cornflakes. The Indian consumer usually holds extremely strong cultural values and turns down to let off traditional eating habits on a regular basis.

The most important lesson to be learnt out of this is that globalization may be an ever-increasing movement, but provincial distinctiveness, customs, and tastes are diverse as ever. It would, perhaps, be more prospective if the companies 'Think Globally, Act Locally'.

(This case was published on the basis of inputs from published sources and the views of the author. It is intended to be used as a basis for classroom discussion. It is neither intended to be used to illustrate either effective or ineffective handling of a management situation; nor as a primary information source.)

Questions

1. Why did *Kellogg's* cereals have a tough ride in India?
2. Suggest repositioning strategy for *Kellogg's* in India.

Summary

Consumer behaviour is still a young discipline and most of the research now available has been generalized only during the past 15 years or so. Innovations such as the lifestyle concept and AIO research represent ways to move the study of consumers away from isolated, often unrelated projects towards broader integrated systems and research techniques. VALS—short for values and lifestyles—is a way of viewing people on the basis of their attitudes, needs, wants, beliefs, and demographics. The VALS programme was created by SRI International in an attempt to 'put people' into the thinking of those of us trying to understand the trends of our times in the marketplace, economically, politically, sociologically, and humanly. VALS 1 typology was further renovated by Strategic Business Units. Now it portrays eight types of lifestyle segments vide VALS™ classification. Thereafter attempt has been made to understand how lifestyle is important in context of formulation of marketing strategies in India.

Key Terms

Value Values are deeply held views about good, desirable, valuable, and worthwhile.

Core value The culture, heritage, beliefs, and social practice develop some set of values amongst the residents of any country. This may be referred as core value.

Lifestyle It refers to the person's pattern of living in the world as expressed in his activities, interests, and opinions.

AIO Activity–interest–opinion classification of lifestyle.

VALS Typology of customer segments based on value and lifestyle.

Questions

1. How core values are different from values? Write a short note on Indian values and how they have been used by marketers in the last decade.
2. What do you understand by the concept of lifestyle? Analyze the VALS I and VALS™ classification in Indian context.
3. Examine how lifestyle is an important parameter for marketing strategy formulation.
4. Differentiate between inner- and outer-directed types. If you are a seller of female apparels in Indian market, how can you segment the market by using AIO inventories.

Critical Assignment

1. Examine the lifestyle segments of Indian male population in context of choosing cosmetics. As a marketer of male fairness cream, what promotion strategy would you design which may have mass appeal?
2. Examine the recent print advertisement for packaged food and apparel to determine how the product is represented in each and is being positioned?
3. Imagine yourself as a retailer for female junk jewelry and propose how you would use lifestyle approach to succeed in your venture?

Section III

Environmental Determinants of Consumer Behaviour

Chapter **10**

Influence of Culture on Consumer Behaviour

Chapter Goals

After completing this chapter, you will be able to understand

- the meaning, elements, and characteristics of culture
- cultural identities in India
- the various sub-cultural factors shaping up consumer behaviour
- cultural adoption process
- influences of culture and sub-culture on consumers and marketers
- cross-cultural influences and their marketing implications

Opening Vignette

Facebook in Soup in Pakistan

In mid-May 2010, Justice Ijaz Chaudhry of the Lahore High Court issued an order for a temporary block of the popular social networking site *Facebook* till May 31, 2010. The Islamic Lawyers Association of Pakistan filed a petition for its permanent ban. Even the Lahore High Court directed the Foreign Ministry of Pakistan to raise the issue and also asked the Foreign Secretary to register a protest with the concerned countries. The basic issue was that this social networking site in one of its Web pages featured some blasphemous caricatures of the founder of Islam.

Acting on the court's order, the Information Technology Ministry directed the Pakistan Telecom Authority (PTA) to block *Facebook* and all 'other Internet links displaying sacrilegious caricatures' of the founder of Islam. The ministry also directed the PTA to 'remain alert and watchful and block all such links displaying the profane caricatures immediately'. PTA responded by developing a 'crisis cell' to monitor objectionable content on various Web sites.

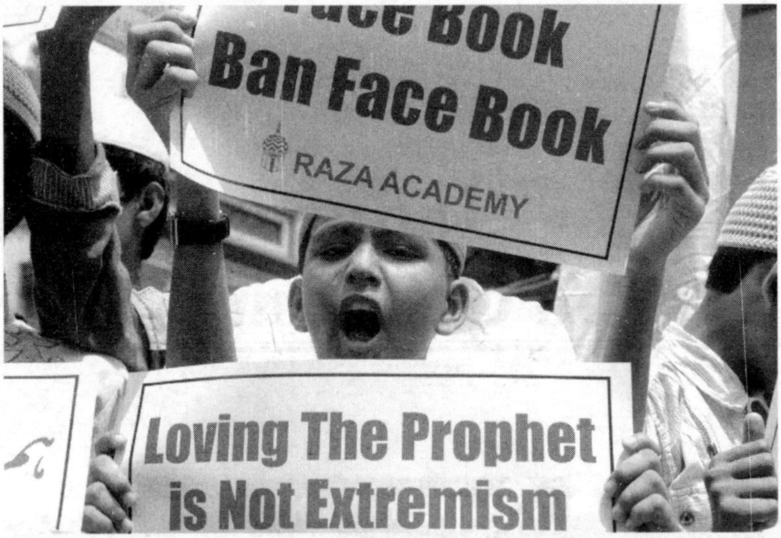

© Indiatodayimages.com

Public protest against *Facebook* in Pakistan

Thousands of *Facebook* users launched a protest campaign demanding a boycott of the Web site over the offending Web page. The offending page in question invited people to send in caricatures of the founder of the Islam religion till May 20, 2010. According to the Islamic rules, the depiction of the founder of this religion in any form is strictly prohibited. One may recall that the entire Pakistan had already witnessed violent protests after such caricatures and blasphemous cartoons were published in some European newspapers in 2005. Similar sentiments stirred the Pakistani people, because of this offending Web page on *Facebook*.

As a result, *Facebook* users across Pakistan were unable to access the Web site till late afternoon on May 20, 2010. This incident highlights the need on the part of the marketers to be sensitive to the religious and cultural sentiments of its intended and expected consumers. This is more important for MNCs that operate across many countries and cultures.

INTRODUCTION

To identify the environmental factors impinging upon the consumers, the chapter starts with focussing on the most enduring factor of consumer behaviour—culture. The aforesaid case illustrates how the existence of *Facebook* was challenged in Pakistan as it overlooked the country's religious ideology. In this chapter, the role and usefulness of cultural analysis in the development of marketing strategies would be investigated. After defining and characterizing culture, the basic cultural values of the Indian consumers and different sub-cultures prevailing in India would be analyzed. By recognizing the existence of the cultural variations in India, further stress is imposed on understanding the cultural changes going around and their impact on the behaviour of the Indian consumers. Finally, cross-cultural consumer behaviour and its impact on global marketing strategies would be outlined.

CULTURE DEFINED

It is indeed very difficult to present an all inclusive definition of culture; nonetheless, sociologists use the term 'culture' to describe the physical and social environment which results in shared attitudes and behaviours that interest marketers. However, amongst the varied definitions of culture, the following two can be considered to be authentic:

- Culture is 'that complex whole that includes knowledge, belief, art, morals, law, custom, and any other capabilities and habits acquired by man as a member of society', Edward B. Tylor (1871).
- Culture is 'the distinctive way of life of a group of people, their complete design for living', Clyde Kluchohn (1951).

Therefore, culture is the collective programming of the human mind that distinguishes the members of one human group from those of another. In other words, culture is the system of collectively held values. Culture is almost everything that is socially learned and shared by the members of a particular society.

CHARACTERISTICS OF CULTURE

Several aspects of culture need special attention.

- Culture is a comprehensive concept. It includes everything that influences an individual's thought processes and behaviour. While culture does not determine the nature or frequency of biological drives, such as hunger or sex, it does influence if, when, and how these drives will be gratified. It not only influences our preferences, but also suggests how we make our decisions and even on our perception about the world around us.
- Culture is acquired. It does not include inherited responses and predispositions. Nonetheless, since most human behaviour is learned rather than innate; culture does not affect a wide array of behaviour.
- Culture is learned by interacting with the other members of the cultural group to which an individual belongs.
- Culture is transferred from one generation to another, with new influences being added to the cultural soup. Thus, culture is always cumulative.
- Culture is adaptive. It changes in response to the needs of the society.

Cultural influences are such that consumers are seldom aware of them. An individual behaves, thinks, and feels in a manner consistent with the other members of the same culture because it seems appropriate to do so. The influence of culture is similar to the air we breathe; it is everywhere and is generally taken for granted unless there is a fairly rapid change in nature. Culture operates primarily by setting loose bondages among an individual's behavioural patterns by influencing his/her function within the family structure or society as a whole or mass media. Basically, culture provides a broad framework within which both the individual's and his/her household lifestyles evolve.

ELEMENTS OF CULTURE

Culture consists of material and non-material components. Non-material culture includes the words people use; the ideas, customs, and beliefs they share; and the habits they pursue. Material culture consists of all physical substances that have been changed and used by people, such as furniture, automobiles, farms, etc. The next sections will focus upon non-material artefacts of behavioural dimensions of life. The elements can be as follows.

Languages and Symbols

Both languages and symbols act as communication media amongst and within the cultures. This communication may be verbal or non-verbal, using images that convey ideas directly or indirectly. The MNCs operating in multilingual regions must be aware of the implications of each word they use in their advertising campaign and brand nomenclature. Besides, languages and symbols may carry, sometimes, different meanings and associations in different countries. For example, owl symbolizes wisdom in West but stupidity in India.

A classic example of frictions in language was identified in the case of *Matsushita Electric's* promo of a Japanese PC for Internet users in courtesy of *Panasonic*. A huge marketing campaign for USA was waiting on the row for *Matsushita*. But almost at the eleventh hour, they had to cancel the same. The reason was related to the selection of words. Actually, *Panasonic* resorted to a cartoon character named 'Woody Woodpecker' and the ad carried the slogan *Touch Woody—The Internet Pecker*. Needless to say, in America 'touch woody' and 'pecker' were considered as slang. This incident was considered amongst one of the world's most erroneous branding moves! Hence, the crossborder marketers should be very careful in choosing words while operating in multilingual regions.

Customs and Rituals

Customs are the established 'rules' of behaviour within a society. They define what is or is not acceptable. In American culture, a ceremony is a joyous and humourous event; in India, it is a solemn affair.

Rituals are patterns of behaviour, quite often complex, which are shared by a group. Rituals may include burning incense sticks during *puja* or buying a new dress on *Durga Puja*. Customs and rituals often represent a substantial marketing opportunity if it is possible to associate an object/event (commonly referred as artefacts) with the festivals. For example, *Archies Gallery* designs cards for various specific occasions.

Norms and Sanctions

The boundaries that culture sets in the behaviour of its subjects are called norms. To be more precise, norms are those set of rules that specify or prohibit certain behaviours in specific situations, based on or derived from cultural values. Although it is the norm in France or the USA to kiss any acquaintance just to greet (in Japan, Maori greetings involve touching of noses), in India physical contact for greeting is not accepable. Rather performing a *namaste* or *namaskar* by just folding hands is a practice in India and bowing is a practice to greet each other in Japan.

Marketers also need to take a note of the social norms of the country in which they are operating. For example, the use of female models for solely males' usable products is not acceptable in Saudi Arabia, whereas it is just a common practice in the USA or India.

Conformity to social norms is often developed in the process of socialization. In the process of consumer socialization, the child learns the cultural practices and gradually adopts it. On the other hand, when a person, because of geographic migration/marriage/other influences, adapts a new culture, it is known as *acculturation*. Both the processes of socialization and acculturation generate certain ideas of cultural sanctions among the people. They start feeling that violation of cultural norms may result in sanctions or penalties. The degree of such penalties corresponds to the degree of violation, and it may go to the extent of banishment from the group.

Values

Values represent the deepest level of culture. They are broad feelings about what is good or bad, clean or dirty, beautiful or ugly, rational or irrational, etc. Values are mental images that affect and, in turn, influence the way a person is likely to respond to specific offers by the companies.

For example, surveys show that the Indian youths are traditional in mind but full of optimism. Taking this clue, *Nescafé* has used the sense of optimism amongst the Indian youth in its new advertising campaign. *Barcardi Rum* is tapping into the ebullient youth imagery. A detailed discussion on values has already been done in Chapter 9.

BRIEF OVERVIEW OF INDIAN CULTURE

With the dawn of the early 21st century, the Indian consumer market was flooded with many new products. No doubt, the economic liberalization of the Indian government in the early 1990s had resulted in the 'globalization' of the Indian markets with manifold increase in the number of foreign players in both the FMCG and durables segments. The new cosmopolitan entrants, with the imbibed cultural traits of their respective homeland, have generated a cross-cultural mix amongst the Indian customers, especially among the generation Y. Technology is also on an upsurge. One such example was found in the jubilant transition of the consumer's preference from the desktop PC to laptop, palmtop, and even iPad. However, the basic ethos of Indian culture is still capitalized by marketers. For example,

Toshiba laptops, in their recent advertisement, focus on the long-lasting disciplined career of Sachin Tendulkar to convey their own consistency over a decade.

Entertainment industry has undergone a sea change with the change in the consumer's lifestyle. With a recent upsurge in a number of international music, sports, and entertainment channels, the world has become a very small place.

The fashion industry in India has been radically changed since the last decade. This has happened due to cross-cultural adaptability and 'globalization'. Nonetheless, the fashion industry always had elongated and rich traditions in India. In a study, by Joy and Wallendorf (1996), it was noted that since ages, dress has always been the indicator of the social status of the individual and the group. As per this study, 'Cloth and cloth transactions acquire meaning because they symbolize status, they record changes in status, and they transform the moral and physical bearing of the wearer'. To exemplify, it could be mentioned that Mahatma Gandhi encouraged Indians to buy Indian-made *Khadi* clothes to support the Indian economy as well as to cultivate the sense of national identity at the time of India's freedom struggle against Britishers.

However, today the non-*Khadi* fabrics are in line with neo-fashion trends in India. Moreover, after 64 years of independence, insistence on *Khadi* is not that way related to patriotic sentiments. Now even the traditional garments such as saris are found in non-indigenous fabrics such as polyester. But Indians till date hold some basic rituals and customs. According to Joy and Wallendorf (1996), 'The ones [saris] that are preferred are those with traditional colours and prints, which suggests that the incorporation process is guided by acceptable cultural norms and principles rather than mere emulation. Further, although polyester is used for day-to-day activities, it is not acceptable for ritual activities'. Nevertheless, this does not imply total rejection of Western influences on clothing pattern but an acceptance of the modernity within the boundaries of culture and heritage.

However, this contemporary Western influence on clothing and fashion in India has altered the consumer's perceptions about boutiques and designer dresses in India. In another study on Indian fashion industry, Bullis (1997) claimed that India recently adopted the concept of *haute couture* along with the traditional clothing like *sari* or *salwar kameez*. Of late, the designer clothing in India has changed to adapt Western influences along with a trendy mix of Indian fabric (hand-painted trousers). This reflection of cultural amalgamation is termed as 'fusion fashion' in India. This mode encompasses Western styles with Indian fabric and attempts to give traditional styles a Western look (e.g., typical Indian bead needlework on a Western-cut shirt). The 'fusion' feature of this fashion statement demonstrates the adaptation of Western influences to indigenize them within the Indian tradition and culture.

In the case of *McDonalds*, the Hamburger was replaced by '*Maharaja Mac*' for India. In this case, the company understood that with a majority of Hindu population in India, it would have been difficult to penetrate the Indian market with beef-made products. Mintz (1997) claimed that some standardized food always gets acceptance by a limited number of consumers almost everywhere across the nation. Nevertheless, to catch hold of the substantial share in Indian restaurant business, *McDonalds* withdrew all beef products from product mix for Indian market and added more vegetarian dishes and mutton/

chicken burgers. Similarly, KFC introduced '*Thali*' for Indian market realizing that the typical Indian lunch/dinner needs to be little heavy with traditional courses.

It was clear to *McDonalds* and KFC that Indians correlate culture, religion, and rituals with food. They look for some Indian touch in Western food items too. *McDonalds* and KFC have tailored their menu considerably to ameliorate their business in India. They have made a fantastic amalgamation of the choice frame of Indian customers in terms of fast-food selection. Hence, while *McDonalds* is most confidently shifting some facets of Indian eating behaviour, the Indian culture too has compelled *McDonalds* into Indianizing its offerings.

Exhibit 10.1: Event Management Emerging

Ravi Kumar is very busy these days because of his daughter's wedding. Both Ravi and his wife are working couple so they are hardly getting any time for the necessary arrangements of the ceremony. But when things reach at a tipping point, they decide to take the bull by the horns and find a suitable *tentwala* for the wedding.

Their neighbour gives them the address of a *tentwala* and advises them to bargain well. After a long discussion with the *tentwala*, they arrive at a price for the *shamiana*. Then Ravi asks the *tentwala* about the discount. The *tentwala* answers ingeniously 'Sir, there is no discount, but the price will be less if you choose a combo pack'. Taken aback, Ravi enquires about the combo deal. According to the *tentawala* the combo deal consists of 'all normal services plus furniture, decoration, and catering'. He further informs them of his collaboration with all these service providers and all Ravi has to do is make a full payment to him and the rest would be assured.

The concept of event management in a mini format is emerging and becoming affordable to the middle income Indian customers. With the changing demography, where more and more families are relying on double income, 'time' is becoming the most precious element of life. Event management today is not only the luxury of the richer sections but also a necessity for the middle class. Ravi Kumar's story is thus not a mere exception.

(The characters of this short ca e let are fictitious. Any resemblance with any person or incidence is highly coincidental.)

INFLUENCE OF CULTURE AND SUB-CULTURE AND THEIR IMPLICATIONS ON MARKETERS

Consumers buy products in a way to acquire meanings to use in establishing their self-identities. The cultural process model depicted in Fig.10.1 shows that the meanings consumers acquire can be transferred to the broad cultural environment through their social behaviour. In a society consisting of many individuals living and working together, culture (shared meaning) is created by the actions of the people. In other words, the cultural environment results from an automatic consequence of daily social interactions among people.

In India, modernization (combination of westernization, industrialization, and secularization) is supported by the Indian elite so long as the traditional value system is not affected negatively. So an Indian welcomes *McDonald's* but rejects hamburger as it does not suit the religious ideology of the Hindus. *McDonald's* had to convert hamburger into 'Maharaja Mac' with chicken stuffing while introducing the *Thali* meal depending on the demand pattern in India.

Figure 10.1 depicts a clear picture of how cultural meaning is transferred by the actions of organizations (business, government, religion, and education) and by individuals in the society. Cultural meaning may be transferred in two ways in a consumption-oriented society. First, marketing strategies are designed to move cultural environments into products and services in an attempt to motivate and persuade the customers via fashion and advertising systems, sales promotion techniques, branding strategies, and other marketing tools. Second, consumers actively seek to acquire these cultural meanings in products to establish desirable personal identity or self-concept.

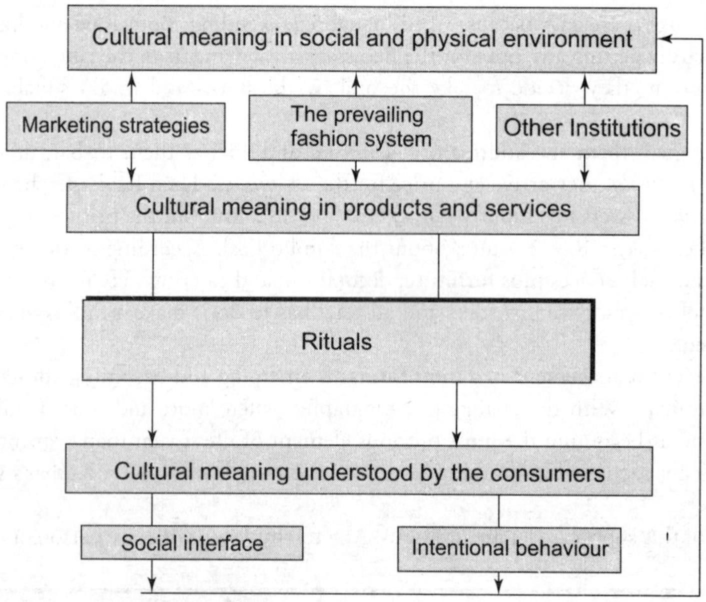

Figure 10.1 A model of cultural process

'Here and now' philosophy among the Indian youth exists but the deep-rooted tenacious traditions have not been abandoned. He/she simultaneously wants to break free from traditions yet wishes to be attached to them. So Indipop sells. In brief, there exists a core culture, yet away from the core there is a spectrum of variation. Consequently, *Maggi* noodles were accepted because the company wisely did not promote them as a part of the main menu. Products, stores, and brand as a whole express both cultural and symbolic meanings. For instance, certain brands have meaning concerning the gender and age groups for which they are appropriate: *Virginia Slims* are for women; *Camels* are for men; roller blades and T-shirts are for young people; gardening tools and laxatives for the elders.

In America, *Cooper Storm* collection includes high-quality reproductions of baseball team jerseys, jackets, and hats of defunct teams like Washington Senators.

The cultural meanings of products are likely to vary across different societies. For instance, most societies have favourite foods that represent important meanings in that culture—Danes love eel, Mexicans love chilies, Irish love Guiness, French love cheese, Americans like hamburgers, etc.

In the second step, the model identifies rituals as important interpreters of cultural meanings from products to consumers. Rituals are symbolic actions performed by consumers to create, affirm, evoke, or revise certain cultural meanings. Buying new clothes at the time of *Durga Puja* in east India, *Pongal* in south India, *Diwali* and *Dussera* in north India typifies buying habits emerging from rituals.

Table 10.1 *Value system and marketing lessons*

Value	***Meaning***	***Indian situation***	***Lesson for multinational marketer***
(A) *Self-oriented values*			
(1) Materialism	Importance attached to materialistic acquisitions	Earlier generation would not approve; now accepted	Lifestyle is still not fully oriented towards materialistic possessions
(2) Immediate/ delayed gratification	Do people live for today?	Earlier saving was a virtue; it still is, but no harm borrowing	Credit-driven sales are possible; 'here and now' messages will work
(3) Sexual mores	Perception towards sex	Sex is a 'closed door' affair	Sexually explicit messages are unlikely to be accepted
(4) Hard work/ leisure	Is working harder (than is economically necessary) a virtue in itself?	No, having leisure and time for oneself is very important, though hard work sometimes precedes enjoyment of life	Role models who only work hard but are not able to enjoy fruits of their labour are not likely to be acceptable
(B) *Other oriented values*			
(5) Individualism/ collectivism	Are individual activities and initiative valued more?	Indians are not team oriented; only one person can occupy top position	Comparative advertising will succeed, since only one brand can be the 'best'
(6) Romantic orientation	Is romance platonic or with sexual innuendoes?	Romance in India has nothing to do with sexual permissiveness. However, with the dawn of 21st century the romantic orientations are gradually moving in reverse directions too	Message of intimacy is not a sure-shot strategy to help promote a product
(7) Adult/child role	Do children act as deciders/influencers?	At least in upper-income classes, children decide about products of direct consumption but with parental sanction	Marketer must sell the product to both, the child and the parents; child cannot independently decide for most categories

(8) Male/female dominance	Who decides: man or woman?	India is still a male-dominated society	Messages that show independence of women will appeal to only niche segment; man still a provider, woman a nurturer
(9) Competition	Is cooperation or competition valued?	Although, in India competition is valued, but the concept of cooperation is never back-seated	Competition oriented messages will succeed
(10) Age	Seniority or merit?	In India, competition is valued. In India, wisdom is synonymous with age	Messages when 'parents know better' will work
(C) *Environment-oriented values*			
(11) Cleanliness	Hygiene consciousness	Rather limited	Products oriented towards maintaining hygiene will have only limited access
(12) Performance/status	Is performance more important or ascribed status?	In India, status is more important	Only well-established products will succeed
(13) Tradition/change	Is change welcome?	No, fundamentally Indians are traditionalist	Consumers are not crusaders. Icons work within the system
(14) Risk taking	Is risk taking a desirable trait?	Yes or no: calculated risk taking is acceptable	Some consumers accept 'entrepreneurial' role
(15) Control over nature	Nature governs me or can I tame it?	There is some 'supra authority'	Many things/events cannot be understood/conquered

CROSS-CULTURAL INFLUENCES ON MARKETERS

The last decade of the 20th century was the dawn of the most stimulating and opportunistic years in the marketing history. The changing political dynamics and trading patterns across the globe at a time showered ample opportunities and threats on today's marketers across the globe.

On the first place, the concept of 'mass marketing' has been outweighed by tailored and customized marketing efforts of the 21st century. Especially, with the call for high level of customization, the organizations involved in electronic, global, and cross-cultural marketing simultaneously faced challenges and opportunities much more than the yesteryears.

With the advent of new marketing techniques like e-commerce, m-commerce, etc., the electronic marketing unearthed almost all chapters of marketing in terms of electronic media, e-mail, CD-ROMs, Internet, rapidly growing infomercials, etc. It is expected that in the 21st century the marketplace will be flooded with almost all innovative marketing tools which, in turn, will generate volume sales for a number of retails and industries as a whole.

Nonetheless, with rapid globalization, marketers need to thoroughly examine the pros and cons of 'borderless' markets to formulate effective economic plans and marketing strategies. However, understanding cultural borders is still relevant especially for the products and services that are 'culture bound' (e.g., food, clothes, etc.). In fact, national culture is one decisive factor behind many aspects of economic development, demographic characteristics, and general business policies across the globe.

The cross-border marketers also need to appreciate that cross-cultural issues not only have an impact on international front but also shape the domestic markets. For instance, with large group of population immigrating across different parts of the world, in this new multicultural 21st century, the US citizens can have a Vietnamese, Chinese, Japanese, Bangladeshi, Pakistani, Russian, Bosnian, Native American, or Indian ethnic origin. Therefore, with the mix and match of culture amongst various ethnicities, the domestic markets are also bound to change to a large extent. Therefore, nowadays, even for dealing with domestic plants and domestic customers, understanding of cross-cultural influences has become extremely essential. Particularly, for the export houses, bankers, retail chains, and food courts having a clear notion about the cross-border influences is almost compulsory.

Exhibit 10.2: The Japanese Television Market

In the 1980s, the Chinese television market was predominantly captured by the Japanese colour televisions. Keeping this fact into consideration, in the early 1980s, a number of Japanese and European television manufacturers conducted an inclusive analysis of the Chinese market as a whole. The European manufacturers reasoned out that given the low per capita income in China, the European high-end luxury televisions would find it pretty difficult to catch hold of the Chinese market. Therefore, the initial research findings discouraged the European manufacturers to enter into the Chinese market.

Nonetheless, Japanese manufacturers comprehended the findings in a different way. They identified that the cultural tradition of China was to pass on the savings across generations. They realized, unlike the European culture, the Chinese lived more in future. Further, the research revealed that the Chinese consumers have a fair inclination towards the imported products with a certain price range. The research also put forth that the Chinese families were capable to accumulate money over a period of time and purchase imported Japanese colour TV sets after a few years. These deeper realizations about the Chinese culture made the Japanese colour TV brands extremely successful in Chinese market both in terms of penetration and profit. On the other hand, their European counterparts completely missed out the opportunities for the lack of such understanding.

Source: http://www.infosciencetoday.org/type/research-type/cross-cultural-issues-in-the-21st-century-marketing.html, accessed on October 22, 2010.

In short, cross-cultural problems definitely provide more challenges and opportunities to marketers in the 21st century although they might not be totally new in the marketing area. There are many unsolved problems or issues that need to be solved and discussed by the scholars and marketing professionals in theories and in practice as well. In the theoretic area, the following themes and issues need to be probed and discussed:

1. Culture impacts on markets: International versus domestic marketing
2. Standardization versus adaptation in cross-cultural marketing
3. Cross-cultural dimensions of marketing research
4. Cross-cultural aspects of marketing mix (products, price, promotion, and distribution)
5. Cross-cultural aspects of service marketing
6. Cross-cultural implications on the aftermarket
7. Cross-cultural marketing of education and professional training

These seven topics or themes can be viewed as guidelines for further theoretic studies although they may not be treated as exclusive for the marketing scholars. More themes and topics are likely to be discovered as the theoretic discussions go on. As marketing professionals, we need to clearly know that although the marketing principals will remain the same, there must be some new challenges to the marketing in the 21st century. In terms of marketing practice, the following points might be taken as guidelines for marketers to minimize the possible cross-cultural marketing mistakes:

1. Be sensitive to do's and taboos. Develop cultural empathy.
2. Recognize, understand, and respect another's culture and difference.
3. Be culturally neutral and realize that difference in culture is not necessarily better or worse.
4. Never assume transferability of a concept from one culture to another. For instance, if local businessmen in developing countries tell you that they do not like Americans, they may not mean that they do not want to buy American goods. It simply means they are expected to say certain things in public, nonetheless may operate differently in private.
5. Get cultural informants involved into the decision makings. Cultural informants could be local businessmen or very well-trained anthropologists. As already claimed, anthropological approach is among the best theories to understand the gamut of the cross-cultural marketing.

In fact, although the anthropological approaches to marketing by no means are entirely new to the business world, these days they are becoming more popular and are perceived more reliable by business leaders and marketers. Nonetheless, how to apply anthropological approaches into marketing practice should be looked at beyond anthropology, to be specific in the whole marketing theoretic areas. The potentials of anthropological approaches to marketing are unlimited and still need to be dug out by the anthropologists and marketers together.

Closing Case

Virginia Blues

Romit Verma was appointed as the National Sales Manager of the Tobacco Division of FTC Ltd., a famous multinational FMCG giant. Cigarette manufacturing is the company's flagship business and the most profitable strategic business unit too. After his appointment, he was looking at the last year's sales records. He found that cigarette sales were as high as he expected in the last sales year. Two of its flagship brands, *Fiffo Army Cut* filter cigarettes and *Fiffo Jumbo King Size* cigars had earned a profit of ₹200 crore altogether. The growth trajectory also looked very fine.

However, his eyes were stuck on the precarious figures of the newly launched *Virginia* ciggis. The brand was launched almost a year back in the month of May 2009. Surprisingly, the sales had never increased in any of the months in the last one year. Romit called a sales meeting with the regional sales managers on June 3, 2010. In the one-hour closed-door meeting nothing was really resolved as Romit found that the company had done its level best and made lots of investment to promote the brand. Ramola, Romit's secretary, prepared the minutes of the meeting. The key points of the minutes were as follows:

- *Virginia* ciggis were principally targeted at the upper- and middle-class female smokers with lower percentage of nicotine in it.
- The price of a 10 ciggi packet was set as ₹25; the house considered that the price was quite affordable.
- As the tobacco advertisement in public media is banned in the country, the company resorted to the point-of purchase displays. In the beetle shops, grocery shops, stationery shops everywhere signboards, cut-outs, and danglers were placed. The shopkeepers used to get higher margins for *Virginia*, as compared to any other cigarette brand. It was even higher than the *Fiffo* brands of the company itself.
- As the company had a very wide distribution network, the brand at one shot reached at all corners of the country.
- The company sponsored the last year's one-day Tri-nation Cricket Tournament amongst India, Sri Lanka, and Pakistan and thereby increased the brand's visibility by all means.
- Six months after the launch of the brand, the company opted for a sales promotion method in the form of quantity discount (two additional ciggis in a 10 ciggi pack). The offer continued for about three months without any fruitful results.

The fact was clear to Romit now and he understood that the brand had vehemently failed. Clueless as he was, he asked FTC's market research division, Kalpa Research, to conduct a survey on the retailers and prospective consumers. The Kalpa Research conducted a survey in Delhi, Kolkata, Mumbai, and Chennai and submitted the report to Romit within 45 days. The research report was surprising! Ramola once again jotted down the salient points and presented the report on his desk. The salient points were as follows:

- About 36% of the surveyed women said that they smoked regularly.
- Out of these 36% smokers, only 2% agreed that they purchased ciggis for themselves.
- They often asked their male peons, male servants, or their husbands to buy ciggis.
- These male buyers were not normally interested in 'female' brands. They felt awkward to ask for 'female' brands from shops. Needless to mention that in all the signboards, cutouts, and even on the packet of *Virginia*, a female face was portrayed and in that way, the brand had been strongly positioned with feminine identity.
- According to the middle-class women, they were not comfortable to buy cigars from shops, especially from their localities. They did not want their neighbours, parents, or relatives to know that they consume cigars.

- They had no prejudice against cigar consumption, but wanted to be represented as a buyer. Keeping in mind the Indian tradition, they felt that their image might get tarnished in the society, if their neighbours spotted them buying cigars.
- Out of 36% female cigarette users, 12% said that they really did not want any female brands of cigar. They felt cigarette smoking gave them a sense of masculinity and they felt at par with their male counterparts in that way. But simultaneously, they could not buy cigars from the shops like their male counterparts as they did not want to be disclosed as smokers in the society.

Looking at these peculiar findings, Romit now was really in a soup. He now questioned himself, whether to withdraw the brand from the market or somehow reposition it. Romit also thought how to break the cultural myth and convert these 'users' into 'buyers and users'. Is it really possible?

(This is a fictitious case designed to stimulate discussions in the MBA classrooms. Any resemblance to any company or character is purely unintentional and coincidental.)

Questions

1. If you were Romit, would you have withdrawn the brand or repositioned it?
2. What marketing strategy would you have adopted to make the brand a success in the Indian market?

Summary

Culture is composed of the value systems, beliefs, and learned behaviours shared by members of a society. A culture evolves over time and adapts to meet the changing needs of members. Culture includes almost everything that influences an individual's thought process and behaviours.

A person living in India is influenced by the oriental, Indian, and various regional sub-cultures.The customs and rituals of these cultures are shared by him/her along with many others. Widespread cultures like this are referred as macro culture. Sub-cultures exist within the macro culture and they could be identified on the basis of (a) regionalism, (b) age, (c) religion, (d) gender, and (e) social class and occupation.

Sub-culture is any cultural patterning that preserves important features of the dominant society but provides individuals with values, beliefs, norms, and behaviours of its own. Sub-cultures exist to provide a source of psychological group identification to offer a support network and to service as a frame of reference for evaluating the dominant culture.

Human societies are socially stratified. The roles performed by various people are valued differently. Differentiation among roles and their relative evaluation lead to the stratification of the society. Social classes are easily identifiable market segments which can be reached with relative ease since they have distinctly defined media habits.

Key Terms

Culture It is the collective programming of human mind that distinguishes the members of one human group from those of another.

Values Values are mental images that affect and, in turn, influence the way a person is likely to respond to specific situations.

Customs Customs are the established 'rules' of behaviour within a society.

Rituals Rituals are patterns of behaviour, quite often complex, which are shared by a group.

Norms The boundaries that culture sets on behaviour are called norms.

Materialism Importance attached to materialistic acquisitions.

Questions

1. Define culture. What are the most important characteristics of culture that reflect its nature?
2. What are the core values held by the Indian culture? Why is an understanding of the foreign culture especially important to an international marketer?
3. A myth is a special kind of story. What makes it special? Give an example of a modern myth.
4. Distinguish between beliefs, values, and customs. Illustrate how the clothing of a person at different times and purposes differ. How is it relevant to marketers?

Critical Assignment

1. Summarize an episode of a weekly soap and enumerate how it conveys the values, myths, and rituals of a particular sub-culture.
2. Select and describe three commercials that were broadcasted during the programme mentioned above. Do these commercials have any influence to shape the culture? Illustrate.

Chapter **11**

Group Influences on Consumption

Chapter Goals

After completing this chapter, you will be able to understand

- what is a group
- types of group
- parameters of group conformity
- impact of reference group on consumer decision making
- impact of reference groups on marketing strategy formulation

Opening Vignette

Boost: The Perfect User of Aspirational Reference Group

Boost, developed by the Research and Development division of *GlaxoSmeethKline,* is one of the major players in the ₹1400 crore Indian Health Food Drink (HFD) market. It was launched in 1977 in India. The brand started becoming popular during the 1980s. However, it was still trailing behind the market leader *Horlicks* and also some other HFD players like *Viva* and *Maltova.*

The Indian HFD market has two categories of health drinks—brown powder segment and white powder segment. The white powder drinks like *Horlicks, Complan,* etc. are the key players in the market. *Boost* is a chocolate flavoured malt-based milk additive and has a share of around 12% in the HFD market.

Principally, *Boost* targets the preteens and the teens. The brand realized that the upper- and middle-class markets are easy to target as the parents of these classes feel the need for some kind of energy drink for their kids as a nutritional supplement to their regular food.

Boost positioned itself as an energy drink by using the tagline 'Boost is the secret of my energy'. The tagline, uttered by the celebrity endorsers for a number of years, has derived a considerable extent of brand recall amongst the target customers. *Boost* was the path-breaker to introduce the concept of celebrity-endorsement in the HFD market.

Experiencing the initial growth phase, the brand's product lifecycle entered a maturity phase in the mid-eighties. At this phase, taking into consideration, the changing dynamics of the target market, the brand crafted an inclusive repositioning strategy.

During 1980s, the iconic Indian Cricket star, Kapil Dev, was roped in as the brand ambassador for *Boost*. This move amplified the success of the brand.

During 1990s, the youngster, Sachin Tendulkar joined Kapil to endorse the brand and the slogan was rephrased as 'Boost is the secret of our energy'. Gradually, only Sachin, the demigod of Indian Cricket, replaced the Kapil–Sachin pair. In 2000, the brand also roped in another successful Cricketer, Virender Sehwag, to endorse the brand. At that time Sehwag–Sachin was the most successful opening pair. Later in 2008, Cricket superstar M.S. Dhoni became the brand ambassador for *Boost*. Over the years, the brand has been positioned and repositioned by being innovative not only in the promotion front but also in product and packaging improvements. The packaging of the product became contemporary and stylish. Boost did so in tune with the changing perceptual map of the consumer. Therefore, to become successful, marketers need to be visionary and use appropriate reference groups across the years.

Source: http://marketingpractice.blogspot.com/2007/01/boost-is-secret-of-our-energy.html, www.en.wikipedia.org/wiki/Boost_(health_food), www.boost.com

GROUPS DEFINED

Aristotle, the Greek philosopher, once said 'Man is a social animal'. In pursuant to this proclamation, it can be said that excluding those very small numbers of people who are classified as hermits, most individuals have a general tendency to interact with other people on a daily basis. An individual's social behaviour and relationships are often motivated by the social and safety needs as described by Abraham Maslow in his need hierarchy. A person might become a Boy Scout or a Girl Scout leader to satisfy the need for community service and recognition. Most of the individuals want to share their success or failure with friends, peers, and family. Some may seek social approval for certain activities, like marriage and *upanayan*. Some individuals might join a warehouse membership club to obtain the benefits of group buying or bargaining power. Workers form union to increase negotiation power to fulfill their unmet common goals and demands. These are just a few of the number of reasons why people interact and be with others. This chapter discusses the basic concepts of social interaction and group dynamics.

A group may be defined as two or more people working together to achieve either individual or mutual goals. The wider scope of this definition ranges from an intimate group of two next-door neighbours who do their daily grocery shopping together to a bigger and more formal group, such as a trade union whose members are equally concerned with the benefits of the work force.

TYPES OF GROUPS

Groups can be classified in a number of ways or dimensions, including functions, degree of perceived importance, and degree of organization. Sometimes groups are even classified in terms of size or complexity, but it is not easy to identify which group must be considered as large or small. It is often observed that in certain large groups one member knows only a few other members and is not fully aware of the roles and activities of all the members of the group (though they are in the same group because of some common interest); whereas in small groups all the members know each other personally and are also aware of the roles and activities of the other members within the group. For example, each member of a college science club is likely to know the roles and responsibilities of all other members. Sometimes, even many large groups are well-knit and well-organized. The groups can be classified on different parameters as shown in Table 11.1.

Table 11.1 *Classification of groups*

Dimensions	*Types of groups*	*Definition*	*Example*
Content or function	Family	This group is dependent on the size and the type of relationships that exist in the family	Joint family, nuclear family, etc.
	Ethnic origin	This group depends on the genetic country—origin of the individuals	American, Hispanic, etc.
	Age	This group shows how individuals can be classified according to their age	30–40, 50–60, etc.
	Sex	This group is gender-specific	Male, female
	Others	This group considers many other factors like education, occupation, etc. Sometimes social networking groups are also considered under this kind of group	www.linkedin.com, University Professors Association, etc.
Degree of personal involvement and perceived importance	Primary group	It consists of those interpersonal relationships which take place generally at one to one level, with high rate of occurrence and on an intimate level. These groups have shared norms and interlinking roles	Families, work groups, and some entertaining groups
	Secondary group	If a person interacts only intermittently with others and does not reflect in their opinions too seriously, the group is called a secondary group	Guardian's forum, citizen's forum, etc.
Degree of organization	Formal group	If a group has a highly defined structure (for example, a formal membership list), specific roles and authority levels (e.g., a president, treasurer, and secretary), and specific goals (e.g., to assist the elderly, anti-smoking), then it may be called a formal group	Rotary, lions, Jaycees, labour unions, social clubs and societies, etc.

	Informal group	An informal group is usually a primary group, featured by a somewhat loose structure, a lack of clearly defined goals or objectives, unstructured interface, and understood rules. Because of the degree of its influence on individuals' values and activities, informal group is perhaps of greater importance to us in the process of understanding consumer behaviour	Peer group, local clubs, etc.
Degree of attachment	Membership group	It is a group to which a person either belongs or qualifies for the membership	The marketing practitioners in American Marketing Association, members of booksellers' guild
	Symbolic group	It is a group in which it is improbable to receive a membership for an individual, despite acting like a member by adopting the group's values, attitudes, and behaviour	Young boys wearing Indian Cricket jerseys and cap feel their association with the team but do not belong to it
Degree of association	Aspirational group	It is a group in which the individuals aspire to be someone	Former Miss World Aishwarya Rai symbolizes beauty and hence is in the aspirational group of young Indian ladies. *Lux*, which has positioned itself as beauty soap used Aishwarya as their brand endorser
	Dissociative group	It is the group in which the individuals do not like to be associated with someone	Traditionalists may not like bare bodied portrayal of John Abraham and thereby avoid the brands endorsed by him as they might think that those brands will clash with their self-image of traditionality

Of all these, the most significant type of groups is the reference group that serves as a point of reference for attitude formation by many individuals. The features and types of these groups have been discussed in the subsequent sections.

GROUP CONFORMITY

The two principle aspects of group behaviour are conformity and compliance. Both these aspects are prevalent in all types of groups, but the term 'conformity' is supposed to be more in formulation of an individual's behaviour. Conformity within a group guides the members in changing or forming their attitudes and beliefs in such a way that they easily fit in with the group norms and standards. In fact, it can be stated that those who conform to the group norms are considered to be more compliant. In order to conform, a group member must attribute someone as having the authority and integrity to lead or influence the group's behaviour. In the absence of this 'leader', conformity toward the group's goals will be less prevalent. If a member of the group does not conform to the group's needs, he/she would lose his trustworthiness in the group.

Though the concepts of compliance sound similar to conformity, nonetheless, they are, to some extent, diverse. For compliance to occur within groups, one must adapt his/her actions to group's wishes or rules. A person that conforms must have a temperament that allows him/her to acquiesce to others. Need for an act of compliance exists in everyone's life. Simply asking someone to perform a task is a request for compliance. The most effectual method to achieve compliance is through rational persuasion and motivation. The central aspect of conformity is that the person being influenced by the group changes his/her attitudes and/or beliefs while the main point of compliance is the attainment of some specified task.

On the other hand, obedience is the act of following orders without question because they come from a legal authority. There are many rightful authorities in a person's life, for example, their parents, professors at college, and even their religious leaders. As a matter of fact, almost at every point of life, many of the individuals follow a superior without questioning why and what they are doing! For example, we never question why we take tests in school. We never asked anybody why to say '*namaskar*' when introduced with somebody. We do it as we have seen our elders doing the same. With this, it becomes evident that 'Man is a social animal' and is scared of any social exclusion.

REFERENCE GROUPS—CONCEPT AND TYPES

The concept of reference group is explicated in many ways. To elucidate the term in simplistic way, we may resort to the following definitions provided by the eminent consumer scientists.

- Reference group is 'an actual or imaginary individual or group conceived of having significant relevance upon an individual's evaluations, aspirations, or behaviour' (Park and Lessig, 1977).
- Reference group is a person or a group that has considerable influence on the behaviour of an individual (Bearden and Etzel, 1982).
- Reference groups are usually conformed by the social network of an individual: family members, friends, colleagues, and inspirational figures (Bachmann, John, and Rao, 1993).
- Reference groups are the source of brand associations that mold the self image of a consumer (Escalas and Bettman, 2003).

However, in diverse cultural context and customs, it is quite understood that the characteristics of the social network are likely to vary. This, in turn, generates variation in the extent of reference group influence (Childers and Rao, 1992). Furthermore, some researchers had identified that in context of public services consumption, reference groups served as the most powerful influencer over a significant period of time (Chapman and Cowdell, 1998; Guzmán, 2005; Lovelock and Weinberg, 1984).

Reference groups come in several different forms:

- *Aspirational reference group* refers to those members of the society like whom an individual aspires to become. For example, many firms use athletes or movie stars as their spokespersons to fuel the individual's unmet aspirations. Sony used the World Cup winning Cricket Captain M.S. Dhoni as their brand ambassador.

Cricketer M.S. Dhoni promoting for *Sony Bravia*

- *Associative reference group* includes people who more pragmatically symbolize the individuals' present equals or near-equals—e.g., coworkers, neighbours, or members of churches, clubs, and organizations. In this context, we may refer to the study of Paco Underhill, a former anthropologist turned retail consultant and author of the book *Why We Buy*. He had concluded that for most of the teenagers, the process of buying apparels follows a two-stage process. In the first place, they seek approval from their peer group (the influencers of the purchase) for the choice made. Secondly, they seek permission from the parents (the payers of the purchase). Though it is a two-stage process, the first stage is comparatively prolonged than the latter.
- *Dissociative reference group* includes people like whom the individuals do not aspire to be. For example, the store literally named 'The Gap' was quite popular as it addressed the generation gap successfully.

Reference groups exert several kinds of influences on the consumers. Primary reference groups impart a profuse level of influence on most of the individual choice behaviour. The family members ideally constitute this type of reference group. On the contrary, the secondary reference groups (mostly the peers, colleagues, people in aspiration) impart less influence on the individuals. For example, the members of a golf club meet only on weekends or other holidays and are probable to have their impact on consumption restricted to that time period only.

Nonetheless, all these reference groups have a significant influence on consumer purchase behaviour as well as on formulation of marketing strategies. These have been elaborated in the subsequent sections.

IMPORTANCE OF REFERENCE GROUPS IN CONSUMER BEHAVIOUR

The significance of studying reference groups is to understand the interfaces among the group members who transform their behaviour in order to make that compliant with the group behaviour. Therefore, it is imperative to make a careful distinction among these as the marketing strategies must be formulated based on the type of influences imparted by the group. There are broadly three types of reference group influences which are as follows:

- *Informational influence*: In this case, an individual adapts the behaviour and opinion of the reference group members as constructive bits of information. In such a case conformity is simply the result of interpersonal trust and reliance on the information shared by the group members. For example, one may like to try a new burger introduced by *McDonald's* because friends with similar tastes recommended it. Some select a movie for the weekend based on the peer group's recommendation.
- *Normative influence*: Sometimes referred even as utilitarian influence, it has an impact when an individual works in accordance to the group expectations to gain a direct reward or to avoid being the odd-man-out. One may thus wear *Reebok* shoes and not *Action* brand to avoid mockery by other members of the group who are the loyal consumers of the first one and vice versa.
- *Identification influence*: Also known as the value expressive influence, it occurs when an individual conforms to the perceived group norms and values as a guide for his own attitude and values. Thus, the individual perceives the group norms as the reference point for his own self image.

A reference group influences consumption behaviour through various means: through norms providing information and through influencing the value expressive needs of the consumers. They influence consumption by bringing about a change in the attitude pattern through encouraging expression of certain shared values by the group. To be more specific, the more an individual feels a sense of identification with a group, the greater will be the psychological or material advantage from being associated with that group. There are three levels at which an individual may be involved with a group:

- *Compliance*: This involves an overt behaviour on the part of an individual. Compliance to the group norms necessarily modifies the individual's beliefs and attitudes. Thus, one may be formally attired for a job, because he feels that this is the only acceptable way to dress up, rather than thinking that this is the best way to do so.

- *Identification*: This represents a closer, more dependent relationship than that expected under compliance. Here an individual complies with a social relationship through adjustments in beliefs and attitudes. Thus, if a group of friends thinks that *Pepsi* is a better choice, then even though your personal preference is *Coke*, you may opt for *Pepsi* due to the group pressure. However, you may like to consume *Coke* when you are alone.
- *Internalization*: Here an individual internalizes the value system of a group so much so that he puts into effect these values even in the absence of the group. The purchase of religious books by the disciples of *Ramakrishna Mission* is a common phenomenon.

REASONS FOR ACCEPTANCE OF GROUP INFLUENCE

By and large, consumers admit group influence because of the perceived benefits in doing so. The nature and degree of the social interface between individuals is determined by an individual's perception of the effectiveness of such interaction. The outcome of interaction may sometimes occur in terms of rewards like friendship, information, satisfaction, etc. Nevertheless, it may also haul out costs like time lost, money spent, and activities being sacrificed. There is always a tendency by an individual to trade-off between these rewards and costs. Thus, an individual chooses his group and interacts with the members of that chosen group based upon his perception of the net reward out of his exchange.

The rationales for accepting group influence are best understood by taking into consideration the benefits derived:

- *Informational benefits*: One of the reasons of accepting reference group influence is that by doing so the consumer feels that his knowledge will improve. Consumers most willingly accept those sources of information that are thought to be most convincing. A consumer, using an informational reference group, may enthusiastically search information from opinion leaders or group members having suitable know–how about a particular product; or arrive at a conclusion through observing the behaviours of others.
- *Utilitarian benefits*: This reason refers to the force on the individual to conform to the preferences or expectations of another individual/group. In a product purchase situation, a customer will conform if he thinks that his behaviour is observable or will be known to others. Sometimes he perceives that others can reject him in case he does not comply with group norms, and this induces his motivation to grasp the reward or sanction.
- *Value-expressive benefit*: This relates to the individual's choice/motive to augment or prop up his self-concept by associating himself with positive reference groups and/or dissociating from negative referents.

MARKETING STRATEGIES AND REFERENCE GROUPS

It is apparent that a marketer may take advantage of reference group phenomenon while designing promotional messages.

- *Personal selling strategies*: In group demonstration and selling situations of direct marketing (like *Tupperware*, *Amway*, etc.), a salesperson may use a 'party' situation to sell a product. The sales people often target school teachers and working ladies in their offices. On each participant, at that time, there is a great deal of social pressure to buy as she thinks that she is being observed by others. A salesperson may by now identify the first prospective customer (by promising her a higher discount/freebie). Once she becomes the first buyer, she acts as an associative referent.
- *Advertising strategies*: A marketer uses celebrities, experts, or a simple spokesperson as a referent in his advertising message hoping that they form either associative or aspirational group. Thus *Lux* uses Aishwarya Rai, *Boost* uses Sachin, and so on. These reference groups increase brand awareness and create favourable attitude in the minds of the customers. One may recall the advertisement of *Horlicks Lite* in this context. The advertisement portrays a middle-class housewife who is concerned about her mid-aged husband's lethargic attitude as this may indicate some health problem. *Horlicks Lite* may provide solution to this problem with low cholesterol ingredients in it. The housewives find their slice of life in this advertisement. Thus, *Horlicks Lite* perfectly uses associative reference group in the advertisement. Simultaneously, with due importance, a marketer has to ensure that he does not associate his brand with negative reference group. For example, while dropping down Peaches Geldof from their commercials due to several sex scandals, Michelle Mone, the founder of the Miss Ultimo lingerie brand categorically stated 'We've given this a lot of thought, but there's a point where a business must stick to its principles and as a brand that targets young women, we feel it is impossible for Peaches Geldof to continue to work with us as the face of Miss Ultimo lingerie.'

EFFECTIVENESS OF CELEBRITY ENDORSEMENT AS A PART OF MARKETING STRATEGY

'Celebrity endorsement on overall brand' is no doubt an important concept. The upsurge of celebrities endorsing brands has been gradually escalating across the decades. Marketers overtly admit the persuasion power of celebrities in influencing consumer-purchasing decisions. It is almost everywhere accepted that celebrity endorsement can bequeath special traits upon a product that it may have required for augmenting its brand value. Therefore, a celebrity may endorse any brand, but to consistently associate the right brand with the right celebrity and in the right way is more important.

The last three years of the 1980s experienced the burgeoning trend of celebrity endorsement. Most of the brands, which had enough financial capability, made no delay in roping Bollywood stars as well as popular cricketers to endorse their brands. Advertisements featuring stars like Tabassum (*Prestige* pressure cookers), Jalal Agha (*Pan Parag*), Kapil Dev (*Palmolive* shaving cream), and Sunil Gavaskar (*Dinesh Suitings*) were some of the very popular advertisements of that time. However, the pioneering brand that encashed on celebrity power as a part of both strategic positioning and long-term mission statement was probably *Lux* soap. Mostly due to its association with the Bollywood divas, *Lux* has been amongst the top three soap brands in the country till date.

Of late, we have seen Shahrukh Khan, the Bollywood superstar in *Santro* campaign with the objective of extenuating the hindrance that an unfamiliar Korean brand faced in the Indian market. No doubt that the intention of *Santro* was to harvest faster brand recall and recognition, association, and emotional ties with the prospective customers. Effective celebrity–brand association can no doubt create magic in the present consumer-centric era. This was further proved by successful endorsement done by Shahrukh for *Pepsi*, *Clinic All Clear*, and *Santro* down the time line. This is the reason why Bollywood stars Bipasha Basu and John Abraham had been used to launch the *Clinic All Clear* advertisement in Mumbai.

Bollywood actor John Abraham launching the *Clinic All Clear* advertisement at Infiniti Mall in Mumbai

Advantages of Celebrity Endorsement

Since the last few decades, many brands have been leveraging celebrity appeal to increase their recall and recognition effect, and as a consequence to increase sales. As soon as players or movie stars become popular, there is a general tendency on the part of the advertisers to queue up to have it splashed all over. The spectacular rise of visibility in several endorsements by Mahendra Singh Dhoni, the Skipper of the Indian Cricket Team, and Sachin Tendulkar is a recent phenomenon. The augmentation of celebrity endorsements is also quite reasonable by the following advantages bestowed on the overall brand:

- *Augmenting credibility*: Endorsement of a brand by star augments credibility for that brand among the target audience—particularly in case of new products. Shahrukh Khan's association from the very initiation stage facilitated *Santro* to amplify the 'brand recall' in India.
- *Breaking the clutter*: Celebrities break the clutter of advertisements and draw attention of the target group.
- *PR coverage*: Managers recognize the importance of celebrities to craft high PR coverage. In this context, one may recall the campaigns of the Spice Girls—one of the world's leading pop group. This group, apart from featuring in *Pepsi*'s advertisements, as part of endorsement also appeared in their several product launch and PR activities.
- *Amplifying recall effect*: Association of celebrities with the brands often augmented the recall effect for the last. Amitabh Bachchan, in India, endorsed *Parker* pens, which subsequently increased its sale. Similarly, the *Idea* mobiles roped in Abhishek Bachchan to enhance their brand recall. Needless to say, this has also been a successful attempt so far.
- *Reinstating tarnished image*: *Cadbury* India wanted to reinstate the consumer's assurance in its chocolate brands after the high-pitch worm's hullabaloo. So the company roped in Amitabh

Bachchan to endorse the brand. Last year, when things started getting worse for both the cola giants (due to negative press and word of mouth), both the companies resorted to more glossy damage control advertisements casting the then top Bollywood celebrities. While Aamir Khan escorted the *Coke* retaliation as a suspicious and persnickety Bengali man who ultimately accepts that 'Coke is safe', *PepsiCo* used the gala combination of Bollywood Badshah Shahrukh Khan and the Cricket God Sachin Tendulkar in the commercials to convince the customers about the safety aspect of the bottled beverages.

- *Psychographic connect*: Celebrities are normally appreciated and venerated by their fans and advertisers utilize stars to make the most of these feelings to influence the fans towards their brand.
- *Demographic connect*: Acceptability of various stars varies across the demographic (age, gender, class, geography, etc.) segments.
- *Wider appeal*: Some celebrities have widespread appeal and thus companies use them as a good stake to engender attention among the masses.
- *Rejuvenating a stagnant brand*: Sometimes, to rejuvenate the recall of certain stagnant brands, the companies resort to incorporate celebrities in their promotional acts. For example, *Dabur* India roped in Bachchan, and *Emami* the then Indian Cricket skipper Sourav Ganguly for the purpose.
- *For recompensing the lack of pioneering ideas*: Several detergents, toilet soaps, and hair oils rope female movie stars just to attract the audience without any innovative and pioneering idea. In these cases, except the faces of the celebrities, most of the advertising themes are almost similar. Rituparna Sengupta and Vidya Balan's casting in *Nihar* natural hair oil can be a portrayal of this phenomenon.

Disadvantages of Celebrity Endorsement

The contemporary advertising world is also characterized by a number of severe mismatches between the celebrity and the brands they endorse. Amitabh with *Parker* and Shahrukh with *Santro* may be really good matches; however, Amitabh with *Dabur Hajmola*, *Navratna Hair Oil*, and Shahrukh with *Pepsodent* seem to be perplexing. If Pierce Brosnan, whose image is that of a perfect gentleman, endorses a brand of casual apparels, it will be a perfect mismatch. As a celebrity himself comes with a strong iconic brand, the mismatch can be counteractive for the brand. The celebrity should be selected in such a way that his/her uniqueness and the unique selling proposition of the brand could create a synergy.

The celebrity approach, therefore, is not free from risk. Some such risks are mentioned below:

- *The vampire effect*: This jargon puts forward a very pertinent issue of a celebrity overriding a brand. If there is no match between the celebrity and the brand, then it may induce 'celebrity recall' instead of 'brand recall'. In this context, one may recall the association of Leonard Rossiter and *Cinzano*. The association of *Visacard* and Sachin; *Castrol* and Rahul Dravid are also some of the examples of the vampire effect.
- *Effects of image fluctuation of celebrity*: If the celebrity's image is tarnished over a period of time due to his/her under-performance or any other reason, the associated brand is bound to

suffer. For example, O.J. Simpson's indictment and later exoneration on murder charges; Pepsi Cola's series of shambles with three marked celebrities—Mike Tyson, Madonna, and Michael Jackson; and impact of Tiger Wood's scandals on *Accenture* imply that celebrity endorsers may sometimes turn out to be burden to the brands they endorse.

- *Discrepancy in the professional popularity of the celebrity*: Celebrity may mislay his or her fame because of some trails in professional presentations. For example, when Yuvraj and Sehwag suffered from under-performance, they were found occasionally in advertisements. But after the gorgeous World Cup victory of India, in 2011, things got revamped for Yuvraj (man of the series) and Sehwag (one of the leading scorers in World Cup 2011).
- *Celebrities endorsing one brand and consuming (competitor) another*: Living celebrities invite problems when they get caught consuming competitor's brand. The brand–celebrity association turns out to be a failure in that case.
- *Multibrand endorsements by the same celebrity would result in overexposure*: The uniqueness of a celebrity endorsement gets watered down if he does too many endorsements across varied product categories. Amitabh Bachchan endorses for *Navratna* hair oil, *BoroPlus* antiseptic, *Parker* pens, *Tide* detergent, *Reid & Taylor* suitings, and many more. Sachin, Shahrukh, and Amir are also adopting the same practice. Therefore, the exclusiveness of celebrity–brand association gets diluted and the situation results in 'commoditization of celebrities'.
- *Disparity between celebrity and the image of the brand*: Every celebrity has a distinctive image. While resorting to celebrity endorsement, the marketers must take into account the compatibility of the celebrity and brand persona. For example, Aishwarya Rai's elegant beauty is well captivated in *Loreal* hair colour advertisement. But Big B using *Pudin hara* or *Navaratna* oil is a hard to believe phenomenon.

A brief appraisal of the present market situation indicates that celebrity endorsement strategies can, under appropriate situations, definitely justify bearing the high costs associated with them. Nevertheless, it would be too presuming to believe that the celebrity endorsement is the universal remedy for all marketing problems. Celebrity endorsement, if used successfully, may derive a lot of mileage for the brands, specifically in terms of brand recall and selection. But to achieve this, the marketer needs to be really careful while selecting a celebrity. This is to be remembered that a 'celebrity is a means to an end, and not an end in himself/herself'.

Closing Case

Mayur—A Mess on Celebrity Endorsements

Rajasthan Spinning & Weaving Mills (RSWM) is one of the largest textile manufacturers in the country with a turnover of ₹1500 crore. *Mayur* Suitings is a textile brand launched by RSWM almost 30 years back. Till 2007, *Mayur* captured a steady market share of about 7% in the ₹10,000 crore Indian suitings market. *Mayur* was especially famous for its predilection for celebrity endorsements. In 1980s, *Dinesh* (endorsed by Sunil Gavaskar) started this practice in the purview of garment manufacturing industry. *Siyaram* also followed the same footsteps. Nowadays, they have roped in M.S. Dhoni, the Indian Cricket skipper, to endorse their brand.

Mayur, the major competitor of *Dinesh* and *Siyaram*, became noticeable since 1995, when they roped in Shahrukh Khan, the matinee idol of Bollywood to endorse the brand. Although at that point of time Shahrukh was not a superstar, he had already shown the prospect of reigning the Bollywood for the years to come. He endorsed *Mayur* for four years from 1995 to 1999 with a tagline, Shahrukh '*Mayur*' Khan. The advertisement was a hit which drove *Mayur* to the big league. The brand gradually became very popular.

Across the years, the brand was endorsed by Chandrachur Singh, Sharad Kapoor, Lisa Ray, and Virender Sehwag. *Mayur* is a typical case of celebrity endorsement which portrays both positive as well as negative aspects of using a celebrity. *Mayur* has always highlighted its celebrity endorser and not any unique selling proposition. Probably so, when Shahrukh was withdrawn from the advertisement copies, the brand was not able to uphold the impetus. With Shahrukh, the company entrusted on the idea of catching the potential stars to hit the market. That may be one of the reasons why Chandrachur Singh was roped in after the success of his debut film '*Machis*'. But in the long run Chandrachur failed to gain the stardom like Shahrukh.

Later on the brand moved from movies to cricket and signed a contract with Virender Sehwag, who was in peak of his career at that time. In 2007, when Virender Sehwag was passing through a bad patch in cricket career, he was dropped and Salman Khan became the endorser. It needs to be mentioned that in 2007, the brand went on for a massive expansion. Mr. Riju Jhunjhunwala, Joint Managing Director, RSWM Ltd., said, 'We plan to undertake several initiatives over the next two to three years to make *Mayur* an affordable and favoured brand in the country'. He further added that at that time the brand was sold through 100 distributors and almost 1500 authorized outlets across India. The company planned to augment the numbers of distributors and retail points radically by 2010. In this context, the company assumed Salman to be the perfect fit for the brand as he enjoyed a great aspirational connect with consumers across all segments. The company, for its new advertisement planned to double its promotional budget. *Mayur Suitings*, which was a ₹100 crore brand in 2007, hoped to clock a turnover of ₹300 crore in the next three years.

The brand was so captivated to the celebrity concept that they even used a tagline '*Stars ki Pasand*'. Nonetheless, this tagline did not add much value to the advertisement, perhaps because this tagline was a perfect mismatch with their 'value for money' positioning.

One may recall the '*Sitaron ka soundarya sabun*' concept of *Lux*, which was the brand's DNA. Mayur failed to create this brand–celebrity association even after 30 years of existence. Actually, *Lux* had always been endorsed by the well-ranked female stars in Bollywood. It was not possible for *Mayur* to afford that lavishness. It had used only one celebrity at a time. Moreover, the failure of the celebrity to execute and outshine also acted against the brand as the brand solely depended on the celebrities to develop its brand value. In other words, the brand failed to stand on its own. *Lux* and *Pepsi* also used celebrities to endorse their brands, but their entire brand positioning did not depend only on the celebrities. No doubt, with the rising stars, their advertisements too looked very glossy, but the celebrities for them helped to break the advertising clutter and draw attention of the customer towards the brands.

Mayur envisages the critical issue of finding out a significant differentiation based on the brand's unique selling proposition rather than focusing only on the celebrity. The market is fiercely competitive with brands like *Raymonds*, *Grasim*, and *Reid & Taylor*. Moreover, the ex-icon for *Mayur*, Shahrukh, is presently under contract with another brand *Belmonte* from *Skumars*. Even though *Mayur* is targeting a much lower end of the garment market cluster, yet the brand has to relive itself to arrive at its aspiration.

Questions

1. Do you think *Mayur* can reach its target with the same strategy?
2. If not, suggest appropriate strategies for *Mayur* to rejuvenate its brand image.

Source: http://www.thehindubusinessline.com/2007/02/14/stories/2007021403510500.htm, Mayur Suitings signs on Salman, February 14, 2007, exchange4media News Service; Mayur Suitings: Stars ki Pasand, February 20, 2007, http://marketingpractice.blogspot.com/2007/02/mayur-suitings-stars-ki-pasand.html, accessed on January 21, 2011.

Summary

This chapter has described the social-group influences on the consumers of 21st century. Groups may be classified on the basis of various dimensions like functions, degree of perceived importance, and degree of organization. The two principle aspects in group dynamics are conformity and compliance. Conformity within a group guides the members in changing or forming their attitudes and beliefs in such a way that they easily fit in with the group norms and standards. For compliance to occur within groups, one must adapt his/her actions to the group's wishes or rules.

The most important concept in terms of group dynamics is the 'reference group'. A reference group is defined as an actual or imaginary individual or group conceived of having significant relevance upon an individual's evaluations, aspirations, or behaviour. Reference groups are of several types, like associative or dissociative, informational or aspirational, etc. The marketing implications of reference group have been elaborated in the chapter by discussing factors related to their level of influence and by citing their relevance in consumer decision making. Finally, the chapter addressed the difficulty a marketer may face in identifying the consumer's relevant reference groups. In this context, focus was given on the use of aspirational reference group in advertising copies with special emphasis on celebrity endorsements. With careful analysis of the pros and cons of celebrity endorsement, it has been concluded that celebrity endorsement, if used productively, may gain lot of mileage for the brands, specifically in terms of brand recall and selection. But to achieve this, the marketer needs to be really cautious about selecting a celebrity. Therefore, this is to be remembered that a 'celebrity is a means to an end, and not an end in himself/herself'.

Key Terms

Group A group may be defined as two or more people who network to achieve either individual or mutual goals.

Group conformity Conformity within a group guides the members in changing or forming their attitudes and beliefs in such a way that they easily fit in with the group norms and standards.

Group compliance For compliance to occur within groups, one must adapt his/her actions to the group's wishes or rules.

Reference group It is an actual or imaginary individual or group conceived of having significant relevance upon an individual's evaluations, aspirations, or behaviour.

Celebrity endorsement When the famous people, who are in our aspiration, are used in advertising of different brands, we call it celebrity endorsement.

Questions

1. Identify three reference groups that influence your consumer behaviour in different situations. Why do you think you conform to this group's behaviour?
2. Describe the types of reference groups and identify how they influence purchase decisions in the market place.
3. If you become a manager of a multinational company selling toothpaste, what aspects would you take into consideration in selecting a celebrity to endorse your brand?

Critical Assignment

1. Select five products of your choice and find out how are you influenced by the reference groups for the choice of brands in product categories.
2. Identify three cases of proper association of brands and choice of celebrity and three cases where you feel there is a mismatch between the celebrity and the brand persona.

Chapter **12**

Family Buying Decisions

Chapter Goals

After completing this chapter, you will be able to understand

- the concepts of family and household
- the types of families
- buying roles in a family
- the concept of family life cycle
- the family buying decision model
- conflict and conflict resolution in family buying

Opening Vignette

Domains of Decision-Making in Mr. Acharya's Family

Mr. Ravikant and Mrs. Janaki Acharya reside in Serampore, a suburb town 20 km (approximately) away from Kolkata in West Bengal, India. They cohabit with their two children (Romi and Mohan) and their parents (Sushma and Janardan Acharya).

Janaki, a renowned pediatrician, is posted in a private tertiary care super-specialty hospital in Kolkata. She needs to travel to her hospital every day in the early morning and even at late hours of night when any patient is in critical condition. Local trains run up to 23.30–12.00 hrs at night. Thereafter, it becomes difficult for her to travel. The hospital authority is very much annoyed with her on the issue of the death of a patient at night, around 2.30 a.m. as she could not attend the case. Hence, Janaki tells Ravikant that they either have to buy a car or an apartment in city Kolkata.

Twelve years old Romi is in VIIth standard in a local school. She needs to travel by school bus every morning at 8.30 a.m. and normally returns at 5.30 p.m. She is not that eager to shift the residence as most of her friends reside nearby. Moreover, she has a strong sentiment for her granny and grandpa, and wants to reside with them only. However, she is very interested about the idea of buying a car. She enthusiastically says, 'Mama my friend Rohan's papa has bought a *Tata Nano* and even Vicky's parents bought a car last month… wait ... I think it's *Maruti Alto*'.

Mohan, a software engineering student of Kolkata, is strongly in favour of buying a residence in Kolkata. He says, 'Papa, even after my college days, it is most likely that I have to work in city offices. So it will be better to have a residence near Rajarhat or Saltlake where most of the software companies are located in the city. Many construction companies are developing dream projects there now...' As parents, Janaki and Ravikant are really anxious about how to provide some relief to their son.

On the other hand, Sushma and Janardan since their three generations have been staying in that small suburban historic town and do not want to shift to the city. They have lots of memories attached with this place and even the house. Janardan is especially very nostalgic about his three-generation-old beautiful house on the bank of the holy river Ganges.

Mr. Ravikant is a busy sales manager of a multinational company. Most of the time, he needs to travel a lot across the country. So, he stays in the periphery of Bengal hardly for seven to ten days. Ravikant, however, is also very much attached to the intimate and fond memories of his childhood spent in this house.

Considering the priorities of each of the family members, Mr. Ravikant now has to seriously take a call on whether to buy a residence or a car. Hence, the family decision-making process, being a joint-decision framework, is far more complex than individual buying decision process.

(This is a fictitious case. Any resemblance with any character is purely coincidental.)

CONCEPT OF FAMILY AND HOUSEHOLD

The above case suggests that a consumer, being a member of a family, cannot solely consider his own requirement while buying a product which is to be used by all the members of the family. He has to take care of the entire family's opinion and arrive at a consensus in purchase decision.

The family is not merely a small group of individuals but the 'most' important influencing factor in terms of a consumer's purchase decision.

The consumer research experts define family 'as two or more persons related by blood, marriage, or adoption who reside together'. Some researchers have opined that the family operates as an economic unit in terms of a collective earning and spending of money. Nonetheless, by collective earning and spending, all the family members must ascertain both the individual and shared consumption goals. For an individual, family is the direct, most significant, and persistent influencing factor for buying decision-making. Moreover, the consumer's attitudes toward spending, saving, the choice of product category, and the selection of a particular brand in that category are quite often shaped by his/her family's influence.

Hence, it is imperative to realize the distinction between various terms that are frequently used in terms of the family decision-making. First, we should differentiate between the terms 'family' and 'household' as the information related to demographic and psychographic segments of the market may be collected on these bases.

A household refers to the related family members and all the unrelated persons who dwell in the same lodging unit (whether house, apartment, group of rooms, or others). Clearly, the households may be of two main types: families and non-families. In many medical, engineering, and management schools, the students, i.e., the households, residing in a hostel are no way members of a family. For a household to be considered as a family there must be a group of two or more persons residing together and connected by blood, marriage, or adoption.

Nonetheless, it should be noted that marketers are concerned not only with the idea of families but also of households, since both may shape the foundation of the consumer's buying-decision behaviour. For instance, producer of refrigerators, kitchen chimneys and utensils, television, service providers of cooking gas, dry cleaners, etc., would possibly find households to be the most pertinent dimensions in estimating market size. On the flip side, marketers of children's garments and toys, valentine gifts for spouse would probably be more interested in information on families, rather than simply on households.

TYPES OF FAMILIES

There are different types of families based on marriage, nature of residence, size or structure, or nature of relations.

(a) On the basis of marriage, family has been classified into three major forms as given below:

- *Polygamous family*: A family made up by more than two marital partners of a man.
- *Polyandrous family*: A family where a woman resides with multiple husbands.
- *Monogamous family*: Monogamy refers to a form of marriage in which a person has only one partner at any one time.

(b) On the basis of the nature of residence, family can be classified into three main forms as given below:

- *Family of matrilocal residence*: Matrilocal family exists in the societal system in which a married couple resides with or near the wife's parents. In this type of family, the daughter will stay in or close to the mother's house, thereby, constituting a large clan of families, where three or four generations of a lady reside in the same area.
- *Family of patrilocal residence*: This type of family exists in a social system in which a married couple resides with or near the husband's parents. Location here means a village, town, or clan area. This practice is found in tentatively 69% of the world's cultures.

- *Family of changing residence*: This type of family neither resides in patrilocal nor in the matrilocal areas; it rather stays somewhere else, e.g., close to their workplace. This is of course a changing social pattern of these days. In India, many young Bengali, Gujarati, and Marathi couples are working in Bangalore IT sector, which is neither of the spouses' native place.

(c) On the basis of size or structure, family can be classified into two major types as given below:

- *Nuclear or the single unit family*: In this kind of family, only the couple or couple with their own unmarried children resides together.
- *Joint family*: Joint families are extended families where apart from only husband-wife and children, grandparents, uncles or aunts also stay together. Many of the Indian families support this system.

(d) On the basis of the nature of relations among the family members, family can be classified into two main types as given below:

- *Conjugal family*: This type of family consists of adult members tied by sexual relationship either by marriage or a live-in relationship.
- *Consanguine family*: These kinds of families are formed by the members tied by blood relation and cohabitated in a single household, e.g., brother and sister, father and son, etc.

BUYING ROLES IN A FAMILY

A big pool of market researchers considers an individual's family to be the most important determinant of his/her buying behaviour. A person normally has a natural tendency to follow his parents in terms of the consumption patterns. Actually, an individual's selection of products and brands are often influenced by what his parents or grandparents used to buy and what his wife and children like to use. In many Indian families, the choice of *Colgate Dental Cream* is an automatic one, due to its age-old use. For a new brand of toothpaste, it would be a real challenge to convert these families to the user of their brand. Even sometimes, people are inclined towards a 'brand' of politics (Congress or BJP) as a family practice.

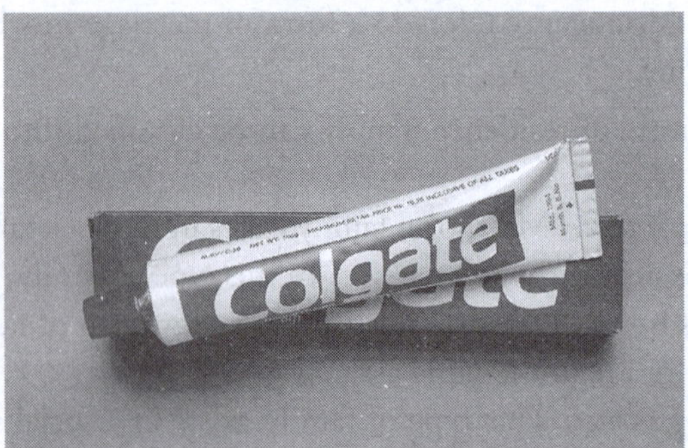

Colgate toothpaste: an age-old family choice

Family buying behaviour nowadays is the focal point of many researchers in the domain of consumer behaviour. Companies are also interested to know the ways by which the family members get influenced over certain purchase decisions of an individual. Children have a great deal of influence by pester power over many household purchases. IKEA used this information to devise their showrooms. The children's bedrooms trait fun beds with attractive quilts so that the children are prompted to ask for the brand by its name.

© Photos.com

A child in her fun bed

Therefore, the marketers need to understand that a set of purchase roles exists and comes into play within the family. If these roles are well noted, it would not be that difficult to understand how each of the family members influences purchase decisions.

The important buying roles are as follows:

- *The initiator*: The initiator first puts forward the idea of a product or service and makes the first move on the purchase process. For example, while walking down the street, the son of a family finds a nice car in the showroom. He walks inside to take the details of the car and shares the information with his family. Or, he may notice a new brand of stereo in his friend's house. It is then talked about at home with the other members of the family (co-decision makers) and the initiation process starts with the discussion on whether the brand suits the family requirements or not. Often the marketer provides some symbolic or significant cue to attract the initiator. Window display, danglers, and cutouts are some of the tools used by the marketers for the purpose. Sometimes, the price discounts on several household items provides significant cue to the marketers.
- *The influencer*: The influencer is someone whose opinion is appreciated in the decision-making process. For example, upon receiving the symbolic and significant cues about the car, both the son and the mother may start influencing the father to purchase a particular brand.

- *The decider*: The decider is the individual who makes the final call on which brand to buy, after considering all aspects such as price, quality, servicing, etc.
- *The buyer*: The buyer is the person who actually purchases the product, takes it home or arranges for the delivery.
- *The payer*: The payer is the person who ultimately pays for the product. The payer may be the earning member of the family (father, mother).
- *The consumers*: They are the ultimate users of the goods or service. As in the case mentioned in the opening vignette, if the car is purchased it would be used by the entire family.

Even though these five buying roles are performed whenever a purchase is made, the individual performing each role may differ from purchase to purchase, and from family to family. Therefore, the number and identity of the family members who fill these roles is often diversified. In any given situation, the same member may take on several or all the roles. For example, when an individual passes by a cigarette stall, and feels the need of having one, he himself becomes the initiator. If he is a 'brand loyal customer', he himself influences his brand choice. Similarly, he only decides the brand, pays for the purchase, and consumes it. Thus, he performs all the buying roles alone.

Sometimes in the family, the decision domains are specified. Especially in case of financial decisions, often the head or the principal earning member of the family is the decision maker. In other cases, a single role may be performed jointly by two or more family members. For example, when a car, music system, or any other household amenity is purchased, normally it is consumed by all the members of the family. Multiple roles, too, may be performed by one of the family members. For purchasing a bottle of jam, the mother may be influenced by the child, but ultimately she is the decider and buyer of it.

The constituents of power within the family are gained from an array of sources mentioned below.

1. *Economic resources*: Here, the highest economic contributor of the family member poses to have the most dominant power over others and thereby becomes the decision-maker.
2. *Cultural norms*: The existing cultural trends may decide who the most dominant partner in the family is. In many patriarchic cultures, the male member is the dominant partner and decisions for several product purchases tend to be more husband-dominant.
3. *Expert power*: One partner may have more knowledge and more detailed information with respect to particular purchases. For example, if the husband is a teacher, there are high chances that his opinion about the child's education will have relatively more importance; or if the wife is a doctor, about the treatment of any member of the family, her opinion will be prioritized.
4. *Legitimate power*: This is the influence that results logically from the expectations in the family regarding one's role. In patriarchic societies, the financial decisions are usually husband-dominant. However, in context of the complex and shifting dynamics of gender roles, nowadays most of the important family decisions are taken on the basis of negotiation rather than legitimate power (Scanzoni,1983)
5. *Bargaining power*: This involves suggesting one member to make a decision favourable to another on the basis of reciprocal arrangement.

6. *Reward/referent power*: Here one spouse may reward the other by accepting the other's choice.
7. *Emotional power*: Sometimes, the purchase decision may be influenced by one partner using his/her emotional influence on the other.

THE STAGES OF FAMILY LIFE CYCLE

Similar to the product types, families too follow a life cycle. The expression 'family life cycle' refers to the sequence of various life stages through which individuals proceed over time. It illustrates, in other words, the course of the family formation and dissolution. Thus, a family may begin for an individual when he moves on from bachelorhood to married life. Thereafter, he passes through a string of stages with new-born babies, grown up children, and so on. Each stage is at variance from the preceding stages in terms of family composition, the financial state, consumption patterns, product needs, and preferences and usage patterns. The life cycle of families has been conceptualized as a series embracing quite a few distinct phases in the following paragraphs.

The bachelor stage (young and single)

In the bachelor stage of the life cycle, income is relatively low as compared to one's future earnings, as the majority of bachelors are at the early stages of their vocation. But, simultaneously, the financial liability is also very little. Therefore, their discretionary incomes are relatively higher than the other stages of family life cycle. They have a propensity to expend considerable amounts on individual consumption items like fast food, trendy apparels, certain luxurious and entertainment goods like walkman, ipods, sunglasses, video games, trendy mobile sets, two wheelers, etc. Some essential furniture items as well as some kitchen apparatus may be acquired. Nonetheless, these purchases often tend to be on a haphazard basis and also least, because they feel these belongings curb their liberty of movement.

The food, detergent, shampoo, etc., marketers also have curbed opportunities in terms of single serving packaging for a wide range of products. Overall, at this stage, the customer demonstrates more individuality syndrome in terms of every purchase decision.

The newly married couples (young, no children)

Marriage changes the needs and preferences. At this stage, life is much more stable. People tend to buy apartments. Need for other household amenities also increase. In addition, in some cases, both partners may be working. Especially in case of the DINK (double income no kids) families, the family income is usually higher than the bachelor stage. Purchases include durable goods such as refrigerators, washing machines, and other appliances, reasonably priced durable furniture, home entertainment items such as television sets, etc. Moreover, holiday packages and restaurant bills are also quite high. With these and many other allied expenses, this stage, therefore, embodies a high expenditure period.

Full nest 1 (young, married, with child)

The influx of a child makes drastic changes in the life further. It is quite likely that some wives may quit their jobs and the family suffers a reduction in overall income. On the flip side, child rearing increases expenses. People are more involved in the purchase of baby furniture, toys, chest rubs, vitamins, baby foods, and medicines. This is also the period when they become discontented with their income and with their incapability to accrue earnings.

Figure 12.1 Family life cycle

Full nest 2 (older, married, with children above five years)

The family's financial state, at this phase starts to perk up because of both career progress and many wives returning to work. They represent a lively market for a wide variety of food products, bicycles, music lessons, computers, laptops, books, magazines, and also tutorial fees for educational services as children are growing up.

Full nest 3 (older, married, with grown up dependent children)

Income is elevated for the family at this stage. Nevertheless, the families now symbolize experienced buyers and are comparatively less fascinated in new product purchases. Expenditures persist to be high due to replacement buying at the end of the stage. Moreover, as children are grown ups now, the educational expenses grow up. The cost of books, apparels, and food also escalates.

Empty nest (Older, married, with no children living with them)

With no children living at home, the financial position becomes stable but savings accumulate. Hobbies also become an important source of pleasure. More money is exhausted on luxury appliances, periodicals, and health products. Key expenditures are on home possession, home improvements, and also on medical care.

Solitary survivor (older, single, retired people)

This is the stage when either of the spouses is passed away. Normally at this stage, people have simple and inexpensive lifestyle. Perhaps, a lower income due to retirement may be a restraining issue. Health care and other services become essential. Normally at this stage pilgrim tours, religious books, spectacles, walking sticks, medicines are more in demand.

Importance of Family Life Cycle to the Marketer

At each stage of family life cycle, there are distinctive sets of desires and demands. Hence, perhaps the family life cycle serves as a better guide to the marketers to understand the consumption patterns than age. For example, it is well known that many household amenities like cots, wardrobes, store wells, freezer, and washing machines are bought at the early phase of marriage.

The family life cycle stages, therefore, serve as a useful tool to analyze and segment the markets. This concept takes into account the family incomes, dynamics of power structure in a family, their joint needs, and mutual influences on each other. The analysis, thus, allows the marketers to segment families into smaller subgroups to develop products and services to meet the explicit needs of families at each stage, and to plan promotional strategies for their particular target segment.

The presence of children influences the family purchase decision a lot. In most of the nuclear families, a huge chunk of disposable income gets spent in fulfilling children's needs. However, the conventional view of the family life cycle has been challenged for failing to identify that a single family unit may not exist throughout the span of an individual's life. There can be breakups of marital relationship and chances of remarriage. Secondly, the traditional model did not take into account the cases of single parent households. But in reality, they exist in huge numbers. In the modern families, the existence of working women makes the family dynamics furthermore complicated and many new types of services like crèche or day boarding schools for the children have gained momentum. Third, the conventional concept of family life cycle still uses demographic variables to segment the market and, therefore, ignores the psychographic variables. Hence, the important psychographic parameters like attitude and perception are often overlooked.

Nonetheless, the family life cycle is a significant aspect in scheming consumption patterns, leisure time, family expenditure patterns for services, etc.

INFLUENCE OF CHILDREN IN FAMILY BUYING DECISION

The entry of a child in the family raises demand for a wide variety of products. Besides, the children persuade the buying decision of several products both directly and indirectly. Especially when we consider child-centred Indian families, children tend to spectacularly influence the family budget.

© Photos.com

A happy family shopping

The moment children build up the basic skills to commune, they try to use pester power to dominate many family purchase decisions. Older children, as the opening vignette suggests, partake even more openly in the decision processes. Though it still remains to be parental prerogative to allocate the family budget but the grown up children influence almost all major dimensions of the decision-making exercise.

They often assume the roles of initiators and influencers especially in case of the products they consume along with others in the family. For example, the purchase of breakfast cereal, brand of toothpaste, and other toiletries are often dominated by them. Once they pass the phase of adolescence, they may take bigger degree of control on several decisions like amusement parks, restaurants, and even sometimes vacations. The influence is clearly much higher in case of products of their exclusive use.

The role of children, however, diverges across the product categories, and even across familial compositions and power structure. As families are different in their traditions, the discretion that is acceptable to children may vary across families and would influence the degree of pressure that children can put forth on the family's purchase decision. In addition, children are also subjective by their families through the process of 'consumer socialization'. In the background of consumer behaviour, the parent-child bond may be assumed as an influence versus yield situation. Children, mostly playing the role of the initiator or influencer, try to manipulate their parents to make a favourable decision towards a particular product/brand (to yield). Thereafter, the reaction of the parent may be tailored by facilitating situations, or a contradictory order of spending preference.

FAMILY BUYING DECISION MODEL OF JAGDISH SHETH

Family decision-making, with its unique approach, is standalone amongst the emerging research areas in social sciences. No doubt, various facets from sociology, social anthropology, psychology, economics, and marketing have contributed in the development of the theory of 'Family decision-making' by the acclaimed marketing guru Jagdish Sheth.

The total consumption of a family may be grouped in three types, namely, consumption by the individual members, the family as a whole, and the household unit. For example, cigarette may be exclusively consumed by the father, lipstick by the mother, and toys by the child. On the other hand, vegetables and curry powder may be transformed into curry by mother and consumed by the entire family. Products like home theatre, car, music system, and air conditioners are also consumed by the entire family as a part of shared consumption items.

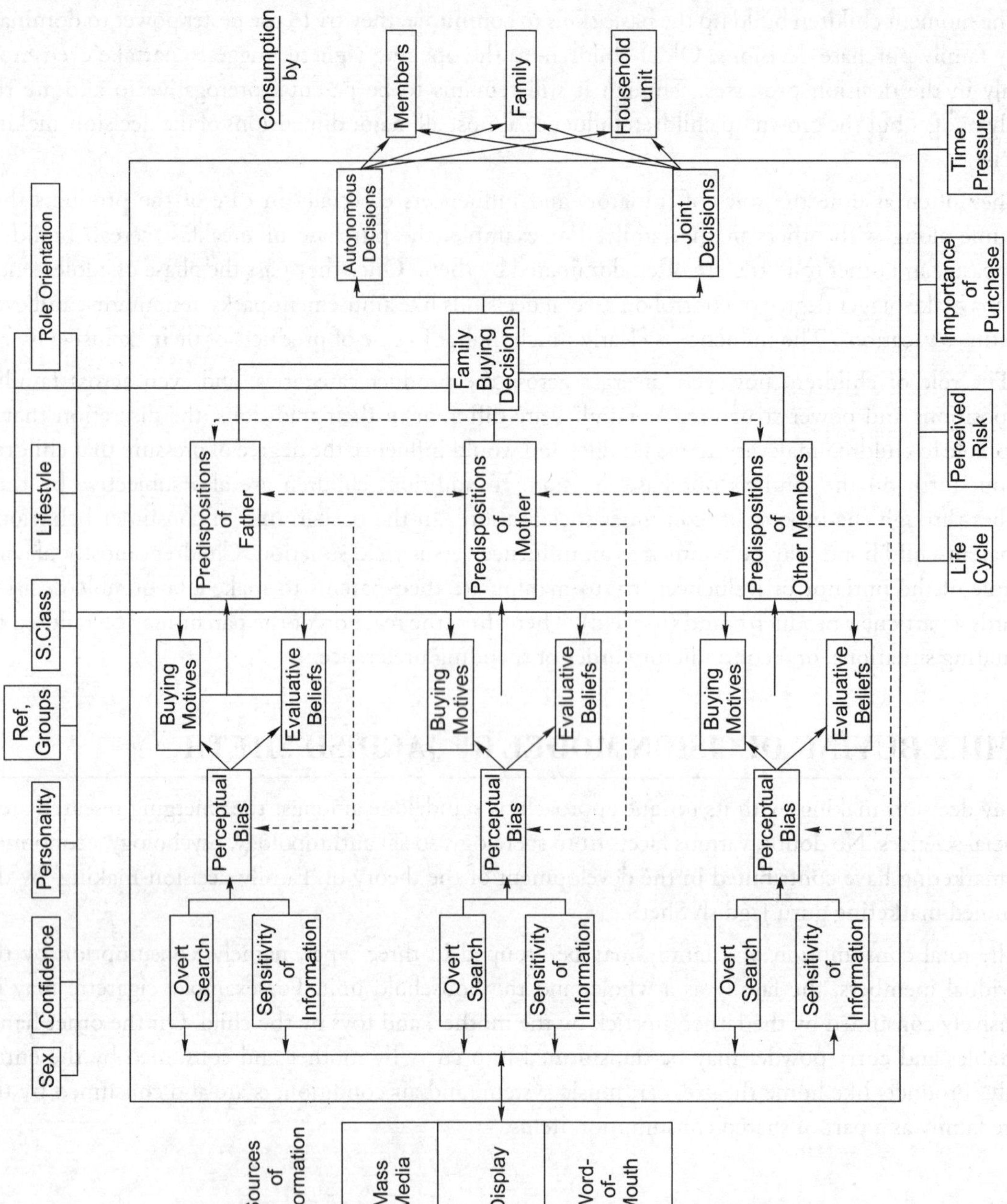

Figure 12.2 Family decision-making model of Jagdish Sheth

Source: http://www.jagsheth.net/docs/A%20Theory%20of%20Family%20Buying%20Decisions.pdf, published with courtesy and permission from Prof. Jagdish N. Sheth.

The family consumption behaviour may often be considered to be the offshoot of family buying decisions. Consequently, consumption cropping up from gifts, rentals, and possession by means other than buying is not overtly taken into consideration. Family buying decisions, according to Jagdish Sheth, are considered to be of mainly two types—autonomous (husband or wife dominant) and joint (by several or all members of the family). The task of specific members of the family that has been described in the earlier sections has a definite impact on the overall buying behaviour. When a person stays alone, he himself may decide to buy apparel or go for frozen foods, based on only his own needs. The situation becomes complex, when that person gets married and has children. At this moment, the decisions may be taken by the husband or wife individually or jointly regarding the various aspects. Nonetheless, the decisions have to be based on the needs and requirements of the family. Lots of influencing factors like the pester power of children and the preference of the previous generation also has to be taken care of.

Since there exist various underlying factors influencing the correlation between consumption and nature of family decision-making, it is highly imperative to properly interpret the determinants of joint versus autonomous decision-making. Hence, the theory of family decision-making comprises the four major sub-sections, which have been illustrated below.

Cognitive Aspects of Individual Members

Each member of a family has his/her own set of positive and negative predispositions regarding some products and particular brands in that product category. These predispositions are assumed to be diverse in many cases due to the existence of disparity in motives and perceptions of all the individual entities involved in the process of making buying decisions. For example, in case of buying an apartment, the husband may prefer to buy a 2000 square feet flat close to his office while the wife may prefer a high-priced small apartment in her matrilocal area so as to stay closer to her aged parents. Within each of these cases, the members may perceive the advantages of specific apartments in a different way.

Therefore, a member's predisposition is a function of his buying motives and evaluative perceptions (beliefs) of specific brands in accomplishing or barring his buying motives. Motives are mostly derived from biogenic or psychogenic needs, wants or desires of the person in buying and consuming a product or service. However, most buying motives are generated from learned predisposition curved out of the consumer's past experiences and acculturation.

One more determining factor of a family member's formation of predisposition is his own evaluative belief about particular brand choice options as to whether they obstruct or aid the attainment of buying motives. They exclusively encompass the person's evaluation of an alternative as a perceived gadget to gratify a set of motives.

Determinants of Differences in Predispositions

From the earlier sub-sections, it is quite evident that there are three major factors in this theory which direct a family member's buying motives, evaluate beliefs, and result in a set of predispositions.

The first factor is derived from a chain of exogenous constructs shown at the top of Fig.12.2. This comprises of individual member's personality, lifestyle, perception of his social class, role orientation within the family, and the reference group of the individual family members. The second factor contributing to the cognitive facets of individual members is the exposure to relevant information from an array of sources (encompassing from the mass media and exposure to word-of-mouth communication) in the course of family decision-making. Nonetheless, the members are likely to be at variance in terms of their ease of access to sources, extent of overt search for information, etc. For example, the husband may simply collect information on a particular buying decision from various accessible sources close to his office, and be more sensitive to information obtained from informal sources (colleagues, friends, etc). Therefore, he may involve more rigorously in the search process before reaching the final buying decision than any other members of the family. The child, on the other hand, may be more sensitive towards point-of-purchase displays and television advertisements as compared to the other members. To be more specific, the family members normally tend to be highly diverse even in terms of sensitivity to their information sources and word-of-mouth communication.

Determinants of Autonomous vs. Joint Decision-Making

Another very crucial aspect of family decision-making is the identification of factors that tell about joint decision-making. In Fig.12.2, these factors have been derived from a mixture of sources identified by Prof. Sheth. These are as follows:

- *Social class*: Prof. Sheth has concluded from a number of studies that there is a higher degree of independence of buying decisions among all members in both the upper and lower social classes. However, the prevalence of joint decision-making is expected to take place in middle-class families.
- *Role orientation*: This refers to the explicit or implicit roles fixed to the members of the family in the course of constant interface.
- *Life cycle of family*: The chance in joint decision is inversely related to the age of the family. Clearly, the probability of joint decision-making is more common among the newly married couple and comparatively less prevalent amongst the couples in 'Empty Nest'.
- *Perceived risk in buying decisions*: Greater the perceived risk of making a wrong decision for the family, higher is the chance of joint decision-making among the members of the family.
- *Importance of purchase to the family*: Greater the importance of a specific buying decision to the family, higher is the probability that the decision would be joint, with majority of the family members partaking in it.
- *Time pressure*: If the time pressure for decision-making is high, the incidence of joint decision-making is likely to be increased. The increase in number of working wives and the resultant fast life in this era is probably one of the reasons of time pressure.

Process of Joint Decision-Making

The nucleus of the theory of family buying decisions is, no doubt, the process of joint decision-making. Some issues partaking with joint decision are as follows:

- *Who is the initiator in the buying process*? Prof. Sheth opined that it mainly depends on lifestyle and role-orientation of the family that who will act as an initiator of a particular purchase decision.
- *Who is the information provider related to the joint buying decision*? As per the analytical insight of Prof. Sheth, drawn out of several studies, it may be stated that all the members share the task of information provider depending on their expertise in different facets of a particular decision. For example, the fathers or uncles are supposed to contemplate on mechanical and financial aspects of the product, as ideally they are also the payers. On the other hand, the mothers or the elderly ladies of the house tend to focus more on ornamental and showy aspects, and the children on societal aspects (due to high belongingness need) of buying decision. It is, nonetheless observed that in these days the children, predominantly the teen-aged children, have been the major source of information for a numerous joint decisions even including those of cars, home theatres, apartments, and vacations.
- *Who is the buyer or shopper*? Many a times, contrary to the common belief, the lady of the house buys apparels and many other personal items for the male members. Many working ladies nowadays take their financial decisions independently.
- *What are the issues of conflict in joint decision-making*? The *issue of conflict* may arise in most of the joint buying decisions. According to Prof. Sheth, the conceptual framework of interpersonal conflict presented by March and Simon (1959) seems extremely pertinent to the family decision-making. Under different situations, each of the family members assumes the role of the head. Particularly for cheap and more individualistic items, decisions are often likely to be autonomic and any of the partners is held responsible for the purchase. The more expensive the items are, greater is the chance of joint decision-making. As the family resources are limited and everybody in the family wants to derive maximum satisfaction out of its utilization, many a times family members disagree about the goals and differ in perceptions about the goal objects. This situation leads to the state of conflict. Therefore, the family decisions may either be consensual or accommodative. For consensual decisions, everyone in the family may be in agreement with the preferred conclusion. Nevertheless, accommodative decisions become essential especially to resolve conflict situations.

There are basically four ways that families usually use to resolve conflict.

- *Problem-solving*. In case of problem-solving, the need for more and more information is prioritized. The natural and immediate consequence of using this tool is to aggressively search for more information or focus more on available information. Thereafter, lots of information is gathered from reliable personal sources. Finally, attempts are made to find out the fresh set of options which have not yet been considered in the course of joint decision-making.

- *Persuasion*: Sometimes, a situation of conflict arises amongst the family members regarding those particular criteria by which evaluation of alternatives is done. Normally, these conflicts are resolved by efforts of persuasion. For example, the wife may initiate the thought of buying a new car, while the other family members may persuade her that buying an apartment is the call for the day.
- *Bargaining*: If, by persuasion, the incongruity over buying motives is not dissolved, then the gadget of bargaining is resorted. For example, the father may be allowed to buy a new laptop for his business activities, but he will have to provide some desirable alternatives to the other members of the family in return. This is almost a give-and-take arrangement.
- *Politics*: When the members of a family not only vary in terms of particular buying motives, but also, essentially, on maximum lifestyle components, the constant conflict is expected to be resolved either by the break-up of the family structure or by politics. Many of the Indian joint families are broken as a result of such family politics and disagreement in motives and varying lifestyles resulting from the generation gap. The later generally results in development of coalitions or subgroups with common motive in an attempt to segregate the member who is identified as the key one behind the conflict. Even though this kind of conflict resolution technique in buying decisions is not expected to be pervasive, it is not absolutely exceptional. To be specific, in the children-centric Indian families, children are often taken as coalition partners of one parent against the other. These days, we even observe coalition subgroup formed by teenaged children against their parents, especially in case of buying expensive mobile handsets or television sets.

Nevertheless, there is no doubt that any type of conflict within a family is detrimental from the social welfare perspective. Still, because of difference in buying motives and different individual predispositions, cent percent avoidance of conflict is simply not possible in this changing socio-dynamics in 21st century. Nonetheless, it is better to resolve conflicts by the process of problem-solving and persuasion, as they are less damaging tools than bargaining and politics.

Closing Case

National Kiosk—Targeting the Niche

Sashikant Verma is the Sales Manager of National Kiosk, an eminent 53-year-old Tours and Travels Company in Delhi, India. It principally arranges nationwide tours. Its famous tour packages comprise Andaman tours, Rajasthan tours, Delhi–Agra and Uttaranchal trips, different South India tours (14, 16, 17, and 19 days tours), and Porbandar–Somnath trip. National Kiosk has tie-ups with many major deluxe hotels across the nation. So ideally, they target the upper income class to be their prospective customers.

Recently, there has been a problem with its Andaman tours division. For the last four years, its business has been in downtrend. Shashikant has had an interaction with the sales officers of the division and they have cited several problems. In the first place, they blame the company for fixing high price for the said tour. Secondly, they mention about the reluctance of the Indian families about their brand. Finally, they put the blame on their superiors for imposing too much work pressure on them. They feel due to that pressure, they have not been able to concentrate on potential clients properly. Being highly confused by their dissimilar responses, Shashikant takes a break from his office and goes to Mr. Sumangal Sheth's house for a discussion. Mr. Sheth is a busy corporate executive from Delhi and resides in a joint family consisting of his wife, son, brother, sister-in-law, and their daughter. They belong to the upper class segment of the capital city. Every year they go for a tour through National Kiosk. So Shashikant has a long-term association with them.

Cellular jail in Andaman depicts the patriotic and nostalgic attraction of the place

In the evening in Sumangal Sheth's house, as the discussion in the issue proceeds, Ravikant has kept on surprising.

'The Singapore–Bangkok–Kuala Lumpur trip now costs just ₹50,000–55,000, whereas a 12 days Andaman tour consisting of Havelock–Ross–Viper–Neil–Baratang–Jolly boy–Port Blair costs almost ₹40,000. If that so, who will not prefer to go to abroad?' claims Sumangal.

Rajani, his sister-in-law, continues, 'Last month my friend Raima went for continental tour and those are affordable too these days… now if I go to the Andaman, what will Raima and all think about me? So I will definitely see that my husband plans for a foreign trip, like Singapore or Bangkok.'

'But one must agree that Andaman Islands are comparable in terms of beauty with any other foreign nations, moreover Port Blair has a lot of patriotic sentiments and historical values…', exclaims Rajnish, Sumangal's brother and an Army officer.

'But Papa, some of my friends are visiting Bangkok this year… you cannot compare it with Andaman… after all it is a national tour', claims Sati, Rajnish's daughter.

'I agree with her', Umesh, Sumangal's son comes forward.

'But won't there be hassles for arranging visa', Jyoti, Sumangal's wife joins the discussion.

'Not at all mom', says Umesh, 'most of the tour companies are making all such arrangements for clients'.

'But National Heritage Cellular Jail is something worth to visit. The memories of Veer Savarkar and Ullaskar Dutta are attached with it', Jyoti tries to convince… 'Moreover the corals of Jolly boy are worth seeing. Radhanagar Beach in Havelock has been rated as World's seventh most beautiful beach.'

Radhanagar beach in Havelock, Andaman

'But after all Bangkok would be a foreign tour', say Umesh and Sumangal together. 'Moreover when Umesh and Sati want to go abroad, we should accept that. After all they are younger and this is their time to enjoy life. Further, with just a difference of ₹10,000 if a foreign trip is possible then that would be a good trade-off.'

'No', says Jyoti, 'Children should also have some patriotic feelings. They should know their country first. Moreover, I want to see the cellular jail at least once in my lifetime.'

The discussion goes on and Shashikant remains a silent listener. While coming back home, the discussion reverberates in his mind and he thinks that this might be the scenario of any child-centric Indian family. Shashikant is now in quandary—How to promote their star package 'Andaman tours'?

Question

1. If you were Sashikant, how would you design your pack so as to convince all the family members?
2. What positioning and promotional strategy would you design for the purpose?

Summary

A family has an organized position in the bigger society and endows with the background for consumer socialization, whereby children also learn consumer tastes, preferences, and purchasing patterns. Therefore, developing the targeting strategies, the marketers must lay proper emphasis on familial influence on each purchase situations.

No doubt, the parents play a significant role in the process of consumer socialization, especially in providing information on the logical facets of consumption. However, their impact varies with the nature of the product and across the stages of the decision process.

Moreover, there are different roles performed by the individuals in a family, namely, initiators, influencers, gatekeepers, deciders, buyers, and users. The buying role of the member is fashioned partly by cultural and social determinants, particularly the mass culture, sub-cultural influences, social class and reference groups.

Decisions within the family can be categorized into four major types, namely, wife-dominant, husband-dominant, syncratic, and autonomic. These types depend on the degree to which the husband and wife act separately or together in making purchases. Children, in many cases, become the major influencing factor in many purchase decisions.

The family also has a life cycle that determines its needs and expenditure patterns at various phases of an individual's life span. The family life cycle principally encompasses nine stages which illustrate changes in the family's buying and behaviour patterns over a period of time. This poises great inference for segmenting families into various markets.

Key Terms

Household A group of people living under one roof.

Nuclear family A family consisting of husband, wife, and offspring.

Extended family A family consisting of the nuclear family plus the husband and/or wife's mother, father and/or other relative.

Family life cycle The idea that families move through a series of stages in a developmental fashion over a time line.

Purchase roles These include the various roles performed by family members or industrial buying groups in the buying decision process.

Syncratic decision Important decisions in which husband and wife participate jointly.

Autonomic decisions Decisions of lesser importance that either the husband or wife may make independently.

Family decision stages The steps in the decision process used by a family to purchase products or services.

Consumer socialization Processes by which children acquire skills, knowledge, and attitudes relevant to their functioning as future consumers in the market place.

Questions

1. Distinguish between the terms 'household' and 'family'.
2. Illustrate how the process of a complex buying decision might operate for a college student who wants to buy a laptop?
3. State the possible purchase decision process that may take place in your family at the time of purchasing a washing machine? Which individuals in your family have the roles of gatekeeper, influencer, decider, buyer, and user? To what extent do these roles change across different product categories in your family?

Critical Assignment

1. Prepare a list of about three durable products and fast moving consumer goods consumed by your family. In case of each product, try to identify the dominant player and the kind of power he/she asserts in the decision process.
2. Select a family from your locality and some items used by male, female, and child and show how the family decision-making is performed in each case.

Section IV

Consumer Decision-Making and Consumer Behaviour Models

Chapter **13**

Diffusion of Innovations and Opinion Leadership

Chapter Goals

After completing this chapter, you will be able to understand

- **what diffusion of innovation means**
- **the diffusion process**
- **the adoption process**
- **the impact of personal influence and opinion leadership on diffusion of innovations**

Opening Vignette

Fevistik—Unique Innovation in India

Pidilite Industries Limited is an Indian company that enjoyed remarkable achievement since its inception in 1959. It was the pioneer in innovative adhesives in India. With the flagship brand *Fevicol*, with its all other brand extensions *Fevikwik*, *Fevibond*, *Fevigum*, *Fevistik*, and *Fevicryl*, the company's constantly swayed over 70% of the total market share in adhesive category. It must be noted that in 2005, *Fevicol* stood 24th among the top 150 Indian brands. *Pidilite's Fevistik* could be considered as a brand extension of *Fevicol*. This glue stick was normally used for gluing paper to plastics, rubber, ceramic, and metals. It was used as an adhesive even for the absorbent stuffs like wood, leather, cardboard, thermocole, plywood, fabrics, etc. *Fevistik* had a unique advantage of instant bonding and was tolerant to temperature ranging from –40°C to 90°C. Its clog-resistant nozzle prevented it from unnecessary wastage and also from splitting here and there.

Although *Fevistik* pioneered in selling this product, the innovation of glue stick was owed to the brand *Pritt* of the *Henkel* group. In fact, it was long back in 1969, *Henkel*'s R&D division invented *Pritt* glue stick. Nonetheless, *Fevistik* might be considered as the Indian edition of *Pritt*. Therefore, although *Pritt* might be the market leader in the adhesives category across the globe, *Fevistik* was the pioneer to bring in the glue stick product in the Indian adhesive market. In fact, being the exemplar of consumer-centric innovation, *Fevistik*, gradually became the market leader with little more than 90% market share in this huge ₹35 crore glue stick market in India.

One could remember the messiness of the bottled-liquid or tubed glue used in the offices, schools, and homes. Users found their papers becoming untidy, the hands used to get grimy and sometimes even the applicator set on the cap of the glue bottle used to fall inside the bottle. *Fevistik*, in a single shot, solved these problems. With the innovation of *Fevistik*, *Pidilite* made a revolution in the entire adhesive segment by changing the dynamics of this product category and changed the customers' usage pattern of adhesives.

Glue stick: a novel concept in India

However, there were several other factors that contributed to the success of the brand in India. The company was using different customized promotional campaigns aimed at both home and office sectors. Moreover, *Fevistik*'s new small portable pack '*Fevistik Pocket*' priced only ₹10 turned out as a miracle in the household segment. *Fevistik* also had 8 gm, 15 gm, and 22 gm packs for targeting the multiple user segments. Its unique selling proposition claiming easily portable, safe for kids, excellent quality, and non-messiness and tidiness, etc., positioned it as an 'easy to use novel adhesive'. The storage of this product also became simple. Moreover, an additional foreign manufacturing unit of *Fevistik* had provided this small brand a global image. Therefore, in order to make the innovation successful, the marketers need to ensure its diffusion amongst the target group. The entire process of diffusion of innovation is discussed with suitable examples in this chapter.

Source: http://marketingpractice.blogspot.com/2007/09/fevistik-clean-sticking.html; http://www.slideshare.net/amit_k102/product-branding-of-fevistik-and-komfo-by-amit-singh; Chopra Komal, Pidilite Industries: Fevicol Success Story; http://www.ibscdc.org/Case_Studies/Marketing/Marketing%20Strategies/MKS0072P.htm, accessed on March 6, 2011.

CONCEPT OF DIFFUSION OF INNOVATIONS

Today's marketers by and large depend on new products to amplify their sales volume. The implication of the term 'new product' is, however, manifold. First, this may refer to a product which is totally *new to the market and no firm has ever delivered such product*. For example, *Apple* invented i-pads or tablet PCs. New products may also mean those *products which are new to the company. Secondly, new product may also mean product that had been invented much before, but the company is reshaping it in its own way.* For example, *Saffola* caters to a special need of cholesterol-free oil in the edible oil segment. Thirdly, the products may be *new to the particular segment—e.g.,* cellular phones and mobile connections were initially targeted towards the urban elite segment. But gradually as these segments were saturated, the mobile hanset manufacturers and service providers moved down the line even to the bottom of the pyramid with cheaper sets and easy filling top-ups.

The *diffusion of innovation* refers to the propensity of new products, practices, or ideas to be stretched among people. Generally, as soon as the new products or ideas enter the market, a small group of people, referred as the innovators and experimentals, as mentioned in the VALS classifications, try the product. Then gradually many others adopt it.

Therefore, diffusion may be referred as an inclusive course concerned with the reach of a new product (alternatively an innovation) from its producer to the consumers. The process of diffusion, therefore, identifies the rate of product acceptance and, consequently, mirrors the product life cycle (PLC). It attempts to spot out the innovators in the introduction period of the product life cycle, the early adopters during the growth phase, and late adopters and laggards during the maturity and decline stages, respectively.

The study on this subject, however, achieved its present importance since 1962, as soon as Prof. Everett Rogers, a professor of rural sociology, published his famous book *Diffusion of Innovations.* In the book, Rogers blended researches from over 508 diffusion studies and shaped the most contemporary theory for the adoption of innovations for both individuals and business houses.

The four major influencing constructs of diffusion of innovation proposed in Rogers' book are *innovation, communication channels, time, and a social system.* In other words, diffusion refers to the 'process by which an innovation is communicated through certain channels over time among the members of a social system'. To be more specific, generally the individuals proceed through five key phases of adoption, namely, *knowledge, persuasion, decision, implementation, and confirmation.* Now, the moment an innovation (a new product, new service, new idea, and new practice) happens, it broadens its reach by means of several marketing communication channels (mass media, sales people, and informal communications). Lastly, the social systems (target market) in which the innovation took place determines the rate and speed of adoption, norms on diffusion, roles of opinion leaders and change agents, restraining factors, and also the consequences of adoption of innovation.

Thus, the four basic elements of the diffusion process are as follows:

- Innovation
- Channels of communication
- Social system
- Time

These concepts are elaborated in the next few sections.

CONCEPT OF INNOVATION

Every product passes through a *life cycle*. The concept of product life cycle is well-knit with the occurrence of diffusion of innovation. In fact, it has been already observed in VALS classification that when a new product is launched, not all the consumers are likely to adopt it first. Only the group of people who are more innovative than others, willing to pay a premium price for novel products, and ready to take a risk on untried technology will buy it initially. Hence, it is essential on the part of the marketers to form a positive attitude and also ensure post-purchase satisfaction of the innovators. It is quite obvious that all the rest categories are likely to follow their footsteps and believe in the word-of mouth spread by them. For example, now in the urban areas of South Asia, almost every middle-class and lower-middle-class household has at least one mobile hand-set. Nowadays, with the invention of new hi-tech products, many products are entering into their *decline stage*. For example, Remington Rand, the famous typewriters faced huge decline in sales with the invention of computer. Nowadays, personal computers are gradually being replaced by the laptops, palmtops, and even ipads. Figures 13.1 and 13.2 depict this scenario well.

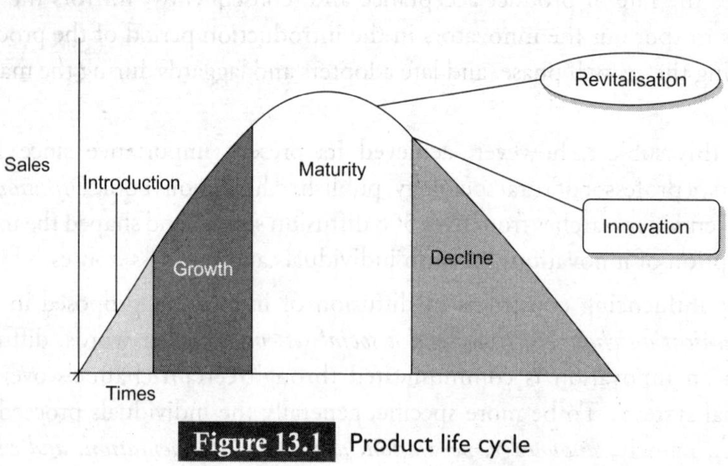

Figure 13.1 Product life cycle

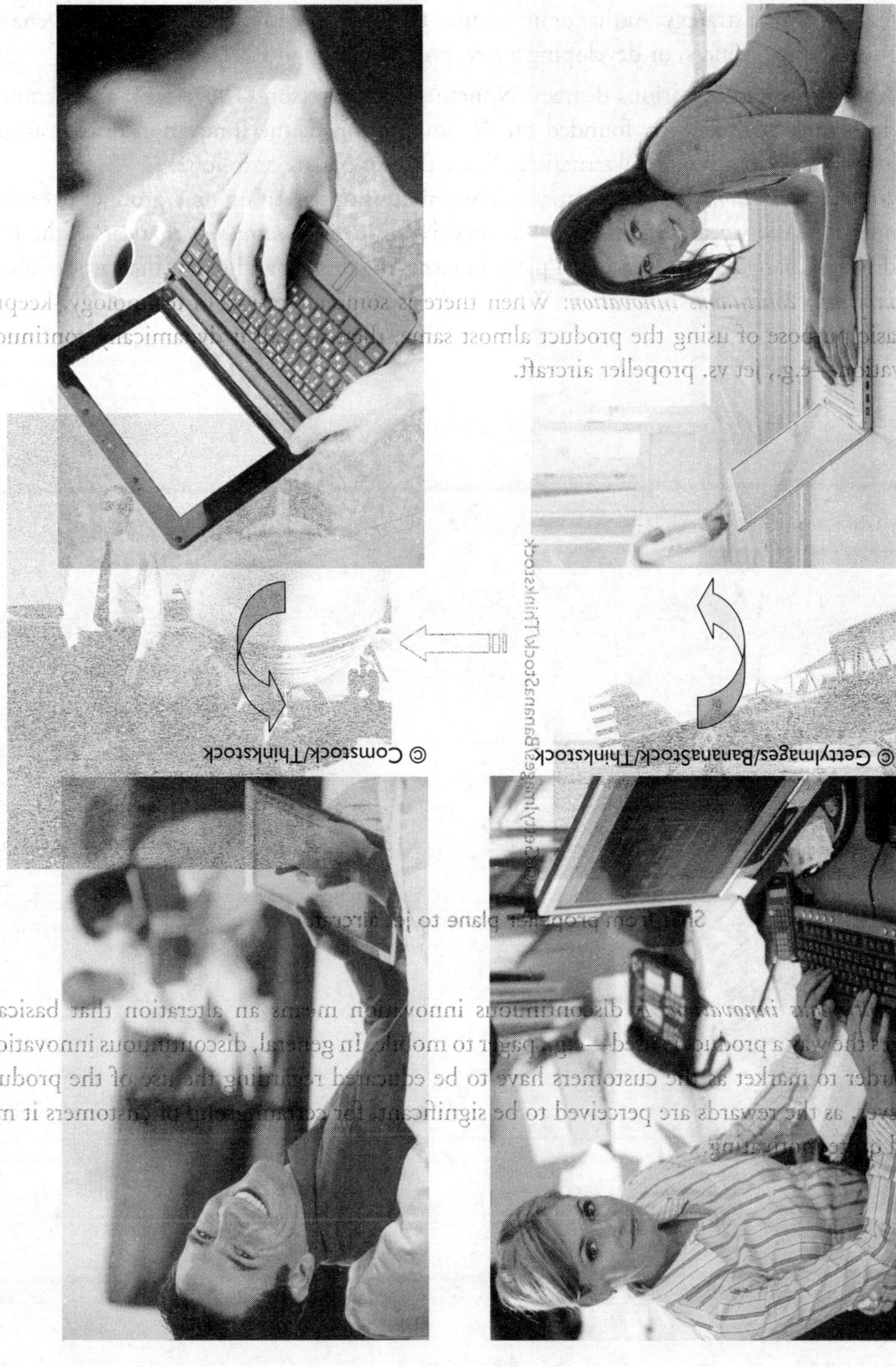

© Jupiterimages/BananaStock/Thinkstock
© iStockphoto/Thinkstock
© GettyImages/BananaStock/Thinkstock
© Comstock/Thinkstock

Figure 13.2 A gradual move from desktops—laptops—palmtops—tablets

No sooner than the product life cycle reaches to the decline stage, the marketers call for modifying their existing marketing mix strategy. At that point of time, they are left with three options: rejuvenating the product, quitting the business, or developing a new product through R&D.

Innovations are generated in various degrees. Nonetheless, Robertson (1967) took an attempt to classify them into three major types, founded on the implication of the innovation on consumer's behavioural pattern in his existing social structure. These three types are as follows:

- *A continuous innovation*: This encompasses continuous improvisation on a product over time. Cars improvise every year, the cars of 1990s are driven much the same way that cars of the 1950 were driven. Changes have only taken place in terms of comfort and use of the car models.
- *A dynamically continuous innovation*: When there is some alteration in technology, keeping the basic purpose of using the product almost same, then we call it dynamically continuous innovation—e.g., jet vs. propeller aircraft.

© GettyImages/BananaStock/Thinkstock

© Ryan McVay/Digital Vision/Thinkstock

Shift from propeller plane to jet aircraft

- *A discontinuous innovation*: A discontinuous innovation means an alteration that basically changes the way a product is used—e.g., pager to mobile. In general, discontinuous innovations are harder to market as the customers have to be educated regarding the use of the product. However, as the rewards are perceived to be significant, for certain group of customers it may sound quite motivating.

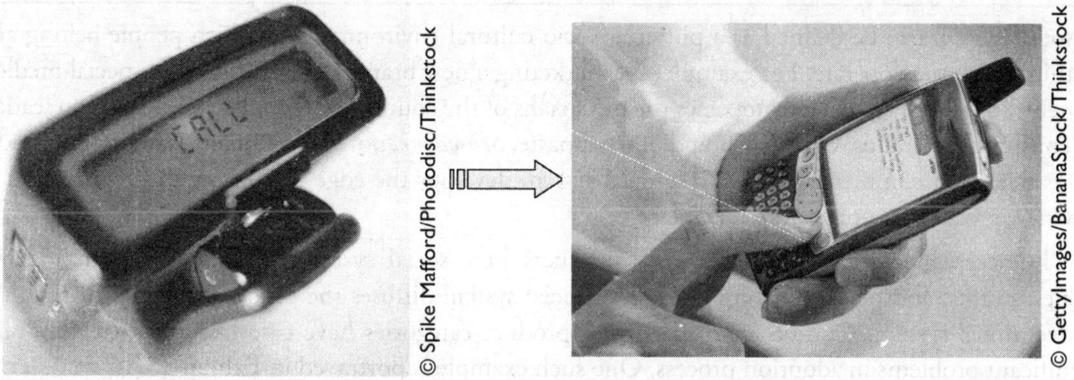

© Spike Mafford/Photodisc/Thinkstock

© GettyImages/BananaStock/Thinkstock

Transition from pager to *BlackBerry* mobiles

CHANNELS OF COMMUNICATION

The launching of the product instantly calls for communication from the marketer to the consumer to generate awareness about the innovation and to endow them with sufficient product-related information. Communication, therefore, is the route of flow of information from marketers by which awareness and knowledge of consumers are developed about the innovation. In fact, through communication the consumers and marketers share necessary product related information with each other to arrive at a mutual understanding.

Marketers looking for diffusion of their innovations usually concentrate on how the product-related information is extended to the target group through different channels of communication. They are also concerned about understanding the implications of their communication messages on the adoption or rejection of new products. In fact, once the awareness is shaped and more and more information reaches the market, the early adopters develop their interest on the product. They usually depend on their friends and relatives (specially the innovators) to assist in their new product evaluation process. This implies that the influence on the end customer occurs from two sources, the impersonal source (marketer's promotional materials or publicities) and the interpersonal source (reference groups, opinion leaders, mainly the innovators). Hence, it is clear at this point that the exposure to marketing communications through mass media (newspapers, television, etc.) is quite higher amongst the early adopters than the late adopters.

SOCIAL SYSTEM

A social system can be defined as a physical, socio-cultural environment to which people belong and within which they operate. For example, for marketing a new brand of herbal tea with special medical benefits, the social system encompasses the physicians of the country, who may serve as opinion leaders to consume the brands. One new brand of toothpaste, *Sensodyne*, portrays a doctor as an opinion leader in its television commercial. Thus, the social system develops the edge within which the diffusion of any new product is supposed to take place.

The acceptance and rejection of new products in a social system largely varies with its own values, norms, and practices. A more modern social system diffuses the innovations quicker than the conventional system. Quite a lot of particular product categories have case histories that exemplify significant problems in adoption process. One such example is portrayed in Exhibit 13.1.

Exhibit 13.1: The Battle of *Scotch Brite* Kitchen Scrubber

Scotch Brite kitchen scrubber created by Minnesota Mining and Manufacturing Co. (3M) was launched in India in 1990. *Scotch Brite* is basically a scrubber slowly entering into the Indian kitchens. The brand principally targeted the upper class and the middle-income households of the country. As it was an innovation in Indian context, rather than facing competition from any rival brands, it had to compete with the traditional practice of cleaning the utensils. The principal buyers, i.e., the homemakers never considered it to be a very essential product. The home makers in most of the households were habituated in using either plastics, nylon scrubs, or sometimes steel wools (for heavy utensils) with a soap bar for the purpose. Coconut fibre was the common scrubber used by the rural housewives. The key barrier for the brand to penetrate the market was primarily the existing dishwashing practices of the customers. Another important challenge for the brand was that in urban upper or middle class households, most of the utensil and wash basin cleaning jobs were done by the maid servants. Therefore, the company realized that it is not sufficient to motivate just the buyers (housewives) but also the users (housemaid) to accept the product as well as the brand.

©iStockphoto/Thinkstock

Cleaning wash basin with *Scotch Brite*

Keeping the importance of the 'primary users' into consideration 3M in 2006 embarked on a huge promotion targeting the maids. In Pune, it prearranged a walk by *Bais* (the maid servants) and vowed through them the use of *Scotch Brite* for cleaning. The participants were also rewarded with gifts. *Scotch Brite* is, therefore, an archetypal customer-centric innovation.

IMPACT OF TIME

Time factor in the diffusion process refers to the moment in which the new product information is hovered in the market and also the moment of purchase. The implication of time in the process of diffusion of innovation is three-faceted. The facets may be elaborated as follows:

(a) *Purchase time*: Purchase time refers to the period between the first product-related information floated to consumers and their purchase/rejection point. The length of this time span determines the diffusion rate of any innovation. In international market, it will determine whether to go for a 'waterfall' or 'sprinkler' strategy. One more significant implication of the 'time' is the trend line on which an innovation gradually becomes a necessity in the minds of early and late adopters within a society over a period of time. One may recollect the case of *Aquaguard* water purifier in India launched by *Eureka Forbes*. It replaced the traditional non-electrical water purifiers and became a necessity to every middle or upper class Indian household or private and public organization.

(b) *Adopter classes*: Rogers, the eminent professor, classified the adopters by time and rate of adoption. His researches portrayed five classes/categories of adopters: (i) Innovators, (ii) Early adopters, (iii) Early majority, (iv) Late majority, and (v) Laggards. Ideally, Rogers' division of adopter classes (Fig. 13.3) is also highly correlated with the gradual movement of the product through its life cycle.

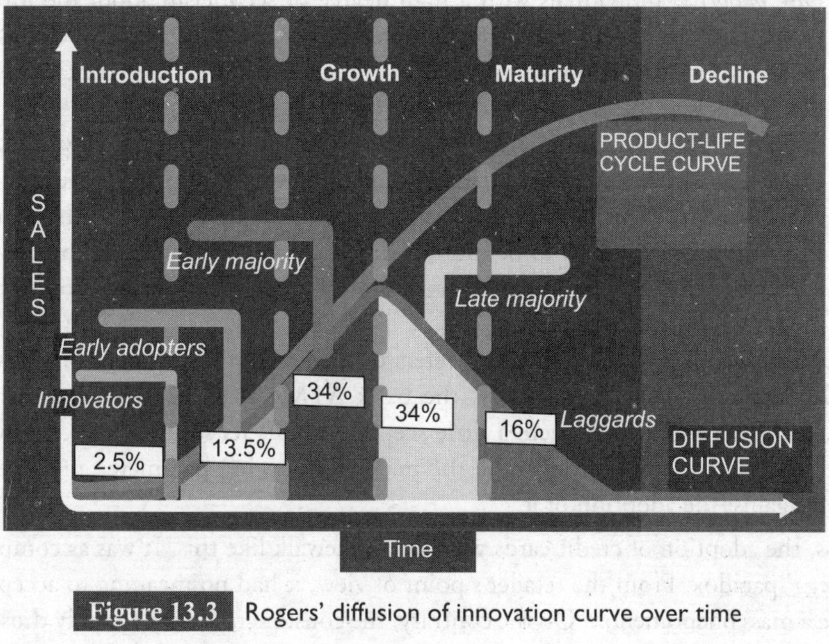

Figure 13.3 Rogers' diffusion of innovation curve over time

The PLC curve deviates from the adoption curve in a way that the former represents sales levels on the vertical axis and the latter depicts the percentage of adopters over the adoption period. Based on this concept, the adopter classes are illustrated as follows:

(i) *Innovators*: Innovators are the first category to welcome and adopt a new product in the market place. Usually this group comprises of younger generations from well-to-do families. They are by nature risk-takers, tech-savvy, and normally have proximity to scientific sources and greater interface with other innovators. They are usually 2.5% of all those who ultimately adopt the product over time.

(ii) *Early adopters*: This is the second group to adopt an innovation after the innovators. In comparison to the innovators, these individuals have a greater chance to become opinion leaders. They too, like the innovators, are usually younger in age, with higher social status, affluence, and relatively higher educational background. They are generally more socially interactive than the remaining adopter classes (except the innovators). However, they are very much selective and rational in product/brand choice unlike the innovators and develop certain firm evaluative criteria.

(iii) *Early majority*: Once the innovation succeeds in the early majority class, people with average social status, education, and relatively risk-averse start adopting it. It needs no mention that for these types of adopters, the time of adoption is considerably longer than the innovators and early adopters.

(iv) *Late majority*: Individuals with a high degree of scepticism adopt the innovation after the majority of society has already adopted it. Late majority usually belongs to the below average social status and has low level of affluence. They do keep contact with others, but not as much as the opinion leaders.

(v) *Laggards*: They form the last consumer category to adopt an innovation. Contrasting to all the earlier categories, the consumers of this group have aversion towards the change-agents. This cluster of the customers normally belongs to the older age group. Laggards naturally tend to be more inclined towards maintaining the age-old 'customs and traditions'. Some of them are economically weak, have interaction only with family members and close friends.

(c) *Rate of adoption:* The rate of adoption refers to the speed of acceptance of a new product by the ultimate adopters. To exemplify, the bank ATM cards experienced a fast adoption in India. Initially some people were a little sceptical about its security aspect; but later on the convenience factors turned out to be the major influencing parameter and ruled out all the barriers against the adoption of it.

Nonetheless, the adoption of credit cards was not a cakewalk like this. It was as complicated as the 'chicken-and-egg' paradox. From the retailer's point of view, it had no meaning to accept credit cards until it became a mass phenomenon. On the contrary, the consumers looked for only those cards which were largely accepted by most of the retailers. Consequently, it was also essential to expedite the process by roping large corporate accounts into the net. This attempt made the credit cards acceptable by both the retailers and consumers.

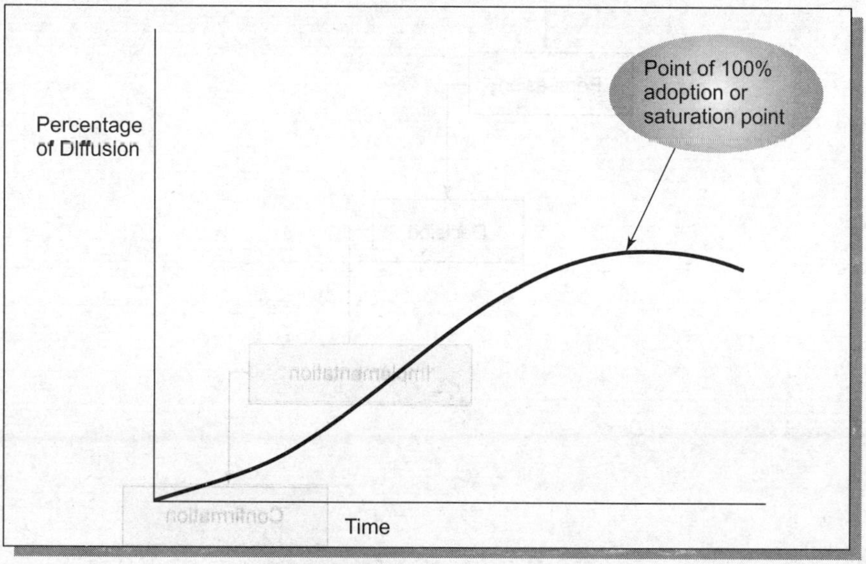

Figure 13.4 The adoption rate

The nightclubs and discos in metro-cities in India spread quickly among urban well-to-do youths at large because of its apparently *bona fide* portrayal of a striking urban lifestyle.

However, the bell-shaped curve often demonstrates the rate of adoption of a new product. In fact, the S-shaped curve reveals the snowballing of the adoptions across customer segments. The *saturation point* is the greatest fraction of consumers probable to adopt a product over a certain time period.

In case of television in the Indian sub-continent, the saturation level in the desired target market is almost cent percent. Nonetheless, at times innovations may *not be adopted*. Like, some young individuals due to low propensity of ailment do not adopt medical insurance policies as they do not use them much.

PROCESS OF ADOPTION

Rogers (2003) depicts the innovation-decision procedure as 'an information-seeking and information-processing activity, where an individual is motivated to reduce uncertainty about the advantages and disadvantages of an innovation'. According to Rogers (2003), the innovation-decision process comprises five basic phases, namely, (i) knowledge, (ii) persuasion, (iii) decision, (iv) implementation, and (v) confirmation. These stages are normally sequential. The stages are demonstrated in Fig. 13.5.

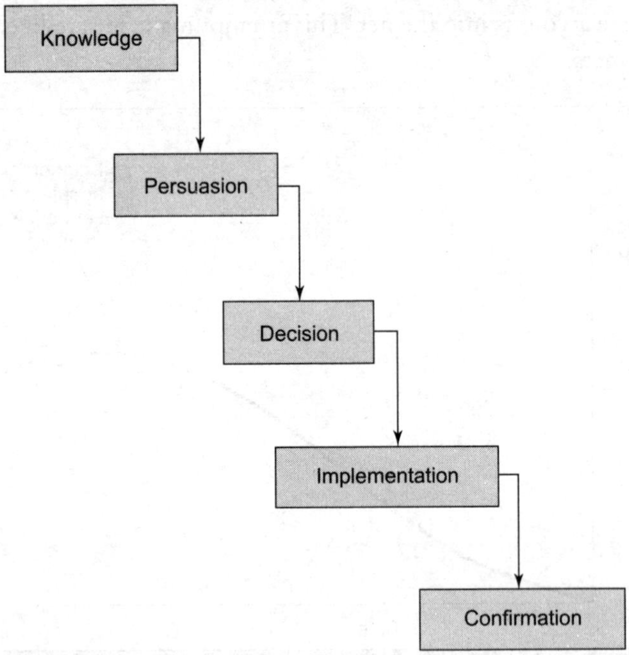

Figure 13.5 A model of five stages in the innovation-decision process

Knowledge Stage

The first stage of innovation-decision process is the knowledge stage. In this step, consumers gradually learn about the occurrence of innovation and deliberately search for information from the environment comprising reference groups, opinion leaders, and several marketing stimuli. The information typically sought at this stage is about the nature of innovation, how to use it, the purpose of using it, and also how to acquire it. According to Rogers, all these aspects constitute three major types of knowledge, namely, (1) awareness-knowledge, (2) how-to-knowledge, and (3) principles-knowledge. They are discussed in the following paragraphs.

- *Awareness-knowledge*: Awareness-knowledge stands for the knowledge of the innovation's occurrence. Ideally, this kind of knowledge may stimulate the consumer to seek for more information about the innovation, develop more knowledge about it, and finally adopt it.
- *How-to-knowledge*: The second kind of knowledge, namely, how-to-knowledge, seeks information about how to use an innovation properly. According to Rogers, this knowledge is a very important parameter in the innovation-decision process. To augment the possibility of adoption of an innovation, a customer should have an adequate level of how-to-knowledge before the trial of the innovation. Especially for complex technical innovation, this knowledge is very crucial.
- *Principles-knowledge*: Principles-knowledge encompasses the execution principles unfolding how and why an innovation has to be used. An innovation may even be adopted without this

knowledge; in that case, there remains a high chance of misuse of the innovation. This misuse will bar the users to properly understand the convenience of the product-usage and lead to its discontinuance.

Persuasion Stage

The second step of the diffusion of innovation process is persuasion. This step takes place when the individual has a strong negative or positive attitude toward the innovation, but 'the formation of a favourable or unfavourable attitude toward an innovation does not always lead directly or indirectly to an adoption or rejection' (Rogers, 2003). The individual shapes his or her attitude after he or she knows about the innovation, so the persuasion stage follows the knowledge stage in the innovation-decision process. Moreover, Rogers claims, unlike the cognitive (or knowing) centred knowledge stage, the persuasion stage is more affective (or feeling) centred. In this phase, the consumer is more concerned about the degree of uncertainty of the performance of the new product and also the social consequence of its usage. Therefore, the social reinforcement from others (friends, peers, neighbours, etc.) influences the individual's attitude and beliefs about the innovation. The customers at this stage keep on searching for information to evaluate the innovation and related promotional messages through the decision stage. Therefore, the marketers not only need to innovate in terms of the products, but also require taking a serious call on mix and match of effective combinations of other marketing mix elements.

Decision Stage

At the third stage of the innovation-decision process, namely, the decision stage, the consumer either adopts or rejects the innovation. While adoption means 'full use of an innovation as the best course of action available,' rejection refers to 'not to adopt an innovation' (Rogers, 2003). According to Rogers, greater the chance of trial-ability of the products, higher is their probability of getting adopted quickly. It is our natural tendency to first give a try on the usage of the innovation and then, if it fits with the customer's need, arrive to an adoption decision. The explicit trial sessions can expedite the innovation-decision process. Nonetheless, rejection can also occur at any stage of the innovation-decision process. This particular facet of the consumer psychology is probably the key behind the immense popularity of tiny SKUs (sachets or pouches).

Implementation Stage

At the implementation stage, an innovation is practised. Nevertheless, an innovation brings the novelty in which 'some degree of uncertainty is involved in diffusion' (Rogers, 2003). Uncertainty about the results of the usage of innovation still persists as a predicament at this stage. This results in the dependence of opinion leaders to understand the technical features of the product properly, and thereby, reducing the risk of consequences. But once, the innovators accept the product; the novelty of the innovation gradually reduces. At this point, many other competing brands enter the market and the product moves from growth phase to maturity level.

Reinvention takes place normally at the implementation stage. Reinvention, as Rogers puts, is 'the degree to which an innovation is changed or modified by a user in the process of its adoption and implementation'. Also, Rogers (2003) elucidated the distinction between concept of invention and innovation. He says, 'Invention is the process by which a new idea is discovered or created'; on the contrary, the adoption of an innovation refers to the 'process of using an existing idea'. Rogers adds that the more reinvention happens, the more speedily an innovation is adopted and becomes a practice. For example, as innovations, computers and cell phones are the gadgets with the possibility of multi-faceted value-added usages and, thereby, are more open to reinvention. Reinvention may occur in terms of process reengineering also. In this context, one may recall, the use of Quick Response (QR) code cards as the novel way to amplify sales. *Cottonworld*, a leading apparel brand, adopted this method to develop customized interface with the Generation Y. The popularity of these cards reached even to the sky heights where *Jet Airways* used their in-flight magazines with QR codes to facilitate the consumers to download flight information, sector details, and many other tits and bits. As Kim Saldanha, Vice President (Marketing, Consumer Centria), puts it, 'QR codes are turning out to be the perfect marketing package—a brief, compact, message driver, and engagement tool—all loaded in one single code'.

Confirmation Stage

Though the adoption decision has already been made in the previous stage of innovation-decision, the individual looks for information to sustain his or her decision in the confirmation stage. As Rogers (2003) puts it, the decision can be upturned if the consumer is 'exposed to conflicting messages about the innovation'. Thus, attitude formation reveals as the decisive parameter at the confirmation stage. Based on the aids to stick in adoption of the innovation and the attitude of consumers towards it, later adoption or discontinuance may occur at this stage.

ATTRIBUTES OF INNOVATIONS AND RATE OF ADOPTION

Rogers (2003) illustrates the innovation-diffusion process as 'an uncertainty reduction process' (p. 232), and suggests some attributes of innovations that facilitate to reduce uncertainty of adoption of innovation. Basically, as Rogers suggests, five basic characteristics attribute to the rate of adoption. They are (i) relative advantage, (ii) compatibility, (iii) complexity, (iv) trialability, and (v) observability.

Relative Advantage

Rogers (2003) delineates relative advantage as 'the degree to which an innovation is perceived as being better than the idea it supersedes'. The cost of purchase, social status of the customer, and his motivation aspects of adopting the innovations altogether constitute the term 'relative advantage'. For example, the innovators, early adopters, and early majority are normally more motivated by esteem need for accepting innovations. On the other hand, the late majority and laggards lay huge importance on the economic and the social acceptance of the product.

Compatibility

In some diffusion study, relative advantage and compatibility were treated as similar aspects; nonetheless, they are conceptually quite diverse. Rogers (2003) claims, 'Compatibility is the degree to which an innovation is perceived as consistent with the existing values, past experiences, and needs of potential adopters'. A lack of compatibility of the innovated product with the needs of the customers, sometimes, might dimidiate the customers to use the product. On the other hand, if any innovation matches with the lifestyle and need of the target population, it will turn out to be an innovator.

For example, considering the huge power cuts and low income level of the Indian semi-urban and rural expanses, *Godrej* and *Boyce* launched an innovative low-cost, tiny refrigerator named '*Chotukool*' in 2010. The portable refrigerator has a capacity of 45 litres and is priced only at ₹ 3750. The project is now piloting in Maharashtra, Gujarat, and Karnataka. By the first quarter of 2012, it is expected to roll out commercially across the nation. In its design, the compressor was replaced by a cooling chip and a fan to make it more efficient and economical. It basically is a sort of 'reverse engineering' as claimed by Mr. G. Sunderraman, Vice President of Corporate Development at *Godrej* and *Boyce*. To ensure its visibility and accessibility amongst the rural mass, it was distributed by the members of the micro-finance groups in the rural periphery.

Complexity

The other aspect, complexity, as defined by Rogers (2003), is 'the degree to which an innovation is perceived as relatively difficult to understand and use'. Unlike the other attributes, complexity is usually inversely associated with the rate of adoption. Thus, too much complexity of an innovation is a significant impediment in its fast adoption.

Trialability

Rogers (2003) defines trialability as 'the degree to which an innovation may be experimented within a limited basis'. Hence, trialability is associated with the adoption rate. It has been already mentioned that in the implementation phase of the innovation-decision process, there is a probability that reinvention takes place during the trial stage. This may modify the process of innovation by the prospective adopter. Improvised reinvention may generate quicker adoption of the innovation.

Observability

The fifth characteristic of innovation is observability. Rogers (2003) explained observability as 'the degree to which the results of an innovation are visible to others'. Role modeling (or peer observation) is the primary stimulus in the adoption and diffusion of technology (Parisot, 1997). Analogous to relative advantage, compatibility, and trialability, observability also is directly correlated with the adoption rate of an innovation.

To sum up, Rogers (2003) claims that innovations contributing more relative advantage, compatibility, simplicity, trialability, and observability will be adopted more rapidly than the others.

IMPACT OF OPINION LEADERSHIP IN THE PROCESS OF DIFFUSION OF INNOVATIONS

Opinion leadership is the route by which the opinion leader off the record persuades the dealings or attitudes of the opinion seekers or just opinion recipients. Opinion receivers recognize the opinion leaders as a greatly trustworthy, objective source of product-related information and the people who can help them to trim down their search and evaluation time and also, reduce the perceived risk associated with the purchase.

Opinion leaders are interested to provide information or guidance to others, partly because, by doing so they feel their own status and self image are enhanced and also partly because such counselling may reduce any post-purchase dissonance that they may contain. Other motives consist of product and message linkage or any other involvement. Studies of opinion leadership point that this effect is normally product category specific, in which they are interested or have expertise. For example, a computer engineer may be an opinion leader to his sister studying in XII standard in case of purchase of a computer. *Sensodyne* has portrayed a dentist to show the hygiene and sensitivity-resistant factor of the toothpaste.

An opinion leader of one product series can be an opinion receiver for a different product category. For example, the teacher recommending books for library purchase may be an opinion seeker in case of purchasing a washing machine. By and large, the opinion leaders are extrovert, confident, innovative people who are socially animated. In addition, they may consider themselves distinguished from others and choose to act differently (or public individuation); many a times for this reason, they turn to be innovators or early adopters. They obtain information about their domain of interest and expertise through passionate readership of interest magazines, search engines, or sometimes simply by new product trials.

Market maven is an extreme variety of opinion leadership. These consumers have a broad array of information about several types of products, retails, and other dimensions of markets. They both kick off discussions with other consumers and act in response to requirements for market information over a broader array of products and services. Market mavens are distinguished from other opinion leaders since their authority roots are not so much from product knowledge but more from general awareness or market awareness that allows them to develop an early knowledge about a broader range of new products and services.

The process of opinion leadership generally occurs among friends, neighbours, and colleagues who are in frequent connection and, thus, have an abundant scope to understand and pass on product-related informal discussions.

Diffusion researchers are mainly concerned with two basic communication aspects of the product innovation, first, the channels through which product-related information is spread to the public and second, the kind of messages that persuade the adoption or rejection of new products or services. The two-step flow of communication theory focuses on the role of interpersonal influence in the reach of innovation-information from the mass media to the prospective customers. This theory develops the base for a much-improvised multi-step communication model, which considers the fact that in the two-way process of communication, the opinion leaders both influence and are influenced by opinion receivers.

It is, therefore, imperative for the marketers to segment their prospective market into opinion leaders and opinion receivers for their particular product categories. As a matter of fact, while directing their promotional efforts to the more influential segments of these markets, the marketers can use these opinion leaders to pass on the information to those who search for product-related suggestions. Marketers, therefore, deliberately aim to create and encourage opinion leadership. They have also recognized that they can generate opinion leaders matching with their own products by incorporating socially concerned, active, and influential people in a calculaive manner to augment the diffusion of their innovations.

Closing Case

Destination Bangladesh

© Photos.com

Destination Bangladesh

Maitree Express was a novel attempt by the Government of India and the Bangladesh Government. It was the first passenger train to travel between the two countries. India and Bangladesh were partitioned in the year 1947, almost with the independence of the country. Many people from Bangladesh had to leave their roots due to the communal riots and had to flee in the neighbouring country India. But the love and attraction for the roots and the nostalgia of childhood continued to prevail amongst many middle-aged and older people.

Initially, there were regular train services between Kolkata and Bangladesh. The trains connected Kolkata, Goalanda (India), Dhaka, and Narayanganj (Bangladesh). Specifically, three trains, namely, *East Bengal Mail*, *East Bengal Express*, and the *Barisal Express*, were operative till 1965. But later they were withdrawn because of several security and war issues amongst the two countries.

In 2007, once again, the then Indian Foreign Minister, Mr. Pranab Mukherjee, in his visit to Bangladesh realized the nostalgic need to bond the countries by railways. Consequently, the decision to reestablish the railways between the two countries was initiated at that time. However, the concept of *Maitree Express* became a reality on April 14 (*Poila Baishakh*, Bengali New Years Day), 2008. At present, only two pairs of trains—one pair of Indian Railways and the other one of Bangladesh Railways travel between Kolkata and Dhaka Cantonment station twice a week as an initial attempt.

© Indiatodayimages.com

Railway service: Establishing Indo–Bangladesh bond

In the train run by Indian Railways, there were altogether five passenger coaches and a pantry car. Most similar to this, the train of Bangladesh Railways also consisted of five coaches, including one pantry car. However, keeping the majority of Muslim population into consideration, Bangladesh Railways had added some unique features to the train, including a '*Namaz Ghar*' (prayer room) and an *azukhana* inside the train.

Mr. Subir Adhikari, a ticket checker in the trains since its reinvention was sitting beside the window of the train in one misty morning of January. As usual, the train moved from Gede, the last Indian station and reached Darsana, the first station of Bangladesh. Mr. Adhikari quietly looked at how the coaches started proceeding one after another behind the distant signal. The roars and rumbles of happiness of the passengers reminded him that they had reached their ancestral root. Entering in India under political and communal compulsion with snivelling eyes leaving behind the terror of losing lives was never a spontaneous move for Mr. Bimal Dey, one of the passengers. He told Mr. Adhikari that he still remembered how they left their own house, the *Tulsi Mancha*, the playground, the school, the teachers, the friends, and many other sweet and sour memories behind and reached India. He was just 12 years old at that time but those incidents remained as scars in his heart and would perhaps flow across his next generations. Mr. Bimal Dey was not an exception. The passengers Mr. Adhikari met almost in all trains had more or less the same compassion.

Mr. Dey, who was in his seventies now, expressed his gratitude towards Indian Government for taking such initiative. He looked quite affluent and so Mr. Adhikari asked him, 'Why didn't you come by flight? You are an aged person. This journey is little bit dreary; you have to bear the long stopovers on both sides of the border for immigration check.'

Mr. Dey said, 'That way you may consider *Maitree Express* as just another mode of transport. But the feeling of reaching my erstwhile motherland is somewhat different. You know, the sights and sounds of my country foster my recollection of childhood days—the same dust and mud, trees and ponds, everything.'

Mr. Adhikari that day was talking to an Indian travel agent Mr. Maitra, who frequently arranges tours to Bangladesh. He asked, 'In spite of so much nostalgic appeal, I wonder why this 360-seater *Maitree Express* never carries passengers to its full capacity.' He continued, 'Mr. Maitra, I am surprised that on the introductory run, the train carried only 65 passengers. You know, sometimes, there were only 10 to 15 people on board.' Shaiful, a Bangladeshi policeman said, 'Adhikarida, you will see that most of the passengers are above sixties. We hardly find the younger generation in this travel.'

Mr. Dey said actually even if the aged people were keen to visit their nostalgic birthplace which they considered as pilgrimage, their children were born in independent India, and at the core of the heart were attached to India only. 'In today's cosmopolitan and global era, my son really does not feel that attraction for his ancestral root. It is just a tour for him and for that he wants to come by flight only. Don't forget, being a corporate executive, time is also an immensely significant factor in his busy schedule', Mr. Dey added.

Mr. Nilmadhab Ghosh, a traveller of the train, looked at Mr. Dey and said, 'There are some other problems too Mr. Dey. See, decades have passed. Everything might have been changed in all these years. I don't know, whether I will really find my village home in Silaidaha and also my childhood school there.' Mr. Ghosh's eyes were filled with tears.

Mr. Adhikari kept mum and started thinking of his uncle who was still alive and was staying in Barisal. For a number of times, the ailing old person had asked him to pay a visit to their ancestral home. But Mr. Adhikari understood, being a government employee, it was not too easy for him to arrange for a visa.

Twice a week the train carries passengers back to their ancestral roots. Similar to any other cross-border tour, stubborn security checks, customs and immigration checks prevail in this journey too. Once the train reaches to Darsana (the first station in Bangladesh), they are taken to the immigration lobby for the necessary checks. At this place, the long halts sometimes become tedious for the older people. Moreover, Mr. Adhikari knows that many travellers feel, they are going to their own country, so their sentiments are somewhat hurt at the time of immigration check. As Mr. Nilmadhab Ghosh puts it, 'Today I am a foreigner to my own country where we used to stay for seven generations.'

After listening to all the discussions Mr. Adhikari looked at Shaiful, the Bangladeshi policeman, and asked, 'Shaiful bhai, I am really astonished even after so much of sentiments and nostalgia attached with this journey, why it is not becoming that popular? Why the train travels with so many vacant seats?' Shaiful agreed, 'Yes dada, it is indeed an innovative attempt on the part of both the Governments, but how to market the service had been hardly thought by both the railways. Till date many people are not aware of the existence of such train. To make this journey popular some sort of marketing push is required'. Mr. Adhikari agreed and all of them reached Dhaka Cantonment station with a wide smile on their faces.

(This case has been designed in the light of the report of Achintyarup Ray and Subhro Maitra titled 'Train of Memories' published in *The Times of India* on March 6, 2011. Nonetheless, the characters of this case are fictitious and resemblance with any person/incident is purely coincidental.)

Questions

1. What according to you were the prime barriers of diffusion of *Maitree Express*?
2. What marketing plans can you suggest for both the railways to make the service popular?
3. What strategies can you suggest for Indian railways to attract the youngsters to this journey?

Summary

Diffusion of innovation refers to the process by which a new product (may be an existing product in the new market or a new item in the product mix from producer's perspective) is adopted by the social system over a time period. The chapter identified that there can be three major types of innovations—continuous innovation, dynamically continuous innovation, and discrete innovation. The concepts have been elaborated in the chapter with real life examples.

The chapter highly draws from Rogers' theory (2003) of diffusion of innovation which clearly categorizes four major elements in the adoption process. These four elements are time, adopter classes, adoption rate, and social system. While time ideally refers to the purchase time, the adopter classes comprise five major categories—innovators, early adopters, late adopters, late majority, and laggards. Innovators, the relatively young, affluent and tech-savvy group, are the primary adopters of the innovation. However, it is the early adopters who are steadier in terms of adoption and finally demonstrate themselves as the opinion leaders. Opinion leaders are referred to those groups of people who have special interest and knowledge for a particular type of product. They facilitate the innovation-decision of late majority and laggards to adopt the product by providing necessary and relevant product-related information to them. The extreme case of opinion-leadership is, however, the market mavens, the very keen people to share product-related and market-related information as they have much more idea about the market place as a whole. Nonetheless, the product adoption rate varies with the relative advantage, compatibility, complexity, trialability, and observability associated with the product purchase and usage. The social system, however, comprises of the target market and the marketing environment in which they operate. Therefore, owing to the Rogers' theory, the chapter discussed in details how an innovation in the market place is diffused or adopted by the en masse in five sequential stages: (i) knowledge, (ii) persuasion, (iii) decision, (iv) implementation, and (v) confirmation.

Key Terms

Innovation It refers to a product which is totally new to the market and no firm has ever delivered such product. It may also refer to those products which are new to the company. A new product may also mean that the product had been invented much before, but the company is reshaping it in its own way.

Diffusion It refers to the propensity of new products, practices, or ideas to be stretched among people.

Adoption When the diffusion forms a permanent purchase pattern, it becomes adoption.

Innovators The relatively young, affluent, and tech-savvy group of customers. They are the primary adopters of the innovation.

Early adopters This is the second group to adopt an innovation after the innovators.

Late adopters Once the product succeeds in the early majority class, the people with average social status, education, and relatively risk-averse adopt an innovation. They are known as late adopters.

Late majority Individuals with a high degree of scepticism adopt an innovation after the majority of society has already adopted it.

Laggards They form the last consumer category to adopt an innovation.

Opinion leader Opinion leaders are referred to as those groups of people who have special interest and knowledge for a particular type of product and convey that information to the other relevant groups.

Market maven The market maven consumers have a broad array of information about several types of products, retails, and other dimensions of markets and disseminate this information at right time and right place.

Questions

1. What do you understand by diffusion of innovation? Explain the following concepts with reference to *Horlicks Foodles*.
   (a) Innovators
   (b) Opinion leaders
   (c) Social system
2. '*Tata Nano* cars till date have just catered to the innovators.' Do you agree? Give reasons.
3. 'Too much complexity of many hi-tech products put them in a situation of premature death.' Do you agree? Explain. State with example, at this stage as a marketer what will you do?
4. Discuss the process of adoption of innovation with respect to an example of your choice. Elucidate how rejection can occur at every stage of the process.

Critical Assignment

1. Follow some ongoing teaser campaigns of your locality and identify whether they are capable to generate innovators.
2. Consider the purchase of *Euroclean Vacuum Cleaner*. From your experience based on the associations and acquaintances you have, write a note on its adoption process. Also elucidate the barriers of adoption that the product faced and identify the role of opinion leaders in this context.

Chapter **14**

Consumer Decision-Making

Chapter Goals

After completing this chapter, you will be able to understand

- the consumer black-box model
- problem recognition process of consumer
- how marketers can utilize the information search process
- how consumers evaluate their choice alternatives
- consumers' purchase situations
- post-purchase behaviour and dissonance patterns of the consumers
- distinction between low- and high-involvement buying decisions

Opening Vignette

BlackBerry—A Perfect Solution to the Needs of 21st Century Customers

In the 21st century, a consumer's lifestyle is going through a faster transition than yesteryears. Today, the urbanized consumers, who face the absolute time crunch, feels the necessity of connecting with their families, friends, colleagues, and business acquaintances instantly at any point of time.

A Canadian company named Research in Motion (RIM) identified one wonderful solution to this customer problem. In 1999, RIM launched *BlackBerry* mobiles across the globe. In India, the brand joined hands with *Airtel* in 2004. Later on, *Reliance* and *Vodafone* also joined the group. *BlackBerry* is a fantastic multi-tasking smartphone, which provides the customers the option to carry one or more applications in the background. According to a *The Times of India* report (March 28, 2011), over 115 million sets had already been sold across the globe by 2010. Over 565 carriers and distribution channels are now in business with *BlackBerry* smartphones in more than 175 nations. The unique selling propositions of *BlackBerry* phones are the real push technology,

PIN-to-PIN messaging, multiple e-mail accounts integration, global positioning system and mapping capacities, high-speed browser, instant Internet access, text messaging, Internet faxing, assimilation with social networking apps such as *Twitter* and *Facebook*, and many more multimedia capacities. It even facilitates the customers to forward e-mails from the desktop to their mobile device and vice versa. By incorporating these features, *BlackBerry* phones have mostly solved the problem of communication of the businessmen who are always busy travelling. For the Indian corporate executives, doctors, and other professionals, it was indeed a welcome proposition.

© Indiatodayimages.com

BlackBerry
(Clamshell Mobile Phone, Cellphone)

Apart from professionals, the product also has gained immense popularity amongst the youngsters, especially those who are staying away from their families in paying guest houses or hostels. Now, they can easily share information with their families by means of pictures and instant messaging. Considering the needs and preferences of the youngsters, *BlackBerry* has undergone a change from its QWERTY keypad look to the stylish *BlackBerry Pearl 8100*, which principally targets the younger generation. Presently, such smartphones are priced at around ₹25,000. This change in the target customer is well reflected in the company's repositioned tagline *Small*, *Smart*, and *Stylish*. The company also facilitates the *Nokia* or *Sony Ericsson* users to access e-mail via *BlackBerry* technology. This has pushed the sales of *BlackBerry* software upwards. The accelerating growth of *BlackBerry*'s market size in India portrays that the company has understood the changing customer's need and evolved its product with complete perfection.

So, to be successful in the market, the firms need to understand the changing nature of the customers' problems and cater to their needs by designing and positioning their products.

Sources: www.blackberry.com; www.wikipedia.com; http://marketingpractice.blogspot.com/2007/02/blackberry-smallsmart-stylish.html, accessed on February 28, 2007; Redefining communication—A consumer connect initiative, *The Times of India*, March 13, 2011.

INTRODUCTION

As discussed, *BlackBerry* clearly conveyed one message—marketers need to understand the 21st century customer. This understanding enables marketers to envisage the characteristics of their target market and facilitates them to formulate appropriate positioning strategy. For example, Ratan Tata observed the change in the Indian socio-economic structure from a pyramidal one to a diamond form with an increasing number of aspirants. He shared his vision 'I observed families riding on two-wheelers—the father driving the scooter, his young kid standing in front of him, his wife seated behind him holding a little baby. It led me to wonder whether one could conceive of a safe, affordable, all-weather form of transport for such a family.' Consequently, *Tata Motors* came out with the innovation of *Nano* to fulfill the dreams of Indian middle-class aspiring to own a car. On unveiling *Nano*, Ratan Tata said, 'We are happy to present the People's Car to India and we hope it brings the joy, pride and utility of owning a car to many families who need personal mobility.' *Horlicks* came out with *Horlicks Lite* and *Women's Horlicks* to cater to the needs of the middle-aged and working women, respectively.

In this context, firstly, the marketers should understand the different types of purchase situations and roles the consumers may encounter. Similarly, they should also have a clear understanding of the factors that may influence the consumer purchase decision. Thirdly, in today's competitive world flooded with innumerous options and alternatives for the customers to choose, it is imperative for the marketers to understand the complex consumers' decision-making process in an appropriate manner. In the following sections attempt has been made to analyze these concepts.

TYPES OF CONSUMER BUYING BEHAVIOUR

Depending on the nature of involvement of the consumers and the type of risk associated with the purchase, the consumer purchase situations may be categorized into three groups which are as follows:

- *Routine response/habitual buying behaviour*: This kind of purchase situation refers to the low involvement in often-purchased low-priced products. Consumers do not put much effort to know about these purchases or evaluate other alternatives. Purchase decisions are often taken when the stock of the product is depleted. For example, a consumer buys a toothpaste pack

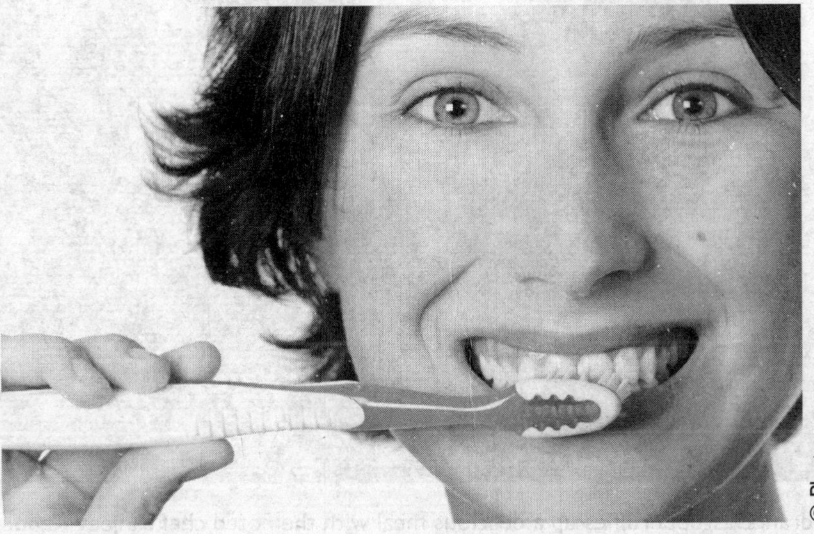

Routine purchase—a toothpaste

once the earlier pack is used. Products such as soft drinks, snacks, milk, biscuits, and other low-cost purchases fall under this type of purchase. As these products are purchased routinely, customers are quite aware of the product/brand features and evaluative criteria. The consumers may have a habit of purchasing a particular brand over the years. *Colgate* toothpaste is used by many Indian families over the generations. As the purchase involves very low-cost products, consumers do not spend much time and effort to purchase them. Hence, ensuring the product's availability intensively is the call for these kinds of products, given the high threat of brand switching.

- *Limited problem-solving behaviour*: A limited problem-solving behaviour encompasses more involvement and effort of the buyer than the routine response behaviour. More specifically, when the product class is known, but the customer is not very sure about the newly launched brand attributes, the limited problem-solving behaviour is quite visible. So, information regarding how the brands score over the consumer's evaluative criteria is quite important and this calls for a moderate amount of time, effort, and involvement to gather information and evaluate the alternatives. When *Saffola* was first launched in India, it was a new variety (cholesterol-free) in the edible oil category. So, customers tried to search information on this 'cholesterol-free' attribute. This executed an example of limited problem-solving behaviour.

© Indiatodayimages.com

Model Indrani Dasgupta ruffles up a delicious meal with the noted chef Sanjeev Kapoor's help at the 'Saffola Losorb Healthy Launch' organized by *Saffola* in New Delhi

- *Extensive decision-making/complex buying behaviour*: The complex buying decision involves the high involvement, unfamiliar, expensive, and/or infrequently bought purchases. This kind of purchasing is normally associated with a high degree of economic, performance-related, or even psychological risk. When an individual buys car, apartment, laptop, jewelry or selects a school for children, he usually seeks a lot of information and gets more involved in terms of time and effort in decision making. Sometimes, the products, which are not expensive but reflect one's personality and social stature, can also fall under this category (buying a wedding dress or wedding gift for sister's marriage). Even, at times when a new technological innovation (e.g., Apple iPad) takes place, the 'innovator' category of the customers seems to be more engrossed in collecting information regarding the product. In fact, all the five stages of the customers buying decision, discussed in Chapter 1, are well visible here.
- *Impulse buying, no conscious planning**: According to the American marketing association, an impulse buying is 'a purchase behaviour that is assumed to be made without prior planning or thought. Often, it is claimed, impulse buying involves an emotional reaction to the stimulus object (product, packaging, point-of-purchase display, or whatever) in addition to the simple acquisition act'.** In other words, impulse buying may also be referred to as a spur-of-the-moment buying. There were two different surveys conducted by the *Yankee Group* and *Ernst & Young* to trace the nature of impulse buying on the Internet. According to the report by *Ernst & Young*, who conducted the study in January 2000, price discounts were the most important motivating factor for almost 88% of the respondents to go for impulse buying. The situation was quite similar to the study conducted by the *Yankee Group* in November, 2000, where 75% of survey respondents claimed that 'price discounts' was the best motivating agent for the consumers.

Many a times, just to satisfy the ephemeral needs such as buying chocolate, chewing gums, junk jewelry, low-priced accessories, even soft-drinks, the consumer goes for impulse buying. This concept has been well viewed in case of shopping malls in the urban areas of India. It is often observed that the food courts, ice-cream parlours, and coffee shops in the shopping malls are more occupied than any other shops. To substantiate this, let us say that in Kolkata a small stationery shop is run by Ramananda Varman. He knows that chocolates and toffees need to be displayed in order to ensure impulse purchase. But in the scorching summer of Kolkata, all the chocolates used to get melt and deformed. The customers made a lot of issues out of it. But he said, 'kids coming along with their parents ask for chocolate principally after seeing it, if I put them in the refrigerator, they won't be able to see it and finally, how will I sell them?' Later on, Ramananda thought of a nice technique to solve this problem—a transparent door refrigerator. Therefore, it may be said that window display is also an important factor to generate impulse buying.

**Source*: http://www.uie.com/publications/whitepapers/ImpulseBuying.pdf, accessed on March 29, 2011.

***Source*: Ramanuj Majumdar, *Consumer Behaviour: Insights from Indian Market*, PHI Learning Pvt. Ltd., 2010, p. 204.

© Indiatodayimages.com

A chocolate shop in Bangalore, India

Moreover, the transition of the Indian society from the pyramidal to the diamond structure, the potential growth in GDP, and the increased purchasing power are also some of the contributing factors for the rise in impulse buying.

However, one should consider that the categorization of routine, limited problem solving, and extended problem-solving behaviours varies across the type of customers also.

For example, for a busy corporate executive, travelling across the country and thereby purchasing air-tickets and selecting hotels may appear to be the routine responsive behaviour, so it is quite obvious that he/she might have an association/tie-up with a fixed travel agency to take care of his/her travel plan. But selecting hotels, buying air-tickets, or even selecting a travel agency for the purpose may be the complex buying behaviour for a teacher couple planning their honeymoon tour.

Keeping all these buying patterns into consideration, the next section focuses on the 'consumer black-box model' envisaged by Professor Phillip Kotler in 1990. This model depicts the human mind as a black box containing all facets that come into play to arrive at a purchase decision.

CONSUMER BUYING DECISION MODEL

The 'consumer black-box model' propounded by Professor Phillip Kotler in 1990 was a pathfinder to understand the most complex individual buying decision process. The model portrays that the consumers will react by certain behavioural constructs in response to various stimuli (either received from the external environment or the stimuli deliberately provided by the marketer to catch the attention of the customer) and thereafter 'process' those stimuli in their minds. Specifically, the model depicts that although the external ambience in which the customer resides or the promotional activities of the marketers may work as a stimulus for consumer's decision making, the consumer's individual characteristics and the five-stage decision-making process will also intermingle with the stimulus before a certain behavioural outcome is caused.

However, the existence of an interface and/or exchange between the external stimuli and human mind can only be assumed because we are yet to know how really the human mind works. Therefore, processing of the stimuli in the human mind has been referred in this model as the 'black box'. As far as consumer behaviour is concerned, it is not that difficult to make out the major internal influences and the main stages in the consumer decision-making process, but how consumers convert all these data into their relevant information and how they interpret that information to generate particular responses are yet to be understood by the consumer psychologists.

As of now, it is clear that there are three major constructs of the consumer black-box model—stimuli, transformer, and response. Schiffman and Kanuk (2004) have elaborated the buying decision-making model as input–process–output model. In the following three sections, an attempt has been made to integrate both these concepts.

Stimuli Influencing Buyer Behaviour—Inputs for the Consumer's Black Box

There are certain external factors influencing the consumer buying decision process. Some of them are endogenous variables developed by marketers and some are exogenous uncontrollable factors. The factors are discussed below.

Marketing Mix Factors

These factors are deliberately created by marketers, namely—the product or service itself, price, place, and promotion. These are known as 'marketing mix' variables. Let us suppose, a person is transferred from one place to another. At that point, his/her prime necessity is to shift all his/her furniture, electrical equipments, and all other belongings to the new place. *Packers and Movers*, one of the most renowned providers of relocation solutions, offers an all-inclusive and cost-effective solution to all kinds of relocation and transportation needs in all major cities and town of India. For the purpose, they have their own widespread networks and associates in almost all the major cities across the nation and service providers at the customer's doorway to eliminate the botherations associated with the relocation and logistics issues. In this case, the service itself is the stimuli for the customer at the point of relocation. How price incentive works as stimuli, specially to the price-sensitive Indian customers, is well reflected in case of the weekend price discounts offered by many departmental stores such as *Big Bazaar*, *Reliance Trends*, *More*, etc. Quite often, the marketers work on cutouts, danglers, and several other point-of-purchase displays to attract the attention of the customers. Exhibit 14.1 displays how the price stimuli are usually provided by the marketers.

Exhibit 14.1: Price—The Most Lucrative Factor for Travel Plan in India

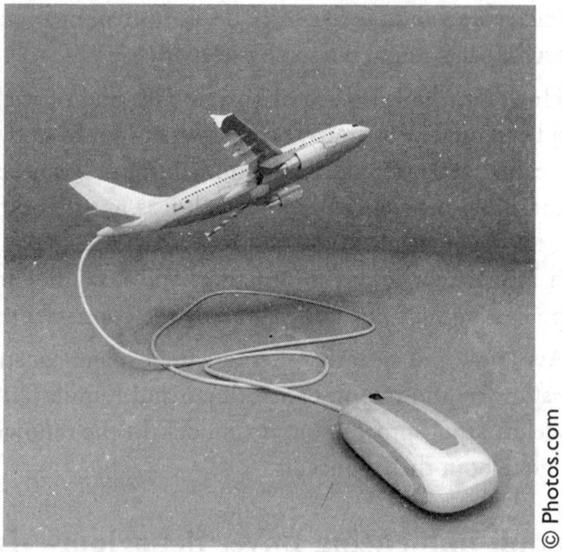

Online air-ticket booking

According to a report published in *The Times of India* dated March 16, 2011, whenever an Indian family plans for a holiday trip, their most searched online items include the cheaper air-tickets, rail tickets, and even bus tickets. A report by *Experian Hitwise Travel* showed how Internet is used as an information source before a travel plan. The report claimed that some tech-savvy customers even go for an extensive search on Internet to read other people's experiences in travelling to the same place. The aforesaid study covering 2 lakh Web sites, 119 industries, and over 60 lakh search items exposed that these sites offered the benefit to compare the prices and also other features (such as time) amongst various airlines, hotels, etc.

The report also projected that *IndiGo* tops the list of the most visited Web sites in case of travel plans in domestic periphery. *IndiGo* is one of the most preferred domestic and international Indian Airlines which always offers, on time and hassle-free operations at low cost, discounted air-tickets, and thereby cheap flights to India and abroad.

Social networking through *Facebook* or *Twitter* is on an upsurge and therefore many travel companies are directly targeting the potential customers through these portals by providing tips, photos, videos, and other relevant suggestions on the travel itinerary and so on.

The report suggested that Indian customers also prefer to bargain deals while booking rooms in hotels. Therefore, needless to mention that the marketers should know which stimulus in terms of marketing mix draws maximum attention of the customer and what kind of information is processed in the black box so as to result in desire and action in favour of a particular product/service/brand.

Source: Indians search for the most cheap air ticket, *The Times of India*, March 16, 2011.

Demographic, Economic, Situational, and Social Parameters

Apart from these deliberately provided stimuli by the marketers, there are several other external environmental factors which have considerable impact on the processing of stimuli in the consumer's black box. These factors are discussed below:

- *Demographic factors*: Consumers' demographic factors encompass their age, gender, education, occupation, stage in family lifecycle, disposable income, etc. Undoubtedly, all these factors have significant impact on the consumers' buying decision and are thereby quite relevant in context to the study of consumer behaviour. For example, for marketing a global brand of nail polish, the marketer needs to target the upper-income urban women, while for some tech-savvy youths a new brand of hi-tech mobile is an attractive product. Similarly, pilgrim tours or walking sticks are principally targeted towards the elderly people, but candies are mainly targeted towards the children. *Horlicks* has very effectively used the demographic parameters for their product differentiation in the form of *Junior Horlicks* (for kids), *Horlicks Lite* (for middle-aged people), *Women's Horlicks* (for women), *Mother's Horlicks* (for lactating mothers), and so on. In summary, the understanding of all such magnitudes of the buyers' attention and interest will give a fair idea to marketers about their needs and wants and facilitate the marketers to design their marketing mix components accordingly.

- *Economic factors*: If the economy is booming, the employment, salaries, and the purchasing power will rise. The reverse happens at the time of recession. One may recall the sensex crush from 21,000 to 8,000 points in January, 2008. The world economy at this point experienced a huge economic downturn and resulted in recession, retrenchments, and so on. Even if customers have favourable attitude towards a product, their economic situation may not permit them to convert the 'desire' into 'action'.
- *Situational factors*: The situational factors that impact the buying behaviour are mainly the time pressure involved in the decision making, the ambience of the retail outlet/restaurant/ hospital, purpose of purchase (wedding, regular wear, parties, games, formal wear, and so on), etc. For example, for minor cuts and wounds, one may go to a local dispensary but in case of a heart attack, a patient would go to the expensive *Breach Candy Hospital*, as the heart attack is perceived as an exigency.
- *Social factors*: Consumers' decisions are strongly influenced by social conditions prevailing around them. Generally, we may specify that the cultural condition, impact of reference groups, and the families are the main social factors that affect the consumer's buying decision.

In American culture, a ceremony is ideally a joyous and hilarious event. In case of India or Pakistan, it is usually a solemn affair. The use of *agarbatti* in *Puja* or buying new dress at the time of *Diwali* has evolved as a part of tradition. Similarly, rice is a staple food in West Bengal and Bangladesh, whereas in north India people prefer the wheat-made *roti* or *chapati*. The garment markets may especially experience boom at the time of *Durga Puja* in West Bengal, *Diwali* in North India, *Pongal* in Andhra Pradesh, *Bihu* in Assam, or *Onam* in Kerala.

The reference groups may steer the choice of a product or the brand. Sometimes, peer pressure has been identified as a dominant factor for arriving at a purchase decision by customers. For example, a person may prefer *Coke*, but when he is with his friends, he may surrender to his friends' choice. The comprehension of reference group behaviour facilitates marketers not only in offering product substitutes and brand extension but also in pricing and positioning (even repositioning) them. Nonetheless, there are also 'dissociative' reference groups like the people whom the consumers do not want to replicate. For example, The *Gap* store chain in the USA actively dissociated itself from Generation X to attract Generation Y.

A consumer's family is another major influencing factor on the consumer decision making. The family consumption behaviour largely varies with the stages of the family lifecycle (refer Chapter 12) consisting of bachelorhood, newly married, parenthood with growing or grown up children, post-parenthood, and solitary surviving. For example, for the tourism companies it is important to take a note of the elderly people's choice while designing pilgrim tours and the young couples' choice at the time of scheduling honeymoon packages. The marketers should also understand that who in the family plays what role in the purchase decision. In case of *Horlicks Lite* advertisement, the anxiety of a housewife towards her husband's health has depicted her as the probable decider and buyer of the product.

Transformation—The Black Box Under Process

In the black-box model, there are two key constructs, namely, the customer's internal influences and his five-stage decision-making process. These constructs are explained as follows.

Internal Influencing Factors of Consumer Decision Making

The internal influencing factors of the customer consist of customer's perception, attitude, motivation, lifestyle, personality, learning constructs, etc. The impacts of these factors are elaborated below:

- *Perception*: It is the process by which individuals select, organize, and interpret the obtained information so as to develop a meaningful and long-term impression in their minds. For example, if a buyer's experience with the credit card of a particular bank is disappointing, he may perceive the entire organization as non-productive and it requires harder efforts from the sales person to convince the buyer once again.
- *Attitude*: An attitude is a learned predisposition formed in the customer's mind to retort in a consistently favourable or unfavourable way to an offer (any product, brand, communication message, discounts, and so on) made by the marketers. Nonetheless, attitude is manifested under certain conditions and might be altered by constant and deliberate attempt by the marketers (refer Chapter 8). However, attitude towards a product has to be interpreted in context of the purpose and capability of the purchase of the buyers; otherwise, marketers may come up with distorted prediction of this behaviour. For example, someone may have a highly favourable attitude towards *Mercedes-Benz* cars but may not have the purchasing power to buy it.
- *Lifestyle factor*: Lifestyle-based segments portray distinction in the way people spend on various products. Understanding the lifestyle and some of the important psychographic variables facilitates marketer to identify the consumer's needs and design the advertising campaign accordingly. *Mountain Dew* has resorted to Salman Khan's 'macho' image in their advertisement campaign.
- *Motivation*: Motivation is the driving force in our subconscious to fulfill certain unmet needs (refer Chapter 4). For example, person having a three-year-old kid would be most interested in searching for a good day-boarding school. An executive in a travel agency would be a frequent visitor of *www.yatra.com*, the travel portal, as he/she will be rewarded for doing his/her job better.

- *Personality*: Personality (refer Chapter 6) can be elucidated as the psychological and behavioural trait of an individual. Marketers should select appropriate brand-ambassadors to convey their messages to the target group. For example, the association of Amitabh Bachchan with *Reid & Taylor* shows the brand's elegance and hence may be liked by the people characterized by elitism. Similarly, Shahrukh Khan's youthfulness has been used in a convincing fashion by *Pepsi* to target the jubilant youths.

Stages in the Buying Process

Conventionally, consumer researchers have analyzed the consumers' buying decision-making process from a rational angle. This aspect is developed on the assumption that consumers are more cognitive (i.e., problem solving) and less emotional. Such a view is reflected in the five-stage buying model elaborated by Kotler (1990). Nonetheless, not in all buying situations the five stages are equally prominent, but in case of complex buying behaviour, all the stages are highly visible.

Stage 1: Need or problem recognition

The problem recognition is the condition of human mind in which at a particular time, the desired state is perceived to be more pleasant than the actual state. This generates the feeling of unmet needs in consumer's mind. For example, Mr. Ravi Kant, due to the hectic commutation to office in the crowded city buses, is attracted to a showroom that displays medium-priced cars in front of his office. Now, he feels the need of a car.

However, in case of impulse purchase, needs are recognized and fulfilled on the spot. Figure 14.1 elucidates the underlying factors behind such need recognition.

It is evident from Fig. 14.1 that an unmet need or problem identification can be defined as the 'perceived gap or discrepancy between the existing and the desired consumer positions for a given product and service'. The consumer's present state of mind reveals his feelings, perception, and attitude towards the firm's offerings. On the flip side, the desired consumer situation ideally refers to the consumer's expected satisfaction to be obtained from the consumption of a particular product and service. If this perceived gap is wide enough to lie within the consumer's perceptual threshold, then it develops a kind of tension in the consumer's mind and thereby the unmet need is realized by the customer. As a person moves upwards in his/her lifecycle and grows physically, financially, and psychologically, he/she will experience several perceived gaps between the current and desired situations. For example, he/she may desire at the age of three to six a tricycle, at his/her teens a bicycle, in his youth a motor cycle, and gradually a car.

Sometimes, marketers may calculatingly induce dissonance in the consumers towards their currently used product bundle. Normally, marketers resort to the ideas such as 'style obsolescence' or 'technology obsolescence' for this purpose only. Apple in that way has moved on from desktop PCs to laptops, palmtops, and now to iPads. The insurance service provider *Aegon Religare* had resorted to the attractive teaser sequel '*Kam insurance lene ki bimari*' to elevate a sense of 'unmet need' in customer's mind in terms of insurance products.

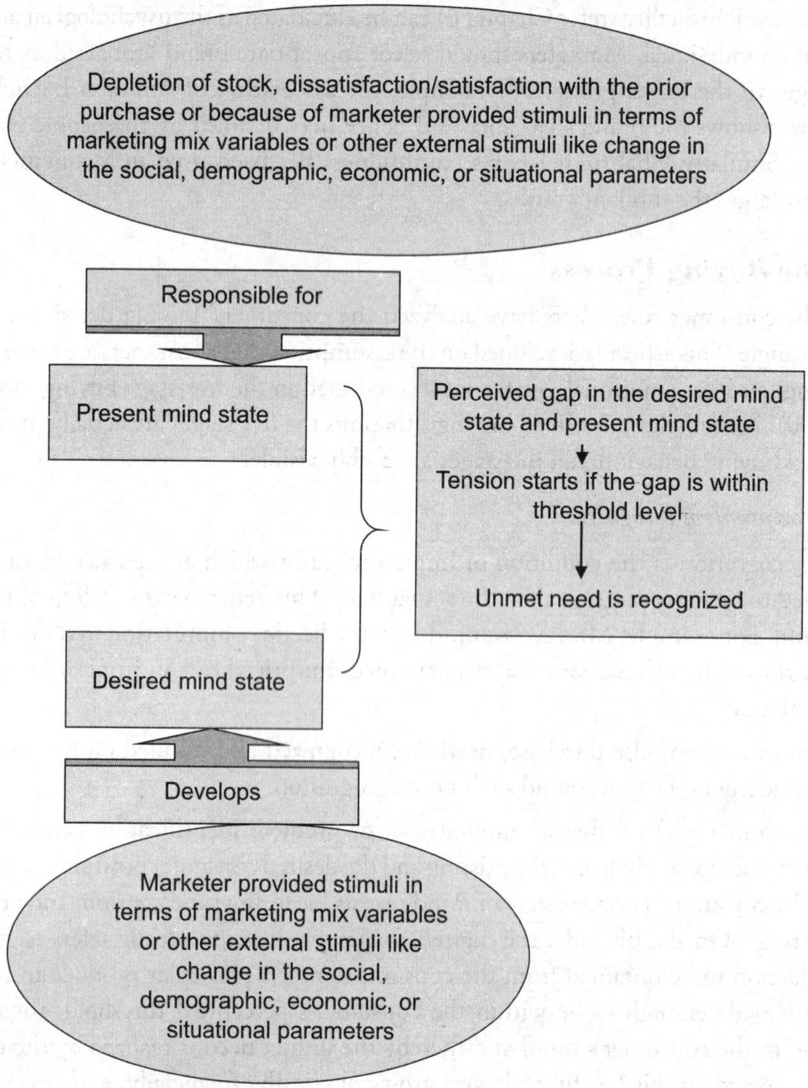

Figure 14.1 Need/problem recognition process

Stage 2: Search for information

Once consumers recognize their needs, they start searching for the relevant information regarding products or services. The information search can be of two types—external and internal search. In case of a routine response behaviour or loyalty decisions, it is sufficient for the consumers to scan their memories as they are already accustomed to the product.

Nonetheless, in case of complex buying situations, customers exert a deliberate search for information from the outer world apart from just internal search. This is referred to as external search which is a controlled, designed, and rational quest of information.

Today's consumers are exposed to multifarious information sources ranging from the non-personal sources such as advertising, in-store promotion, newspapers, dealer information, package information to personal sources such as sales personnel, friends, relatives, neighbours, and Internet (especially social networking). Internet shopping Web sites such as *Amazon.com* and *ebay.com* not only provide information about the product, but also provide the customers' review on the same.

However, this phase is much shorter in case of impulse buying where such external stimuli (principally marketer-designed stimuli) such as the attractive point-of-purchase displays, packaging, discount offers, and other free gifts stimulate the need of the consumers to move from the present state to the desired state.

It may be stated that in case of a high-involvement purchase, as the perceived risk is very high, the search for information would be quite high as well. The other factors which may expand the stage of information search are the product-related factors such as long inter-purchase time (time between two purchases, e.g., time lag between the purchases of two cars by an individual), high price (jewelry), frequent price changes, amount of purchase, availability of various alternatives (insurance), etc. Some situational factors also play a dominating role in expanding the span of pre-purchase information search. If the purchase is discretionary (when an individual is buying an additional car) rather than necessary (buying a medicine when one is sick), the search process is extended. The purpose of purchase (gift or personal consumption) is also an important situational parameter which prolongs the search process. The demographic (age, income) and psychographic parameters (such as perception, personality, motivation, self-concept, attitude, etc.) also influence the purchase decision. For example, the low-income people are likely to be more price-sensitive.

Stage 3*: *Evaluation of alternatives

For the evaluation of the available alternatives, however, three basic aspects are to be taken care of by consumers. They are as follows.

(a) *The evoked set*: The evoked set is often referred as the list of brands or sometimes models of a particular brand, from which the customer is likely to choose the best suited one for him/her. In other words, the evoked set encompasses only those brands, with which customers are familiar with. These brands are somewhat acceptable as well. However, one should not confuse between the evoked set and the inept or inert set. Inept set comprises those brands which consumers feel unacceptable and exclude them from the decision-making process. The inert set encompasses those products about which customers are indifferent, as they do not appeal to the desired state of the customer. Such brands are often overlooked by customers and fail to get into the customer's evoked set.

In each case, it is the task of marketers to plan the promotional strategies in such a way that convey the relevant and favourable product and brand-related information to the target customer. Some value-added attributes of the product or some sales promotion techniques may induce the brands from the inert set to the evoked set.

(b) *Evaluative criteria*: Evaluative criteria are those characteristics of the product which are used by customers to select a brand (from the evoked set), which suits them the best. These criteria may be price, availability, style, design, brand equity, etc.

(c) *Decision rules/heuristics*: Once the evoked set of brands or models are identified and the evaluative criteria are recognized according to their relative importance, consumers exert to their relevant decision rules or heuristics to select the best suited one. There are two broad categories of decision rules, namely, the compensatory and non-compensatory decision rules (Schiffman and Kanuk, 2004). To make the concepts clear, we may recall the example of selecting a small car by Umesh Nair for his family and also for his travelling from office to residence (Refer Exhibit 8.2 in Chapter 8). For convenience, let us once again see Table 8.1 to explain the decision rules.

- Compensatory decision rule: In the compensatory decision rule, first consumers assign weight to several evaluative criteria. Then they evaluate a brand or model in terms of the relevant evaluative criteria, and a weighted sum for each alternative is, thereafter, calculated.

Table: 8.1 *The evaluation table*

Criteria	***Weights of criteria***	***Maruti 800 Std BSIII***	***Tata Nano Std BSIII***	***Maruti Alto Std***	***Tata Indica V2 Xeta GL***	***Hyundai Santro Xing (non-AC)***
Price of the car (C_1)	.32	4	5	3	2	2
Fuel efficiency	.28	3	4	3	4	3
Warranty period	.18	3	4	3	3	3
Dealer's Proximity	.12	5	2	5	4	3
Bank loan	.06	4	4	4	5	5
Wife's choice	.04	1	2	3	3	5
Preference for brands	$\Sigma W_i = 1$	*3.54*	4	*3.26*	*3.20*	*2.88*

According to the compensatory rule from Table 8.1, the highest summated score is obtained for the brand *Tata Nano* car, and hence the brand/model is found to be the best-preferred alternative. The most distinctive attribute of the compensatory decision rule is that it simultaneously considers all the positive and negative aspects of the brands in the evoked set.

- Non-compensatory decision rules: On the contrary, consumers cannot balance the negative features of a brand with some positive aspects in case of non-compensatory decision rules. There are three major non-compensatory rules, namely, conjunctive rule, disjunctive rule, and lexicographic rule.

In the *conjunctive decision rule*, consumers establish a minimum point of cutoff for each attribute. If any brand falls below the cutoff point in terms of the selected attributes, it is eliminated from the choice set. In case of Mr. Umesh Nair, if he sets a cutoff point of 3 for all the choice attributes, then we find, except *Maruti Alto* Std, all other cars have scores below 3 in some attributes. Hence, *Maruti Alto* would be chosen by Mr. Nair, if he follows the *conjunctive decision rule*.

Table 8.2 *Evaluation table*

Criteria	*Weights of criteria*	*Maruti 800 Std BSIII*	*Tata Nano Std BSIII*	*Maruti Alto Std*	*Tata Indica V2 Xeta GL*	*Hyundai Santro Xing (non-AC)*
Price of the car (C_1)	.32	4	5	3	2	2
Fuel efficiency	.28	3	4	3	4	3
Warranty period	.18	3	4	3	3	3
Dealer's proximity	.12	5	2	5	4	3
Bank loan	.06	4	4	4	5	5
Wife's choice	.04	1	2	3	3	5

However, in this rule, there is a high probability that more than one brand still remains in the evoked set. In that case, additional decision rule has to be applied to arrive at the final conclusion. So, it may be stated that this rule is reasonably helpful in reducing the large number of alternatives in the evoked set. Nonetheless, this rule has to be sophisticated by any other choice rule to arrive at the final choice.

The second type of non-compensatory decision rule, namely, the *disjunctive rule*, is just the reverse of the conjunctive rule. Similar to the conjunctive decision-making rule, here also a minimum cutoff level for each attribute is set. According to this rule, Mr. Nair will choose the alternative which may satisfy his minimum cutoff in terms of any choice criteria. Usually, this cutoff is set little above the cutoff value set in conjunctive rule. In this case, let us assume the cut-off is 4.

Table 8.3 *Evaluation table*

Criteria	*Weights of criteria*	*Maruti 800 Std BSIII*	*Tata Nano Std BSIII*	*Maruti Alto Std*	*Tata Indica V2 Xeta GL*	*Hyundai Santro Xing (non-AC)*
Price of the car (C_1)	.32	4	5	3	2	2
Fuel efficiency	.28	3	4	3	4	3
Warranty period	.18	3	4	3	3	3
Dealer's proximity	.12	5	2	5	4	3
Bank loan	.06	4	4	4	5	5
Wife's choice	.04	1	2	3	3	5

Now, in Table 8.3, as all the brands are meeting the cutoff, all of them still remain in the evoked set. Therefore, consumers once again need to resort to some other decision rule to arrive at a choice of their most preferred brand/model. So the problem of less sophistication, which, we found in the conjunctive heuristics, is also present in the disjunctive heuristics.

However, in case of *lexicographic heuristics*, consumers first order the attributes according to their perceived importance. For example, in case of Mr. Nair, according to his relative importance, the evaluative criteria can be ranked as price (1st), fuel efficiency (2nd), warranty period (3rd), dealer's proximity (4th), bank loan (5th), and wife's choice (6th). Now, consumers compare all the brands' score in terms of the most important criteria set by them in single/multiple iterations till the most preferred alternative is identified. Here, Mr. Nair has selected price as the most important attribute. Now *Tata Nano Std BSIII* scores the highest (5) as compared to the other brands in terms of price criteria and hence would be considered as the best-suited alternative for Mr. Nair.

Table 8.4 *Evaluation table*

Criteria	*Weights of criteria*	*Maruti 800 Std BSIII*	*Tata Nano Std BSIII*	*Maruti Alto Std*	*Tata Indica V2 Xeta GL*	*Hyundai Santro Xing (non-AC)*
Price of the car (C_1)	.32	4	5	3	2	2
Fuel efficiency	.28	3	4	3	4	3
Warranty period	.18	3	4	3	3	3
Dealer's proximity	.12	5	2	5	4	3
Bank loan	.06	4	4	4	5	5
Wife's choice	.04	1	2	3	3	5

In case, more than one brand scores 5 (highest score) in terms of the most important criterion, then those few brands are compared in the same terms of the second important criterion and if required the process moves on to the next important attribute till the point of the single brand selection.

The lexicographic heuristics sound very significant while studying the consumer's shopping orientation. For example, Mr. Nair ranked price of the car as the most important criterion, so it may be concluded that he is a price-sensitive customer in terms of car purchase. However, Mr. Nair may not appear as a price-sensitive customer while selecting a school for his son. At that point of time, irrespective of tution fees (price), quality of education may be his topmost priority and he may expose himself as a quality-conscious buyer.

Nonetheless, there are several other decision rules used to select the most preferred brand by the customer. We have just mentioned some basic rules here. In many cases, these basic rules are mixed to derive a new choice rule, like if there are too many brands in the evoked set, then *conjunctive–compensatory* or *disjunctive–lexicographic* may appear to be appropriate. This type of combined choice heuristics is called the *after-referral decision rule* and this is perhaps the most popular choice heuristics. Understanding of the consumer's choice heuristics is extremely important from the marketer's point of view especially for launching a new model of a known brand or designing a promotional message.

Responses—The Outcome of Black-Box Processing

The response in the consumer decision-making model relates to the purchase and post-purchase behaviour of the consumers. However, after the post-purchase behaviour, there may be an alteration in the evoked set. For example, after using *Tata Nano* car, if Mr. Nair has some negative experience of the product, then he may drop this alternative from his evoked set, in case of further purchase or replacement purchase of a car. Now let us discuss about the stages of purchase and post-purchase behaviours.

Stage 4: Product choice and purchase

At the purchase stage, the consumer undergoes any of the three purchase situations—trial, repeat, and long-term commitment purchase. For example, if a new brand of detergent or shampoo enters into the market one may buy a trial pack or sachet of the product. If he/she finds it suitable, the user may become a repeat purchaser of the product and, in the longer term, may appear to be a brand-loyal customer of the product. His/her purchase volume may also significantly increase while moving from trial purchase to repeat purchase. However, trial and repeat purchase may be applicable in case of routine response behaviour or to some extent in limited problem-solving behaviour. For example, in case of purchasing a toothpaste pack, packet of biscuits, or shampoo, the consumer may opt for a trial when a new brand is launched or the company is providing some special offers or in any such circumstances. Nonetheless, a trial purchase is not possible for most of the durable products such as refrigerators, television sets, air conditioners, etc. or the products related to complex buying behaviour such as house, car, etc., as these items are quite expensive. In these cases, the selection of a brand/model directly results in a long-term commitment without a trial.

At the purchase stage, not only the product/brand but also the price, the point of purchase, and the method of payment are taken into consideration given the alternatives. For example, once Mr. Nair has selected a *Tata Nano* car, his next decision should be related to the method of payment (whether to go for cash purchase, bank loan with initial small down payment, number of installments, etc.).

There may be many such situations where the consumer does not undergo actual purchase, even after the brand/model choice is made. Many situational factors play a major role for this decision of no purchase. For example, after witnessing the most attractive advertisement of *Horlicks Foodles* if the consumer wishes to buy the same but does not find it in the nearest shop, he may drop the decision of purchasing the product.

Stage 5: Post-purchase use and evaluation

After using the product, the customer may experience any of the following three states of mind:

- The actual performance of the product may exceed the expected performance of the same and the customer may feel satisfied. He/she may, thereby, engage in repeat purchase and gradually become a brand-loyal customer.
- The actual performance matches with the expected performance of the product and the customer is neutral. Even if the actual performance is closer to the expected performance, the customer usually does not complain.
- But if the actual performance of the product is much lower than the expected performance, the customer may experience some sort of tension or disturbances in his mind. He/she may feel that the choice of product was not appropriate at all. This stage is referred as the *post-purchase cognitive dissonance* stage. The obvious actions of the customers here are normally seeking more information about the product. He/she, at this phase, gets more involved in watching or reading the commercials of the brand and avoids those of the competing brands to reassure his/her choice. Sometimes, the customer may try to persuade his acquaintances to purchase the product to confirm their own choice and, thereby, seek reassurance for their chosen brands.

However, the persistent post-purchase cognitive dissonance may be dangerous from the marketer's point of view as it may also result in negative word-of-mouth communication and push away a lot of potential customers by refraining them from purchasing the brand or model. Hence, the company carries out various correction measures to prevent buyer's dissonance. For low-priced products, the marketers might offer a money back guarantee. Otherwise, they might reassure the customers by highlighting more and more on the brand's USP through advertisement or sales people.

The entire process discussed in this section can be summated and presented in Fig. 14.2.

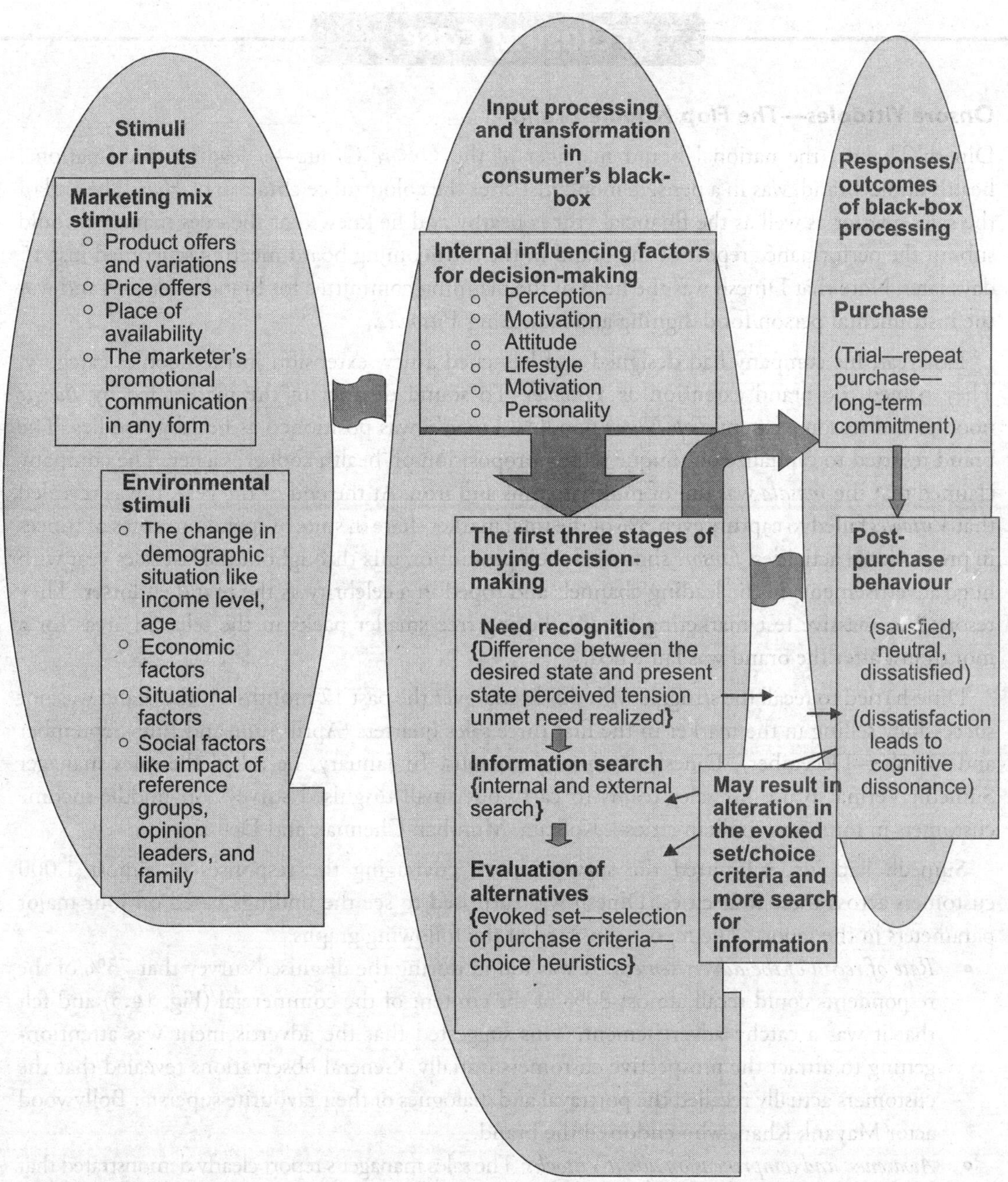

Figure 14.2 Consumer decision-making process (the figure is drawn on the basis of the idea of Schiffman and Kanuk, *Consumer Behaviour*, sixth edition, Figure 13-3, Simple decision-making model, page 565, PHI Pvt. Ltd.)

Closing Case

Onsore Vittooles—The Flop Noodle Brand

Dinesh Thakur, the national brand manager of the *Onsore* Group—a leading multi-national health drinks brand, was in a pensive mood just after the colourful celebration of *Holi*. The end of the sales quarter as well as the financial year is nearby and he knew that the sales manager would submit the performance report of the brand in the forthcoming board meeting scheduled just 15 days later. Note that Dinesh was the head of the planning committee for brand extension and was the instrumental person for designing and launching *Vittooles*.

Last year, his company had designed and launched a new extension in the noodles category. They named the brand extension as *Vittooles*. To sound distinct in the market led by *Boogie* noodles and to some extent *Top Notch* noodles, *Vittooles* was positioned as healthy noodles. The brand resorted to capitalize on unique selling proposition of 'health cooker' sachet. The company claimed that the *masala* was full of multivitamins and iron. At the end of the year, it was revealed that *Vittooles* failed to capture even 3% of the total market share in spite of spending crores of rupees in promotional activities. *Onsore* showered their promotion mix throughout the last sales year with huge advertisements in the leading channels and roped in a celebrity as the brand endorser. They resorted to massive test marketing by distributing free smaller packs in the selected areas for a month just after the brand was launched.

Dinesh tried to recall the struggle with this brand over the past 12 months. As the brand was not successfully selling in the market in the first three sales quarters (April–June and July–September and October–December), Dinesh was pretty anxious. In January, he asked the sales manager Sumedh Verma to use his sales teams to carry out small disguised surveys on middle-income customers in four metropolitan cities—Kolkata, Mumbai, Chennai, and Delhi.

Sumedh had just submitted the survey report, envisaging the responses of almost 1,000 customers across these four cities. Dinesh was surprised to see the findings based on four major parameters in the report. The report consisted of the following graphs.

- *Rate of recall of the advertisement*: It was found during the disguised survey that 73% of the respondents could recall almost 80% of the content of the commercial (Fig. 14.3) and felt that it was a catchy advertisement. This suggested that the advertisement was attention-getting to attract the prospective customers initially. General observations revealed that the customers actually recalled the portrayal and dialogues of their favourite superstar Bollywood actor Mayank Khan, who endorsed the brand.
- *Awareness and comprehension about Vittooles*: The sales manager's report clearly demonstrated that *Vittooles* was a well-known brand (80% of the respondents knew what it was) (Fig. 14.4).
- *'Generic brand' image of Boogie in the category*: In Fig. 14.5, it was quite obvious that *Boogie* acted as almost a 'generic brand' in the noodles category. *Vittooles*, in spite of its rigorous promotion, failed to break that myth.

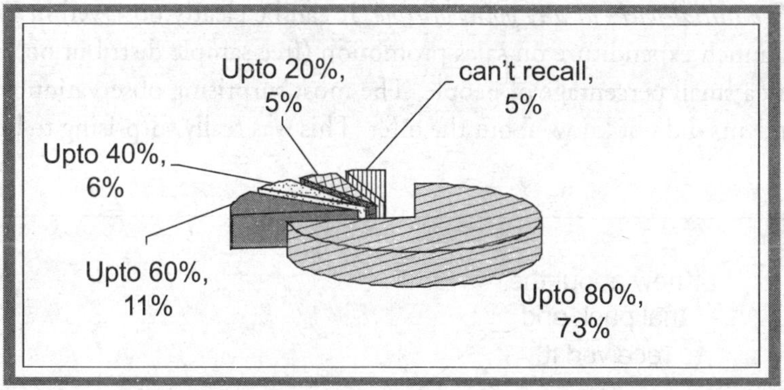

Figure 14.3 Recall rate of the *Vittooles*

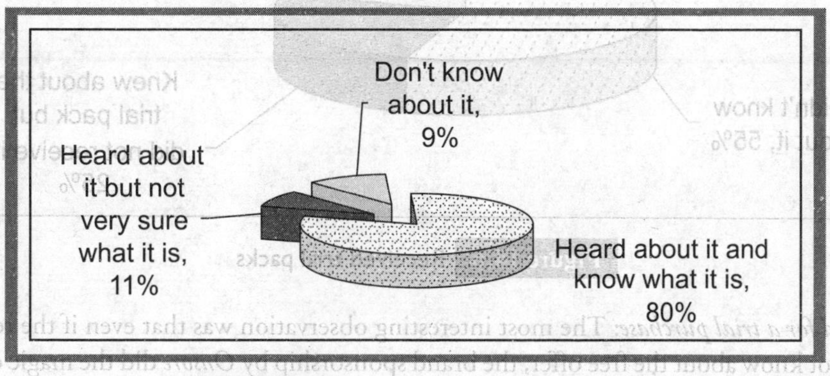

Figure 14.4 Awareness about *Vittooles*

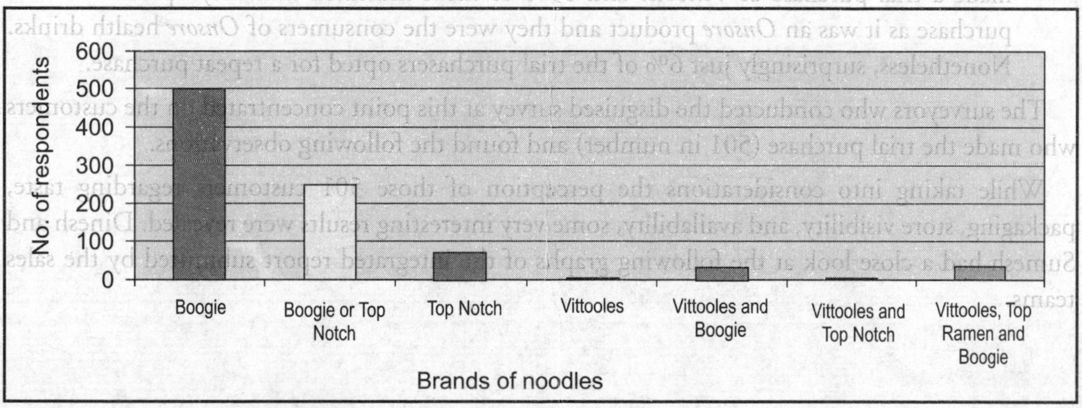

Figure 14.5 Generic identity of various brands of noodles

- *Received free initial packs at any point of time*: It can be clearly observed in Fig. 14.6 that in spite of so much expenditure on sales promotion (free sample distribution), the packs were received by a small percentage of people. The most surprising observation was that 55% of the respondents did not know about the offer. This was really surprising to both Dinesh and Sumedh.

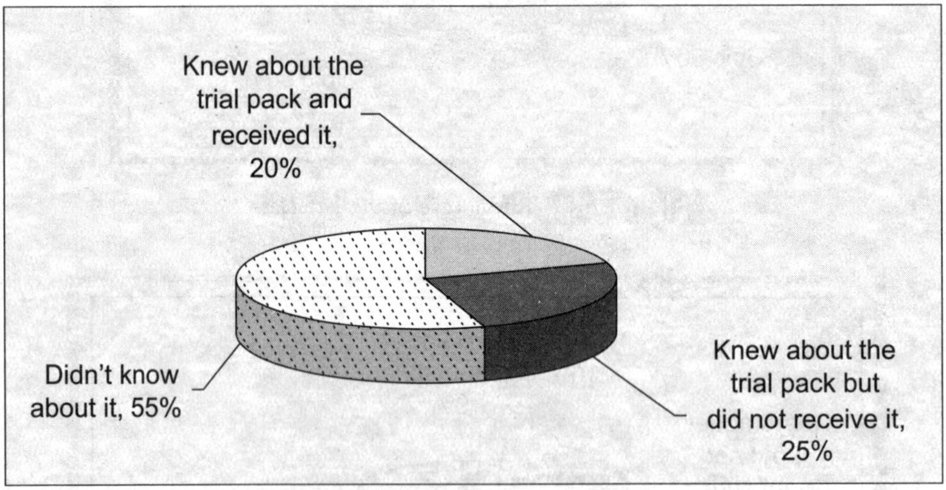

Figure 14.6 Received trial packs

- *Opted for a trial purchase*: The most interesting observation was that even if the respondents did not know about the free offer, the brand sponsorship by *Onsore* did the magic of reaching at least to the segment of innovators. It was observed that almost 50% of the respondents made a trial purchase of *Vittooles* and 85% of them indicated that they opted for a trial purchase as it was an *Onsore* product and they were the consumers of *Onsore* health drinks. Nonetheless, surprisingly just 6% of the trial purchasers opted for a repeat purchase.

The surveyors who conducted the disguised survey at this point concentrated on the customers who made the trial purchase (501 in number) and found the following observations.

While taking into considerations the perception of those 501 customers regarding taste, packaging, store visibility, and availability, some very interesting results were revealed. Dinesh and Sumesh had a close look at the following graphs of the integrated report submitted by the sales teams.

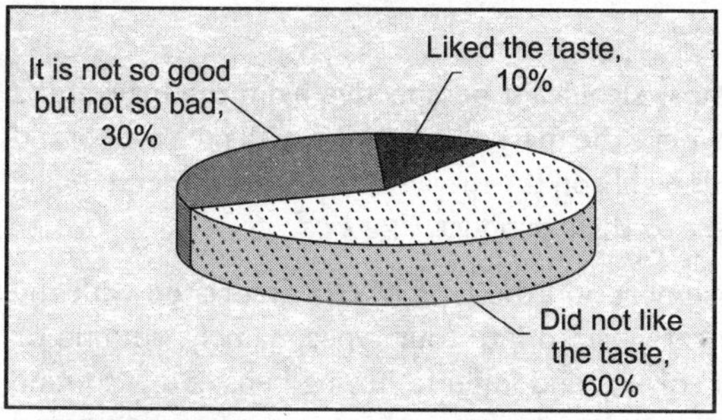

Figure 14.7 Likings of taste of *Vittooles*

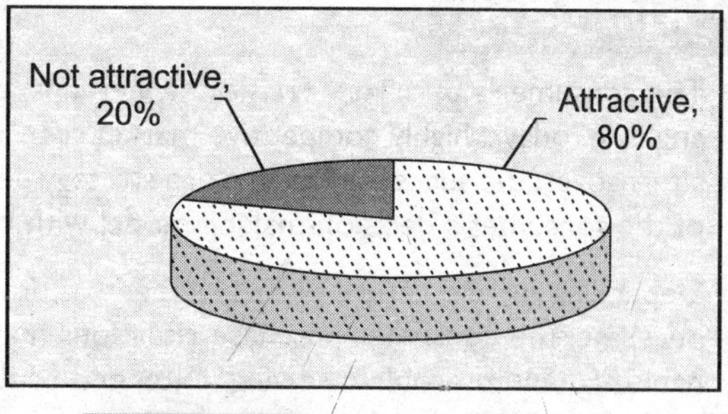

Figure 14.8 Packaging of *Vittooles*

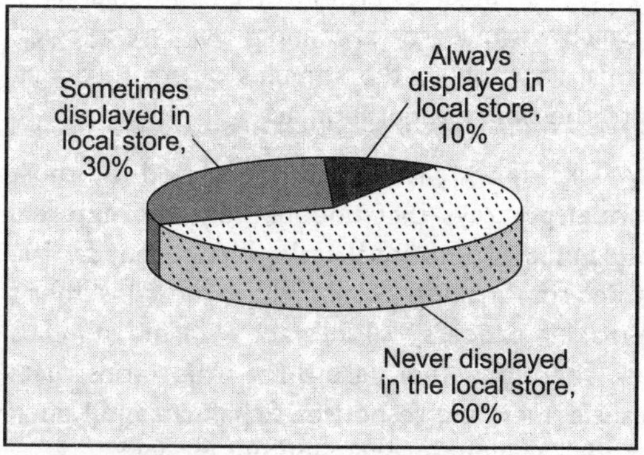

Figure 14.9 Visibility in the local stores

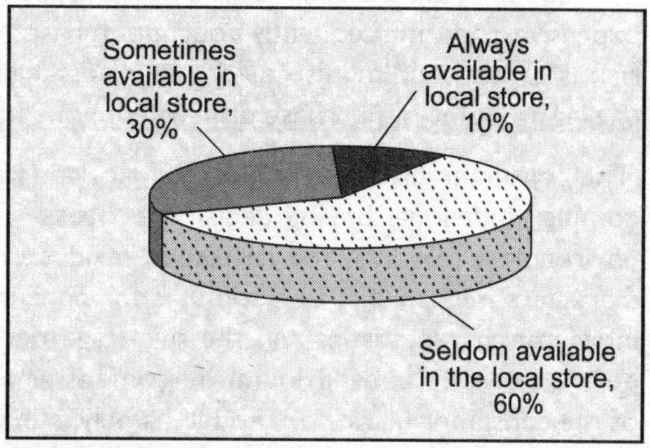

Figure 14.10 Availability at the local stores

Dinesh was perplexed and sat down on his desk to develop further strategies.

(This is a fictitious case developed in order to stimulate classroom discussions at MBA level. Any resemblance with any person or organization is purely coincidental.)

Questions

1. In spite of so much promotion and strong umbrella brand of *Onsore*, why did *Vittooles* failed to succeed in the market?
2. Had you been Dinesh, what strategies would have you taken to convert the interest of the consumers into purchase?

Summary

The consumer's purchase decision is, perhaps, the most significant perspective from the marketer's angle. In today's highly competitive market scenario, where the market is flooded with plenty of brand alternatives, the success or failure of a strategy depends highly on the marketer's proper understanding of the consumer's decision-making model with respect to their product.

Depending on the nature of involvement of the consumers and the type of risk associated with the purchase, the consumer purchase situations may be categorized into four types, namely, routine or habitual, limited problem solving, extended problem solving, and impulse buying behaviour. Routine response behaviour refers to the purchase situations related to the low involvement often-purchased low-priced products where the purchase decisions are usually taken when the stock of the product is depleted. A limited problem solving encompasses more involvement and effort of the buyer than the routine response behaviour. The complex buying decision involves high involvement, unfamiliar, expensive, and/or infrequently bought purchases with which a high degree of economic or psychological risk is associated. Impulse buying involves an emotional reaction to the stimulus object (product, packaging, point-of-purchase display, etc.) in addition to the simple acquisition act.

'The consumer black-box model' by Kotler (1990) was really a trailblazer to understand the most complex individual buying decision process. The model portrays that undoubtedly, the external environment in which the customer resides or the planned promotional tasks carried out by the marketers might work as a stimulus for consumer's decision making. Nonetheless, the consumer's individual characteristics and the five-stage decision-making process will interact with the stimulus before a particular behavioural outcome is generated. Therefore, there are three major constructs of the consumer black-box model, namely, stimuli, transformer, and responses. Schiffman and Kanuk (2004) have elaborated the 'buying decision-making model' as input–process–output model.

As far as consumer behaviour is concerned, it is not that intricate to make out the key internal influencing agents and the main stages in the consumer decision-making process. Nonetheless, how consumers transform all these data into their pertinent information, how they interpret that information to generate particular responses are yet to be understood by the consumer psychologists and hence referred as 'black box' by Kotler.

Key Terms

Information search The act of acquiring, processing, and using relevant information for a consumption decision.

External search The act of deliberately collecting and using information for a given purchase decision.

Internal search The act of regaining information from stored memory.

Impulse purchases It refers to the unplanned purchases made at the point of purchase.

Involvement The level of perceived importance evoked by the entire present set of stimulus in a given situation.

Obsolescence Out-of-date.

Problem recognition The realization by the consumer that there is a difference between the present and desired states of satisfaction.

Stimuli The symbolic or significant cues or actions that evoke/stimulate a reaction from the receiver.

Threshold level The stimulus reception level within an upper and lower limit at which an individual can experience a sensation.

Routine response behaviour It refers to the purchase situations related to the low involvement in 'often-purchased low-priced products' where the purchase decisions are often taken when the stock of the product is depleted.

A limited problem solving behaviour It encompasses more involvement and effort of the buyer than the routine response behaviour.

The complex buying decision This involves the high involvement, unfamiliar, expensive and/or infrequently bought purchases with which a high degree of economic or psychological risk is associated.

Impulse buying This involves an emotional reaction to the stimulus object (product, packaging, point-of-purchase display, etc.) in addition to the simple acquisition act.

Heuristics The choice rule of the customers given various alternatives.

Evoked set The bundle of acceptable alternatives.

Evaluative criteria The criteria based on which the brands are evaluated.

Questions

1. How do you categorize the types of consumer purchases based on low- and high-involvement situations? How need recognition varies in each of the buying situations? What are the marketing implications of such variations?
2. Explain with examples why the marketing mix and situational factors are considered to be so important to marketers?
4. Being a marketer of a fitness organization such as VLCC, how would you develop awareness for fitness among the customers?
5. Briefly describe the buying process taking the example of 'home loan' and 'educational loan'.

Critical Assignment

1. Identify at least three brands of cell phones offered by the multinational companies and conduct a small but focused group interview to identify the effectiveness of their marketing messages in terms of consumer's five-stage decision-making process.
2. Name five products which need rigorous pre-purchase search by a consumer. Make out the types of perceived risks associated with each of the purchase. Being a marketer, do you feel you can diminish these perceived risks? If so, how?
3. For a long time, your brand of jewelry is not working well in the market as compared to your competitors. You wish to change the evaluative criteria of the customers so that your USPs are noticed and your brand becomes acceptable by the consumers. How will you proceed?

Chapter **15**

Models of Consumer Behaviour

Chapter Goals

After completing this chapter, you will be able to understand

- **the facets of consumer behaviour as the sub-sets of human behaviour**
- **the basic elements of a consumer behaviour model**
- **the nature, scope, and areas of application of consumer behaviour models**
- **the use of consumer model in explaining buyer behaviour**
- **the critical evaluation and comparison of the existing models**

Opening Vignette

Teaser Campaigns—Mix and Match of Success and Failure

The most contemporary version of promotion is perhaps the teaser campaign, to which the marketers of 21st century resorted to magnetize the audience and to boost up hype about a product within a very short course of time. These attempts are principally undertaken to break the clutter of formal advertisements and draw attention of the prospects and, thereby, induce the action to purchase. One may recall the latest 'Digen Verma' campaign of *Frooti* which was considered as one of the most successful teaser campaigns in India in terms of its 'recall' effect. This teaser campaign started in February 2001 and lasted for almost 15 days. The campaign was all about an undisclosed person named as Digen Verma. The market was ushered with posters and hoardings consisting of messages like 'Who is Digen Verma?', 'Digen Verma was here', etc. This enticed the kids and youth market specially and 'Digen Verma' gained immense popularity. Nonetheless, the propaganda executed by Everest Communications was not decoded to the long-term brand loyalty of the customers.

One more example of such teaser campaigns was run by Population Studies International—a reputed NGO for the purpose of awareness against HIV-AIDS. It featured a fictitious protagonist named Balbir Pasha. This campaign, because of its catchy theme, also attracted the audience and generated lot of buzz in the country. Though the Balbir Pasha teaser commercials were popular but as of now, the consciousness about HIV has not properly generated. The social stigma still prevails.

Therefore, it is important to analyze the market and the target audience prior to shaping any marketing strategy, be it promotion, distribution, or launching of a new product. In other words, the key challenge of the marketer is to be aware of the target audience before launching any marketing plan. Therefore, it is imperative to learn the existing models to comprehend how really the customers make up their mind to take a decision.

Source: http://www.brandbhai.com/relaunch-of-frooti-the-digen-verma-campaign; http://marketingpractice.blogspot.com/2006/03/frooti-fresh-n-juicy.html, accessed on August 23, 2010.

INTRODUCTION

Marketers are often unsure about the variables that may influence the consumers' buying decision-making and to what extent they do so. It is also necessary for the marketers to understand how these variables intermingle amongst each other. These variables may be internal (like motivation or attitudes), external (such as the demographic, socio-cultural, and geographic variations across the country), observable (marketer's stimuli like sales promotion offers), and latent (like predisposition). Even if the variables are understood, their accurate characteristics and the relative strength of their influence are not so obvious. Given the complex set of behaviour of the contemporary consumers, from the marketer's point of view, formulation of a model incorporating all the possible equations and correlations amongst the relevant variables may sound very useful to understand how consumers behave in the market place. This understanding would help them to design appropriate strategies and operate in the market accordingly.

A model, here, may be interpreted as a simplified realistic version of the actual actions performed by the consumers in their own mind and its reflection in the market place. Since consumer behaviour has been defined as a blueprint of the decision process, models that focus on this process will be of substantial interest to us.

MODELLING BEHAVIOUR

In order to appreciate the underlying constructs of the consumers' choice decisions and the extent to which they contour the choice process, marketers often resort to some established models of consumer behaviour. Models are sometimes designed by verbal illustrations, by portraying with the help of diagrams or mathematical symbols, or by describing with some physical process. In consumer behaviour, the existing models may be segregated into two different schools—the traditional models and the contemporary models. These models are elaborated in the next sections.

Traditional Models

While attempting to have a clear comprehension about the economic system, it was the economists who emerged as the pioneers to develop the basic consumer decision models. Ideally, the priori assumptions of the economic models pivot around allocation of limited resources across unlimited needs and wants. Two of its key facets, namely, microeconomics and macroeconomics have contributed in different ways to analyze the process of consumer's decision making. Even though these models have been criticized for being over-simplistic, nonetheless, after several modifications over the decades, these pioneering models still contribute a lot towards the development of contemporary theories.

Microeconomic Models

The classical microeconomic approach, propounded in the first quarter of the 19th century by Alfred Marshall, principally focused on the type of goods (normal, necessary, or giffen) and prevailing price structure in the country. The underlying assumptions of the Marshallian model are as follows.

- It is not possible to satisfy the consumers as they have unlimited needs and wants.
- Consumers are restrained by a budget line and thereby they try to allocate available purchase budget in a way that maximizes their utility.
- Consumers autonomously build up their own preferences in the absence of any external influence and their preference pattern is consistent over time.
- Consumers have perfect knowledge about the utility of a product, i.e., they are fully aware of the level of satisfaction they can derive from the use of the product.
- The law of diminishing marginal utility prevails which means the proportion of increase in utility gradually diminishes with the consumption of additional units of the product.
- Price is the only determinant of purchase preference.
- Consumers are perfectly rational in a sense that given the individual's choice criteria, they will always act in a conscious and calculated way to maximize their utility.

Based on these assumptions, economists conclude that perfectly rational consumers choose the product bundle for which the perceived cost-benefit ratio is maximum. For any particular item, the benefit/cost ratio can be measured as a ratio (MU/P) of its marginal utility (MU) to price (P). Hence, the consumer would try to realize a position where the following equation is valid for any number (*n*) of goods.

This means

$$\frac{MU_1}{P_1} = \frac{MU_2}{P_2} = \frac{MU_3}{P_3} = \ldots = \frac{MU_n}{P_n}$$

The economists noted that if a product's perceived marginal utility to price ratio is higher than the others, the consumer will be able to obtain higher level of satisfaction per unit of money from it and will opt for purchasing additional units of it. Given the adequacy of budget, the consumer will keep on purchasing additional units of the product until its marginal utility declines to the level where the product's MU/P ratio settles in an equal position to all other products' MU/P ratios.

Critical Evaluation

Although the microeconomic models are the pioneering attempts to understand the choice processes, due to their several unrealistic assumptions, their applications are highly restricted. The concept of utility maximization does not always hold true in case of the 'bottom-of-the-pyramid' consumers who usually strive for acceptable levels of satisfaction. Besides, in many cases the consumers lack perfect knowledge regarding products, and they frequently manipulate each other's preferences. Also, today's customers are subjected to many variables in addition to the price to assess a product's cost. Finally, consumers simply do not appear to be perfectly rational in all their purchase decisions. In reality, lots of psychological and social variables influence each other before a customer reaches his/her final buying decision. These impracticable assumptions may not have totally mired the worth of this model in explaining the behaviour of an entire economic system, but they are certainly not useful in understanding how actually the individual consumers behave in specific purchase situations.

Nonetheless, in spite of several shortcomings, the microeconomic models have been useful in providing a pioneering perspective which has built the base to comprehend the contemporary models of the consumer behaviour. Finally, because economists have restructured some critical aspects of the microeconomic models, it continues to exert significant influence on the contemporary thinking of the consumer behaviour.

Macroeconomic Viewpoints

Macroeconomics school of thought, on the other hand, stresses on the summative flows in the economy in terms of the monetary value of goods and resources, the directions, and the extent of their change over time. Given the knowledge of these aggregate flows, the macroeconomic school attempts to analyze the behavioural responses of the consumers who stimulate and direct the extent of financial flows. Even though the school did not produce a full-proof model of consumer buying behaviour, it has successfully provided some food for thought to analyze the contemporary models formulated in the latter half of the 20th century.

One particular aspect which has been stressed in macro-models pivots around how consumers allocate their income between consumption and savings. The underlying assumption of the macro-models is—higher the income of the families, smaller is their marginal propensity to consume and, thereby, they spend relatively lower proportion of their disposable income than the lower-income families on consumption.

In his relative-income hypothesis, James Duesenberry (1949) opined that people's consumption levels are primarily governed by their peers and social groups rather than their own absolute income levels. Therefore, an individual's marginal propensity to consume is likely to change only when he moves in an upward/downward direction in terms of social class. Nonetheless, with an equal rise in income of all the groups of the society, the marginal propensity to consume is not expected to change for any of the groups.

On the flip side, the permanent-income hypothesis proposed by Milton Friedman (1957) centres around the notion that the consumption of a family/individual/social class depends on what they consider as their 'normal' income. In doing this, they try to retain a reasonably stable standard of living even though their incomes may vary considerably over time. As a consequence, the change in income that people perceive as impermanent has modest effect on their consumption spending.

Contrary to the microeconomic models, the macro-models consider a pool of other variables like consumer's income, previous income experience, accumulated liquid assets (Friedman, 1957), variations in taxes or credits, and also increase in relative income (Duesenberry, 1949) as influencing parameters of consumer purchase decision. Nonetheless, most of the significant and symbolic cues used by the marketers as stimuli along with the psychological and social variables are overlooked in all the macroeconomic models. However, on a pragmatic note, the customers are often exposed to these variables while forming their attitude or arriving at the final buying decision.

Furthermore, both the micro- and macroeconomic models crop up as a result of their focus on the particular act of purchase. However, substantial search for information precedes it, and purchase evaluation as well as repeat purchase can tag on it. Since the economic models do not deal with these activities, they may not be accepted as all-inclusive illustration of the consumer behaviour.

Thus, the study of consumer behaviour gradually evolved as a distinctive discipline while several new approaches emerged to illustrate the process of consumer decision-making. These contemporary views are quite diverse from the earlier models because of their focus on the decision process that consumers undertake while choosing products and services. Therefore, contrary to the economic models, in these models, importance is placed on the mental process that transpires before, during, and after the purchases are made. Secondly, the contemporary models largely draw analogies from various domains of behavioural sciences. In fact, a large number of the variables used in these models are borrowed from the fields of psychology and sociology.

Quite a few contemporary consumer models have been evolved varying in terms of their sophistication, precision, domain, and scope. However, due to the scope of the syllabi only a few of the widely quoted models will be reviewed in the following sections.

Contemporary Models

Since consumer behaviour has emerged as a separate discipline, several attempts have been made to conceptualize the buying behaviour through comprehensive models. Nonetheless, five major comprehensive contemporary models are most coveted in the arena of consumer behaviour. The models range from the oldest Andreason model (1965) to the latest Engel–Kollat–Miniard and Sheth–Newman–Gross models (1991). The five models are discussed in this chapter.

Andreason Model (1965)

One of the earliest models of consumer decision-making was proposed by Andreason (1965) whose model focuses on the acceptance and interpretation of information in the consumer decision-making process. It is assumed that messages reach the consumer's memory through five basic senses. The messages can either be personal or non-personal (i.e., either word of mouth or advertisements designed by the marketers). Thereafter, a filter is created by individual's perception, with attitudes as determining factor, through which the information flows. Nonetheless, the model seems to have laid too much emphasis on the aspect of attitude while ignoring its relevance in terms of repeat purchase situations. However, attitudes can be altered in several ways. For example, when a person interacts within a group, he/she is often subject to different group norms. Further, the new information obtained would certainly have some influence on the individual's attitude, beliefs, and feelings. Cultural values, personality, experience, and wants will also shape the information processing of an individual and thereby arriving at the final choice.

Critical evaluation

For most of the complex buying models, the decision-making process starts much before the information search stage. Even Kotler's black-box model begins with the 'need-recognition' of the customers due to marketer-provided, environmental, and other stimuli. In reality, if these stimuli reach the perceptual threshold of the customers, then and only then the customer will be attentive towards the marketing communication and search for information regarding the intrinsic or extrinsic benefits of the products or brands. Secondly, the model is devoid of detailed analogy of repeat purchase situations or impulse buying situations. Thirdly, it is difficult to generalize the model in the absence of any validation methods used.

Nicosia Model (1966)

Nicosia's model (1966) focuses on the buying decision, especially for a new product. It is a four-field-model, in which the first three fields elucidate various decision-making steps that the consumers espouse before buying goods or services. Nicosia had resorted to a detailed computer flowchart for this purpose. For ease of comprehension, all the mental situations of the consumer have been classified into various fields and subfields.

Thereafter, all the elements of the model are connected through direct as well as feedback loops. Hence, the model stresses on the association between the firm and its prospective consumers. The firm communicates with consumers through its stimuli (in terms of all the four Ps), and the consumers respond to these messages by forming their attitudes towards the product/brands and finally purchase/reject it. A careful watch on the model may project that the two basic entities of the market place, namely, the firm and the consumer, are neatly connected with each other, and mutually influence each other's strategies and actions. The major fields and subfields of the model are as follows.

Field 1: The consumer's attitude based on the firm's messages

The first field that deals with the consumer's initial attitude after being exposed to the firm's message is sub-divided into two subfields.

The first subfield explains how the firm's marketing environment and communication effort are shaped by its attributes and traits, given the existing competitive environment and features of the target market. The second subfield portrays the consumer's individual characteristics, e.g., experience, personality, and how he perceives the marketer's communications regarding the product. In this phase, the consumer develops his attitude toward the firm's product depending on the way he interprets the firm's message.

Field 2: Search and evaluation

In the second phase, the consumer begins to search for attributes of other firm's offerings and compares them with the concerned firm's brand. At this phase, it is the task of the marketer to provide adequate information about the product, highlight their USPs, shape the customer's evaluative criteria (as Nicosia talks about new purchase only), and motivate them in favour of its brands through its promotional messages.

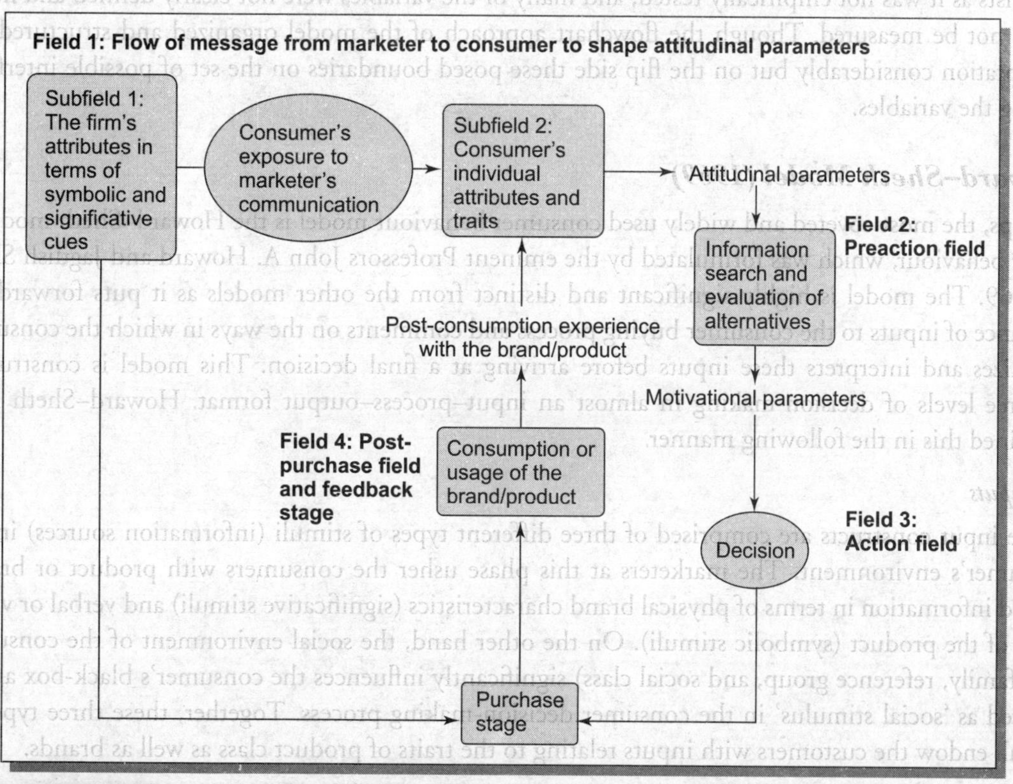

Figure 15.1 Diagrammatic interpretation of Nicosia's model of consumer decision process

Source: Loudon D.A. and Della Bitta A., *Consumer Behaviour*, TMH Publications, 2001.

Field 3: The act of the purchase

At this stage, the motivated customers are convinced to purchase the firm's products from a specific distributing point.

Field 4: Feedback

Finally, the model interprets the post-purchase feedback of the consumers. The firm may use the sales data as a feedback and modify the brands' traits or promotion/distribution strategies if required, and the consumer is supposed to use his experience to develop notions about the product/firm.

Critical evaluation

The worth of Nicosia's model, however, rests on the integration of insights about the 'non-action' kind of variables present in the environment and the ways they prompt actions from the consumers. But it does not unveil the impact of the internal factors on the consumer and the ways they shape the consumer's attitude toward the product. Moreover, the Nicosia model overlooks the aspects of predisposition and perceptual bias—the two most crucial aspects of understanding the customer's expectation from a product or brand. Besides, this model has been severely criticized by the behavioural scientists as it was not empirically tested, and many of the variables were not clearly defined and hence could not be measured. Though the flowchart approach of the model organized and structured the presentation considerably but on the flip side these posed boundaries on the set of possible interfaces among the variables.

Howard–Sheth Model (1969)

Perhaps, the most coveted and widely used consumer behaviour model is the Howard–Sheth model of buyer behaviour, which was formulated by the eminent Professors John A. Howard and Jagdish Sheth in 1969. The model is highly significant and distinct from the other models as it puts forward the relevance of inputs to the consumer buying process and comments on the ways in which the consumer organizes and interprets these inputs before arriving at a final decision. This model is constructed in three levels of decision-making in almost an input–process–output format. Howard–Sheth have explained this in the following manner.

(a) *Inputs*

These input constructs are comprised of three different types of stimuli (information sources) in the consumer's environment. The marketers at this phase usher the consumers with product or brand-related information in terms of physical brand characteristics (significative stimuli) and verbal or visual traits of the product (symbolic stimuli). On the other hand, the social environment of the consumer (e.g. family, reference group, and social class) significantly influences the consumer's black-box and is referred as 'social stimulus' in the consumer decision-making process. Together, these three types of stimuli endow the customers with inputs relating to the traits of product class as well as brands.

(b) *Processing of inputs*

Similar to the consumer black-box concept, the most fundamental part of this model too consists of several psychological variables involved when the consumer is envisioning a decision.. The perceptual variables determine how the consumer interprets the information from the input stimuli, memory and other sources. Improper comprehension of the environmental stimuli results in 'stimulus ambiguity'. Further consequence of stimulus ambiguity is 'perceptual bias' which is formed when the consumer distorts the information received in a way it fits with his established needs or experience. While mentally processing the information or stimuli received from the environment, the consumer may resort to some other decision-making parameters which Sheth *et al.* referred as learning constructs. The learning constructs include confidence on the product/brand, intention to purchase, motives behind the choice, choice criteria, brand comprehension, and level of perceived satisfaction from the product/brand. The possible interface amongst the perceptual and learning constructs endows the model with considerable improvement over the traditional models.

However, some exogenous variables, which are not direct part of the decision-making process, pose some influence on the importance of the purchase, consumer's personality traits, religion, time pressure, etc.

(c) *Outputs*

The outputs are the resultant behaviours of the consumers exposed in the market place based on their interpretation of the received environmental stimuli through the interface of the perceptual and learning constructs. These response behaviours can be measured in terms of attention, brand comprehension, attitudes, and intention.

Critical evaluation

Howard–Sheth model focuses on three input stages—significative, symbolic, and social stimuli. While explaining both the significative and symbolic stimuli, the model has over-emphasized on the material aspects, such as price and quality. Conversely, at the point of interpretation of the social stimuli, the model fails to explain how the dynamics of social variables differ across the societies and even geographic regions and in particular how those changes in social dynamics influence the decision-making process. For example, the family values and influences of the Indian rural bottom-of-the-pyramid customers are significantly different from that of the double income urban literate customers. Moreover, the model has mentioned about various input-processing variables, but has not mentioned how they intermingle and correlate amongst themselves to develop the perceptual bias or predispositions of the customers. Finally, no direct relation has been drawn on the role of religion in influencing the consumer's decision-making process. Religion is evaluated just as an external factor without any real sway on the consumer and, therefore, might be considered as the palpable weakness while interpreting this model. In a country like India, where many of the social stimuli, like family structure, festivals, etc., vary with religion, the model may significantly fail to explain the pragmatic situation, especially in the rural context. In particular, while targeting the rural bottom-of-the-pyramid customers, having clear-cut idea about the level of literacy, prevailing myths, and superstitions about the adoptability of a particular product are the calls for the day. Another weakness stems from the fact that there being ample of measurement errors, the theory cannot be practically tested. The distinction between the exogenous and endogenous variables is also not unambiguous. Some of these constructs are really difficult to practically measure (for example, perceptual bias and attitude). While Howard and Sheth attempted to generalize their conclusions, Loudon *et al.* (1993) pondered over its unsuitability in explaining joint or group decision-making. Jagdish Sheth, later on propounded his 'family decision-making model' (1974), but there too, he had mentioned about several individual and group constructs that influence a family-purchase behaviour. But once again, the measurement methods of these variables were not clear and hence, this model too, could hardly be generalized.

Exhibit 15.1: Analysis of the Constructs of Howard–Sheth Model with Respect to Purchase of Hi-tech Mobiles Amongst the Indian Youths of 21st Century: An Empirical Research

Recently a study was conducted to analyze the constructs of the Howard–Sheth model with respect to the purchase of hi-tech mobiles amongst the 21st century youths of Kolkata, one of the biggest metropolitan cities in the world.

For the purpose, 4 focus group interviews were conducted with 36 respondents and the observations were explained with the Howard–Sheth model of consumer behaviour. The respondents were of the age group 24–37, high salaried management graduates or engineers working mainly in Sector V, Salt Lake City, Kolkata. The survey results can be grouped into the following sub-sections.

Level of problem solving

Hi-tech mobile phones are relatively high priced and, therefore, by nature are high involvement products. Thus, as is the case with all such high priced and high involvement products, this purchase may also be categorized as the extensive problem-solving behaviour.

Inputs

The Sheth model specifies three types of stimuli, namely, significative, symbolic, and social. In this case, the two most important stimuli were the social and significative cues. It was also identified that the significative and symbolic stimuli have been imbibed mainly from the family, reference groups (specially the peer group), and several non-personal information sources (Internet, advertisements, etc.). As the concerned age group was mainly in their late 20s and early 30s, it was not surprising to see that the main source of information for them comprised the Internet and the peer group.

The kinds of stimuli that motivated the customers were mainly designs, features, trend, and value-added services of the mobiles. Significative cues were the price and quality. Moreover, staying in one of the biggest metropolitan cities, availability of a new model is more or less ensured, and hence, this parameter was not a matter of concern for them. However, esteem need seemed to be prioritized amongst 80% of the respondents.

(Contd.)

Exhibit 15.1 *(Contd.)*

Perceptual constructs

- *Overt search*: After gathering information from different sources, the respondents completed their overt search and then formed a consideration set which included shortlisted brands and models of mobiles.
- *Stimulus ambiguity*: It is evident from the study that the respondents grasped pretty well the information obtained from various sources regarding the mobile phones. There was no point of confusion about certain features in the phone or the way they were represented. Thus, it could be safely claimed that the stimulus ambiguity in this case was zero or nil.
- *Attention*: It is important to know how much attention the respondents pay while receiving different input stimuli from different sources. It is important as without any proper attention, the respondent will not be able to comprehend the brand attributes to reach a clear decision about his/her preference and choice of brands/models. To assess the level of attention that the respondents paid to the different input stimulus, the following two aspects were considered.
  - *Do they remember the logo of their preferred brand of mobile phones?*
    Thirty-two out of the 36 respondents showed that they paid due attention to the different input stimuli.
  - *Do they remember the brand ambassador of their preferred mobile phone brand?*
    The result here was pretty interesting as 22 out of the 36 respondents were not able to remember the brand ambassador of their preferred brand whereas 13–14 respondents were able to remember the brand ambassadors. But this does not necessarily mean that the respondents were not clear about their choice of brands. Almost 75% of the respondents who were not aware of the brand ambassadors of *Nokia*/*Samsung* preferred those brands. The positioning strategy of *Nokia* is such that they rely mainly on the quality of their phones and the loyal customer base. Brand mascots were found to have little or no impact on the choice of *Nokia* handsets.
- *Perceptual bias*: Perception, as its definition goes, is the process by which an individual selects, organizes, and interprets stimuli into a meaningful and coherent picture of the concerned product. Whenever a consumer is in the process of decision-making to buy a certain product, it is common that he/she distorts the information received in such a way that it fits his/her established needs or experience. The perceptual bias can occur as a result of previous experience or preconceived ideas about something. These perceptual biases usually eliminate some brands or models (according to the propositions of the Howard–Sheth model).
  In this study, the following perceptual biases were observed:
  - Twenty-two respondents preferred *Nokia*/*Samsung* and considered them as their only brand of consideration.
  - Eleven respondents did not want mobile phones with a flip, as they did not have a good past experience.
  - Twenty-three respondents did not want mobiles with touch screen as they thought it would malfunction sooner than later.

Thus, it is observed that the majority of the respondents wanted *Nokia* and some of them did prefer phones with flip or touch screen, and accordingly the consideration set of the consumer was formed.

Learning constructs

- *Motives*: It is important to know about the motives for which a consumer is contemplating to buy a certain good. In the present study, an attempt was made to identify the motive/s of the respondents

(Contd.)

Exhibit 15.1 *(Contd.)*

for which they wanted to buy a hi-tech phone. Motive can also be termed as the need for which the respondents want to buy a phone. From the focus group interview, the following needs were observed among the respondents.

- *Esteem needs*: Seventy-five percent respondents agreed that the motive of buying a hi-tech phone was to use it as a status symbol.
- *Social needs*: Some of the respondents also acknowledged the fact that the motive behind their purchase was to keep in touch with their near and dear ones.

- *Choice criterion*: The following choice criteria in terms of mobile phones were revealed during the study.
  - *Price:* Price was revealed as an important criterion for choosing a brand of mobile phone. In this study, 80% of the respondents found ₹10,000–20,000 as the accepted price range for their hi-tech phones whereas 10% of the respondents found ₹20,000 and above as the accepted price range. The rest 10% respondent thought that ₹7000–10,000 was the accepted range. Thus, it can be claimed that, for the majority, the accepted price was above ₹10,000.
  - *Functionality*: Choice of the different functionalities greatly influences the preference of one model of mobile phone over the other. In this study, it was observed that the majority of the respondents wanted camera, music player, and FM in their phones. Apart from these, they also somewhat preferred the facilities like surfing the Internet from the mobile (such as 3G or Wi-Fi). This result is not surprising as it has already been observed that, for majority, the motive to buy a mobile was either related to one's esteem or belongingness.
  - *Availability of service centres*: Fifty percent of the respondents were found to be indifferent to this aspect and assumed it is not so important to have a service centre in the vicinity of their residence. But the rest of the consumers felt the importance of having a service centre near their residence. As a matter of fact, as the respondents resided in Kolkata, one of the biggest metropolitan cities in India, they knew that they would in any case find a service centre in proximity for almost all mobile brands.
  - *Brand name*: Brand name was revealed as an important parameter for 85% of the respondents as they steadily recalled the brand names like *Nokia*, *Samsung*, *Sony Ericsson*, etc.
  - *Other criteria*: There were certain other criteria which crept up in course of the interview. Majority of the respondents wanted the mobile phone to have a good battery life and some even preferred the phone to be sleek in appearance and light-weighted. Another criterion which came into light was that some respondents wanted the keypad to be smooth and easy to use.
- *Brand comprehension*: Based on the motives and the choice criteria, the different brands under consideration were comprehended. In the present study, majority of the respondents had a positive brand comprehension about *Nokia* followed by *Samsung*, *Sony Ericsson*, and *Micromax*. The result could be easily interpreted as majority of the respondents had a bias towards *Nokia* as it offered the functionalities that they wanted and at the same time fulfilled their buying motives.
- *Attitude*: Although in this study, majority of the respondents had a positive attitude towards *Nokia*, i.e., they liked the brand; it may not necessarily ensure that they had the intention to buy it.
- *Confidence*: Before a consumer develops an intention to buy a product, he must have the confidence in it. As the present study is concerned with only hi-end and high priced mobile phones (which were high-involvement products), so the confidence of the customers on the chosen brand was extremely crucial. Most of the respondents took the decision to buy the mobile themselves and the time gap.

(Contd.)

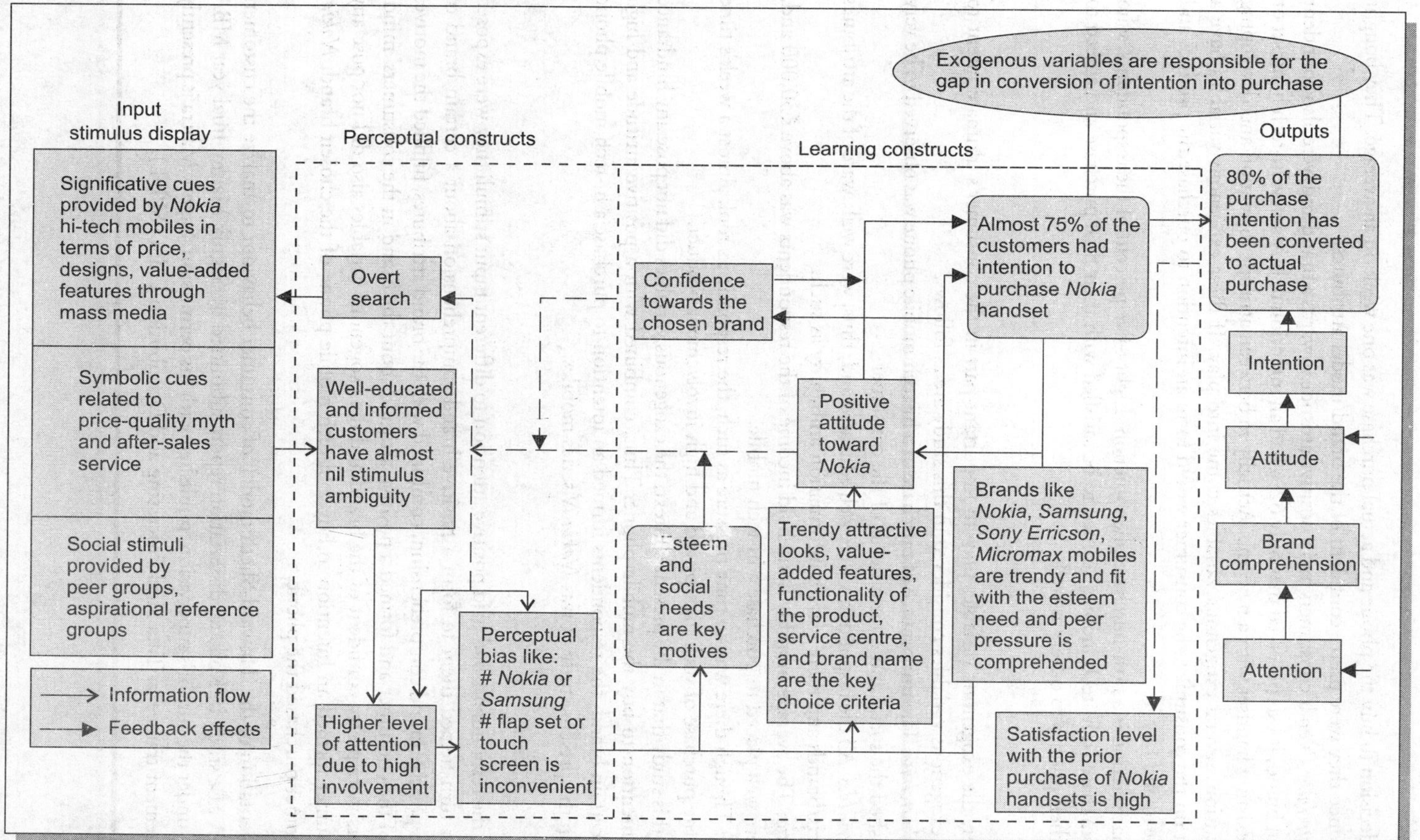

Figure 15.2 A simplified version of consumer decision-making model regarding hi-tech mobiles in the light of Howard–Sheth model

Source: Howard, John A. and Sheth, Jagdish, *The Theory of Buyer Behaviour*, John Wiley, 1969; Loudon and Della Bitta, *Consumer Behaviour—Concepts and Applications*, Tata McGraw Hill, 2002, p. 608; http://www.churcher.com/FOSM/foundations-of-senior-management-10013.htm

Exhibit 15.1 *(Contd.)*

between the decision to buy the phone and actual purchase was one week on an average. They bought the handsets once they were pretty confident of the brand/model attributes.

- *Intention to purchase*: Even if consumers had a positive attitude towards a brand and were also confident of their chosen brand, it was observed that only 62% had an intention to buy a new hi-tech hand set or replace their existing handset with a new one. Actually in between attitude formation and developing purchase intention, several exogenous variables come into play. If these exogenous variables have a positive effect on the consumer, the consumer would form an intention to purchase the product and he may go ahead and buy it.
- *Satisfaction*: Satisfaction is a post-purchase phenomenon. Eighty-five percent of the respondents, who had already purchased a hi-tech mobile, seemed to be satisfied with their final purchase and agreed to recommend their phones to others as well.

Exogenous variables

As mentioned earlier, the exogenous variables play an important part in the consumer's ultimate intent to buy a product. The exogenous variables considered in this study are as follows.

- *Importance of purchase*: The importance of purchase of a hi-tech mobile phone was observed to be very high as it satisfied the social and esteem needs of the consumer.
- *Personality variables*: All the respondents were well educated and, thus, were well aware of the attributes of the products/brands and there was no information ambiguity as such.
- *Financial status*: The average monthly household income of the respondents was above ₹30,000 and, thus, they were well placed to purchase a hi-tech mobile.
- *Time pressure*: Though there was no time pressure as such, the respondents took almost a week's time to decide on the purchase of such high priced and high involvement product.

It was clear from this study that in the present context, the exogenous variables did not pose any hindrance in the consumer's intention to buy the mobile phone. Thus, combined with a positive attitude and high confidence about a certain brand, the respondents formed an intention to purchase a hi-tech mobile phone of a certain brand. In the present study, it was *Nokia N* series mobiles.

Output

As discussed earlier, the respondents had paid positive attention to different input stimuli they were exposed to. These stimuli in turn helped them to form a positive brand comprehension about a certain brand of mobile phones. This positive brand comprehension, combined with the brand attributes, fulfilled the motives and choice criteria of the consumer and formed a positive attitude about the brand in the consumers' mind. When the consumers were pretty confident of the brand and the exogenous variables also did not pose any hindrance, the consumer formed an intention to buy a hi-tech mobile phone of the chosen brand, *Nokia*. Thereafter, the customer purchased the phone.

Source: The implementation of the 'Howard-Sheth model' of consumer behaviour to analyze the customers of hi-tech mobiles–A case study in Kolkata, dissertation report submitted by Sagnik Maitra, final year MBA student 2009–2011 under the author's supervision, published with his permission. Sagnik Maitra is presently working as a management trainee in Tata Steel Processing and Distribution Ltd. (TSPDL).

Engel–Kollat–Blackwell Model (1972)

Engel–Kollat–Blackwell (EKB) model, as other basic models of consumer behaviour, has undergone several modifications and improvisations to enhance its evocative power of the basic relationships between constructs and sub-constructs. The latest version coined up was the Engel–Kollat–Miniard (EKM) model, which principally portrays the four stages explained below.

First stage: Decision-process stage

The pivotal point of the model is the five stage basic decision-process—problem recognition, search for alternatives, alternate evaluation (at some point in which consumer's beliefs may lead to formation of attitude and subsequently purchase intention), purchase, and outcomes (in terms of satisfaction or dissatisfaction). Nonetheless, as discussed in the earlier chapter, in all purchase situations the consumers are not passed through all five stages; only in case of extended problem-solving behaviour, all the five stages are visible. In case of the choice of hi-tech and hi-end mobiles, as discussed in the earlier case study (high-involvement purchase), the consumer will behave as an extended problem-solving situation and undergo all five relevant stages of decision-making.

Second stage: Information input

This stage is quite similar to the stimulus-input stage mentioned in the Howard–Sheth model. At this stage, the consumer first tries to recollect the product or brand related information from his own memory, which is referred to as 'internal search'. For example, in case of choosing a hi-tech mobile, the prospect first tries to remember the advertisements to which he is exposed to in recent past, which sets his peer group has used recently, and what the features of the product/brand are. If this internal search is not sufficient, then the consumer deliberately searches information from outside. He obtains information from several marketing (promotions or retailers) and non-marketing sources (peers, family reference groups, opinion leaders). At times the situation is the other way round. Sometimes the external stimulus generates the problem recognition stage of the decision-making process.

Many a times, to reduce the post-purchase dissonance, the consumer strives for searching the external information to confirm his choice.

Third stage: Information processing

This phase of consumer decision-making encompasses the following stages—consumer's exposure to the marketer's stimuli (advertisements or any other marketer's communication), attention (if the product has any relevance to the consumer), perception (once the marketer's communications fall within the consumer's perceptual threshold), acceptance to the information, and retention of the perceived and accepted information in the memory (initially short term, then gradually long term). For example, the prospective buyer of the hi-tech mobile may have to undergo through the following stages of information processing.

- Initially today's young prospective buyer of a hi-tech mobile is ushered with information through television commercials, hoardings, banners, and also from his peer group.
- Thereafter, he allocates space for this information.

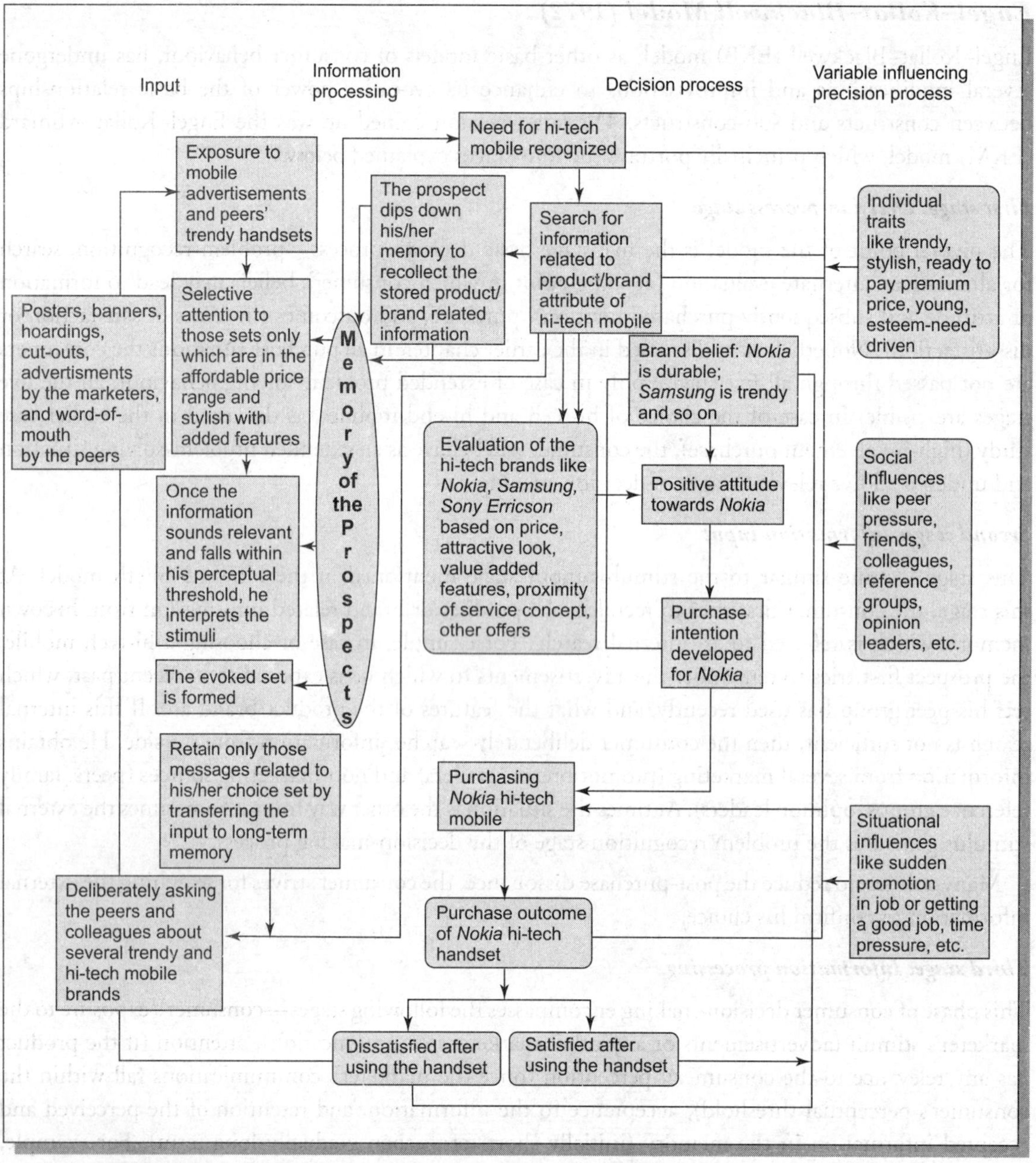

Figure 15.3 The Engel–Kollat–Blackwell model of consumer behaviour for hi-tech and hi-priced mobile handsets

Source: Engel, J.F., Blackwell, R.D. and Miniard, P.W., *Consumer Behavior*, Cengage Learning, 1995, p. 95.

- Once the information sounds relevant to him and falls within his perceptual threshold (in terms of price preference, trend, style, design, features, availability, celebrity endorsement, catchy music, or colours in the advertisements), he interprets the stimuli.
- After interpretation, the prospective buyer can shape his evoked set and retain messages related to his choice set by transferring the input to the long-term memory.

Fourth stage: Variables influencing the decision process

In the fourth stage, Miniard *et al.* spoke of the individual and environmental influences on all five stages of the decision process. Similar to the Howard–Sheth model, here too, individual characteristics include motives, values, lifestyle, and personality. The social influences, like culture, reference groups, and family, and the situational factors (such as a consumer's financial condition) also influence the decision process. About the hi-tech mobile users, once again, it is well understood from the explanation of the Howard–Sheth model, mentioned in the earlier section, that the young high-income prospective consumers are more influenced by both the social and the individual variables like esteem needs, social needs, trendy lifestyle, happy-go-lucky, or chic-urbanite personality, etc.

This model, therefore, incorporates many important individual and social parameters such as values, lifestyle, personality, and culture, which significantly influence the consumer decision-making.

Critical Evaluation

Majority of the contemporary models shaped in the 1960s and 1970s lacked strong theoretical background as the discipline of consumer behaviour was in its nascent stage at that time (Du Plessis, Rousseau *et al.*, 1991). This concern might have been partially eliminated by the modernizing of some of the contemporary models like the EKB model. The so-called 'grand model' has been revised and renamed as EKM model which has categorically and explicitly encompassed several individuals and environmental constructs of consumer decision-making, such as values, lifestyle, personality, and culture. Nonetheless, the environmental and individual variables mentioned in the model have been ushered with severe criticisms due to the vagueness of their definitions and their roles within the decision-making process (Loudon and Della Bitta, 1993). To be more specific, the influences of the environmental variables are well identified, but their roles in influencing the buyer behaviour are not very comprehensively elucidated. Further, the model fails to showcase which factors will shape these individual and social variables, and why different types of personality traits result in differences in consumer's choice processes. In countries like India, Pakistan, or Bangladesh, religion can also play a major role to elucidate some behavioural characteristics of the consumer, and, thereby, lead to better understanding of the model. However, this link is completely missing in the model.

Further, the roles of individual purchase motives are only considered to be constructive for need recognition, and, thereby, this crucial theoretical aspect seems to be undervalued in analyzing the decision-making process (Bagozzi, Gurhan-Cantli *et al.*, 2002; Loudon *et al.*, 1993). The model has also been criticized for its mechanistic treatment with highly flexible psychological and social constructs (Loudon *et al.*, 1993).

Sheth–Newman–Gross Model of Consumption Values (1991)

Much after the acclaimed Howard–Sheth model formulated in 1969, Prof. Sheth, along with Newman and Gross, developed another advanced and comprehensive model of consumer behaviour comprising of five consumption values influencing consumer choice behaviour. These values are functional, social, conditional, emotional, and epistemic in nature. These behavioural scientists claimed that any or all of the five consumption values play their own roles while the consumer contemplates to a decision. Sheth *et al.* (1991) claimed that most of the theories behind this model have been drawn from studies and research findings across the diversified disciplines of economics, sociology, and several branches of psychology, marketing, and consumer behaviour. Most of the consumption values mentioned in the model are consistent with several constituents of the theories propounded by Maslow (1970), Katona (1971), and Katz (1960). Sheth *et al.* have articulated the five consumption values, namely, functional, social, conditional, emotional, and epistemic values to shape the centroid of this model.

The first value: Functional value

> *'The perceived utility acquired from an alternative for functional, utilitarian, or physical performance. An alternative acquires functional value through the possession of salient functional, utilitarian, or physical attributes. Functional value is measured on a profile of choice attributes'*
>
> (Sheth, Newman, and Gross, 1991)

Sheth *et al.* claimed that the functional values, being the most important parameter behind the consumer's final choice, deserve special analytical focus. This presumption is very much in line with the Marshallian economic utility theory. The Marshallian economic theory (1890) more often articulates the consumer as a 'rational economic man'. Ferber (1973) took the 'rational economic man' concept a step further by concluding that the brand options are often evaluated in terms of their various functional traits, such as reliability, durability, and price. For example, the decision to purchase a particular brand of laptop may be based on its price, proximity of the service centre, and service records.

On the other hand, according to Solomon (1996), once the most attractive functional trait of a product perceived by the customers is recognized, marketers are in a position to determine which of their unique selling propositions can motivate the prospects. Accordingly, the communication message and packaging strategies can be formulated highlighting the already identified functional traits. For example, the recent advertisement of *Hajmola* highlights the need to be protected from indigestions while enjoying the festivals and ceremonies. Many companies announce festive bonazas during October–November which are considered to be the festive season of the country with *Navratri*, *Durga Puja*, *Dussehra*, and *Diwali* being celebrated during this period.

Katz (1960) has further enhanced the functional theory by his own contribution. He has defined four specific functional values based on the particular attitudinal parameters of the customers. These functions are enumerated below.

1. *Utilitarian function*: The utilitarian function is based on the very basic propositions of reward and punishment. In most of the cases, the customers form their attitude based on the perceived satisfaction or dissatisfaction generated from the consumption of the products.

2. *Value-expressive function*: The market place responses of the customers are often influenced by his/her core value, self-concept, or even extended-self. Therefore, following Katz it may be stated that the value-expressive function, sometime or the other, outweighs the objective benefits a person may derive from the use of the products.
3. *Ego-defensive function*: When a consumer seeks protection for self, either from external environmental embarrassments or internal feelings, he often resorts to an ego-defensive function. Marketers, while designing their advertising message, often use the ego-defensive cues. For example, one may recollect most of the campaigns of anti-dandruff shampoos which stress on the awful and awkward situations faced by the individuals for dandruff in offices (as in the *Garnier* shampoo advertisement) or other public places (as in the *Chik* shampoo advertisement).
4. *Knowledge function*: It has been argued by Katz that attitude is often developed as a consequence of a need for order, structure, or meaning. Knowledge function is particularly relevant when a person is in an ambiguous situation or wants to use a new product. For example, when a person wants to buy a laptop or car, he often resorts to extensive search for information from his opinion leaders and several marketing sources as he is not conversant with the technology in-built in those products.

The second value: Social value

> *'The perceived utility acquired from an alternative association with one or more specific social groups. An alternative acquires social value through association with positively or negatively stereotyped demographic, socioeconomic, and cultural-ethnic groups. Social value is measured on a profile choice imagery'*
> (Sheth, Newman, and Gross, 1991)

The term 'Social imagery' envisages all pertinent primary and secondary reference groups which are expected to be the driving forces for the product's usage. Consumers are positively or negatively typecast depending on how they intermingle with varied demographic (age, gender, stage of family life cycle, etc.), economic (disposable income), psychographic (attitude, motivation), or religious/ethnic groups of people.

Generally, the consumer decision heuristics for the products which reflect individual's personality traits or social class due to their high visibility (e.g., apparels, watches, accessories) and the products to be gifted or shared with other members of the group are influenced by consumer's social values. For example, *Raymond*'s suiting may be chosen for the social image it evokes ('The Complete Man') than its functional or utilitarian performance. Many a times, even selection of products/brands which are likely to be governed more by their functional traits are finally chosen on the basis of their social values.

The third value: Emotional value

> *'The perceived utility acquired from an alternative's capacity to arouse feelings or affective states. An alternative acquires emotional value when associated with specific feelings or when precipitating those feelings. Emotional values are measured on a profile of feelings associated with the alternative'*
> (Sheth, Newman, and Gross, 1991)

The authors have showcased the consumer's perceived utility as a set of emotional reactions extracted particularly in the course of the product usage or consumption experience. The concept of consumption emotion has been explained either by the particular types of emotional experience and responses (e.g., bliss, resentment, and anxiety) or by the structural dimensions forming the core emotion categories, such as comfortable/uncomfortable, leisure/action, or serenity/exhilaration. Subsequently the marketers often resort to the customer's probable emotional responses (e.g., the sense of jubilation arising out of viewing a gala party in any television show) associated with the product to design the product as well as its communication message. The nostalgia associated with the advertisement of *Titan* or the sense of fulfilment associated with the commercial of *Life Insurance Corporation of India* are some such exemplars. The emotional values can also be generated from the aesthetic orientation of the product. Sometimes, the emotional values, similar to social values, outweigh the tangibles and functional traits of the products even when the product apparently seems to be a utilitarian one. For example, some pens or ties arouse a feeling of placate through their association with first job experiences.

Time and again, behavioural scientists have tried to categorize the various emotional values that play a dominant role at the time of consumer decision-making. In one such study, the eminent behavioural scientist, Izard (1977), propounded the classification of affective experiences which elaborate the underlying emotions attached to certain kinds of purchase. Izard *et al.* (1984) identified ten basic emotions to explain such affective experience process. These emotions are sadness, anger, interest, joy, surprise, fear, shame, disgust, contempt, and guilt. Izard's study appeared to be a foundation for the future consumer researches on emotional values.

The fourth value: Epistemic value

> *'The perceived utility acquired from an alternative capacity to arouse curiosity, provide novelty, and/or satisfy a desire for knowledge. An alternative acquires epistemic value by items referring to curiosity, novelty, and knowledge'* (Sheth, Newman, and Gross, 1991)

Epistemic issues mean the set of values that could validate and enhance the customer's perceived satisfaction level obtainable from a novel product by fulfilling the curiosity, knowledge, and exploratory needs. Alternatively, even a simple change of product can also generate epistemic value, like product differentiation offers. Sometimes, just to break the monotony of food habits, clothing styles, etc., the customer may exert to epistemic values by trying out something different.

The fifth value: Conditional value

> *'The perceived utility acquired by an alternative is the result of the specific situation or set of circumstances facing the choice maker. An alternative acquires conditional value in the presence of antecedent physical or social contingencies that enhance its functional or social value. Conditional value is measured on a profile of choice contingencies'* (Sheth, Newman, and Gross, 1991)

Based on the concept of stimulus dynamism advocated by Howard (1969), in this model too the conditional value proposition emphasizes on the process of learning that takes place as a result of experience with a given situation. This Sheth, Newman, and Gross model refers that consumers may also evaluate a product/brand's utility based on situation. For example, a consumer may just go to a local shop to buy a dress for ₹500 for going to college or office. The same customer may be ready to buy a dress for ₹2000 to wear in his sister's wedding.

Thus, the five consumption values recognized in the Sheth, Newman, and Gross model play as differentiators of consumer choice in case of any particular product/brand. For example, to a first-time car buyer, the purchase of a car might provide functional value (comfortable travel to his office), social values (many of peers and colleagues are possessing cars), emotional values (the consumer feels secure in owning a car so that his child may be dropped to school safely), epistemic value (the novelty involved in purchasing a new car is pleasant), and conditional value (the new office is quite distant and it is too hectic to travel by the crowded buses).

Critical evaluation

According to Sheth, Newman, and Gross (1991), customer's choice decisions are based on five major values, namely, functional value, emotional value, social value, conditional value, and epistemic value. Functional value is assumed to be the most important influencing variable of consumer choice. This assumption is derived from the Marshallian 'utility theory' (1890) which most often considers the customer as 'rational economic man'. However, as mentioned earlier, since 1980s, the researchers are vehemently arguing over the concept of rationality of the consumer actions. Quite often, the rational information processing approach of the model falls short to interpret the non-conscious behaviours of the customers. Similarly, the emotional constructs and the role of choice heuristics (in purchase phase) are not well encompassed in the concepts of functional and emotional value. Moreover, the model has explicitly spoken of the factors which may shape the decision, but how they form a linear or non-linear equation for the actual decision making is not well analyzed.

It may be concluded that a common concern of all the 'analytic' models principally underlies with the latent nature of many of the variables (Loudon and Della Bitta, 1993). Therefore, it is still difficult to assure whether the existing models do represent the pragmatic process of buyer decision-making in the market place at all. It is also difficult to predict the accurate values of all the observable and latent variables.

Closing Case

Eden City—Struggling to Convert Purchase Intention into Purchase Action

Kolkata-based Eden Group, a ₹300-crore well-known real-estate developer with more than 100 projects in its portfolio, initiated a teaser campaign featuring Konkona Sen Sharma, actress and daughter of the celebrity director and actress Aparna Sen. Perhaps, this was a pioneering attempt by the company to build its brand. With the help of a teaser campaign, the company desired to ignite a buzz which in due course would decipher into its brand-building.

The teaser campaign was run for six days. A hidden survey was conducted on 10 high salaried individuals for 10 days from the opening of this teaser campaign. The observation was based on four parameters—attention, interest, desire, action (AIDA model). It was recorded in a checklist form and the ratings were given in a 10-point staple scale.

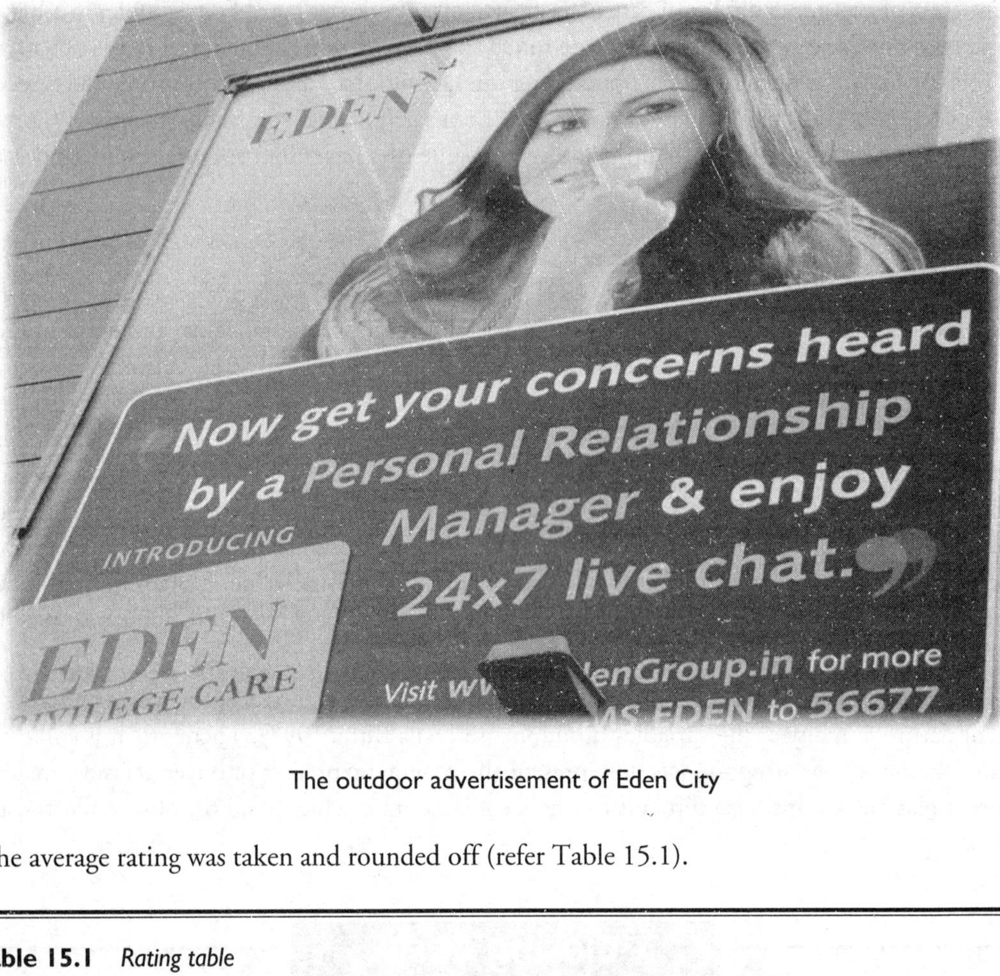

The outdoor advertisement of Eden City

The average rating was taken and rounded off (refer Table 15.1).

Table 15.1 *Rating table*

Days / *Interest*	*1*	*2*	*3*	*4*	*5*	*6 (Day of disclosure)*	*7*	*8*	*9*	*10*
Attention	3	4	5	6	7	7	6	5	4	2
Interest	2	3	5	6	7	8	8	8	8	8
Desire						6	7	8	8	8
Action										

Ratings were based on 10 being the best and 1 being the worst.

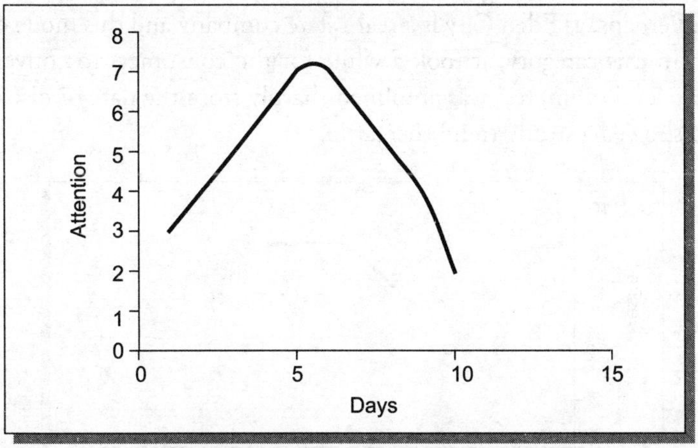

Figure 15.4 The attention graph

From the *attention* graph, we can observe that in the initial days the audience did not pay much attention, however, the level of attention increased sharply and got stabilized for a short period after reaching the peak on the seventh day, and thereafter, it started declining as the initial hype was over.

Nevertheless, some catchy lines like 'Why doesn't the builder listen to me after I book my home?' and the presence of Konkona Sen Sharma provoked curiosity and the viewers' attraction kept on increasing for about a week. Therefore, it can be said that the company was successful in creating the initial buzz, however, as soon as the product was disclosed and the charm of the teaser was over the audience became less attentive.

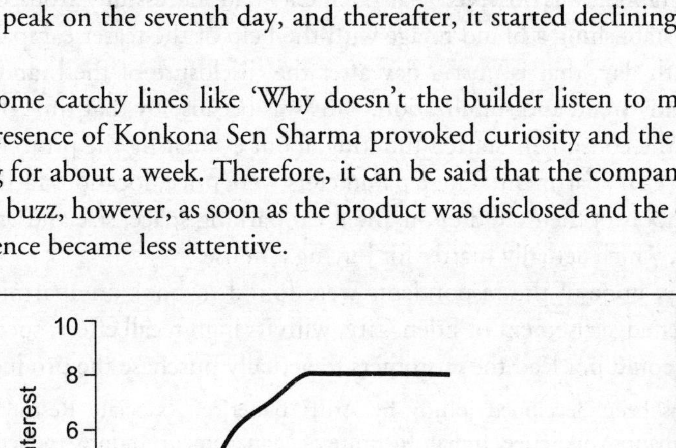

Figure 15.5 The interest graph

The *interest* curve shows more or less a steady increase. At the beginning of the campaign, the interest level was very low, but as it gained attention it evoked curiosity and viewers' interest level started increasing. Perhaps, as Eden City is a real-estate company and this mode of promotion was not very common in this category, it took a while for the consumers to convert their attention into interest. So the level of interest was amplified sharply from the date of disclosure. It attained maturity level and showed a steady trend thereafter.

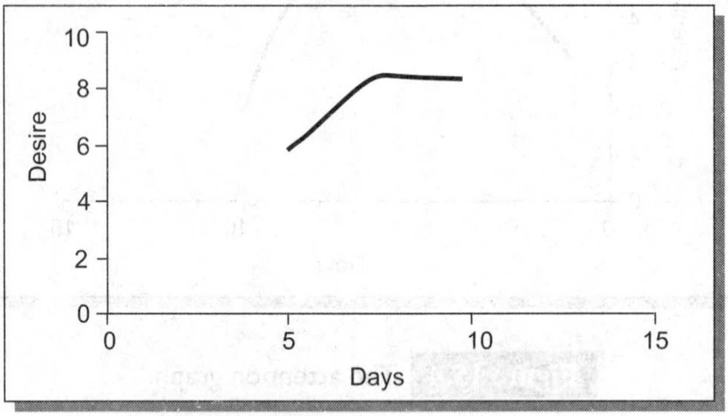

Figure 15.6 The desire graph

From the *desire* graph, it was observed that Eden City had successfully aroused the desire among the consumers by establishing a brand image with the help of the teaser campaign from the sixth day. After the eighth day, that is, just a day after the disclosure of the brand name, the desire graph showed a steady trend and stabilization. This was because by that time the initial hype was already over. Now the consumers started thinking about evaluating the project on the pragmatic parameters to choose an apartment. These parameters were price, location, facilities, proximity to their offices and schools of their children, market, car parking space, size and *vastu* compliance of the apartment, etc., which actually matter for buying a house.

By the tenth day, none of the respondents were found to book an apartment in Eden City. Therefore, the teaser advertisement of Eden City, with its high recall effect, successfully tantalized the customers, but could not lead the customers to actually purchase the product.

Source: This case has been developed jointly by Aritri Banerjee, Associate Research Manager, IMRB International and Srabanti Mukherjee, Indian Institute of Management, Indore. In fact, Eden City later on became popular for its attractive designs, locations, price, and many other facilities. But the case considers only the phase of its teaser campaigns based on hidden survey on selective respondents of Kolkata. So some amount of bias might be associated with it due to inadequacy of data. The intention of this case is to simply stimulate discussions in the classroom.

Questions

1. Had you been the Marketing Manager of Eden City, would you feel that your 'teaser campaign' strategy was wrong?
2. What strategy would you suggest for Eden City to convert intention to action given the present situation?

Summary

The basic intention of this chapter is to bring forward the underlying assumptions, characteristics, and reviews of several consumer behaviour models propounded by eminent behavioural scientists. The interested reader may find it useful to combine this material with a review of Chapter 14 which has explained the Kotler's consumer black-box model in an elaborative manner. Finally, this chapter focuses on some critical issues which may be considered as the research gaps while brazening out researches in the arena of consumer behaviour.

The chapter has classified consumer behaviour models into the traditional and contemporary versions. The traditional models are primarily the economic models, i.e., basically the Marshallian microeconomic models (based on the law of diminishing marginal utility) and the macroeconomic models (Friedman's permanent income hypothesis and Duesenberry's relative income hypothesis).

In the subsequent sections, five major contemporary models consumer behaviour have been described. All these models primarily considered satisfaction as the final output of the decision process, included it in the feedback process, and correlated it with the predictability to the future behaviour. One of the earliest models was propounded by Andreason (1965) which emphasized on the importance of information in the consumer decision-making process. The importance of Nicosia's model (1966), conversely, rested on the assimilation of insights about non-action kind of variables present in the environment and how they prompt actions at the consumers' end. The most widely used consumer behaviour model, Howard–Sheth model (1969), on the other hand, illustrated three input stages: significance, symbolic and social stimuli, and elaborated the model in an input–process–output format.

However, as most of the contemporary models were developed during the 1960s and 1970s, they lacked strong theoretical background as the discipline of consumer behaviour was in its budding stage at that period. This concern might have been somewhat purged by modernizing of some of the contemporary models like the EKB model. The EKB model was improvised and renamed as EKM model which has categorically and explicitly encompassed several individual and environmental determinants of consumer decision-making such as values, lifestyle, personality, and culture. On the contrary, according to Sheth, Newman, and Gross (1991) choice decisions are based on five major values, namely, functional value, emotional value, social value, conditional value, and epistemic value.

This chapter, however, does not draw any final conclusion about the consumer's decision-making process as this is an emerging field and the researches are still continued from various aspects to unveil the entire process in the widest detail.

Key Terms

Law of diminishing marginal utility This means the proportion of increase in utility gradually diminishes with the consumption of additional units of the product.

Overt search Search for information to develop evoked set.

Stimulus ambiguity Not understanding what the marketer wanted to communicate through stimulus.

Traditional models Economic models.

Contemporary models Behavioural models.

Perceptual bias Sometimes consumer distorts the information received as a result of previous experience or preconceived ideas about something. This is known as perceptual bias.

Learning constructs The learning constructs deal with the stages from the buyer motives to his satisfaction in a buying situation.

Perceptual constructs These attributes deal with the way the individual perceives and responds to the information from the input variables.

Purchase intention It is an outcome of the interplay of buyer's motives and choice criteria.

Brand comprehension Resultant brand attitude and the confidence associated with the purchase decision.

Motives Motives are representatives of the goals that a buyer seeks to achieve in the buying exercise. These may originate from the basis of learned needs.

Exogenous variables These variables are not defined but are taken as constant. For example, the purchase situation, time at the disposal of the buyer, personality traits, financial status, etc.

Functional value The perceived utility acquired from an alternative for functional, utilitarian, or physical performance. An alternative acquires functional value through the possession of salient functional, utilitarian, or physical attributes. Functional value is measured on a profile of choice attributes.

Utilitarian function The utilitarian function is based on the very basic propositions of reward and punishment.

Value-expressive function Attitude that underlies a value-expressive function is assumed to be the consumers' own central value, self-concept, or even extended-self in some issues.

Ego-defensive function Attitude developed for the protection of the self from external environmental embarrassments or internal feelings acts as an ego-defensive function.

Knowledge function It has been argued by Katz that attitude is often developed as a consequence of a need for order, structure, or meaning.

Social values The perceived utility acquired from an alternative association with one or more specific social groups. An alternative acquires social value through association with positively or negatively stereotyped demographic, socioeconomic, and cultural-ethnic groups.

Emotional values The perceived utility acquired from an alternative's capacity to arouse feelings or affective states. Emotional values are measured on a profile of feelings associated with the alternative.

Epistemic values The perceived utility acquired from an alternative capacity to arouse curiosity, provide novelty, and/or satisfy a desire for knowledge.

Conditional values The perceived utility acquired by an alternative is the result of the specific situation or set of circumstances facing the choice maker. Conditional value is measured on a profile of choice contingencies.

Questions

1. What was the basis of formulating consumer behaviour models? How are they important to a marketer? What major contributions do the contemporary models of consumer behaviour make when compared to the traditional models?
2. Explain with reference to Nicosia model, the process of consumer decision-making in case of
   (a) a private regional TV channel
   (b) air-conditioners
3. Compare and contrast the Howard–Sheth model and the EKM model with respect to the choice of retail to buy jewelry for your sister's wedding.
4. Do you feel the Sheth, Newman, and Gross model (1991) is really an improvisation over the original Howard–Sheth model (1969)? Explain the above statement.
5. What according to you are the general shortcomings of the contemporary models as a whole?

Critical Assignment

1. Prepare a checklist and conduct a hidden survey of five of your peers regarding the choice of ready-made apparels. Explain their behaviours with respect to the Nicosia, Howard–Sheth, and EKM models.
2. Survey 10 bottom-of-the-pyramid customers and explain how they behave in terms of seeking food, healthcare, banking, and television by using Sheth–Newman–Gross model.

Chapter **16**

Organizational Buying Behaviour

Chapter Goals

After completing this chapter, you will be able to understand the

- characteristics and importance of B2B market
- components of the business market
- types of industrial purchase
- buying decision process in business
- multiple buying influences and conflicts in buying decision in industrial buying

Opening Vignette

Earthquake in Japan—The Case of Supply-Side Crisis for the Indian Car Market

Japan—one of the topmost automobile manufacturing countries—was literally shaken by the severe earthquake and its aftershocks in March, 2011. As a result of this calamity, the car industry of Japan underwent a severe supply chain disturbance. The most important part was that just before this natural calamity, most of the samurai brands—*Honda*, *Toyota*, *Nissan*, and *Suzuki*—were to implement more aggressive stratagems to have further control on the lucrative and developing Indian car market.

Honda had stopped manufacturing at all the Japanese plants till March 20, 2011 and was in the process of assessing the exact damage. Mr. Jnaneswar Sen, Senior Vice-President (Sales and Marketing) of *Honda Siel Cars India*, claimed, 'There are hundreds of suppliers there, who may have been hit. Unless their fate is clear, nothing can be said with certainty.' Moreover, *Honda* imports many of its important engine parts from Japan. The local units of *Honda* and *Toyota* had already called off most of their promotional actions. *Honda* was about to launch a fabulous promotional event scheduled in the third week of March for its much-awaited compact car *Brio*.

Immediately after the earthquake, the company had to postpone this programme. Nonetheless, they still had components and knocked-down equipment stocks for the time being. However, nothing could be commented at that moment for the future production plans.

The earthquake devastation

Condition was graver for the consumer durables and electronics manufacturers of Japan. No doubt, the Japanese electronic products have led Indian market with much amplified investments. Nonetheless, because of the occurrences of the earthquake and tsunami in Japan, the Indian car market had suffered a major jolt. Japan's major electronic goods exporter *Sony* anticipated the chance of supply side crisis. The company had closed down six of its factories in the coastal areas. *Toshiba*, another diversified manufacturer of electronic products, too apprehended that investments scheduled for the promising Indian market were likely to experience crunch due to the massive damage happened in their country.

It was difficult to recover the damage due to the continuing power failure. As a matter of fact, due to the power failure, it was even impossible to accurately inspect the magnitude of damage occurred at the manufacturing and storage points. Therefore, it was too difficult to state at that point of time, when the damaged factories would be able to recommence their full-fledged operations. Therefore, no doubt, a pool of uncertainty was reigning in the supply side.

Sony, *Toshiba*, and the car manufacturers expected severe supply-side bottlenecks due to the prevailing uncertainty. For example, *Maruti Suzuki* depends on 95% local sub-parts for preparing older models and about 85–93% for manufacturing contemporary models. Although *Suzuki*'s Hamamatsu plant was not affected, *Maruti* imported a number of important components from Japan and hence the crisis hit a number of its Indian vendors also to import in the post-tsunami period. On March 14, 2011, a meeting took place in the Indian head office of *Maruti* to appraise the situation. Mayank Pareek, Managing Executive Officer (Sales & Marketing) of *Maruti Suzuki* briefed, 'We have a buffer stock of two weeks and would not be affected till then. However, the situation is not clear on what happens after that.'

© Indiatodayimages

Maruti Suzuki India Managing Director and CEO Shinzo Nakanishi poses with the newly launched Alto-K10 in New Delhi, India

Even the *Toyota*'s Indian unit, *Toyota Kirloskar Motor*, deferred the launch of its second plant in India. The programme was scheduled for the third week of March only. According to Sandeep Singh, Deputy Managing Director of *Toyota Kirloskar Motor*, 'production in Japan is likely to be shut for the next 2–3 days.'

So, the situation is clear, for both the electronic goods industry and the automobile industry, if the market for spare parts suffers, the production of the finished goods is bound to suffer. Hence, it is imperative to study the nature of the industrial market, behaviour, and factors influencing the behaviour of the industrial consumers.

Source: Sen Gupta, Nandini and Doval, Pankaj, Japanese Car and Electronics Makers Shut Plants, Assess Damage Auto cos may face parts shortage, *The Times of India*, March 15, 2011; Sharma, Samidha, Supply crunch to hit durables cos, *The Times of India*, March 15, 2011.

INTRODUCTION

Apparently, the organizational buying behaviour looks analogous to the consumer buying as it is the people within those organizations who take purchase decisions. Nonetheless, apart from these apparent similarities, there are significant disparities between these two types of purchases. Understanding of these differences properly is very important from the marketer's perspective in order to thrive in the organizational market.

Household consumers buy products to satisfy their as well as their families' needs. But the organizations procure goods and services to produce finished goods, provide a service, or reselling. Organizational buyers are of various types, ranging from commercial business houses and non-profit organizations to government organizations or undertakings. The organizational buying process envisages transactions of spare parts and raw materials for manufacturing the finished product or reselling the finished goods to the next level of marketing channels.

Organizational buying may be defined as the decision-making process by which organizations establish the need for purchased products and services and identify, evaluate, and choose amongst the alternative brands and suppliers.

The dynamics of organizational purchase activities have radically progressed in the world market with the outbreak of World War II. Diverging from just crude clerical operations of industrial purchase (as it was initially), it has now evolved as a more sophisticated process involving a purchasing specialist and several influencing sections, such as engineering, quality control, senior management, and the end user. Nowadays, most of the purchase decisions are taken by harmonizing the organization's requirements and the goals of suppliers and other stake holders in terms of product specifications, trade regulations, price discovery, etc.

COMPONENTS OF BUSINESS MARKET

Various categories of organizational buyers persist in the Indian market. For example, in India, on one hand, we find the mining and extractive industries (e.g., *Hindustan Copper Limited, Coal India Limited, ONGC,* etc.) and on the other hand we get to see material processing industries (e.g., *Tata Steel, Steel Authority of India Limited, Bharat Aluminium Corporation,* etc.). There exist lots of original equipment manufacturers (OEM) or, in other words, the manufacturers of parts and assembly line business houses such as *Bharat Forge, Hindustan Aeronautics Limited, Sundaram Clayton, Semiconductors of India Limited, GEC, Larsen & Toubro,* etc. The contributions of the final assembly manufacturers (*Crompton Greaves*), TV manufacturers (*Samsung, Sony, Sansui*), truck manufacturers (*Mahindra & Mahindra, Ashok Leyland*) in the Indian B2B market are also worth mentioning. On the flip side, in the resellers' market, the most visible industrial buyers are possibly the distributors. They generally buy from the manufacturers and sell to the retailers. Table 16.1 shows the types of industrial buyers. Principally, there are six types of industrial markets, namely:

1. Agriculture market

2. Reseller market
3. Government market
4. Services market
5. 'Non-business' business market
6. International market

These types are explained in the Table 16.1.

Table 16.1 *Types of industrial markets*

Types of industrial market	Characteristics
Agriculture market	Agricultural market envisages the services involved in the movement of the final agricultural produce from the farm gate to the consumer. Several interrelated actions characterize this market, viz., production planning, sowing, reaping and harvesting, grading, packing, transportation, warehousing, food processing, distribution, advertising, and finally selling.
Reseller market	Buyers may procure products to resale them to others. The reseller market consists of wholesalers, retailers, and distributors. Resellers may confine their business to a single product/brand or work as a multi-brand/product dealer or distributor.
Government market	Consumer group comprises central and state government, and other local government units such as municipality, PWD, State Electricity Board, and many more. It must be noted that the government market in aggregate accounts for the maximum amount of purchases by any consumer group in India. All the government concerns together engage in B2B operations worth crores of rupees. They purchase bulk amount of goods and services across the year. Primarily, the government purchases a wide range of products such as food, military equipment, office supplies, buildings, clothing, vehicles, and many other types of equipments.
Services market	Services marketing, in general, refers to both business-to-consumer (B2C) and business-to-business (B2B) services. Services industries include telecommunications services, financial services, hotels, hospitals, aviation, car rental services, personal care services, consultancies, and many more professional services.
'Non-business' business market	Not-for-profit oriented organizations ideally target to provide some goods and services for public well-being.
International market	International marketing (IM) or global marketing refers to the marketing process performed by companies beyond their home country and across countries. This strategy uses an expansion of the system used in the home country of a firm. It refers to the firm-level marketing practices to operate worldwide as well as segmentation and targeting, entry mode selection and determination of right positioning strategy, marketing mix, and of course several strategic decisions to participate in international markets.

As Table 16.1 portrays, 'organizational marketing' is very vast and heterogeneous. Another way to identify the organizational customers is to classify them into three categories. In that sense, the organizational market can be categorized into three groups: industrial buyers (comprising of all manufacturing organizations), institutional buyers (generally comprise service organizations such as universities, hospitals, hotels, distribution firms), and government (CPWD, army, municipalities, etc.).

In this context, it is now the need of the hour to understand the 'typical characteristics' of industrial market. Nonetheless, pragmatically, it is very important to study the organizational buying behaviour for a particular product–market situation. In the next section, we will discuss the characteristics of industrial market.

CHARACTERISTICS AND IMPORTANCE OF B2B MARKET

Webster and Wind, who have done some revolutionary works in the arena of industrial buyer behaviour, described the organizational buying as a multifaceted practice of decision making and communication, which occurs over time, engaging a number of organizational members and many other correlated firms and institutions. According to them, it is not always just a process of straight re-buy by placing an order to the regular suppliers. In that way, organizational buying behaviour may be referred to as the decision-making process by which organizations identify the need for particular products and services, identify the available alternatives of brands and suppliers, and finally evaluate and choose from the most suitable ones. From the aforementioned views by Webster and Wind, the following characteristics of industrial market can be derived.

- Industrial buying is related to the products that are meant for further production, operations, or resale. These purchases are generally like purchase of equipments, raw materials, and semi finished goods.
- There are relatively small numbers of buyers and sellers present in this market; hence, a long-term relationship between suppliers and buyers is very crucial.
- The demand for products by the industrial buyer is often derived from that of the final product. For example, the demand for raw cotton by the textile mills of Ahmedabad will depend on the nation's demand for cotton garments.
- Many a times the organizations depute some professional purchasing agents to complete a purchase on their behalf. They are called the buying specialists.
- A B2B sale often calls for selling several entities within the *buying centre*. For example, some laptops may be used by the employees of an organization; however, their specifications have been designed by the IT department, and purchase has to be sanctioned by the purchase and finance departments. For a huge number of purchases, bids can be called by the purchase department and the final authorization is made by the company CEO.
- As the industrial market is often regulated by specialists, it is more likely that buyers would mention exact specifications of the product. While purchasing office computers in bulk, an organizational buyer is supposed to mention specifications regarding processor speed, memory, hard drive size, etc. prior to bidding price for computers.

- Many agricultural firms often prefer to lease public warehouse space to combat with the fluctuating market demands. Many construction companies lease trucks and other vehicles as they stay in a particular site for short term.
- For any bigger and mass-scale purchase, organizations engage in competitive bidding (alternatively, the price discovery mechanism practiced by *Coal India*, *BSNL*, etc.) and negotiation mentioning the product specifications, delivery, price, payment mode, transportation mode, etc.

INDUSTRIAL vs. CONSUMER MARKET

In marketing practices, the differences between B2B and consumer-goods marketing are shown in Table 16.2.

Table 16.2 *Comparing business-to-business and consumer marketing*

	Business-to-business marketing	***Consumer marketing***
Product	Relatively technological in nature, associated services are very important	Depending on the need of the customer, the product may be standardized or customized. Customers are more interested in the functional attributes of the product rather than simply in the technical ones
Promotion	Emphasis on personal selling as it is easier to explain typical product specification in one-to-one and case-to-case basis	Emphasis on advertising as it is required to communicate in mass scale
Distribution	Relatively shorter, often the direct channels to market	Product passes en route through a number of intermediary links to consumer
Customer relations	Comparatively long term and multifaceted	Comparatively irregular contact; may be special offer or festive bonanzas
Decision-making process	Diverse group of organizational members with diverse goals takes decision	Individual or household unit takes decision
Price	Competitive bidding by calling for tenders for unique items; list prices prevalent only for some standard items	List prices (in most of the cases the maximum retail price or MRP is mentioned)

INDUSTRIAL PURCHASE SITUATIONS

Robinson, Faris, and Wind have classified the various buying situations into three categories:

- *Straight re-buy situations*: This situation is quite alike to the routine response behaviour of consumer/household purchase behaviour. In case of straight re-buy situation, the buyer usually places the order on routine basis with unaltered product specifications (e.g., stationery items, chemicals, lubricants, paints). Here, the buying alternatives are known, and the formal list of 'approved' suppliers is normally maintained by the organizations.

- *Modified re-buy*: In a modified re-buy situation, a buyer may alter the product specifications or may even shift his choice to a substitute product. For example, using aluminium as an alternative to copper wires, push button telephones instead of finger-dial ones, and so on. In this situation, buyers are aware of the buying alternatives but for upgradation or renovation of product, some alteration to the raw materials or equipments may be required.
- *New task*: 'New task' is a situation where the organizational customer buys the product for the first time with no prior experience about its performance (e.g., laptops, photocopiers, fax machines, or may be automation of the entire organization). For example, Indian Railways is undergoing a significant change by opening up new automated reservation counters across the nation. The 'new task' situations envisage the following features.
  (a) Need for the product is not felt by the firm earlier.
  (b) There is minimum or no prior buying experience to aid in the purchasing decision.
  (c) Lot of information is required to arrive at a consensus by the members of the organization involved in the purchase decision.
  (d) There is a chance that at an early stage, mainly at the information search stage, in the decision process the external marketing stimuli may have a huge impact.

CHARACTERISTICS OF BUSINESS MARKET DEMAND

In the B2B market, there exist five major constructs of demand, namely, derived demand, volatile demand, joint demand, elastic or inelastic demand, and inventory adjustments. It is of immense importance to have a clear idea about all these constructs to understand the behavioural pattern of the business market. The explanations of these demand constructs are presented in Table 16.3.

Table 16.3 *Categories of business market demand*

Type of demand	*Definition*
Derived demand	The demand for the equipment and inputs for production of a certain industrial product depends on the demand of the finished goods in the consumer market. So the derived demand refers to the correlation between demand for a company's output and its procurement of inputs such as raw materials, machinery, and other components. Demand for raw jute by the jute mills will depend on the demand for the jute-made articles in the market.
Volatile demand	Derived demand results in ups and downs in business market demand. This is referred to as volatile demand. Especially, the demand for capital resources is sometimes even more volatile than that for consumer demand. For example, the sales volume for a gasoline retailer escalates at an annual rate of 6% and then nosedives with a 4% annual increase. This deceleration may appear to the firm as the real slump and it may keep some of its current gasoline pumps (capital expense) inactive and reinstate them only when market conditions get better.
Joint demand	There are certain complementary products such as printer and cartridge. In this case, the demand for a product depends on the demand for the other which is used in combination with it.

Elastic and inelastic demand	This refers to the sensitivity of demand to a price change, normally following the law of demand. However, in most of the cases, the demand for industrial products are inelastic as the demand here depends more on the demand for finished goods rather than the price of the inputs.
Inventory adjustments	Adjustments in the quantity of inventory that effect business demand are referred to as inventory adjustments. Suppose a textile manufacturer takes a 70-day supply of new materials as the optimal inventory level. In this situation, if suddenly economic conditions or other factors tempt these firms to augment their inventories up to a 100-day supply, then this alteration will result in sharp increase of new orders for the raw-material suppliers. However, in case of just-in-time (JIT) system, the question of inventory does not arise. Normally, in these cases, electronic data interchange services (direct computer-to-computer transactions into vendors' databases and ordering systems) enable organizations to buy different equipments to complete the transaction. JIT II is the most recent inventory trend that heartens suppliers to position representatives at the buyer's place to perform as branch of an integrated and on-site customer–supplier group. In this case, the suppliers design and place orders based on the discussions with the buyer. This reorganization of the inventory management procedure provides a better control of the flow of goods or allows for greater efficiency by cost optimization in the entire supply chain.

DETERMINANTS OF BUSINESS MARKET DEMAND

In the previous sections, discussion has been made on the characteristics of the organizational buying behaviour and the demand constituents of the organizational markets. But it may not be ignored that there are several influencing factors which directly or indirectly control and manipulate the organizational buying decision. A group of economists and marketers consider that it is the economic factor which plays crucial role on industrial buying behaviour, as the rationality assumption holds here. They assume that the lowest price is the only parameter to choose suppliers. However, an all-inclusive view of influencing parameters in organizational buying situations was first developed by Webster and Wind (1967). According to them, there are four major types of criteria—environmental, organizational, interpersonal, and individual—that influence the industrial purchase decisions. These criteria along with their sub-fields are shown in Fig. 16.1.

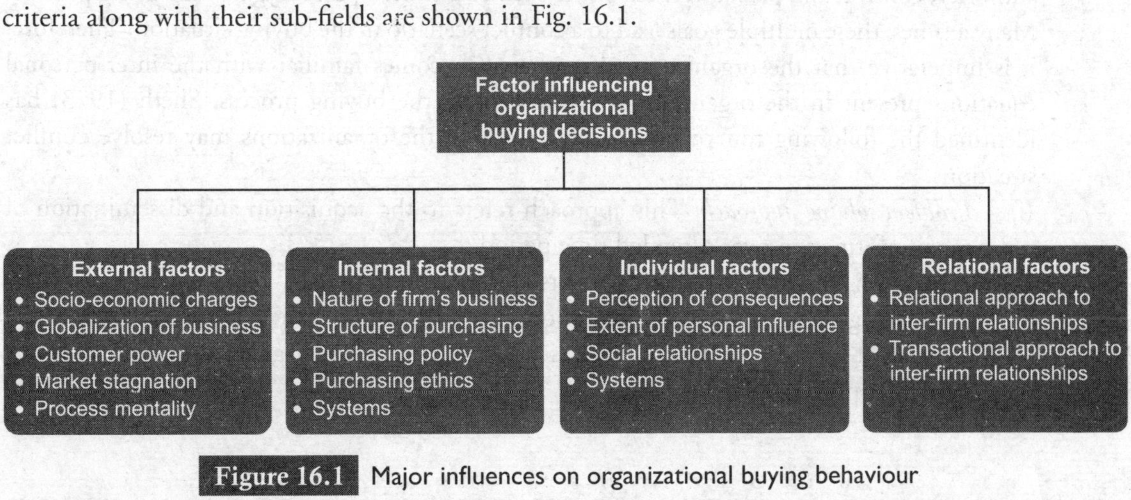

Figure 16.1 Major influences on organizational buying behaviour

The factors shown in the diagram have been elaborated as follows:

- *Environmental factors*: These factors comprise financial, social, political, technological, legal, infrastructural, demographic, and cultural factors. Environmental factors are more country specific rather than industry specific. It is actually the prevailing environment where all the business houses normally operate. The influence of environmental factors can be omnipresent. With the commencement of new economic policy and the globalization initiative in the year 1991, the country was ushered with foreign private investments and the multi-national production units of cars, soft drinks, machineries, etc. An industrial marketer should be fully alert to the changes in all the environmental factors amidst which the business is operating, and accordingly he/she should formulate and fine-tune the marketing strategy.
- *Organizational factors*: Organizational buying behaviour differs from organization to organization as the organizations themselves may be at variance with each other in terms of objectives, procedures, organizational structure, systems, and technology. It is, therefore, imperative to identify and understand the implications of such organizational specific factors on its buying behaviour. In India, some of the contemporary studies portray that there exist some critical parameters influencing the business buying structures and systems. Some of these are as follows.
    (i) Innovativeness involved in the particular purchase
    (ii) Surfacing of 'buyer' as the vital constituent of the 'buying centre' (refer *The Webster and Wind Model*)
    (iii) Centralization and decentralization of input procurement process
    (iv) Automation of the buying process (e.g., electronic data interchange system)
    (v) Involvement of purchase specialists
    (vi) Capacity of the firm to avert detrimental dealings between buyers and sellers
    (vii) Appreciation at the top level
- *Interpersonal factors*: Organizational buying involves multiple individuals in the purchase process. So the process turns out to be even more complicated due to different goals, status, authority, control, and persuasiveness of the each constituent partaking in the buying process. Many a times, these multiple goals lead to a conflict scenario in the buying situation. Therefore, it is imperative that the organizational marketer becomes familiar with the inter-personal equations present in the organization and influences the buying process. Sheth (1973) has identified the following four major routes by which the organizations may resolve conflict situations.
    (i) *Problem solving approach*: This approach refers to the acquisition and dissemination of more information over extended time period.
    (ii) *Persuasion*: Attempt is made to persuade the opinions of rebellious members by influencing them to decrease the importance of the criteria they are using to select the alternative in order to satisfy their as well as organizational goals associated with the particular purchase.

(iii) *Bargaining*: In many cases, conflicts arise due to disparities in basic purchase goals and objectives. This is generally a typical situation in case of new buying situations. In such cases, simply trying to alter the relative importance of the buying criteria may not work to resolve the conflict. Hence, any party is permitted to make an autonomous decision by agreeing to reciprocate at the time of future decisions. This process of conflict resolution is referred to as bargaining.

(iv) *Politicking*: When all the aforesaid steps go in vain, the conflicting bodies may resort to politicking. This route is harmful in context of institutional harmony and may result in casting aspersions on the rebellious members. Sheth (1973) divided all these four conflict resolution techniques into two categories. 'Problem solving' and 'persuasion' have been referred to as rational methods while the other two are considered as non-rational methods.

- *Individual factors*: An industrial marketer should be aware that may it be the suppliers, finance department, or purchase department; the purchase decision would actually be executed by a group of individuals. As these individuals, forming the group, come from diverse socio-economic backgrounds, they have a unique personality, a certain set of learned predispositions, a particular organizational task to execute, and perceptions of the finest route to fulfill both personal and organizational objectives. Possibly, an analytical insight on the 'perceived risk and its management' of the individual stakeholders of the organizations may provide the industrial marketer an opportunity to smoothen the organizational decision-making process.

Principally, there are four factors that shape the individual's purchase risk. They are the characteristics of the purchase problem, characteristics of buyers, organizational environment, and the perceived risk associated with the purchase.

The characteristics of the purchase problem encompass the size (rupee value) of the expenditure, the degree of novelty involved in the type of buying task, degree of product essentiality, factors provoking purchase, etc. On the other hand, the characteristics of buyers comprise product-specific self-confidence level, experience, purchase history, and degree of technical and professional affiliations. The standing of the individual in the organization depends on the extent of decentralization of organization and individual's perceived risk involved in the process.

At this point, the organizational marketer needs to understand that fundamentally in any organization, an individual apprehends two types of perceived risks. One is performance risk, where he/she thinks that the product might be unsuccessful in terms of the performance benchmark. The other is the psychological risk which refers to the individual's anxiety of being held accountable for the decision taken in the group. Both these apprehensions are, however, linked with the fear of choosing a wrong product or vendor ultimately. An industrial marketer must make an effort to appreciate and foresee the possible domains of perceived risks and develop effective selling strategies accordingly.

ORGANIZATIONAL BUYING DECISION PROCESS—EARLIER STUDIES

Organizational buying process is certainly a very complex buying process and several attempts have been taken by researchers across the globe to trace a chain of sequences to explain it. Two of such most important studies are performed by Robinson, Faris, and Wind in 1967 and further by Frederick E. Webster and Yoram Wind in 1972. In 1973, Jagdish Sheth proposed an integrated model of industrial buying decision which was published in the *Journal of Marketing* (vol. 37, October 1973). In the following sections, brief extracts of the abovementioned models are showcased.

Robinson, Faris, and Wind Model (1967)

The industrial decision-making process is not just a single act of order placing and processing. Following the previous section, it may be stated that the industrial decision-making process is an immensely complicated process; therefore, instead of focusing on the individual constructs of industrial buying, it is better to emphasize on the decision process as a whole. On the basis of the various research inputs, Robinson, Faris, and Wind identified eight primary steps in the buying process. According to the buy-phase model (Robinson *et al.*, 1967), the purchase of a product or service starts as soon as the need is felt (Stage 1). Once the need is recognized by the relevant group, the technical and functional characteristics are determined (Step 2). In the third stage, the technical and the functional aspects are converted to performance standards (Stage 3) and the suppliers are asked to submit proposals (Stage 4). Thereafter, the proposals are analyzed based on the benchmarks specified (Stage 5) and the best vendor is chosen (Stage 6). Finally, the order procedures are chosen (Stage 7). Once the product is received and utilized, its performance with respect to the benchmarks is assessed (Stage 8).

Nevertheless, this eight-stage buying process is normally visible in case of new buying (new task situations). For straight re-buy or modified re-buy, the buying procedure is much simpler and expands over a shorter time period. Like for buying stationeries for office, usually, the companies have listed vendors. Therefore, when the need for the product is realized, the order is placed to the selected vendor and the stock is received and utilized. So only stages 1, 7, and 8 are visible in this case. Actually, the way in which the companies carry out their buying actions is influenced by the type of products and the buying situations they are concerned with. The variations in the purchased products have been viewed as the fundamental issue in planning effectual buying practices for organizations. Robinson, Faris, and Wind (1967) identified three types of buying situations, namely, straight re-buy situation, modified re-buy, and new task, which have already been discussed in the *Industrial Purchase Situations* section.

Webster and Wind Model (1972)

In 1972 the industrial marketing Professors Frederick E. Webster and Yoram Wind propagated the 'buying centre' concept to configure large-scale sales in complicated business environments. However, in the beginning of 1980s, Thomas Bonoma, another eminent consumer psychologist, incorporated the role of initiator to further elucidate the initial list of five roles explained by Webster and Wind. In a company, a buying process depends on the individual(s) involved in the buying decision. The tasks of different buying centres are searching and collecting information, developing choice criteria, and based on those choice criteria choosing the most appropriate one amongst the available alternatives.

- *Gatekeepers*: A gatekeeper refers to anyone in the organization who can control and manipulate the flow of information in the buying process. They are actually the transmitting agents of any product-related information and, thereby, can facilitate the passing of messages from the salesperson to the members of the organization. The prospective buyer's escritoires, in this case, are the office clerks of the purchase department. They help the vendor's representative by providing names, telephone numbers of the key deciders and influencers, and their availability schedule.
- *Influencers*: An influencer is usually somebody who exerts considerable influence on the decider or buyer to take a decision on choosing an alternative. Suppose a multi-national company wants to buy 50 cars for their middle level managers posted in India, then some of the company executives themselves, like the purchase manager and even the sales officers of various car companies can act as influencers.
- *Deciders*: Usually the purchase manager may take the decision regarding the selection of brands and the terms and conditions related to the purchase. These deciders are the most crucial people in the buying decision-making process. The decision-making power does not essentially mean that the decider applies any persuasion on the choice. For example, the chief executive officer (CEO) of a company might be the only key entity who is the authorized signatory for all major purchase applications, but for straight or modified re-buy he may not be much involved in the decision-making process apart from merely signing the documents. Therefore, it may be stated that the decider is the entity in business organizations who has the final authority to decide what to purchase.
- *Buyers*: A buyer is someone who finally carries out the deal on behalf of the company. He may or may not be involved in the other phases of the purchase decision making and primarily acts just as the purchasing agent. In the aforesaid car purchase situation, the purchase manager is the buyer on behalf of the company. Therefore, the sales representatives of the car brand should maintain a well-trusted long-term rapport with these people to ensure a smooth final transaction.
- *Users*: The entities who finally derive utility from the purchase are the users of the product. In the above mentioned car purchase situation, the middle-level managers of the concerned MNC who will be benefitted from those cars are the users of the cars.

SIMPLIFIED INDUSTRIAL PROCUREMENT PROCESS

Taking note of the researches and studies by the eminent consumer scientists, we have made an attempt to propose a simplified and integrated framework of industrial buying behaviour.

Consider, a telecom service provider GG Nigam Limited (GGNL) often procures high-value and high-tech equipments, for example, the large size switching equipments, transmission equipments, and push button telephones.

All the procurement maintains a specified quality consideration mentioned by the QA (quality assurance) section. The vendors are selected by fair and transparent, sealed bid procedure. The modified procurement procedure is shown as a flowchart in Fig. 16.2.

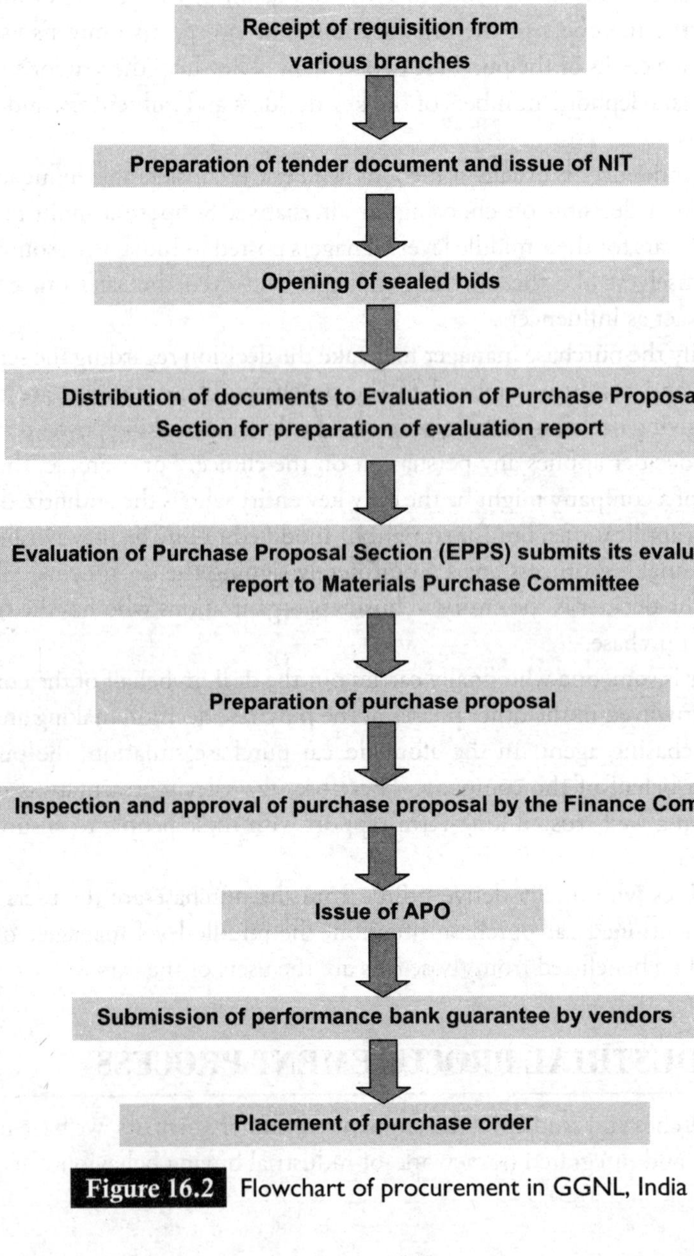

Figure 16.2 Flowchart of procurement in GGNL, India

The principal steps showcased in the flowchart are enumerated in the subsequent paragraphs.

(i) *Receipt of requisition*: The process begins with the receipt of requisition by the GGNL's corporate headquarters for push button telephones from various branch offices across the country.

(ii) *Preparation of tender document and issue of Notice Inviting Tender (NIT)*: Within five working days of receipt of requisition from several branch offices, the purchase section of the headquarter starts preparing the tender document. The approximate quality, quantity, and other technical specifications of the product, the expected lead-time, delivery mode, and payment mode are to be analyzed by the purchase section at this phase. Accordingly, the Notice Inviting Tender (NIT) issued by the corporate headquarter has to be published in any two national and local newspapers and also in the company's Web portal. At the same time, a copy of NIT is sent to the *Indian Trade Journal*, Telecom Equipment Manufacturer's Association (TEMA), and other relevant bodies. The qualified bidders should be only those Indian companies who are registered to produce the push button telephones in India, after getting clearance from the Reserve Bank of India. For this procedure, the company may schedule total 10 days. If the bidders have any query related to this procedure, they have to make it clear within this time period only. The contents of the bid documents such as tender forms, technical specifications, price schedules, security form, performance security bond form, or any other relevant documents mentioned in the NIT are filled up.

(iii) *Opening of the sealed bids*: Once the time period for the submission of the tenders is over, GGNL fixes up a particular date to open the bids. The GGNL's purchase manager and the authorized representatives of the vendors must be present at that time. After opening all the sealed tenders, the bidder's names, quoted price, and other details as specified by the purchaser are announced.

(iv) *Distribution of documents to evaluation of purchase proposal section for preparation of evaluation report*: The purchase manager, who acted as the bid-opening officer here has to submit all the documents to the evaluation of purchase proposal section (EPPS). Within a month's time, the EPPS, considering all technical, payment procedural, delivery mode specific issues, and the financial aspects, may evaluate all the bid documents. The EPPS selects the most appropriate one from them as per the terms and conditions predetermined in the tender document. On the basis of its recommendations, the EPPS will develop a report and submit it to the materials purchase section (MPS). If any clarification from the vendor(s) is required, it can be done during this phase only. In case any modification is required in the tender document regarding any finer technical attribute, it may be mentioned in the report based on the consensus of the EPPS and the vendor.

(v) *Preparation of purchase proposal*: Generally, within 7–10 days of the receipt of the report, the MPS is supposed to prepare a purchase proposal in accordance with the approval of the General Manager (MPS) of GGNL following all terms and conditions in the tender document.

The purchase proposal should contain a brief background of the company; key points in the approved tender (especially the technical specification of the product, size of the order, summary of the recommendations of the EPPS, all amendments specified by the EPPS, price quotations, payment procedure, delivery mode, comments on the recommendations by MPS, and all relevant dates including the NIT date and bid opening date).

While preparing the formal purchase proposal by the MPS, it should be taken into consideration that the following points are not missed anyway:

- Validation of the reasons of selecting particular vendors
- Order amount sanctioned for each and every vendor
- Unit price as well as total price (with discounts, if any) of the push button phones ordered
- Expected financial consequences of the proposal
- If any advance payment is required
- Transportation cost from the vendor's warehouse to GGNL's headquarter
- Details of vendor's proposed bank guarantee, consignee, and paying authority

The proposal, thereafter, is sent to the General Manager (Finance) for the finance committee's approval.

(vi) *Inspection and approval of purchase proposal by the finance committee*: The tender proposal which fulfills all the criteria specified by GGNL with the lowest cost will be selected by the highest rating for the purpose of distribution of push button telephones. The formula that GGNL would follow for the vendor rating is quite similar to the formula that BSNL follows. BSNL, the country's telecom major, is currently a Government of India enterprise. Nonetheless, the weightage of criteria of GGNL varies with that of BSNL.

$$VR = 0.7\ PR + 0.2\ DR + 0.1\ QR$$

where

VR= vendor rating

PR = price rating

DR = delivery rating

QR = quality rating

and summation of weights is equal to 1.

(vii) *Issue of APO*: After the approval of the finance committee and the proposal getting duly signed by the General Manager (Finance), the advanced purchase order (APO) is issued. The following points must be mentioned in the APO:

(a) Number of push button phones with unit price
(b) All the transaction dates, numbers, and reference
(c) All marketing and financial terms and conditions mutually agreed upon
(d) Amount of performance bank guarantee with all the details of bank guarantee provided by the vendor
(e) Delivery and advance payment schedule
(f) Time period to accept the APO and submission of the bank guarantee by the vendor; for GGNL it is 15 days from the receipt of APO by the vendor

(viii) *Submission of performance bank guarantee by vendors*: Once the APO is issued and the formal letter of intent is sent to the vendor, the supplier has to hand over GGNL the bank guarantee on a percentage of total purchase order mutually agreed by both parties within the stipulated time period mentioned in the APO.

(ix) *Placement of purchase order*: Once the bank guarantee and the acceptance of the APO by the vendor are received, the final purchase order is executed.

The entire procedure should be completed by a stipulated time period. For GGNL it is 100 working days.

(This section of the chapter is designed based on one-to-one discussions with a number of engineers employed in several telecom service organizations in India. Although GGNL is a fictitious organization, but most of the government organizations, government undertakings, or even private organizations generally follow similar kind of organizational procurement process. This is, in fact, just an attempt to explain the most complex industrial procurement in India in a simpler way.)

Closing Case

Time to Expand!

Mr. Ravi Narayan Sharma was the managing director at *Sameet Cooperative Works*—a small-sized co-operative firm producing readymade *salwar–suits*. The firm had an annual sales turnover of ₹20 crore. The company earlier depended on its own outlet *Pakija* located at Sahidnagar market. But later, as the product became very popular and its demand started increasing, the company looked for more intensive distribution of its product across the city. There were clearly three alternatives—open up two more outlets of *Pakija*, sell the products at any garment store, or call for tenders to select some franchisees of *Pakija*.

In order to decide among these three alternatives, Ravi formulated a team comprising of sales manager, administrative manager, purchase manager, finance officer, and himself. There was an air of disagreement among the team as the sales manager was in favour of opening up of own outlets as *Pakija* which would be positioned as a distinctive cooperative producing handmade suits. But as this would incur a huge cost, the finance officer did not agree to this proposition. He rather wanted to sell their products through multi-brand outlets as this would increase their sales by just paying the retailers' margin. But as this might dilute the distinctive positioning of line of products under *Pakija*, the other members readily rejected the proposal. The purchase manager understood the relevance of both the points and wanted to use franchisee instead of selling through multi-brand outlets or opening additional company retail. The team agreed upon this option, as this would increase their distribution without incurring additional cost and diluting their brand image. It was decided that two such franchisee units would initially be opened by next Diwali.

On the basis of aforementioned discussion, Mr. Sharma instructed to call for proposals from interested businessmen. Accordingly, in the local newspapers, the advertisement was floated.

Upon receiving a huge number of proposals, the team had another discussion and selected the best five. Now, Mr. Sharma had to select the *best two out of these five*. He jotted down the points in a table. The table looked similar to Table 16.4. But as each proposal had its strong merits, it was difficult for Mr. Sharma to arrive at a decision. He pondered over the table and was in a state of uncertainty.

Table 16.4 *The comparative table for the five options*

Criteria	*Option 1*	*Option 2*	*Option 3*	*Option 4*	*Option 5*
Years of operation in business	5	6	5	9	10
Years of operation in garment business	5	1	3	2	0
Number of parallel business	0	3	1	1	5
Location chosen	Station area	A market place near to their existing *Pakija*	Near movie complex	In a shopping mall	Station area
Possible initial investment to decorate the store	₹10 lakhs	₹15 lakhs	₹10 lakhs	₹5 lakhs	₹13 lakhs
Initial monthly purchase of suits from the company	500 pieces	100 pieces	200 pieces	300 pieces	600 pieces
Projected number of floor staff	5	5	5	8	10
Agreeable investment on promotion of the brand	₹2 lakhs	₹2.5 lakhs	₹3 lakhs	₹3 lakhs	₹5 lakhs
Warehousing the products	Yes	Yes	Yes	Yes	Yes
Percentage of transportation cost to be borne	50	60	10	40	100
If unsold the intended action with the products	Will wait for 6 months and thereafter return to the manufacturer	Will wait for 6 months and thereafter return to the manufacturer	Will wait for 3 months and thereafter return to the manufacturer	Will wait for 6 months and thereafter return to the manufacturer	Will wait for 12 months and thereafter return to the manufacturer
In case of minor defects of the brand	Will repair and sell at discount	Will return back to the manufacturer	Will return back to the manufacturer	Will return back to the manufacturer	Will repair and sell at special discount

Agreeability to bear the stitching cost for fitting as asked by the customers	Yes	Yes	Yes but additional price would be charged from the customer for this purpose	Yes	Yes but additional price would be charged from the customer for this purpose
Agreeable franchisee fee irrespective of the sales volume per year	₹2 lakhs	₹2 lakhs	₹4 lakhs	₹2 lakhs	₹6 lakhs

(This is a fictitious case. All the characters, brands, and places mentioned in the case are imaginary. Therefore, resemblance with any organization's efforts, characters, brands, and places is purely coincidental.)

Question

1. If you were in place of Mr. Sharma, which two options would you select for franchisee and why?

Summary

Organizational buying is the organization's process of procurement of products and services. There are various categories of industrial buyers, namely, agricultural market, reseller market, government market, service market, non-profit market, and the international market. In another way, the organizational buyers are classified into three major categories—institutional buyers, industrial buyers, and service organizations.

Though the decision-making process in consumer and industrial markets looks similar; nevertheless, when analyzed carefully, it is observed that there exists significant difference between the processes and hence studying organizational market separately calls for special attention.

Thereafter, in the chapter, emphasis has been laid on the different buying situations, namely, straight re-buy, modified re-buy, and new-task. Straight re-buy process is quite similar to the routine response behaviour discussed in Chapter 14. However, when some specifications of the product are required by the buyer, it becomes a modified purchase situation. On the other hand, when the organization buys any product for the first time, it becomes a new task. This is the most complex buying situation and the subsequent sections mainly focused on this type of buying situation.

However, the characteristics of the market demand in consumer and industrial markets are quite diverse. The major five constructs of demand in the industrial market are derived demand, joint demand, elastic and inelastic demand, volatile demand, and inventory adjustments. Nonetheless, there are several factors influencing the organizational buying decisions such as external factors (socio-economic changes, extent of globalization, etc.), internal factors (nature and structure of the organization, etc.), inter-personal relationship, and individual factors.

Organizational buying process is, undoubtedly, a complicated procedure and over the years various attempts have been made by researchers across the globe to map out a chain of sequences to explicate it. Two of such most significant studies performed by Robinson, Faris, and Wind in 1967 and further by Frederick E. Webster and Yoram Wind in 1972 have been discussed in the chapter. Some conflict resolution aspects proposed by Jagdish Sheth in the course of the organizational buying decision making have also been explained in the chapter. The chapter concludes with an integrated framework of industrial buying decision process with respect to a dummy organization.

The area is enormous as it includes product market situations, which in some logic may emerge as distinctive and diverse from each other. It is, therefore, recommended to relate some specific situations with the general views discussed in this chapter.

Key Terms

Organizational buying The decision-making process by which organizations establish the need for purchased products and services and identify, evaluate, and choose among alternative brands and suppliers.

Derived demand The demand for industrial goods often depends on the demand of the finished products; this is known as derived demand.

Straight re-buy The regular purchases of the organization such as stationeries.

Modified re-buy The regular purchases with added special features or amendments.

New task The purchase in which the organization has no prior experience.

Buying centre Buying centre encompasses those entities which are directly or indirectly connected with the organizational buying decisions and perform their specific roles.

Influencers The entities related to the business purchase decision which influence the buying decision at any stage are referred to as the influencers.

Users The entities in the organization who would actually use the product–service package to develop the final product or resale it.

Deciders The entities in the organization delegated with the task of making the buying decision.

Buyers The entities in the organization delegated with the task of formalizing the final order and the commercial terms and conditions. Ideally, the buyers are the officials of the purchase department.

Gatekeepers The entities in the organization who control the flow of information within a buying organization.

Buy phases The eight-stage buying decision model explained by Robinson, Faris, and Wind.

Evaluation criteria The criteria such as price, delivery, quality used by the customers to appraise and select the vendors.

Buying influences These include infrastructural, political, organizational, economic, social, and individual factors.

Questions

1. Is there any difference between the organizational buying and household buying practice? Elucidate with examples. Taking the example of purchase of air conditioners at any of your relatives' office, explain how that buying situation differs from that of your household purchase of air conditioners.
2. Discuss the major influencing factors of organizational buying process with respect to any car company.
3. Explain the concept of demand with respect to purchase of raw jute for the jute mills.
4. Enumerate the Webster–Wind model and differentiate that with the Robinson, Faris, and Wind model with respect to purchase of jeeps for Indian Army.
5. What methods has Jagdish Sheth suggested for resolving organizational buying conflicts? Which one do you feel is better and why?
6. Try to identify three or four purchase situations and explain the vendor selection process in each of these situations.

Critical Assignment

1. Visit any organization in your vicinity and try to analyze what are the different purchase situations undergone by this organization. Underline the characteristics of these buying situations. Also analyze two of its new purchases in the last three years.
2. Visit a factory that manufactures local equipments or a local ice-cream producing firm. Looking at their new purchase decisions in the last couple of years, try to find out the influencing factors of the firm's decision making.

Chapter **17**

Dimensions of Consumer Research

Chapter Goals

After completing this chapter, you will be able to understand

- **how the concept of consumer research evolved from modernist era to the era of post-modernism**
- **the consumer research process**
- **scope of consumer research**

Opening Vignette

Pearlpet—Where Research is Needed

Pearlpet is a highly successful brand in the PET bottle category. With the emergence of this brand, the Indian kitchenware market has literally transformed. About two decades back, the kitchens were featured with food items like pulses, rice, biscuits, *bhujia*, etc. stored in glass bottles of *Boost*, *Horlicks* or in metal containers of *Complan*, *Amul Milk Powder*, etc. Now the rows filled with the nice looking transparent plastic containers demonstrate the change in the psychology of the middle class customers in terms of kitchen apparels. *Pearlpet* is one of the major catalysts behind this change.

PET is the acronym of polyethylene tetraphthalate. PET bottles are considered to be extremely safe and convenient storage solution for both industry and households. Therefore, along with the household segments, *Pearlpet* has an immense opportunity to cater the packaging of large scale confectionary or soft drinks market too.

Glass bottles and containers had a shortcoming of being unsafe and breakable and PET jars had a ready solution to these hazards. The trendy look, style, shape, unbreakable nature, and reasonable price gave the sales of *Pearlpet* jars a massive escalation. Malaika Arora, the model for this brand, was also a reason behind the brand's initial popularity.

PET bottles are considered to be safe and convenient for storage

Even in the industrial market segment, the rising number of brands in the FMCG, soft drinks, and confectionery sections amplified the reach of PET products. However, establishing *Pearlpet* in the market was not an easy job. The utmost threat was from the small-scale local firms. As the concept of PET bottles was of recent origin, the consumers failed to differentiate between branded and unbranded products and preferred the low-priced unbranded products or polythene packs. Furthermore, the cheaper Chinese products were flooded in the Indian market. These products were trendy, good looking, and most importantly, very cheap.

In the early 21st century, the story of *Pearlpet* was distressing. In the premium segment, the two marketing giants, *Tupperware* and MNC brand *Rubbermaid* were the leaders. *Tupperware* followed a networking strategy where its agents targeted the working ladies at their respective work places. On the contrary, *Pearlpet* was only available in stores with several other items. So the product did not obtain a perfect 'push' in the market and, therefore, in spite of the first-mover advantage, it failed to get the desired momentum in the Indian market.

In the highly competitive scenario, *Pearlpet* did not look very aggressive on competition. It seemed that the brand was relying on its initial glory. Of late, they are hardly visible in any promotional slots. The unique selling proposition of the brand is hardly identified by the consumers. The brand, therefore, missed out its first-mover advantage and started operating in laissez-faire. Nonetheless, the brand still has an enormous equity which it should cultivate and endow with. Even though the brand led the PET jar market, lack of brand promotion in today's fiercely competitive market could appear as one of the most potential threats for the company.

But how can *Pearlpet* recover its market share once again and what should exactly be its promotional message now? A detailed study on consumer's lifestyle and preference is needed in this context. Here lies the scope for consumer research.

Source: Pearlpet: Har Dil Ka Pet, http://marketingpractice.blogspot.com/2009_04_01_archive.html, April 30, 2009, accessed on June 20, 2010.

HISTORY OF CONSUMER RESEARCH

History of consumer research can be traced with the history of marketing philosophies. The purpose of this chapter is to identify the historical dependence and the adherence of consumer behaviour on various disciplines and practices of marketing. It then endeavors to recollect the earlier trends and forecast the upcoming trends in consumer behaviour research; as a corollary of novel and promising schools of thought.

The arena of consumer research was initially developed as an annex of the field of market research, focusing almost exclusively on consumer behaviour rather than on the other facets of the marketing management. The key rationale behind studying consumer behaviour was to facilitate the marketers to envisage how consumers would respond to their marketing messages, and to introspect their already taken purchase decisions. Marketers assumed that if they understand the nitty-gritty of consumer decision-making process, they can frame the appropriate marketing strategies, especially the promotional messages and the distribution mode that will persuade the consumer in the most preferred way (i.e., to purchase the marketer's product or service). In short, consumer research concept is quite similar to the dimensions of applied economics. To be more specific, the economic man theory holds the assumption that consumers are rational decision makers who logically appraise the goods and services available to them and choose only those which give them optimal utility keeping the cost constraint as it is.

Modernist Phase

The period during which the field of consumer research, in its literal meaning, had been developed is often referred as the modernist era. Researchers who approved the assumptions upon which modernism is based are called positivists. The research methods used in positivist research are derived primarily from the natural sciences and therefore consist of experiments, survey techniques, and observations. Though in these cases, the outcomes are often descriptive and empirical, but if collected randomly, these can be generalized for a bigger set of populations. The data thus collected are, by nature, quantitative and lend themselves to further sophisticated statistical analysis.

Regardless of their assumptions that consumers were rational problem solvers, the earlier researchers found that consumers were not always consciously aware of the reasons behind their decisions. Even when they were aware of their basic motivations, they were not always willing to reveal these reasons.

Ernest Dichter's motivational theory has already been referred in Chapter 4. As a matter of fact, a Viennese psychoanalyst, Dichter, first began to use Freudian psychoanalytic techniques to unveil the latent motivations of consumers. By the late 1950s, his research methodology, which is often referred as motivational research, was extensively adopted by marketers and advertising agencies. Motivational research methods comprise of both projective techniques and in-depth interviews. Nonetheless, the motivational research calls for highly trained interviewer-analysts to collect data and to analyze the research findings. However, due to small sample sizes it is difficult to generalize the findings for the larger populations. Motivational research is highly subjective, because it is usually based on analyst's interpretation. Used primarily to obtain new ideas for promotional campaigns, motivational research is normally used as a part of qualitative research technique.

Nonetheless, being aware of the precincts of motivational research methods, some marketers use a mixture of quantitative and qualitative research to facilitate strategic marketing decisions. They apply qualitative research findings to develop new ideas and consumer insights, and quantitative research findings to forecast consumer actions based on various promotional stimuli.

Post-Modernist Phase

The post-modernist era was characterized with underlying importance on the consumption pattern rather than just the act of buying. May it be the academicians from the fields of consumer behaviour or other social science disciplines; most of them had been interested in the later part. According to them, consumer behaviour is a subset of human behaviour. Concentration in consumer experiences has led to the term experientialism, and the researchers who espoused this archetype were referred as experientialists, post-modernists, or interpretivists.

The interpretivists normally resorted to qualitative research. By and large they made a wide use of ethnography, semiotics, and in-depth interviews as their research tools. Ethnography is a method derived from cultural anthropology in which the researchers consign themselves amidst the society under study in order to understand the sense of various cultural practices. Ethnography lends itself effortlessly to the study of all kinds of consumer behaviours as well as individual purchase patterns of various goods and services. Ethnography has been used in interpretivist's studies to realize the meanings of objects accrued by the homeless. Interpretivists are also paying attention to semiotics—the study of symbols. Consumer researchers principally use the tool, semiotics, to resolve the implication that the non-verbal symbols that augment, rather than slow down, the expressiveness of the message. In-depth interviews are an important part of the interpretivist's research process. Nevertheless, interpretive research findings are often distinctive to the specific researcher–respondent interface, because sometimes the researcher plays an active role in the interview process. However, these days both the aforesaid approaches are used to make practical business decisions.

Marketers have understood that rather than contradiction, these two research dimensions—positivism and interpretivism—are truly complementary in nature. The forecast made by the positivist research and the perspective provided by interpretivist research jointly put forth a better-off and more vigorous profile of consumer behaviour, and permit the marketer to frame more evocative and effectual marketing strategies. Furthermore, positivist and interpretivist research findings, when used simultaneously, offer a strong root for developing non-profit marketing strategies and public policy decisions.

CONSUMER RESEARCH PROCESS

The contemporary process of consumer research encompasses the methodical identification, collection, analysis, and distribution of information to facilitate consumer decision-making. Although the purpose of consumer research varies across cases, nonetheless, the general purpose of gaining intelligence for decision-making remains constant throughout.

Though there are a number of steps in the process of consumer research, each of those steps fits into one of the six major steps of the marketing research process. These six steps are depicted in Fig. 17.1.

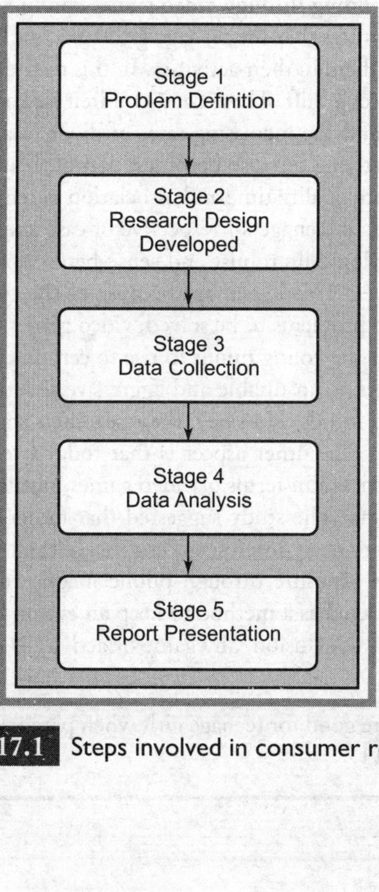

Figure 17.1 Steps involved in consumer research

Step 1: Problem Definition

The first step in any marketing research project is to define the problem. While defining the problem, the researcher must take a careful note of the purpose of the study, the pertinent background information, and exactly what the researchers want to find out. Problem definition engrosses discussion with the decision makers, interviews with industry experts, analysis of secondary data, and perhaps some qualitative research, such as focus group interviews. Only when the problem has been accurately defined, the research can be designed and conducted properly.

In fact, with identification of the problem, research objectives should also be stated carefully. For example, are we about to segment the market for male apparels? Do we want to find out consumer's attitude towards adopting mobile commerce? Sometimes one may even go for exploratory research to figure out family consumption behaviour, etc. One such example is shown in Exhibit 17.1.

Exhibit 17.1: Bonding between Teen Girls and Their Parents through Video Games

An exploratory study on teenage bonding through video games conducted by Brigham Young University's School of Family Life in the US portrays that the teenage girls turn out better behaved with greater familial bonds when their parents join with them in their activities. In this tech-driven era, it is quite natural that the preference of children also experiences a shift. These days, children face a huge generation gap because of the breaking of joint families in India and the increasing rates of divorces across the globe. Today's kids want their parents to not only stay beside them, but also become a part of their daily lives. Thus parenting pattern also demands an alteration. The more quality time and association parents share with their kids, the happier the kids are. Video games stimulate all teenagers irrespective of cast, creed, age, and sex. Researchers opine that the girls turn out to be psychologically robust and sense better domestic attachments if their parents join them while playing video games. This is perhaps because of the rejuvenating pragmatic situations in theatrical ways and posturing tough problems to be solved, video games can be thought-provoking. Playing games with or against a parent helps the young minds to rise to certain challenges.

Some people often carp video games as unsuitable and aggressive substances posing negative influence on the easily-motivated young budding minds. However, the researchers stated that this is so only if the games played do not fit in with their age. The other aspect is that today's teenagers' exposure to this so called 'unsuitable content' is not only restricted in terms of video games, but is also present in many other modes like TV, Internet, music, and cinema. The study suggested that rather than becoming a hard taskmaster, today's parents should actively share their interests. Today's children are very well informed and more matured due to lot of information exposure through public media. In case of video games particularly, parental involvement may be considered as a method to keep an eye on the content and avert gaming from becoming an addictive obsession. In conclusion, any game or activity is a mutual learning experience and a mode of bonding too.

Source: Research says video games are good for teenage girls when parents join the fun: it's caring by sharing, *The Times of India*, February 3, 2011.

Step 2: Development of an Approach to the Problem

This step involves developing the theoretical background, identifying the research questions, forming the hypotheses, etc. This process is conducted primarily by discussions with management professionals or by referring to the existing case studies or pilot survey. This step may be considered as the ground work for formulating research design.

Step 3: Research Design Formulation

Research design is a skeleton or outline for carrying out the consumer research project. It lays down the frame of the detailed actions required to test the research hypotheses and find out possible answers to the research questions. In case of collection of primary data, it is essential to devise a questionnaire and a sampling plan to select appropriate respondents for the study.

More formally, preparing a research design involves the following steps:

(i) Secondary data analysis
(ii) Identifying sources for primary data
(iii) Methods of collecting quantitative data (survey, observation, and experimentation)
(iv) Sampling plan
(v) Scale design and formation of questionnaires
(vi) Plan on analytical tools

Step 4: Field Work or Data Collection

The data collection step requires a field force. The field force may directly operate in the field, as in the case of questionnaire-based survey and personal interviewing (in-home, mall intercept, or computer-assisted personal interviewing). They can also conduct survey from an office by telephone or by online surveys using google docs, etc. Apposite selection, training, supervision, and evaluation of the field force may minimize data-collection errors.

Step 5: Data Preparation and Analysis

Data preparation primarily involves data editing. Data editing includes removal of several redundant data and thereafter, coding, transcription, quality control, and validation of data. Each questionnaire or checklist is thoroughly inspected or edited and, if necessary, corrected. Thereafter, numeric coding is done for each response received through the questionnaire. Data validation ensures the accuracy and fitness of the data for further statistical analysis. The researcher interprets the data and reaches to certain conclusion by several data analysis tools. Normally, while dealing with a single measurement of the sample units, the univariate techniques are used for analysis. On the other hand, multivariate techniques for analyzing the data are used depending on the statistical principle of multivariate statistics, which involves observation and analysis of more than one statistical variable at a time.

Step 6: Report Preparation and Presentation

Once the analysis is over, the research agency/organization develops a written report. The research report addresses the particular research questions identified and mentions the research approach, design, methods of data collection, and tools of data analysis in detail. Thereafter, it presents the obtained results and provides an interpretation of the major findings. The results of the research are presented in a logical arrangement so that they can be readily used in the decision-making process. Apart from these, all relevant facts, figures, tables, etc. are annexed at the end as appendix/enclosure/annexure. Besides, an oral presentation, on requisition by the clients, is made precisely by using tables, figures, and graphs to increase transparency and impact.

Usually research reports are structured in the following sequence:

- Preface
- Executive summary
- Contents
- List of figures and tables
- Introduction
- Theoretical background
- Problem definition
- Research design
- Data analysis
- Discussion on findings
- Recommendations
- Conclusion
- Appendices
- Bibliography

SCOPE OF CONSUMER RESEARCH

The environment of business not only comprises of customers and competitors, but also its suppliers and distributors, if it does not own a distribution network. Additionally, there are certain other segments, such as government departments and legislation, its shareholders, and the labour unions, etc. There are many external and uncontrollable variables influencing the formulation of marketing strategy. All of these sway the character of problems with which the organization has to deal with and thus the products it plans to generate for the target market, sometimes even for determining the target market. The fields where consumer research is usually resorted are discussed in the following sections.

Products and Their Development

All aspects of product development, idea generation or concept testing, production, launch or post-launch decisions call for an extensive consumer research. The first step of idea generation must be researched in terms of trade perception of acceptability and corporate fit as well as consumer perception of the functional and technical benefits accrued from the product and their purpose of purchase. Moreover, packaging strategy, the relationship between quality of the product and its price; the brand equity, positioning and repositioning strategy are also some of the purviews of consumer research. If this stage is not precisely and competently researched, then every decision which follows may be flawed and lead to severe financial penalty for the company.

Identifying the Target Market

This involves identifying the customer groups which are to be catered. It is important to understand the features of the target market in terms of the following questions:

- Why do they purchase certain products or services?
- What is their present pattern of purchasing behaviour, from whom do they buy, and why?
- What kinds of benefits do they seek from the products they buy?
- What are their attitudes and opinions, and how are consumer tastes, and thus needs and wants, shifting?

Therefore, information is sought about changes in fashion and lifestyle trends, which may in turn influence consumer purchase patterns.

Analyzing the Market

The third important area, where consumer research may be conducted is to analyze the size, shape, and characteristics of the target market. Most of the researches in this area are conducted to answer the following questions:

- What kind of the demographic and psychographic framework does the target market have?
- How is the framework getting changed over the timeline? What are the implications of such change to the marketing strategy formulation?

Distribution of Product

Consumer research in this area is primarily targeted to find out the following:

- The available locations and possible opportunities for distributing a product.
- Present methods of distributing products, and possible alternatives and comparatively better methods.

Suitable Sales and Promotion Methods

This aspect involves assessing the following issues:

- Which are the most appealing methods of selling and promoting products to the target customers?
- What should be the optimal coverage and frequency of a media advertisement of the products? Are the commercials viewed by right audience or the promotion has resulted into unnecessary

exposures? What types of media should be used to reach to the desired audiences? Does the product require any celebrity endorsement? If so, which celebrity persona would be appropriate to match with the brand characteristics?

Moreover, customer feedback, both positive and negative, is an extremely useful information for the marketer. The information obtained from customer complaints are often the starting point for modifying products and incorporating value-added services. Therefore, consumer research is important in pursuant with the famous marketing proclamation 'Customer is the King' and the marketers ought to satisfy him.

Closing Case

Margo: Is it Mislaid?

Margo, one of the oldest brands in India, is positioned as a herbal soap for the middle-income populace of the country. The 85-year-old brand is essentially known for its neem content. The product, although well known for its positive effects on the skin, is now almost in a down-turn in the market. During its launch, the product experienced dedicated customer base with its clearly defined unique selling proposition, 'medicinal value.' But over the decades, the brand never judged the customer's psyche associated with a toilet soap and hence never changed its positioning with the change in the customer's choice pattern.

A small survey on toilet soap market in Kolkata identified that a toilet soap is chosen by the customers not only because of one particular ingredient, but also many other factors like, promotional component, shape, price, style statement, advertising frequency, intrinsic features, perceptual and predisposition factors.

Margo failed to appreciate the shifting dynamics of Indian consumers. More and more choices began to unfurl before the consumers and *Margo* was gradually shelved. With the globalization after 1991, countless soap brands invaded the Indian market. Some such brands are as follows.

- *Breeze Scent Magic* is the soap which fulfills the aspirations of women of rural India. Breeze positions as 'beauty at an affordable price,' making the rural lower-middle income ladies look and feel gorgeous. Studies have shown that the yearning for great aroma featured maximum in the daily beauty regime of the discount-soap users.
- *Dove* soap, which was launched by *Unilever* in 1957, has been available in India since 1995. It provides a delectable substitute for any other toilet soap. *Dove* is prepared as pH neutral (pH between 6.5 and 7.5) and, therefore, is supposed to be gentle on skin. This soap provides an idea to the upper and upper-middle class customers that healthy skin is an essential requisite for women. With its ¾ moisturizing substance, *Dove* is fit for all skin types in all seasons.
- *Hamam* is also considered to be the most steadfast option in the Indian soap market. Launched in 1934, *Hamam* has traditionally been a soap that takes care of your skin in a natural way. *Hamam* typically targets the middle-income customers and according to a

market survey conducted by *Indica Research* in May 2003, 78% of doctors in Tamil Nadu officially recommended *Hamam*.

- Making a billion Indians feel secure, safe, and sound by fulfilling their health and hygiene needs is the positioning strategy of *Lifebuoy*. *Lifebuoy*, principally targeting the lower-middle class, is one of the world's largest selling soap. It offers an undeniable health benefit to whole family. Launched in 1895, *Lifebuoy*, for over 100 years, has been considered to be tantamount with health and value. The brick red soap, with its perfume and well-liked *Lifebuoy* jingle, has carried the *Lifebuoy* message of health across the country with explicitly eying on the low-end market.
- For 28 years, *Liril* is perfectly positioned in the Indian middle-class market as synonymous to freshness.
- *Lux*, almost synonymous to beauty and glamour, stands as one of India's most reliable personal care brands. *Lux* continues to be preferred by the cohort of users for the experience of a luxurious and comfortable bath. Since its launch in India in the year 1929, *Lux* offered a variety of diverse colours and fragrances, and also roped most of the top Bollywood actresses to endorse the brand. This in turn showed the brands identity with such personas.

Aishwarya Rai endorsing *Lux*

- Introduced in India in 1902, *Pears* soap is playing well in the Indian market. It is sufficiently placid, even for a baby's skin. *Pears* soap is different from any other toilet soap with an increased glycerin substance retained within the soap, which gives it a transparent look.

Contrary to this, *Margo* was positioned as 'complete skin care soap.' As the market became split with lots of products positioning at various intrinsic characteristics, *Margo* became marginal just as a medicinal soap. Even in that case, it faced fierce competition with *Dettol* and *Savlon* soaps (as these are specifically designed as medicinal brands).

Though the product did not show a good shelf display in shops, it had inherent negative factors coupled with it. Moreover, neither the aroma was attractive nor the shape eye-catching. It was also less lathering compared to its competitors. With the change of ownership from *Shaw Wallace* to *Henkel*, *Margo* was replanted in 2003 with a new fragrance and shape. However it failed to energize the market any more even with the new positioning message '*Margo clear skin.*' A small survey conducted on the shopkeepers of West Bengal in 2010 projected that the brand *Margo* failed to attract the generation Y customers. Moreover, there is now a big doubt whether the brand can change its *avatar* and fight *Lifebuoy* in the health platform?

Source: *Margo*: Lost in the neem trees!, http://marketingpractice.blogspot.com/2006/02/margolost-in-neem-trees.html, February 27, 2006.

Questions

1. What, according to you, went wrong with *Margo*?
2. Define the consumer research problem in this context.
3. If *Margo* asks you to conduct a consumer research and identify the best alternative solution for revival of its brand, how would you proceed?

Summary

The field of consumer research was developed as an extension to the field of marketing research to facilitate marketers to envisage how consumers would respond in the market place. Consumer research undertaken from the managerial perspective to improvise strategic marketing decisions is called positivism. It is generally quantitative in approach, and tries to identify cause and effect relationship in buying situations. It is often supplemented with qualitative research.

A second research point of view, called interpretivism, is by and large more concerned with understanding the act of consumption itself rather than the act of buying (i.e., consumer decision-making). Interpretivists sight consumer behaviour as a subset of human behaviour, and increased understanding as a means to purge some of the ills associated with critical consumer behaviour.

Each theoretical standpoint is based on its own explicit assumptions and usually uses its own research methodologies. Positivists generally use quantitative studies that can be generalized to larger populations. Interpretivists often use subjective studies that view consumption experiences as unique state of affairs that occur at specific moments in time. The two theoretical research orientations, when used together, provide a deeper and more astute understanding of consumer behaviour than either of the approaches used alone.

The consumer research process—whether quantitative or qualitative in approach—generally consists of six steps: defining objectives, collecting secondary data, developing a research design, collecting primary data, analyzing the data, and preparing a report of the findings.

Key Terms

Motivativational research It is the research methodology comprising projective techniques and in-depth interviews used to identify the latent motivation of the customers.

Positivism This branch of consumer research is conducted from managerial perspective to improvise strategic marketing decisions. It is generally quantitative in approach, and tries to identify cause and effect relationship in buying situations.

Interpretivism This branch of consumer research is mostly concerned with understanding the act of consumption itself rather than the act of buying (i.e., consumer decision-making).

Questions

1. Sam Walton once said 'Only the customer can fire us all.' Do you agree with this statement, and how do you relate consumer behaviour to this statement?
2. Differentiate between the schools of thought of the modernist and post-modernist era.
3. Government of India is planning to introduce a new SMS-based medication service. In this case, a consumer may track a low-price substitute of the prescribed drugs. If you are asked to develop an inclusive research plan for the possibility of its success, how would you proceed?

Critical Assignment

1. Government of India has announced Universal Health Insurance Policy in 2004 for covering the health hazards for the poor, wherein, the subsidy amount exceeds the individual's contribution in the premium structure. The policy is yet to derive momentum in the Indian market. Construct a research design to find out the reasons behind this problem.
2. *Ambassador* car brand of *Hindustan Motors* was a market leader in Indian small car segment in 1960s and 1970s. However, since the latter half of 1980s, it started losing its market share. After 1990s, when the economy was opened up and the market was flooded with imported Japanese and US cars, *Ambassador* completely became obsolete. In spite of incorporating improved motor to rejuvenate the cars, nothing really happened. Carry out a pilot survey to identify the underlying reasons behind this event and suggest how to rejuvenate this brand.

Section V

Cases

CASE-I

SHINY SHOE SERVICE: WILL CUSTOMERS PATRONIZE THIS BUSINESS OPPORTUNITY?*

Prof. Ramendra Singh

'Is it real or am I dreaming?' Dilip, the new brand manager of the 'Shiny' brand of shoe polish, thinks as he scratches his head. However, he cannot reconcile how an innocuous looking shoeshine machine inside the toilets of the five star hotels can become an attractive business opportunity. But an exploratory study conducted in Mumbai and New Delhi in 2009 validated that given a modest capital investment a budding entrepreneur can tap this completely virgin market. He is still undecided about the consumer behaviour related to grooming outdoors, especially when it comes to male grooming habits. Till date, a typical Indian male is accustomed with shining his shoes at home, using one of the popular wax based polishes, which lasts only few days. However, given the dust and the Indian climate, sometimes it is necessary to polish the shoes more than once a week. But never has Dilip seen an overwhelming response to shoeshine machines, which are a novelty factor similar to weighing machines put up in public places. There are shoeshine boys, but they are confined to places such as railway stations, and they carry out manual buffing.

What is a Shoeshine Machine?

A shoeshine machine is an electrically driven machine used for buffing and polishing leather shoes. Both men and women can use it, though it is more convenient in usage for men's shoes. Across the world, these machines come in a variety of shapes and sizes, from small portable and dismountable Chinese machines weighing no more than 7 kg to large and heavy Italian 'weighing machine look-alike' sizes. There are typically two brushes (on the same motor shaft)—one for pre-cleaning or buffing and the other for polishing. Polishing is done after cleaning and by putting a small amount of cream on the shoe from the cream dispenser. The shoe cream is mostly neutral (white in colour). Polishing and buffing both can be done independent of each other. Both activities do not take more than a minute, and if the shoe cream is of reasonably good quality, the shine on the shoe is comparable to the 'home-made' shine, without the same effort. The machine itself requires low maintenance and overhead costs. The fastest consumable is the shoe cream, which is easy to replace.

---

*This case has been prepared by Prof. Ramendra Singh, Assistant Professor (Marketing), Indian Institute of Management, Calcutta, and is based on a fictitious situation to stimulate discussion in an MBA classroom. Resemblance to any person or organization's efforts in the market in the past, present, or future is purely coincidental and unintentional. Published with permission.

Current Users

Shoeshine machine in India is about a decade old. In developed countries, it has been in use for a longer time. The usage is still confined to toilets of five star hotels, big clubs, and few corporate offices. Almost every five star hotel in metros, many corporate offices, few clubs, very few paid toilets, and some staff colleges are the current users. At these places the machine is placed generally in toilets, next to the hand dryer and serves the purpose of grooming. In some institutions like clubs in Mumbai, it is also placed at the entrance, next to the reception desk. The machines are meant to be used by hotel/club guests.

Currently the awareness level about the machine and its usage is very low. The plausible reasons being the high prevalence of in-home polishing of shoes, the low awareness levels, and the resistance to change old habits. Hence the numbers of such machines have not increased tremendously, though it has been present in India for a decade. These machines can be used not only in hotels but their business opportunities also lie in using them as vending machines in public places. Currently there are a couple of manufacturers of shoeshine machines, mostly in Mumbai and Delhi. There are others in hospitality trade who may import the machines on particular demands. The machine has consumables like brushes and shoe cream or 'neutral'. There are many manufacturers of neutral across the country. Small regional players supply most of the neutral (shoe cream) that goes into the machines.

Current Market Size and Future Growth Potential

The current market is urban and consists of around 3500–4000 machines. The consumption of shoe cream to these machines is around 3000 kg or 3 tonnes per annum (tpa). But not all of these machines are actively used. The active machines would be around 50–60%. The machines are not serviced properly, wherever they are placed. Most of the machines have been sold in Mumbai, Delhi, and Bangalore. On an average around 400–450 new machines are being sold each year by 2 or 3 manufacturers combined (for the period 2004–2009). The study has shown that in Mumbai and surroundings alone there must be approximately 1000 machines. Delhi would be having around 250–300 machines. The rest of the machines are placed in cities like Lucknow, Pune, Hyderabad, Jaipur, and others. The shoeshine machine market grew at an approximate average compound annual growth rate (CAGR) of 12% in the period 2001–2009 and it has been estimated that the shoe cream consumption will go up to 250 tpa by the end of 2020. Accordingly, the machines too would increase in number. These estimates are based on increasing the number of machines that can be placed at potentially suitable places alone and it does not take into effect the increase due to usage rate or occasions per user.

There are two to three machine manufacturers in India. One of them in Mumbai accounts for 75–80% of all the machines sold in the country. This particular supplier sells to institutions like hotels directly and sources shoe cream from a local supplier. There is an additional revenue source from servicing these machines through annual maintenance contract (AMC). A well known bank's corporate office in Mumbai is a good example of annual maintenance service contracts. Nevertheless, there is no competition in the vending machine type of shoeshine machine. The factors critical to success in this business would be

- Conveniently accessable prime locations where the machines should be placed in case of vending type of machines.
- High service quality.
- Increasing the percentage of polish occasions out of total usage occasions of the machine.
- First mover advantage of the business party.

A Business Opportunity Waiting for Its Customers

The shoeshine machine can also serve value added services like a grooming mirror, cool air face blow, music on demand, wet face towels to improve the customer experience. Further innovations required are the battery-operated machines, various sizes and shapes of machines. The business investment is modest and can be financed either through a bank loan or through one's own capital. The capital investment required is for purchasing machines only. The recurring expenses are of purchasing shoe cream every month and shoe brushes once in 8–10 months depending on the consumption rate. The approximate cost of a standard size shoeshine machine is around ₹8000–10,000.The cost of 1 kg of shoe cream varies from ₹300 to ₹450 depending on the quality of cream. The rates of these would obviously go down when purchased in bulk. The useful life of the machine is 8–10 years. The average consumption of the cream is 1 g per usage occasion. Based on these estimates, the humble shoeshine machine presents a shining business opportunity with low capital investment waiting to be tapped.

However, Dilip's company is currently a market leader in the shoe polish segment with a complete product line of 'Shiny' brand of shoe polishes (used within home, mostly once or twice a week) and is thinking of a brand extension into the area of out-of-home market, which he thinks is largely untapped, except for the shoeshine boys. These shoeshine boys are present mostly in areas like railway stations and bus depots and are largely unorganized. The latent business opportunity for the company is to be the first mover in this segment as its 'Shiny' brand is stagnating in the market with around 45% market share, with its closest competitor having another 25% market share. The rest of the market is divided among local brands. The urge to grow the stagnating brand is the order of the day for the new brand manager. But Dilip is not sure, if the company can really exploit the opportunity successfully, despite being a well known MNC with similar superior brands in other categories besides shoe polishes. If he proposes this opportunity to his VP (Marketing), he must be very sure about the figures he presents and since no official numbers are given to the market (no official market research has been done on the market for shoeshine machine business), he is hesitant to do so. But his hunch, based on 10 years of marketing experience, leads him to believe that there seems to be such an opportunity, as he himself has seen some large shoe companies having a few shoeshine machines at certain locations in the airport, as a brand building exercise. At stake is his own and his company's reputation in the market. Moreover, his career can either takeoff or nosedive depending on the outcome of his recommendation to the company. At the back of his mind, he knows that his company expects him to rejuvenate the stagnating brand through some innovative juggling of the marketing mix, and here he is thinking of presenting a new business opportunity which has the potential of cannibalizing the existing sales of the 'Shiny' brand in the market. All these issues are bugging Dilip.

Questions

1. Will customers really care to shine shoes outside home, specially using these shoeshine machines?
2. Will budding entrepreneurs care to partner with Dilip's company to make the business model successful?
3. Do we understand the customer behaviour in male grooming correctly?
4. Can the shoeshine machine be a value added service provider that can be clubbed with other male grooming services in places such as parlours?
5. Will shoeshine service be a shining business opportunity?

CASE-2

INCOMPLETE PRODUCT DISCLOSURE AND POOR CUSTOMER COMPLAINT HANDLING: A LETHAL COMBINATION AT ABC CELLULAR LTD.*

Dr. Jayashree Dubey

After shifting to Itarsi, in Madhya Pradesh, Mr. Vikhyat took a postpaid mobile connection from one of the top cellular company, ABC Cellular Ltd. He decided to go for plan 'Super 300'. Under this plan, he was initially allotted a monthly limit of ₹500. The plan included monthly free call allowances of 525 calls and 175 SMSes (local and national combined). As he was left with large number of free text messages, on *Diwali*, a big Indian festival, he sent greetings using SMS service to many of his friends and relatives. Next day he got a message from the company that he had exhausted 90% of his monthly limit. As prior to sending greeting messages, he was left with enough balance and did not make many calls, he was surprised as to where his balance had disappeared. On calling to the customer care, the executive informed him that as per the company's policy, text messages were not free, and were rather costly on festive days. Hence the text messages sent by him on *Diwali* were not free, and were charged at the rate of ₹1 for local and ₹1.5 for non-local national messages, costing him a total of ₹175. Obviously, Vikhyat was ignorant of this service condition. He was not informed about this at the time of taking the connection nor was any such information disclosed in any other document provided to him. On enquiring, the customer care executive failed to quote where it is mentioned in black and white. Vikhyat was clueless what to do. It was time for him to leave the matter here, or pursue it to the next level. He chose the latter. But he had to be very sure about the case, and decided to learn more about the service conditions.

Ambiguity in the Service Terms and Conditions of ABC

Upon referring to the company's Web site to know if the information was available in public domain, he found that under the heading 'Terms and Conditions' (T&C) one point was: 'The above mentioned text message rates are not applicable on festival days (ref. Annexure-I). During these days the rates will be ₹1 for local, ₹1.5 for non-local national, and ₹5 for international messages (160 characters)'. As the text message charges mentioned in the tariff plan was ₹0.4 (local and national) and since as per his plan

*This case has been prepared by Dr. Jayashree Dubey, Assistant Professor (Marketing), Indian Institute of Forest Management, Bhopal, and is based on a fictitious situation to stimulate discussion in an MBA classroom. Resemblance to any person or organization's efforts in the market in the past, present, or future is purely coincidental and unintentional. Published with permission.

he was given 175 free SMSes, the rates mentioned should be applicable only once a customer exhausted all his/her free SMS limit. He interpreted the point mentioned under T&C to be applicable only to those who were not given any free SMS allowances or those who had exhausted their limits.

He argued, 'It only means that if your messages are chargeable, the charges will be as mentioned under T&C and not the normal charges (₹0.4). However that point in no way communicates whether or not the opted scheme gives you certain free SMS allowances and it will not be free on the specified festive days'. Vikhyat also observed that there was no disclaimer to the disclosure in T&C, either in the column 'Free call allowances (local + STD Usage)' nor at '550 minutes calling Free, 175 messages free' to specify that certain additional conditions were imposed over and above those in T&C. Disclosure of such disclaimers was often used by companies to caution customers in all cases where additional charges were levied. Convinced that he was wrongly charged, it was time for him to talk to the company officials.

Vikhyat's Attempt to Knock the Door of ABC Cellular

He tried to contact senior staff over phone. However, the call was received by a junior fellow and was asked about the nature of complaint. The junior fellow also gave the same reasoning as given earlier by the customer care executive. He did not find enough substance in the complaint to be passed on to the higher ups and refused to transfer the call to his senior.

By this time, based on his information search, Vikhyat had also got to know that charging text messaging on festive days was common amongst other service providers, but was not convinced with the arguments made by the customer care executives as he had not found similar claims in the T&C disclosure from the company, neither in documents provided to him nor in the company's Web site. He decided to write a mail to the grievance cell, an internal body of the company which was superior to customer care. He hoped to get reply, and a reimbursement.

ABC's Reply

A few days later, he received the following reply from the customer service desk.

Dear Mr. Vikhyat,

Greetings from ABC Cellular Limited.

With reference to your mail and further to previous communication, we would request you to kindly provide us with your alternate contact number to enable us to assist you further as the below mentioned numbers are not getting answered.

We value your association with us, and look forward to your continued patronage.

Customer Service Desk

ABC Cellular Limited

Vikhyat thought that the grievance cell might have passed the complaint to customer care that in turn had sent this message. He gave his alternate number along with the multiple options of time to discuss. Nonetheless, he did not receive any call or any further message.

Further Aggravation of the Problem

After waiting for a couple of days for their call, Vikhyat further wrote, 'In case you don't have any answer to backup your policies on legal ground, kindly specify that to me, so that I can plan to approach other government body to get justice and monitory compensation for the loss in my professional work, loss of pleasure of talking to my relatives, loss of time in communicating to deaf ears, and loss of health thinking over this issue. The claim made will depend upon the delay done at your end'.

This time he got the reply from ABC cellular that said, 'Further to previous communication, I would like to reiterate that SMS charges applicable as per normal rates on festival days for bill dated 15/Nov/2010 was found to be correct and would request you to clear the outstanding amount to restore the services for the phone number #…#. However, the discontent caused is sincerely regretted'.

Vikhyat replied, 'Please don't frame your own rules. Kindly show me where you have mentioned that free text messaging facility will not be available on *Diwali* day. In case you fail to give me a written proof, we will meet in district consumer forum. I wish your team good luck to locate the written information in public domain.'

ABC Cellular kept on arguing, 'We would again like to inform that the required information for the year 2010 is clearly mentioned in the ABC's Web site and postpaid activation form for your perusal.'

Vikhyat replied, 'I failed to find a point mentioning that free messaging facility is not available on *Diwali*. I request you to highlight that portion clearly specifying the same and send me a scanned copy.'

After this mail, he did not get any reply from the grievance cell. He moved to the 'appellate body' of the company that was constituted to address such issues which are not resolved by customer care and grievance cell. This time he did not get any reply at all. His patience was running out. He was particularly pained by the manner of handling such issues by such a top-level service provider. Upping the ante, he decided to go beyond customer care, grievance, and appellate body, reaching to the top management of the company. He wrote a mail to the Chief Corporate Affairs Officer apprising him about the complaint and the responses he got from various levels of customer care executives. He hoped that this time, the matter would be resolved.

However, he was surprised at the twists and turns of the whole event that highlighted several things, right from the gimmicks that the company played to fleece its customers, to a highly incompetent system of managing customer grievances reflecting lack of internal audits and controls on the service levels. Pondering over actions he had taken over the past weeks, he also wondered if he had any better and more effective option to handle such treatment meted out to helpless customers.

The other major complaints which Vikhyat had were that after approaching 90% of the monthly credit limit, the company restricted outgoing calls only to its own network. Once the credit limit was over, a customer could not even make a call to the customer care or use even the free SMSes. The company had a policy of sending a reminder to pay the outstanding amount when he crossed 85% of the monthly credit limit, however, it was not always sent. He learnt about all these policies on enquiry from customer care when his calls and subsequently SMSes were barred. He was not informed earlier either orally or in writing, despite of the fact that he visited the company's office to get the connection. The level of dissatisfaction rose to an extent that now Vikhyat was looking for an appropriate time to port his number and move to some other service provider.

Questions

1. Is ABC cellular on the wrong side?
2. Should the company refund to Mr. Vikhyat and make changes in the public document?
3. Should the company have plans for service recovery to regain customers' confidence?
4. Comment upon the other complaint of Mr. Vikhyat regarding barring even free SMSes after using 100% of the monthly credit limit and barring calls to other network upon exhausting 90% level of credit limit.
5. Is there a need for ABC cellular to improve upon its services to avoid customers' exodus especially when number portability is in place?

Annexure-I Postpaid Plan—Madhya Pradesh

Name of tariff packages	***Super 300***
Monthly rental	₹300
Entry level cost	Activation charges – ₹280 (to be refunded/adjusted in the 5th and 6th bills)*
Commitment fee	Nil
Plan fee	Nil
CLI	Free
Tariff	All local and STD calls @ 50p/min
SMS (local)	₹0.4
SMS (national)	₹0.4
SMS (international)	₹4
Monthly free call allowances (local + STD usage)	525 minutes calling free, 175 SMSes free
Any taxes, in addition to the above	10.30% service tax

Terms and Conditions

*The activation charges of ₹280 will be refunded to the customers @ ₹140/month (or usage amount, whichever is lesser) as discount on the bill value with effect from their 4th bill, for a period of 2 months. Usage done in own network would be considered for the same.

If there is no usage, customer will not be entitled to discount in that particular month and same will be forfeited.

Plan change will get affected in case the number is active at the time of plan change.

STD facility will be available with activation but features like ISD/international roaming will be available as per the policy of company effective at that point of time. This is subject to payment of appropriate deposits.

All the tariff plans are subject to TRAI and/or other regulatory body approval, and may need to be modified, changed, or discontinued based on the guidelines received from time to time.

Security deposit will be refunded within 45 days after adjustment of all your dues.

SMS charges will be levied as 165 characters/SMS.

Free call allowances do not include roaming calls.

The free SMS in all the plans above are not applicable for peer to application (P2A) usage.

The above mentioned SMS rates are not applicable on festival days. During these days SMS rates will be local ₹1, national ₹1.5, and international ₹5 per SMS (160 characters)

New year (eve) (31st Dec), new year (1st Jan), Valentine's day (14th Feb), *Holi* and *Diwali*.

Conditions apply

Date: 5-04-11

CASE-3

BRANDED FRUIT JUICE—CHALLENGES IN FOR THE GLOBAL BEVERAGES LTD.*

Dr. Archana Sharma

Mani Bhushan, Director (Marketing) of Global Beverages Ltd., India, was in a pensive mood. He was trying to create a marketing plan for a pan-India launch of a new brand of packaged fruit juices in the Indian market. He had in his hand the market research report received from a team of researchers he had appointed some time back. As he glanced through the report, the events occurring over the last six months passed through his mind.

Global Beverages Ltd., the company for which Mani had been working for the last 10 years, was a transnational company in the business of non-alcoholic beverages with headquarters in Los Angeles, US. It was a professionally managed, widely held Public Ltd. company with its shares listed at the New York, London, Tokyo as well as Hong Kong stock exchanges. It had its subsidiaries as well as marketing offices in almost all the countries of Europe and North America and was now trying to enter the Asian markets.

Working in various capacities in the company, Mani had been directly involved in the successful launching and marketing of various beverages in the global markets. Before joining Global Beverages, he had worked for various companies in the US for about 15 years since he completed his MBA from IIM-Bangalore and migrated to the US. After the death of his mother, his father had been coercing him to come back to India. So, when Global Beverages opened a marketing office in India to make its presence felt in the emerging market, Mani took this as an opportunity to be with his ailing father as well as undertake the challenge of launching a new product in the Indian market.

Briefing Mani on his new assignment, his boss, the CEO of Global Beverages, stationed at Los Angeles, had advised him to continue with the same tried and tested globalized marketing plan of positioning the fruit juice as a breakfast option. He felt that the 'new global Indian consumer' would be able to relate to a global concept and would associate with the fruit juice brand. After all, the metropolitan Indian loved to consume anything and everything that was American. They wore *Levi*'s jeans, drank *Coca-Cola* and *Pepsi*, watched Harry Potter and Spiderman, and dined at *Pizza Hut, KFC,* and *McDonald*'s! It seemed inevitable that they would also accept the practice of drinking fruit juice in breakfast.

---

*This case has been prepared by Dr. Archana Sharma, Sr. Lecturer (Marketing), Indian Institute of Social Welfare and Business Management, Kolkata, and is based on a fictitious situation to stimulate discussion in an MBA classroom. Resemblance to any person or organization's efforts in the market in the past, present, or future is purely coincidental and unintentional. Published with permission

But after spending the last eight weeks having discussions with his various associates in India, and also remembering his own eating habits as a child and a young adult, he realized that the global positioning stand might not work in India. Even today, closing his eyes, he could almost hear his mother's voice calling him for breakfast, serving him hot '*aaloo ke paranthe*' with butter or sometimes *idlis* with piping hot *sambhar*.

His gut feeling told him that however westernized the modern metropolitan Indian had become, they might not readily accept the concept of drinking fruit juice for breakfast. He also remembered what had happened to the global strategy of *Kellogg*'s initially.

With exactly this in mind, he had appointed a market research firm to conduct a usage and attitudinal study between both juice and non-juice drinkers. He had categorically pointed out that he wanted an in-depth understanding of the Indian morning meal ritual, especially the role of fruit juices in the morning event. In this context, he had mentioned Patricia B. Seybold's research paper titled 'Get Inside the Lives of Your Customers' (HBR, May 2001). This paper talked about the fact that 'most companies have collected and sifted mountains of data on preferences and behaviour, divided buyers into ever-finer segments, and honed their products, services and marketing pitches. But few companies have bothered to look carefully at the broad context in which customers select, buy, and use products and services.'

The primary objectives that Mani had set for the market research team were as follows:

- Develop an understanding of the morning ritual of the Indian consumer with specific stress on the eating habits in the morning.
- Find out current as well as unmet needs in the morning meal occasion.
- Understand the perception of fruit juice among Indian consumers.
- Come up with the points that trigger and work as barriers behind consumption of branded fruit juice.

Following are the excerpts from the market research report.

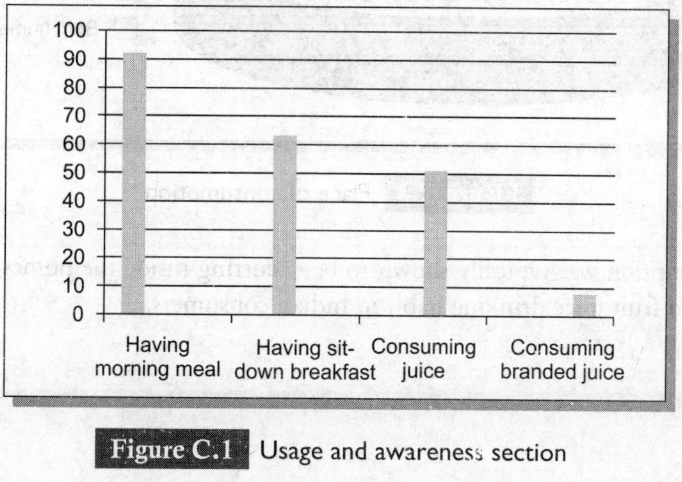

Figure C.1 Usage and awareness section

The research revealed that almost everyone (93% of the respondents) consumed some form of food or beverage, other than water in the morning.

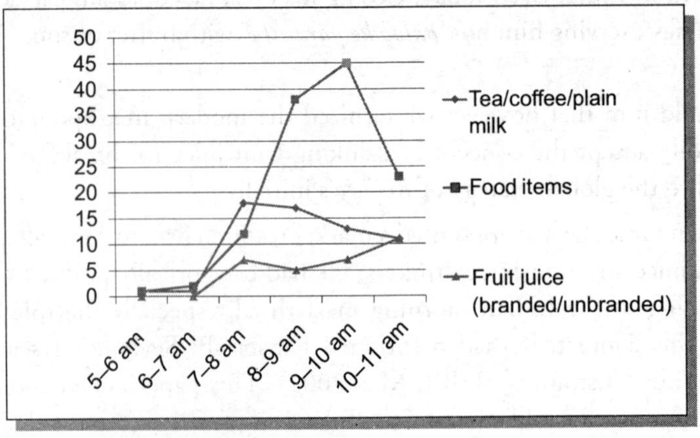

Figure C.2 Time slots of morning meals

Observing the time slots of the consumption during morning meal, it was found that eating of food items was more between 7 am and 8 am whereas drinking of fruit juices, whether home-made or packaged increased during the late morning hours, i.e., 10 am to 11 am, after the heavy meal consumption was over.

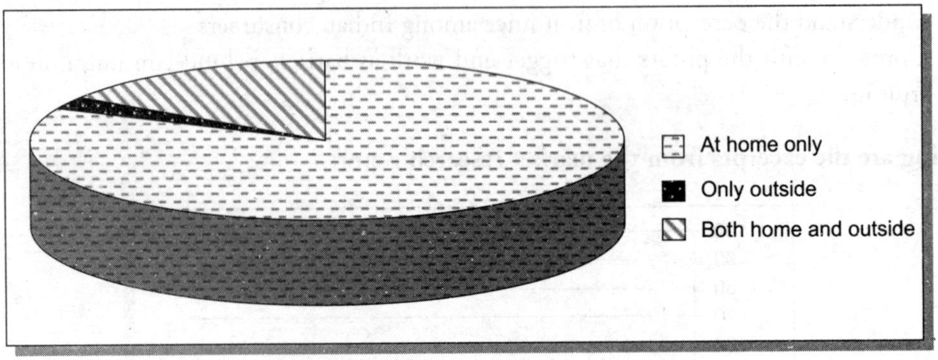

Figure C.3 Place of consumption

Breakfast consumption was typically shown to be occurring inside the homes, a positive signal for cultivating packaged fruit juice drinking habit in Indian consumers.

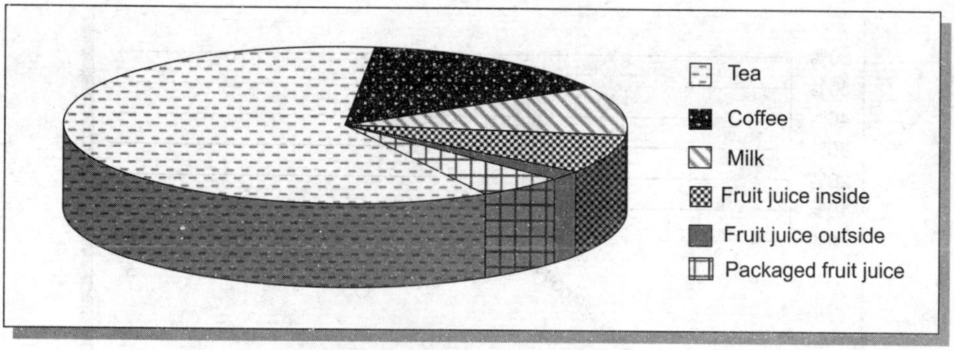

Figure C.4 Share of beverages

Looking at the share of beverages, tea and coffee dominated the scenario and together with plain milk, made up for more than half of the share of beverages, while fruit juices were left with just 10%.

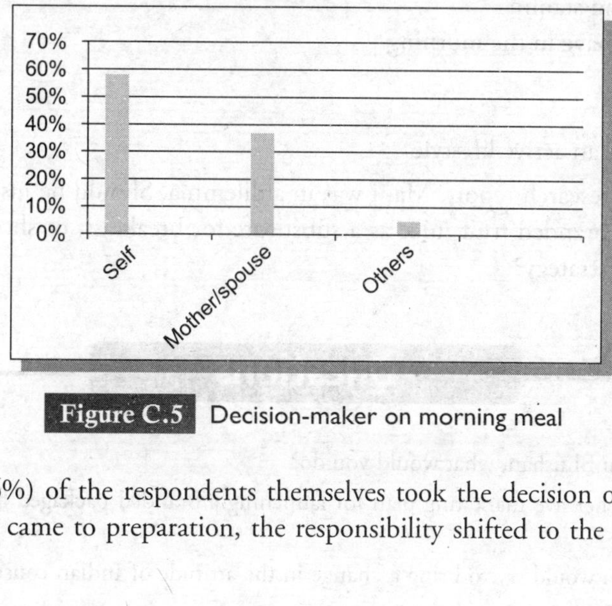

Figure C.5 Decision-maker on morning meal

A major chunk (56%) of the respondents themselves took the decision of what to consume for breakfast, but when it came to preparation, the responsibility shifted to the female members of the family.

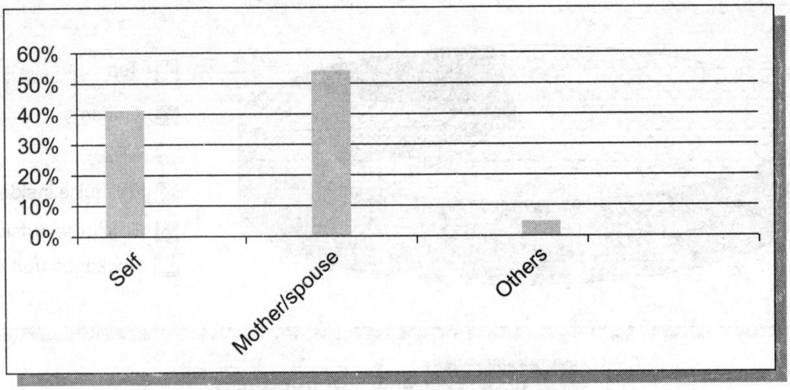

Figure C.6 Preparer of the morning meal

The hierarchy of needs for the morning meal as brought forward by the researchers was as follows:

- Gives energy and stamina
- Convenient to have in the morning
- Filling
- Natural
- Enables to have an active lifestyle

Reading the market research report, Mani was in a dilemma. Should he just obey the orders of his CEO and position the branded fruit juice as a substitute for breakfast, or should he create a distinct and Indian positioning strategy?

Questions

1. If you were Mani Bhushan, what would you do?
2. Create a comprehensive marketing plan for launching a branded packaged fruit juice in the Indian market.
3. Explain how you would try to bring a change in the attitude of Indian consumers towards branded packaged fruit juices.

CASE-4

IMPACT OF TEASER CAMPAIGN ON CONSUMER DECISION MAKING THROUGH AIDA MODEL—A CASE STUDY ON AEGON RELIGARE ON SELECT RESPONDENTS IN KOLKATA*

Aritri Banerjee and Dr. Srabanti Mukherjee

The Indian private insurance giant, *Aegon Religare*, is quite popular in the country for its catchy campaigns. In 2008, it had launched a beguiling campaign provoking people to safeguard themselves against the problem of being under-insured. The tagline of the campaign was '*Kam Insurance Lene Ki Bimari*' (KILB). In January 2011, they released a sequel about inadequate insurance coverage. The sequel portrays the popular actor Irfan Khan once again, teasing people and indicating that they are habituated to inadequacy.

Teaser advertisement of *Aegon Religare*

The well-planned teaser advertisements were carried on in all media till the late second week of January before the revealer advertisement was aired on January 16. The first teaser was a 10-second

*This case has been prepared by Aritri Banerjee, Associate Research Manager, IMRB International, Kolkata and Dr. Srabanti Mukherjee, Indian Institute of Management, Indore. This case is based on a small hidden survey and hence may not be conclusive enough and may contain some amount of sampling bias. This case was designed just to stimulate discussions in MBA classrooms.

television advertisement showcasing Irfan Khan as a shoe salesman, offering his customer a tiny pair of shoes. In the second sequel, Irfan portrayed a waiter in a posh restaurant offering a baby napkin to a customer.

Even in the outdoor campaigns, it was shown that Irfan is holding a tiny helmet, a pair of very small sunglasses, and a mini cup of tea. All these forms of advertisements poked the customers about inadequacy by saying '*Bas itna? Par aapko to aadat hai.*' The second phase of the campaign unveiled that it was mentioning about under-insurance and therefore, the endorser Irfan said, '*Kab tak KILB ke sang jiyoge? Aadat badlo.*' In pursuant with the brand's identity, the attitude and approach of the campaign were educative, where Khan was ideally featured as a concerned, friendly, and sociable opinion leader. They wanted to underpin the notion that along with healthier lifestyles, adequate attention also has to be paid to be sufficiently insured. Consequently, the campaign called for shaping a buzz about the common practice and carry across the '*aadat badlo*' message, thus spurring the respective customers to action.

A hidden survey was conducted on 9 high-salaried individuals (range of income 20–40k per month and in the age group of 35–45 years in Kolkata for 10 days from the starting day of this teaser campaign. The observation was based on four parameters: attention, interest, desire, action (AIDA model). It was recorded in a checklist form and the ratings were given in a 10-point staple scale.

The average ratings were taken and rounded off. These are shown in the table below.

Table 18.1 *Rating table*

Days / ***Attributes***	***1***	***2***	***3***	***4***	***5***	***6 (Day of disclosure)***	***7***	***8***	***9***	***10***
Attention	3	4	5	5	6	6	5	4	4	2
Interest	2	3	3	4	5	5	6	6	6	6
Desire						5	6	7	7	7
Action							2	1	0	0

Ratings are based on 10 being the best and 1 the worst

Ratings of desire and action were given from the day of disclosure (when the brand name was unveiled).

Now let us have a look at the results.

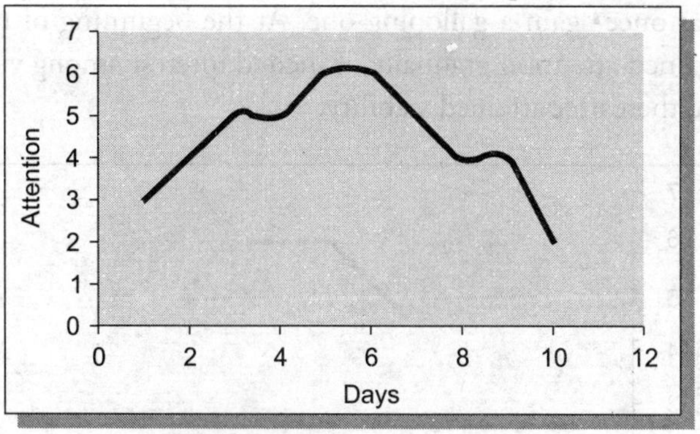

Figure C.7 Attention graph

From the *attention* graph, it could be seen that the attention level did not increase sharply, rather it moved in a galloping manner. The increased curiosity got stabilized between the 3rd and 4th day for a while and again started increasing. It attained the maximum level during the disclosing time (6th day) but after that it went down in a similar fashion. It must be mentioned that '*Kam insurance lene ki bimari*' was not a new one and the viewers were already aware of it. Nonetheless, due to some catchy advertisements, it was successful in drawing the attention of the audience. So the teaser advertisements provoked excitement, but as the idea was not new, the attention curve did not have a sharp rise; it rather moved and fell in a galloping way.

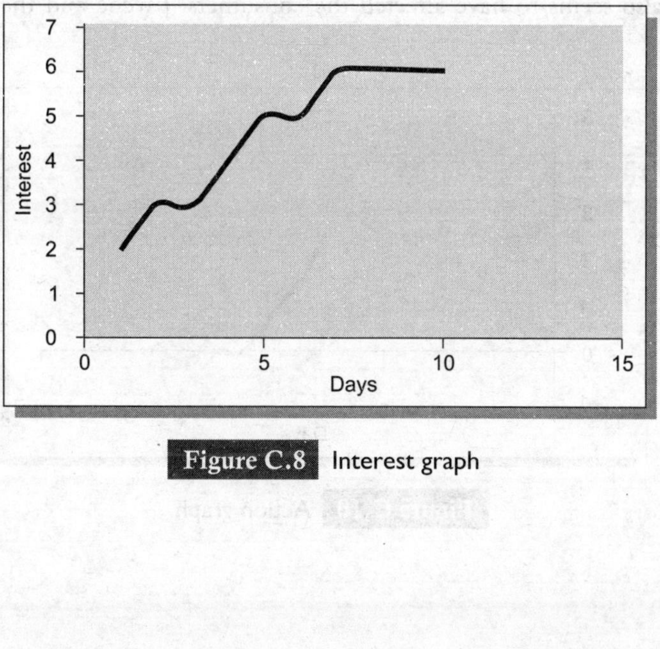

Figure C.8 Interest graph

The *interest* curve was once again a galloping one. At the beginning of the campaign the interest level was low and as it gained attention gradually, it incited interest among viewers so the interest level increased till 7th day and thereafter attained stability.

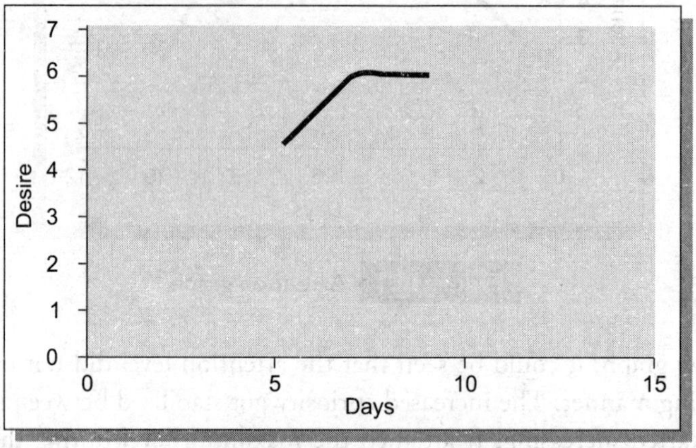

Figure C.9 Desire graph

From the *desire* graph, it was found that the teaser campaign KILB of *Aegon Religare* successfully aroused the desire among the viewers. No doubt, the campaign tone was an educative one directing towards better lifestyles. The notion of the advertisement that one must also pay attention to being sufficiently insured also seems to have affected the consumers' psyche and they started desiring the product.

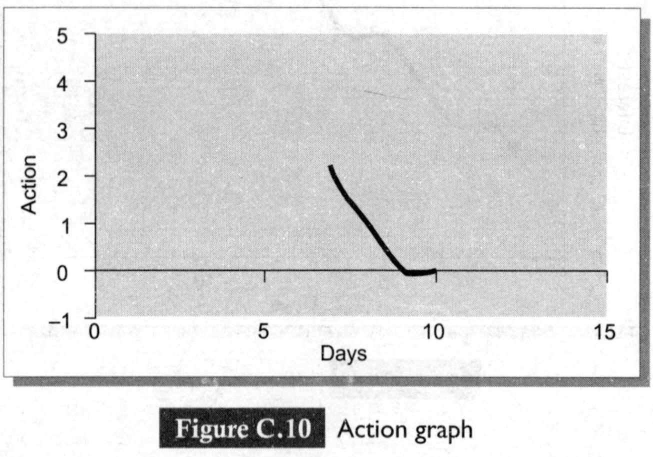

Figure C.10 Action graph

However, from the *action* graph, it could be observed that on the 7th day, i.e., one day after the disclosure of the brand name, only two out of the nine respondents were thoroughly interested in the advertisement and purchased the product. On the 8th day, only one of the respondents enrolled in the scheme and nobody else showed interest to purchase. So the immense interest and subsequent desire for the product in this case did not lead the customers to actually purchase the product. After drawing the graphs of the hidden survey, the respondents were formally put in a focus group discussion to talk about their perception on the teaser campaign and subsequently on their purchase decision. The following dimensions were revealed from their discussion.

(i) The respondents mentioned that the Indian insurance policies were very complicated and difficult to understand just by seeing the commercials. Again these teaser commercials did not talk about the policy features, exclusions, etc. So in order to properly communicate about the insurance schemes and benefits to the customers, the customers needed somebody on behalf of the company to explain them the policy features thoroughly.

(ii) As insurance is a financial proposition, trust for a brand is very important. The respondents mostly agreed that they had more faith on the government undertaking insurance companies than the private ones.

So the major challenge of how to make the teaser campaign effective in terms of purchase still prevails.

Questions

1. Do you feel teaser campaign in general fails to convert attention to action or is it a specific case of *Religare*?
2. If as a Manager (communication) of *Aegon Religare*, you get these results across the country, will you stop teasers and continue with the conventional form of advertising. Or will you think of any other strategies to convert attention to action? Give reasons.

CASE-5

ABN HOSPITAL'S COMMUNICATION PROBLEMS—A CASE STUDY*

Debanjan Guha

ABN hospital was a city based leading corporate hospital. It was a multi-specialty hospital with state-of-the-art infrastructure and latest medical equipments. It had some of the best doctors and surgeons in Kolkata offering quality healthcare services to patients.

It was the morning meeting amongst the Chief Operating Officer (COO) of ABN hospital, Dr. Archana Roy, the General Manager (corporate communications) Mr. S. Basu, and two of their best doctors Dr. P. Mukherjee and Dr. D. Saxena from the cardiology and neurology departments of the hospital, respectively. The discussion centred on the response generated from the advertorials called '*From the Doctor's Desk*' which they have been doing with *The Express Today* newspaper for the last three years.

The COO asked the General Manager, 'Mr. Basu, why are the enquiry emails decreasing over the last few months?' Mr. Basu replied,'Madam, it seems that the readers' interest in sending their inquiries to the doctors is going down.' Mr. Basu presented the following graphical representations to showcase the diminishing response calls as a proof of his proclamation.

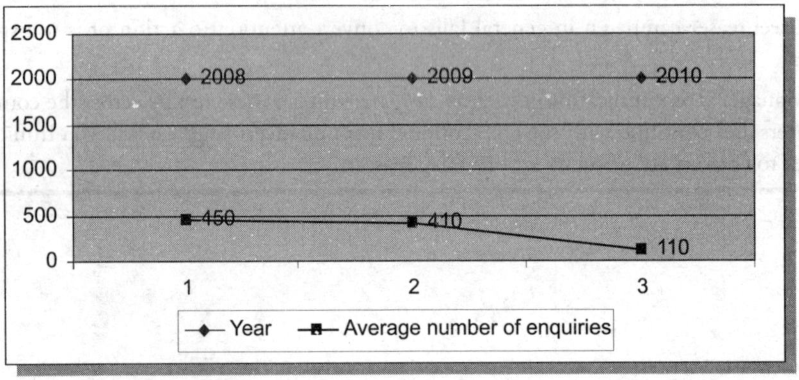

Figure C.11 Average number of enquiries through email

---

*This case has been prepared by Debanjan Guha, Manager (Space Marketing Department), The Indian Express Limited, Kolkata and is based on a fictitious situation to stimulate discussion in an MBA classroom. Any resemblance to any person or organization's efforts in the market in the past, present, or future, is purely coincidental and unintentional. Published with permission.

Dr. Roy asked, 'But what is the reason? Why is such an innovative concept losing its appeal?' Dr. Saxena said 'Madam, we used to get more than 400 email inquiries every week last year. But now it has come down to almost 100 per week!' Mr. Basu said, 'It is perhaps because of the similar kind of promotion by competing hospitals in Kolkata.' He presented the following graphical representation to show the increase in advertorials by other hospitals:

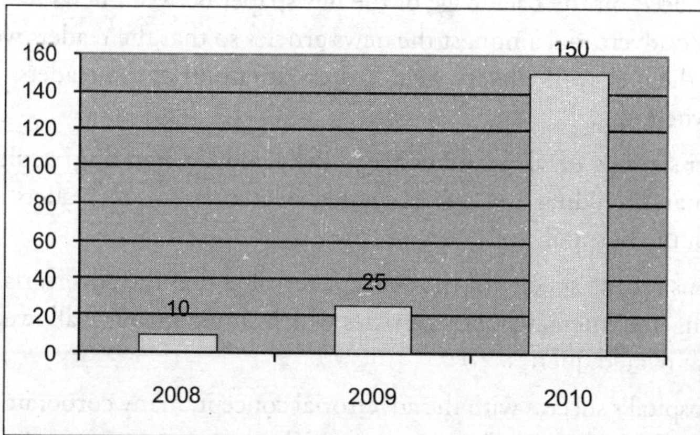

Figure C.12 Increase in advertorials by other hospitals per week

Mr. Basu added further, 'Actually, if we observe the response received over the last three years, we may find that the number of response calls is going down. The apparent reason seems to be the similar advertorials being done by other corporate hospitals in newspapers. In 2008, only 10 advertorials per week from other corporate hospitals appeared in newspapers. But the number of advertorials from other hospitals had increased to 150 per week in 2010. Every day *The Express Today* itself is carrying at least three advertorials from different hospitals. As a result, the readers' are losing interest in advertorials.'

Dr. Mukherjee said, 'Madam, it appears that the readers have started referring the advertorials as advertisements. It seems that they have understood that the main purpose of the advertorials is advertising the hospital's services. Naturally they are losing interest.'

Dr. Roy asked, 'Do you mean to say that advertorials are not working anymore? Do we need to start thinking about innovative concepts again?' Mr. Basu replied, 'Yes madam! I think we must start thinking about new ideas in advertising.'

Dr. Roy started recollecting the context in which the advertorials were planned. Advertorials were thought as an effective form of advertisements in newspapers and thus were extensively used by the healthcare industry in Kolkata. In the year 2008, *The Express Today Space Marketing* team conceptualized a unique form of weekly advertorial of size 10 cm height and 16 cm width for ABN hospital of Kolkata which was published in *The Express Today*, Kolkata edition. Known as 'From the *Doctor's Desk*' the concept involved a question and answer session where a doctor from a particular medical specialty department from the hospital would answer the health related enquiries. The readers would send their enquiries through email. The questions and answers would then be put into a form of an advertorial with the photo, name, and specialty department of the relevant doctor. A bottom strip of the advertorial would carry the logo, name, and phone numbers of the hospital.

Till now many of the corporate hospitals were using this concept as a brand building exercise very effectively. It initially generated tremendous interest among the readers of *The Express Today*. Usually the advertorials were placed on the back page of the newspaper between news items. The idea behind it was to camouflage the advertorial amongst the news articles so that the readers would consider it as a news item. Till 2009, the idea worked very well. It drew attention of the readers. The responses from the readers were overwhelming.

From the advertiser's point of view the concept delivered outstanding results for the corporate hospitals in terms of brand building and also generated awareness among readers about the renowned doctors associated with the hospital.

Analyzing the reasons for the success of the concept revealed that the advertorials were perceived by the readers as interesting and interactive news articles which simultaneously allowed the readers to seek answers for their health related queries.

Visualizing ABN hospital's success with the advertorial concept, many corporate hospitals in Kolkata followed their footsteps. But as more and more advertorials started to appear in the newspapers, readers gradually became aware that they were not news articles but actually advertisements. The innovative appeal of the advertorials was, thus, experiencing 'commoditization'. Advertorial concept was successful probably due to its uniqueness. But extensive use of this concept by corporate hospitals diluted its uniqueness and novelty and perceived to be identical for all hospitals. Subsequently, it was leading to the death of the concept. As a consequence, the effectiveness of the advertorial concept was diminished.

Since '*From the Doctors Desk*' had evolved as an important communication tool for ABN hospital to promote its brand name, it was difficult to replace it with some other concept. The COO of ABN hospital Dr. Roy was concerned about how to replace a successful concept like advertorials with some other innovative concepts. What fresh concept could be conceptualized to generate the kind of reader interest developed by the advertorials?

Questions

1. Should ABN hospital continue with the advertorial concept?
2. What other innovative communication tools can be developed by the hospital so as to form a different set of predispositions in the minds of the customers?

CASE-6

MRS. URBAN INDIA—A BUSINESS OPPORTUNITY WAITING*

Sankara Pillai

Pathfinders India, the research division of Lintas and the forerunner of QED Research, was a pioneer in psychographic segmentation, conducting P:SNAP (Study of Nation's Attitudes and Psychographics) after VALS. There were five rounds conducted in 1985, 1992, 1996, 1999, and 2005. This has been the only systematic and sustained effort at tracking the women psychographics in India. Essentially it classified, based on an attitudinal battery of about 130 statements, the 10,000 housewives who form the main target groups for most FMCG products. Lowe, the communication group of Lintas, termed these five categories as five faces and named their studies as 'Lowe-faces: Mrs. Urban India'.

Lowe's intensive study of how humans accept and adapt to change shows two underlying dimensions that unify or divide people:

Do people really seek change in their lives?

Are they 'traditional' or 'modern' in accepting change?

On one dimension, Lowe saw that people are either change seekers or stability seekers. On the other dimension, they are separated by how modern or how traditional they are.

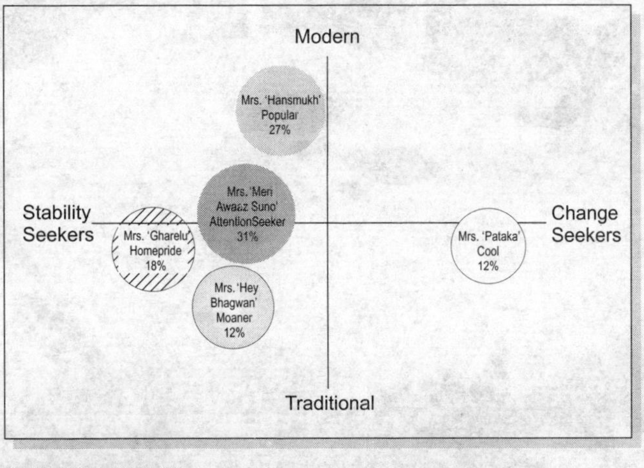

Figure C.13 Psychographics of urban women in India

*This case has been developed by Mr. Sankara Pillai, Mentor QED Research (#9 Belle Vista Commercial Complex, Next to DY Patil University, Belapur, Navi Mumbai 400 614), based on his study as the then Head Quantitative Research, Pathfinders. Published with permission.

In India, the study analyzed over 10,000 married women across 38 urban centres using the P:SNAP (Study of the Nation's Attitudes and Psychographics), conducted by Pathfinders India. Five segments or Faces©, with their own demographic, lifestyle, psychographic and brand skew characteristics emerged and are discussed in the following pages.

Mrs. '*Hasmukh*' Popular

Mrs. '*Hasmukh*' Popular 27%

She treats her life like a must-win popularity contest. She's everybody's friend, a perfect wife, a perfect mother, and a perfect daughter-in-law.

Independent-minded, she is not self-sacrificing, and would love to be a fashion leader among her friends. Yet she is respectful and caring to elders, and has no problems living in a joint family.

Very independent, she is the rock others lean on. She divides her time between husband, children, elders, herself, and her friends. She visits temple as well as beauty parlour. She would rather chat with visitors than do chores. So, she buys products that make housework more convenient.

A roie-model didi, she encourages kids to pursue their own careers, as she herself would like to do what other women don't. She is a wife, a friend, and an asset to her husband.

Skew: Key Demographics

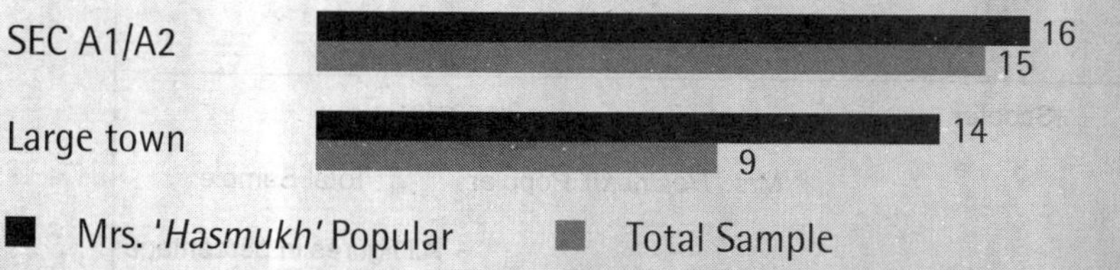

All figures in percentage

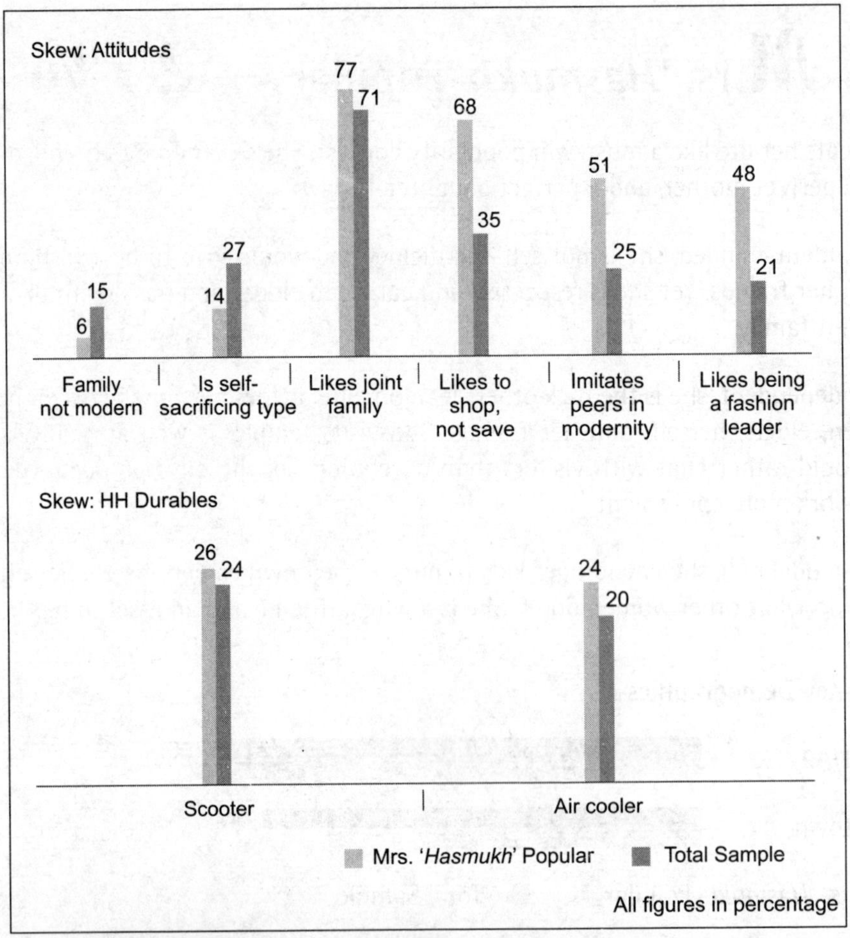

Figure C.14 Preference pattern of Mrs. '*Hasmukh*' Popular

Brand skew for Mrs. '*Hasmukh*' Popular

Mrs. '*Pataka*' Cool

Mrs. '*Pataka*' Cool 12%

She's just too cool. She looks cool, she acts cool. She talks about doing what other women don't, even talks of starting a business if she wins a lottery. Her child goes to the 'best' school. Style matters everywhere, even in her watches and sunglasses. She goes out the most, to the beauty parlour, on holidays, for parent-teacher meetings, to restaurants, even to temples.

She is the cool metro woman, still young, and is consulted by her husband over any decision. But inside this cool woman is a middle-class heart that beats for the family. She even does the housework—with the help of convenient products, that is. She wants her family to approve of any new purchase she makes, even the taste of the new healthy cooking oil and corn flakes.

Skew: Key Demographics

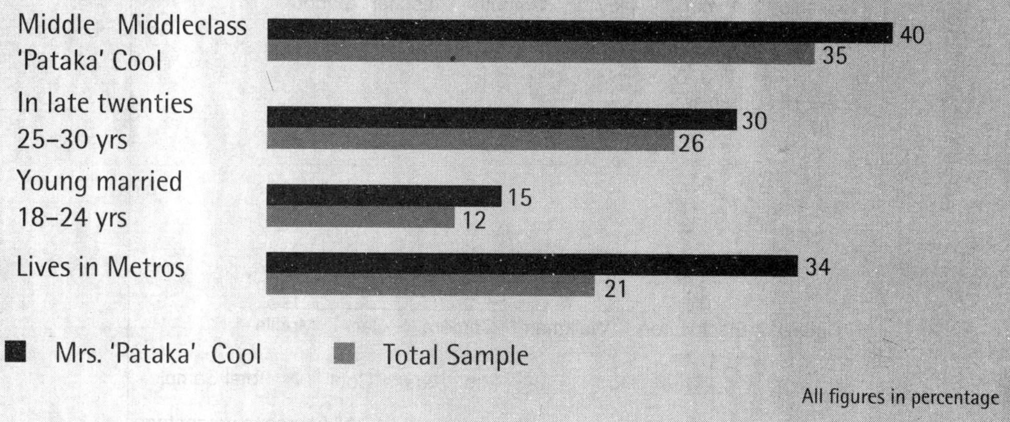

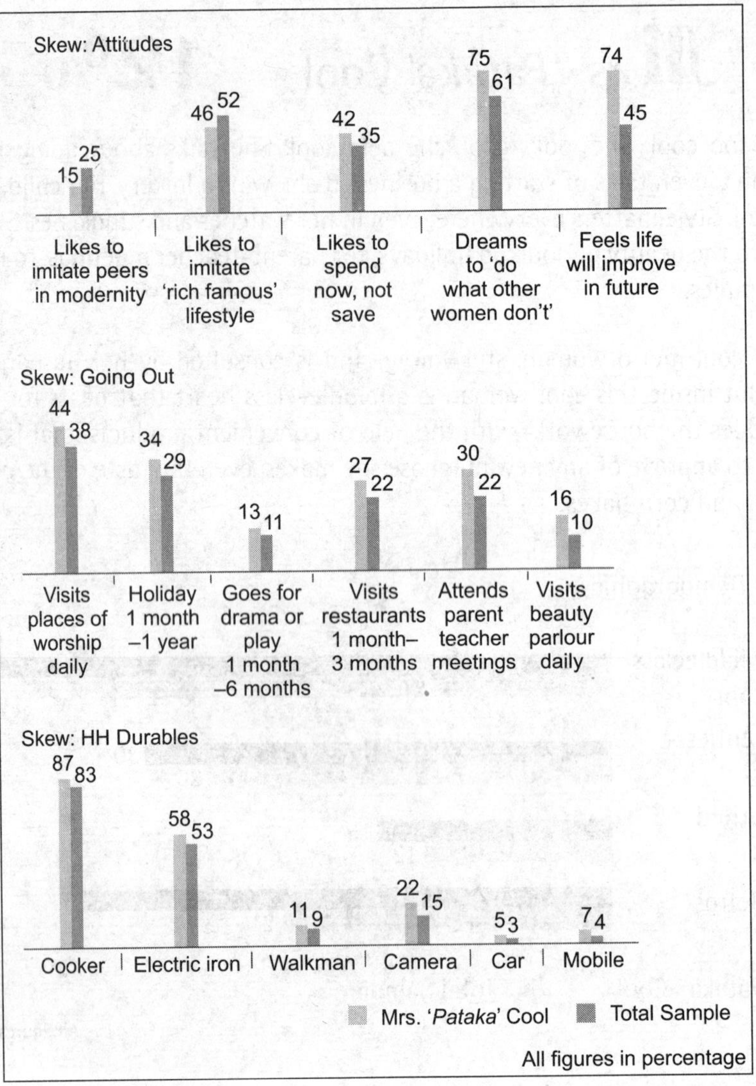

Figure C.15 Preference patterns of Mrs. '*Pataka*' Cool

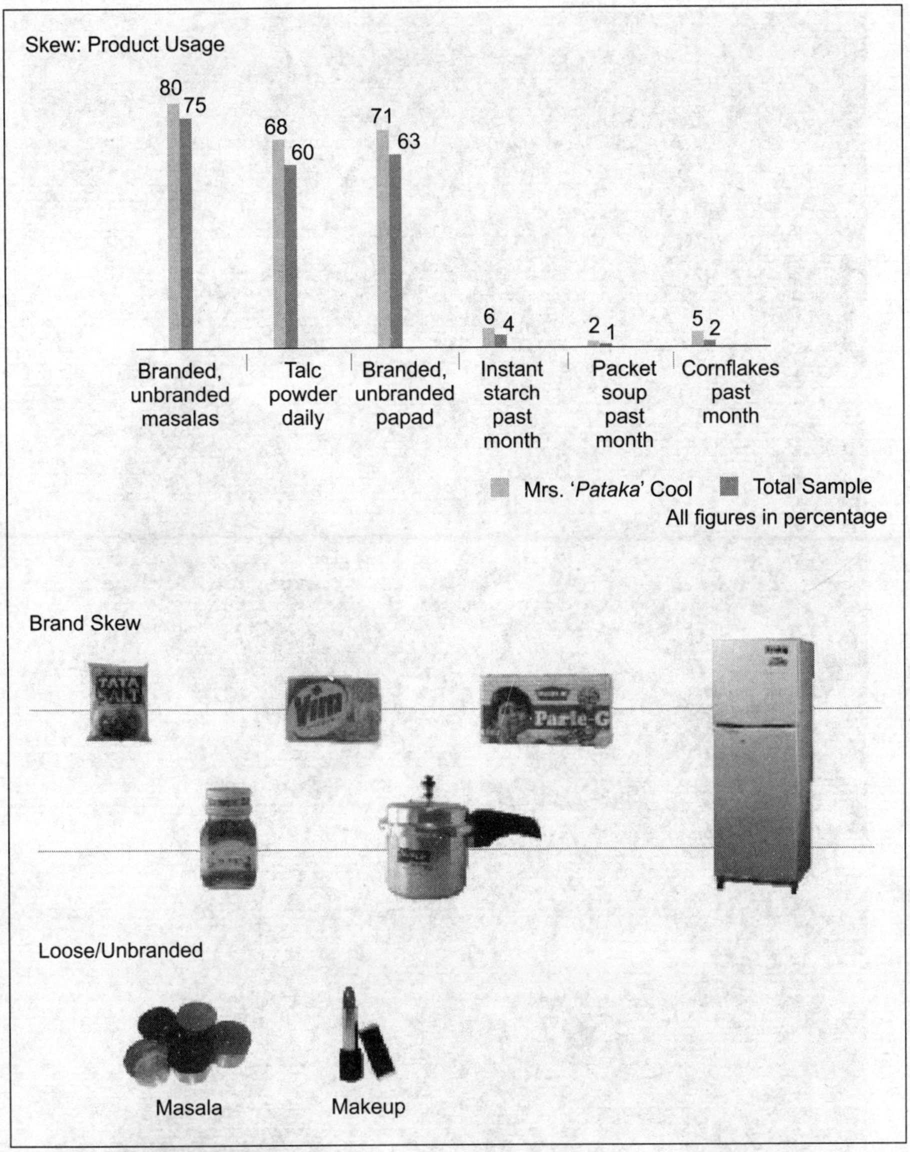

Figure C.16 Product usage patterns of Mrs. '*Pataka*' Cool

Mrs. '*Meri Awaaz Suno*'

Mrs. '*Meri Awaaz Suno*' Attention Seeker 31%

The purpose of her existence is to be noticed. Society places too many restrictions on her, her family is not modern, and she doesn't like the idea of staying in a joint family. Her husband takes major decisions on his own even on issues like family size and monthly budget.

She dresses up even when she goes to the market for vegetables, *Good Knight* mosquito repellent, chips and *Coke*—after all, she doesn't get out anywhere else.

Any money in hand would be spent in buying nail polish to match her latest shoes. She'd be happier if you admired her outfit rather than her cooking. Win a lottery and invest in gold or save in a bank? Never! She'd rather spend the money now that she has it.

Skew: Key Demographics

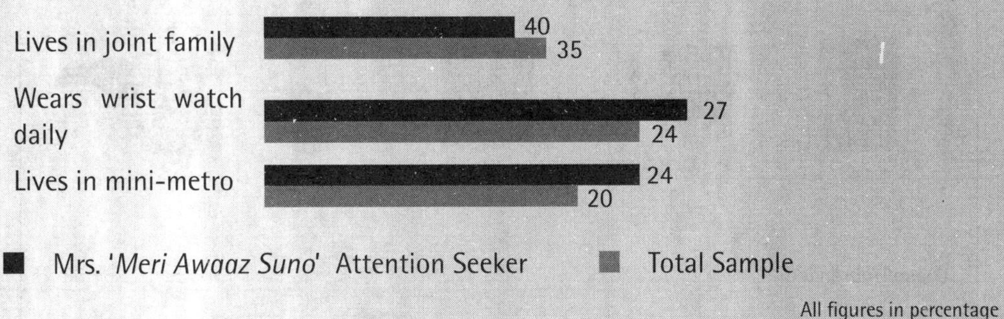

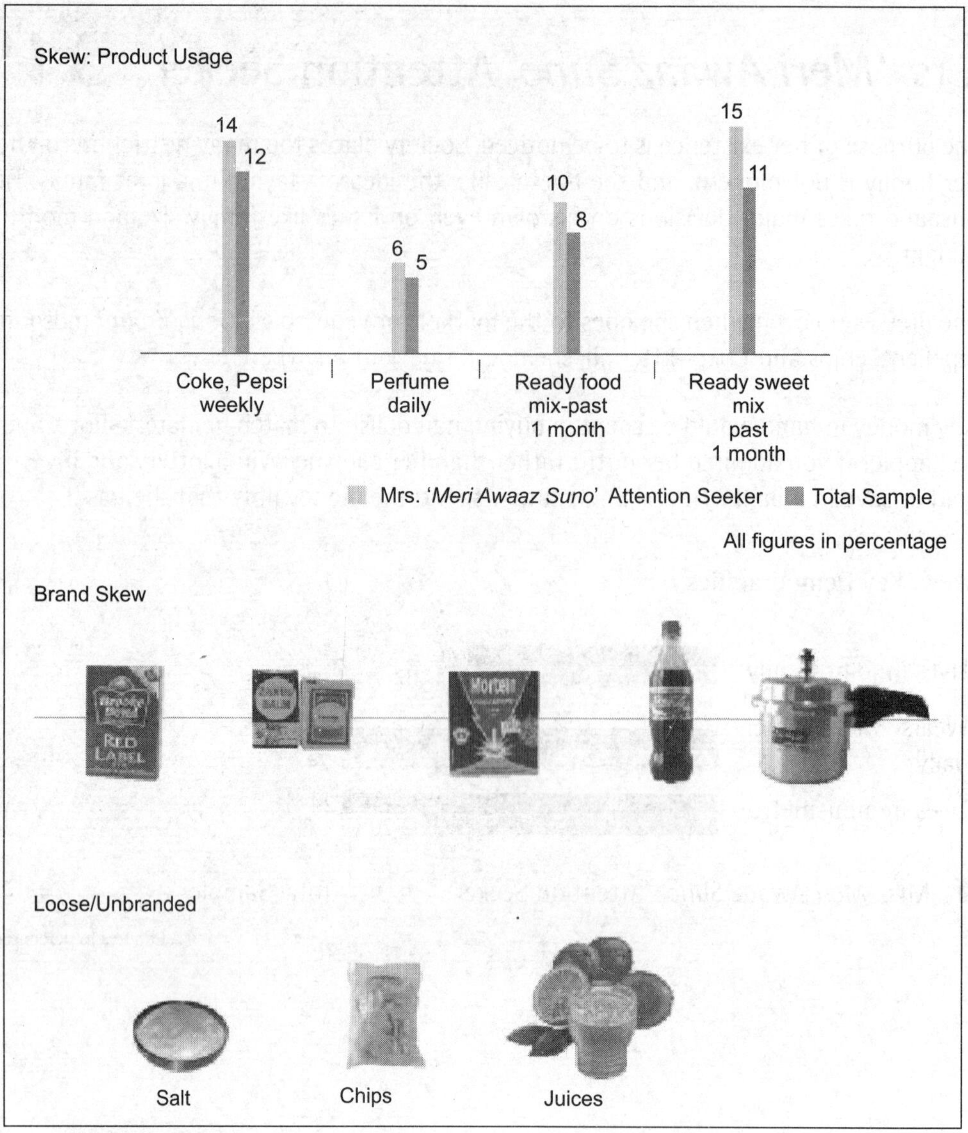

Figure C.17 Product preference and usage pattern of Mrs. '*Meri Awaaz Suno*'

Mrs. '*Gharelu*' Homepride

Mrs. '*Gharelu*' Homepride 18%

The quintessential sacrificing '*maa*', the perfect homemaker.

It's always spotless white clothes and *Maggi* noodles for her kids. Her daughter has to be well groomed; so, liberal use of *Parachute* oil, *Clinic Plus* shampoo, talcum powder, and *Fair & Lovely* is a must.

She's proud of her mixer, water filter, and sewing machine, and loves people asking for second helpings of her food.

Why waste money? She'll make her own pickles and won't drop money into the temple coffers everyday—instead, she'll buy noodles, glucose biscuits, or healthy cooking oil instead. Her husband relies heavily on her wisdom.

The best investment she can make in her kids is to send them to 'expensive' schools. If she wins the lottery, she'd put that into their education. But she's not going to let her kids choose any newfangled, 'unknown' career; her family is not that modern.

Skew: Key Demographics

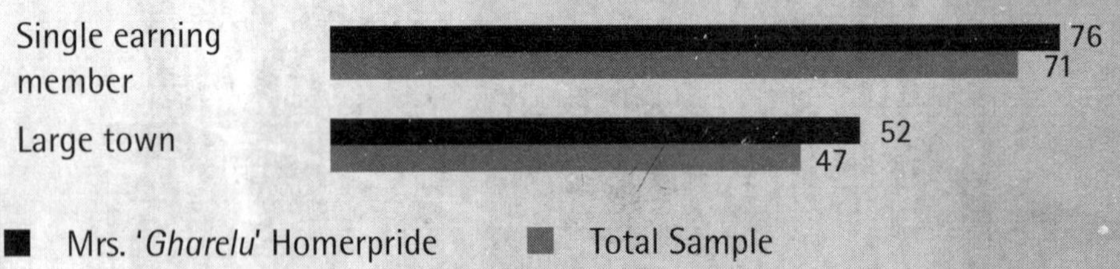

All figures in percentage

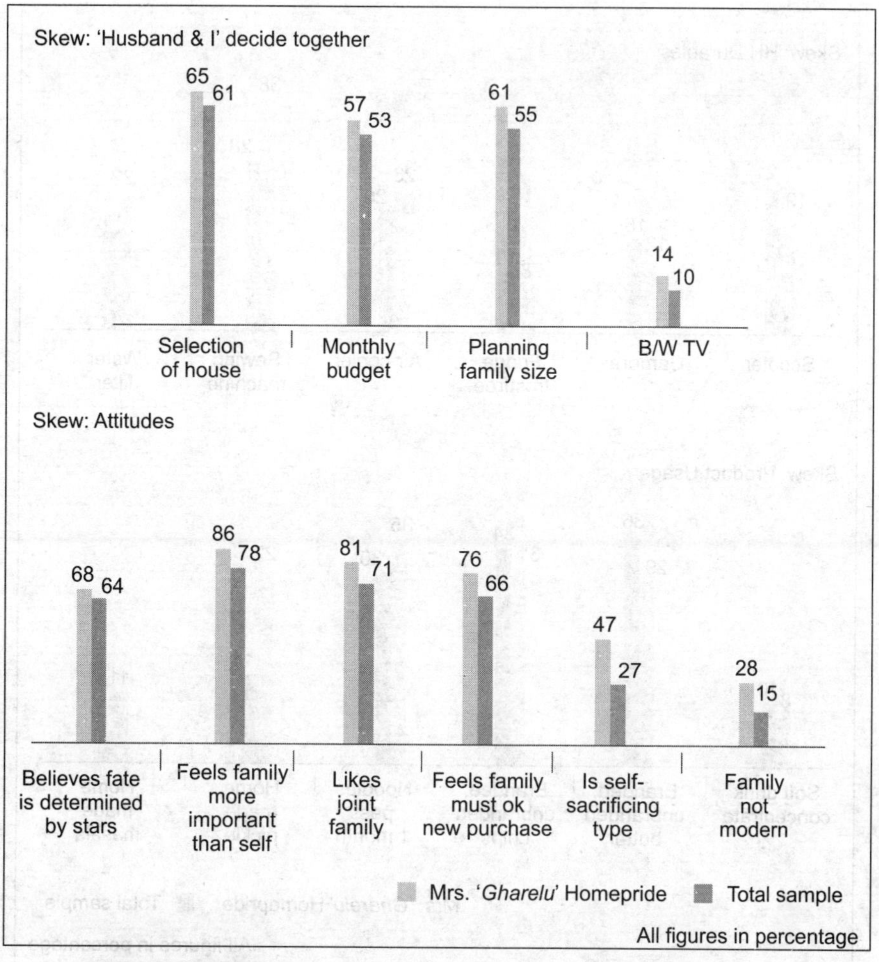

Figure C.18 Mrs. '*Gharelu*' Homerpride's choice parameters

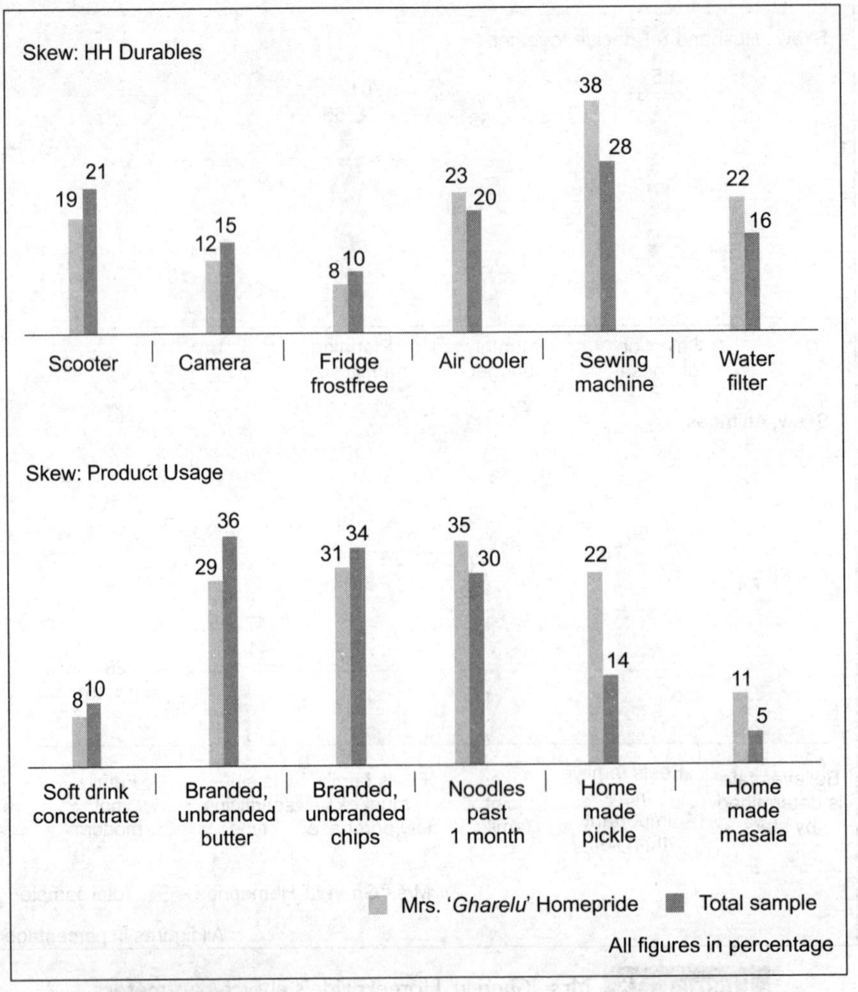

Figure C.19 Mrs. '*Gharelu*' Homerpride's preference pattern

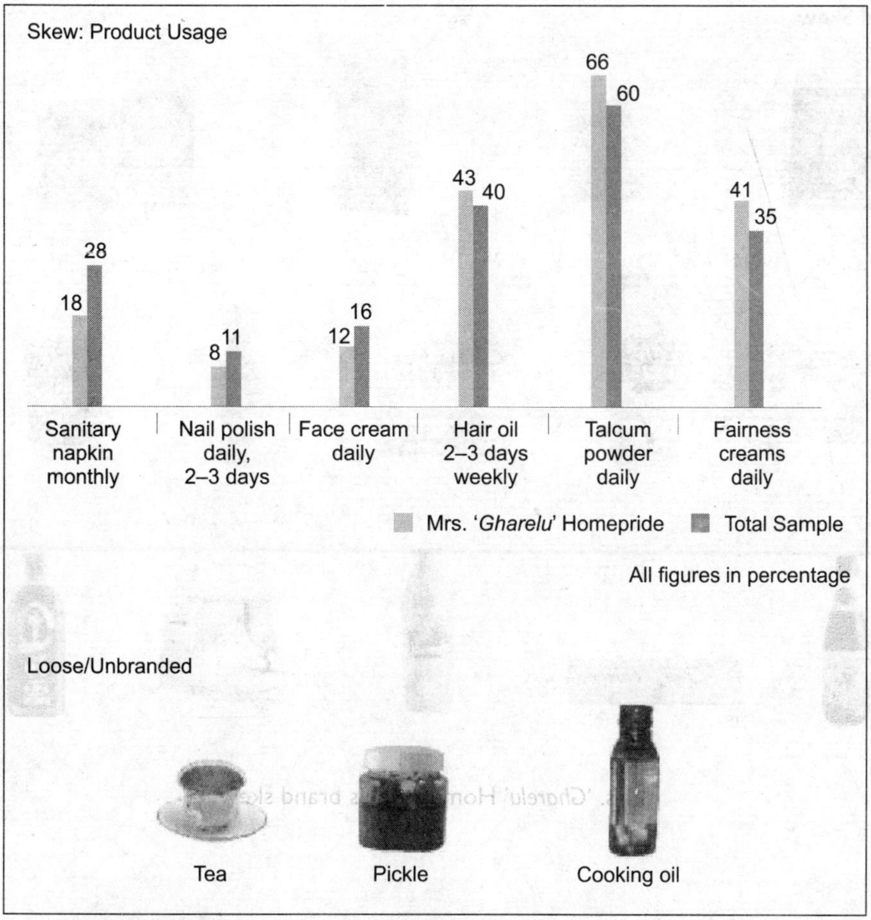

Figure C.20 Mrs. '*Gharelu*' Homerpride's product usage pattern

Brand Skew

Mrs. '*Gharelu*' Homerpride's brand skew

Mrs. '*Hey Bhagwan*' Moaner

Mrs. '*Hey Bhagwan*' Moaner 12%

'Oh, my life is so bad! Poor me! I wasn't educated beyond primary school; otherwise I would have done so much. I don't have money, so I can't send my kids to expensive schools. What's the point in saving and scrounging without even telling my husband? We'll never live the lifestyle of the rich and the famous. My husband hasn't even got me out of this lower middle-class drudgery—how much can a skilled man do in a mini-metro? And the family? Thank God, we don't have to live in a joint family; I'm not prepared to make any more sacrifices. It's bad enough that my husband takes all major decisions by himself. Oh, when will my life change?'

She cooks, cleans, saves, hoards, and dresses plainly. She dreams of winning a lottery, of owning a home, and having gold jewellery. She is fatalistic, but doesn't pray much. She hopes that will somehow improve in the future.

Skew: Key Demographics

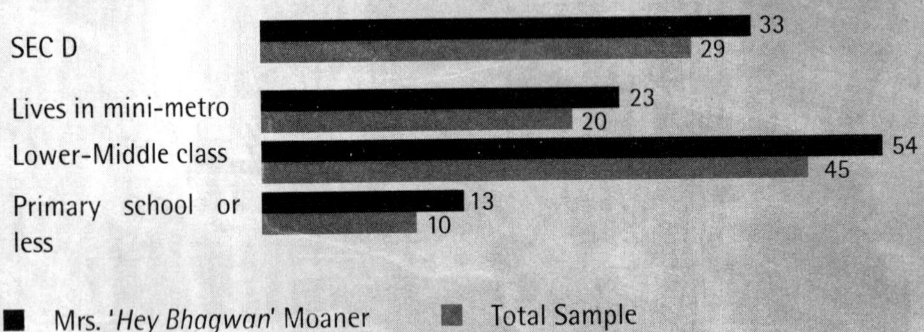

All figures in percentage

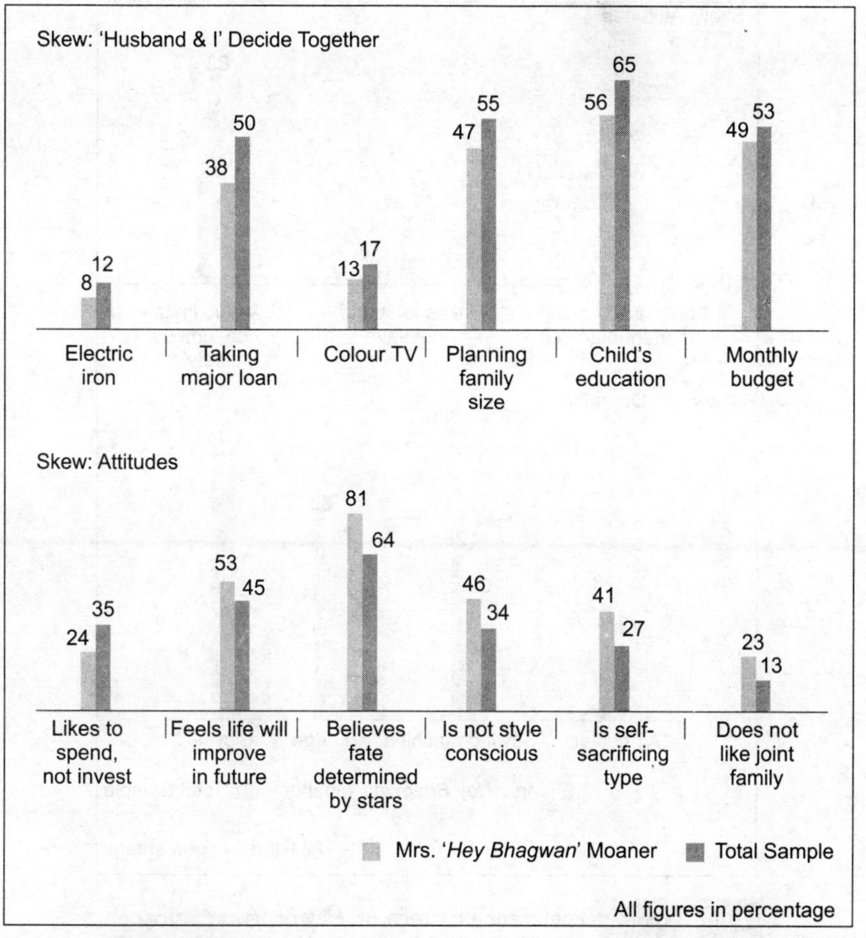

Figure C.21 Choice parameters of '*Hey Bhagwan*' Moaner

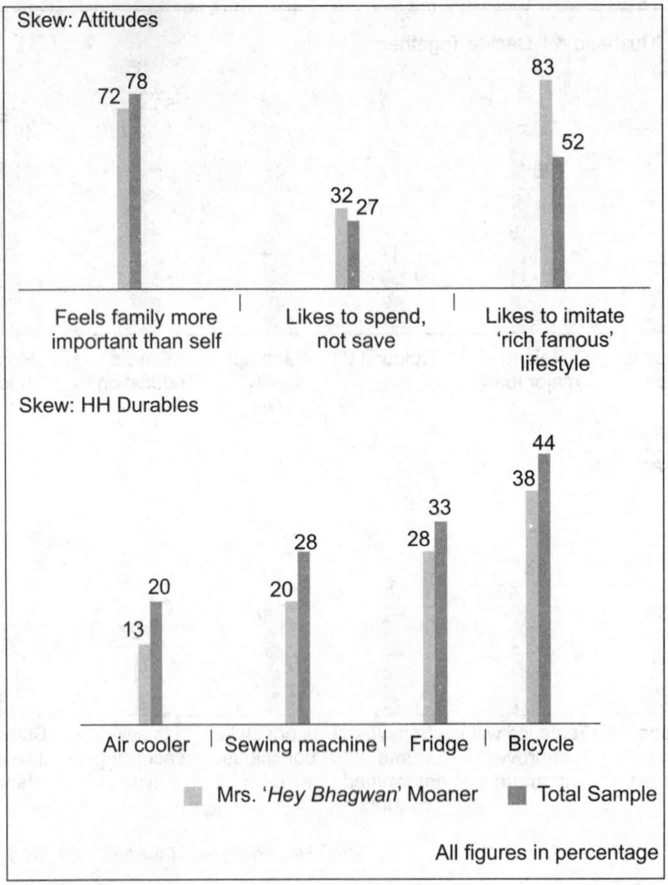

Figure C.22 Preference pattern of '*Hey Bhagwan*' Moaner

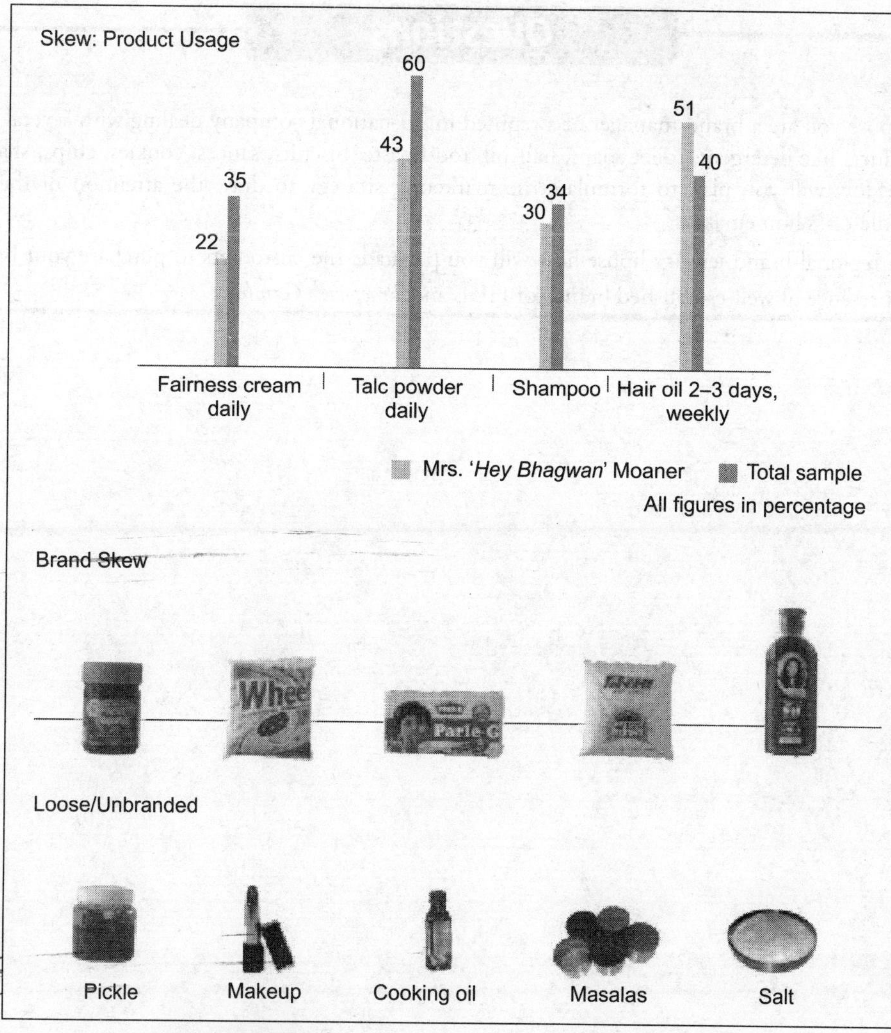

Figure C.23 Brand skew of '*Hey Bhagwan*' Moaner

Questions

1. Suppose you are a brand manager of a reputed multi-national company dealing with several FMCG products like detergent, toilet soaps, hair oil, toothpaste, biscuits, sauces, cookies, chips, shampoos, etc. How will you plan to formulate the marketing strategy to draw the attention of the Indian middle-class homemakers?
2. As a regional-brand jewelry house how will you persuade the customers to purchase your brands in the presence of well-established brands of HUL and *Procter & Gamble*?

CASE-7

PENETRATION IN THE INDIAN RURAL MARKET—THE CASE OF HINDUSTAN OILS LTD.*

Dr. Archana Sharma

The view from the 20th floor office of Nishi Bhargava, Area Sales Manager (Soaps), for West Bengal, Hindustan Oils Ltd., was beautiful with the vast expanse of the Hooghly river before her. The sunlight falling on the waters created a kaleidoscope of colours which never failed in captivating her. But that day she was just not in the right frame of mind to enjoy the scenery.

The sales report for the last quarter was on her desk. She had been expecting a below-target figure, but the report was worse than her expectations. She knew that she would have to undertake some drastic measures to influence the sales in the coming quarter.

Nishi Bhargava had joined HOL as a young management trainee after earning a diploma from a reputed Business School 10 years back. Over the years she had risen in the ranks because of her dedication and perseverance. Nishi prided herself for her knack of understanding the distinct critical success factors of each market, that she was placed in charge of. She had an enviable record of never achieving sales below the target set for her territory. Nishi had been instrumental in launching successfully various brands of cooking oils in both the urban and the rural markets.

Nishi's Task

Six months back, she had been transferred to the company's Soaps Division with the brief to replicate the success she had achieved with the parent organization. But Nishi soon realized that trying to establish a brand name in the personal care industry in a highly competitive market dominated by large, cash rich, multinational organizations such as *Hindustan Unilever Limited*, *Pond*'s, and *Proctor & Gamble* was not an easy task. These companies had existed in the market for almost 75 years and, therefore, had managed to capture top of the mind position for their various brands.

In fact, the Indian personal care category had the largest number of brands, i.e., 21, inclusive of *Lux*, *Lifebuoy*, *Fair & Lovely*, *Pond*'s, etc. There were 11 HUL brands in this 21, aggregating ₹3,799 crores of business or 54% of the business volume of personal care category.

*This case has been prepared by Dr. Archana Sharma, Sr. Lecturer (Marketing), Indian Institute of Social Welfare and Business Management, Kolkata, and is based on a fictitious situation to stimulate discussion in an MBA classroom. Resemblance to any person or organization's efforts in the market in the past, present, or future is purely coincidental and unintentional. Published with permission.

Therefore, it was a tough task to even get the prospective customers to include Hindustan Oils' products in their 'choice set'. The company's think-tank felt that the task would be tougher in the highly cluttered urban markets where the customers already had a strong positive association with the existing companies' brands. It had been, therefore, decided in the last Annual Sales Meet that HOL would try to find the 'Fortune at the bottom of the pyramid' and concentrate its efforts in penetrating the rural markets of India.

About the Company

Hindustan Oils Ltd. was a 25 years old company with headquarters in Kolkata and manufacturing units in the five states of West Bengal, Maharashtra, Gujarat, Orissa, and Madhya Pradesh, and sales offices across India.

It manufactured and sold vegetable oils extracted from mustard, groundnut, and sunflower since its inception. Since the last two years they were also preparing oils from corn and soybeans. Its several brands of vegetable oil were household names across India and Indian housewives. The customers rated the quality of the cooking oil as very high. The company had been successful in capturing and maintaining 65% of the edible oil market in India.

Five years back, the strategic planners of the company decided to diversify their business and entered into the 'personal care and hygiene' industry. New brands of soap, shampoo, and conditioner were launched across India. Two years down the line, the product-mix was extended to include bathing gel and deodorants.

About the Industry

The personal hygiene market in India generated total revenues of $1.5 billion in 2008, representing a compound annual growth rate (CAGR) of 3.5% for the period spanning 2004–2008.The per capita expenditure on personal care products in India was currently the lowest, but the fastest growing among the other BRIC economies. The constant urge among Indians to maximize leisure time at home and also the high costs of professional personal care services had been instrumental in creating a demand for personal care products which could recreate professional quality, while offering the advantage of at-home usage.

As of 2009, Indian consumers in the first income quintile allocated at least a third of what they spent on their grooming needs on styling products and were expected to contribute the most towards the growth of styling products over the next five years.

About the Territory (Rural West Bengal)

Nishi was going through some research reports generated by her company. Her eyes were stuck to the following self-explanatory graphs.

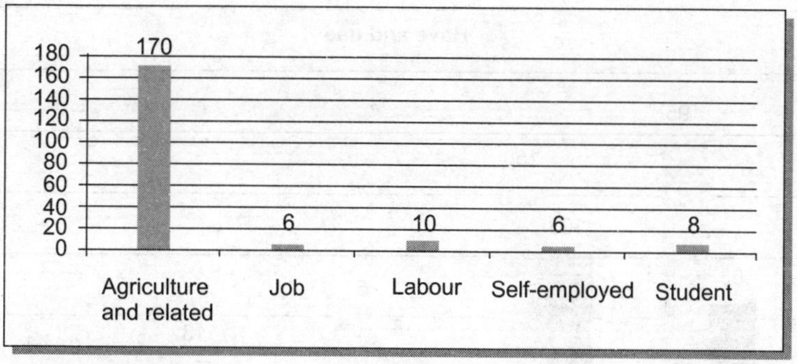

Figure C.24 Occupation pattern of villagers in Nishi's territory

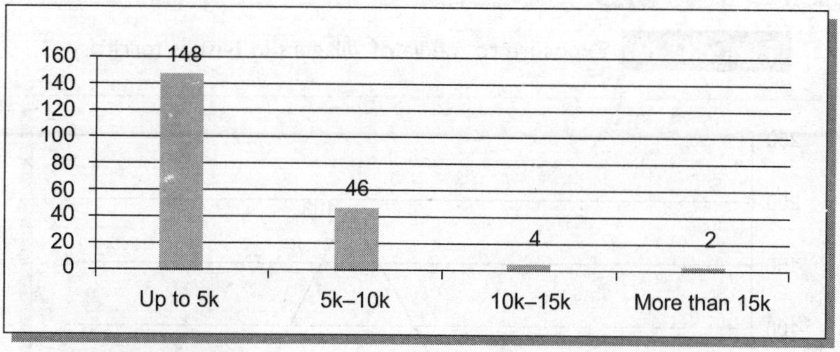

Figure C.25 Income pattern of villagers in Nishi's territory

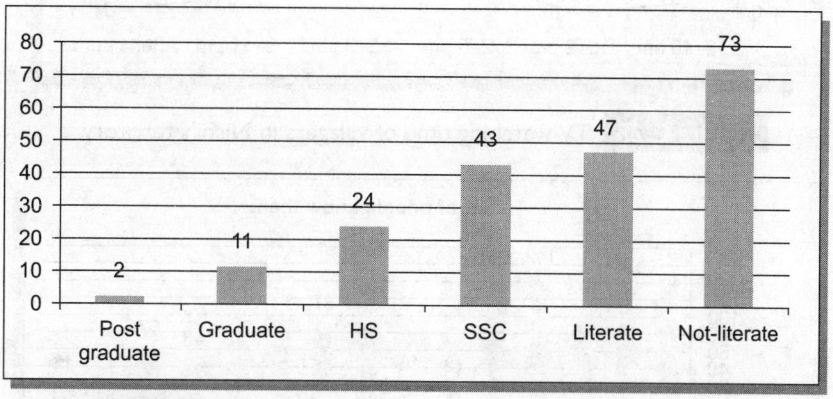

Figure C.26 Educational pattern of villagers in Nishi's territory

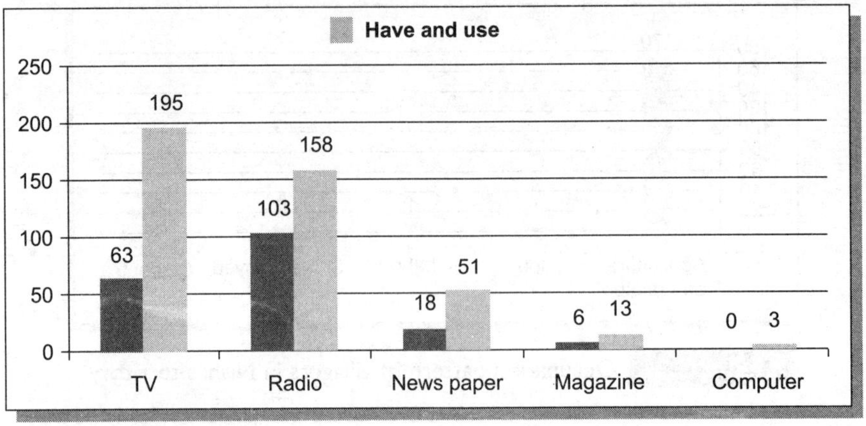

Figure C.27 Exposure to media of villagers in Nishi's territory

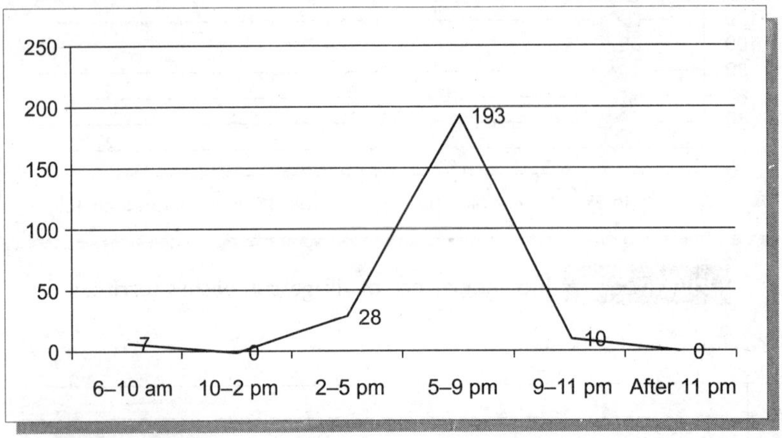

Figure C.28 TV watching time of villagers in Nishi's territory

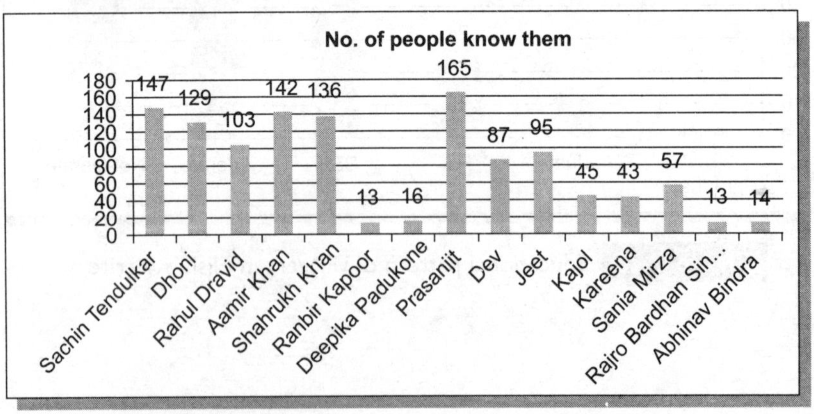

Figure C.29 Popular celebrities in Nishi's territory

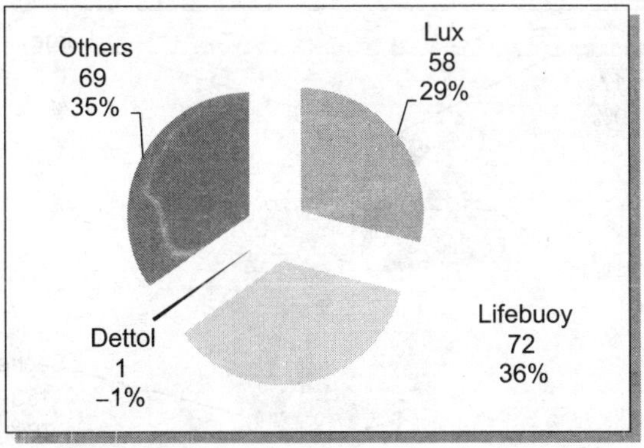

Figure C.30 Popular toilet soaps in Nishi's territory

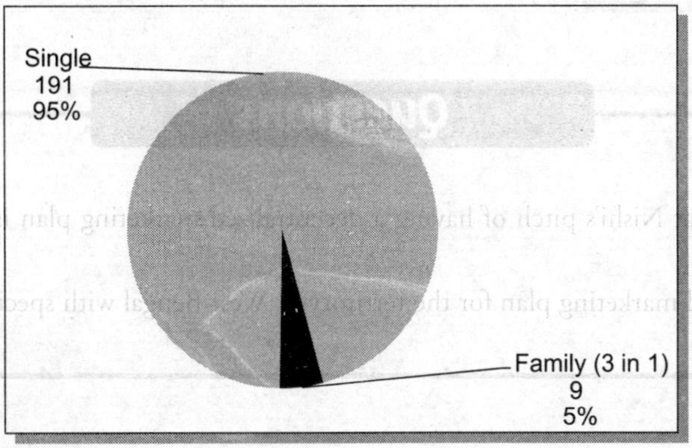

Figure C.31 Preferred pack size of toilet soaps in Nishi's territory

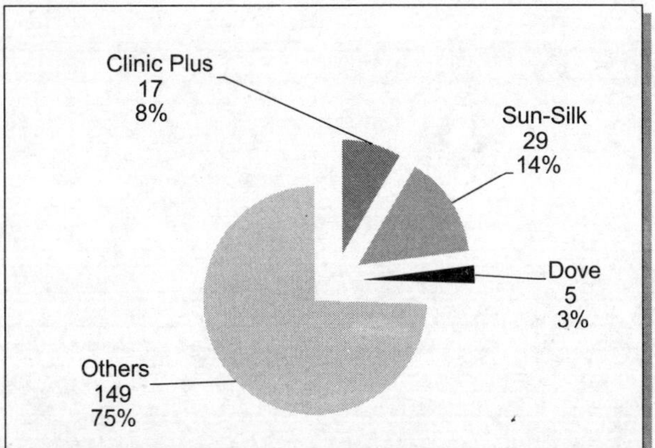

Figure C.32 Popular shampoos in Nishi's territory

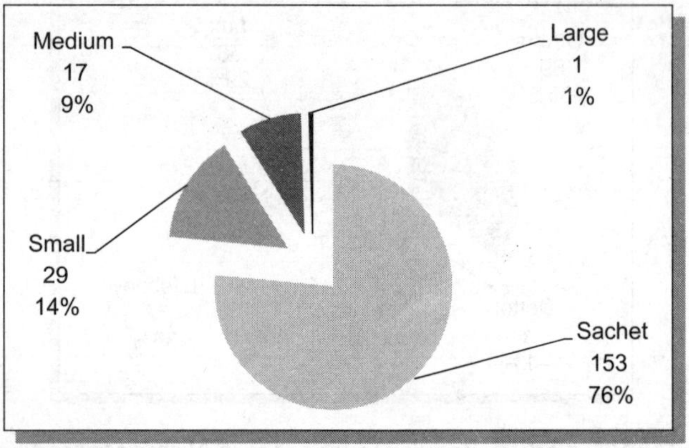

Figure C.33 Preferred pack size of shampoos in Nishi's territory

Questions

1. Do you think that Nishi's pitch of having a decentralized marketing plan is right? Give reasons for your answer.
2. Prepare a detailed marketing plan for the territory of West Bengal with special emphasis on the rural segment

References

Chapter 1

Engel, J.F., Blackwell, R.D., and Miniard, P.W., *Consumer Behavior*, The Dryden Press, 1995.

http://www.articles.economictimes.indiatimes.com/2011-08-09/news/29867320_1_rajan-anandan-e-commerce-internet-users, accessed on August 19, 2011.

http://www.martrural.com/corporate_pilot_implementation.htm, downloaded on July 10, 2009.

http://www.ncaer.org/downloads/medialips/press/rajeshshukla-indiasunnysideup.pdf, accessed on July 27, 2010.

http://www.news.bbc.co.uk/2/hi/business/7957671.stm, downloaded on July 10, 2009.

http://www.thehindubusinessline.com/catalyst/2003/05/29/stories/2003052900020100.htm, downloaded on July 10, 2009.

http://www.thuyha-management.blogspot.com/2008/04/unilever-in-india-hindustan-levers.html, accessed on August 20, 2011.

http://www.210.212.230.219/dde/downloads/markiv_rm.pdf, accessed on August 20, 2011.

Karnani, Aneel, "Fortune at the bottom of the pyramid: A mirage," *California Management Review*, Summer 2007.

Loudon, D.L. and Della Bitta, A.J., *Consumer Behaviour*, fourth edition, Tata Mcgraw-Hill, 2002.

NCAER reports, 2003, 2006, 2010.

"Product market study: Consumer behaviour in India," MATRADE Chennai, October 2005.

Schiffman, J.B. and Kanuk, Lealie Lazar, *Consumer Behavior*, sixth edition, Prentice-Hall, 1997.

Singh, Namrata, "Value vaulters emerge as companies push for premium products," *The Times of India*, April 23, 2011.

Solomon, M.R., *Consumer Behavior*, third edition, Prentice-Hall, Englewood Cliffs, NJ, 1996.

Chapter 2

Annual Report of ITC Limited, 2004.

Higgs, Robert, "From central planning to the market—The American transition, 1945–1947," *The Journal of Economic History*, September 1, 1999.

Hines, Andy, "Consumer trends in three different worlds," *The Futurist*, July–August, 2008.

http://www.countercurrents.org/dsharma210111.htm, accessed on March 12, 2011.

http://www.en.wikipedia.org/wiki/ASEAN, accessed on April 23, 2011.

http://www.en.wikipedia.org/wiki/North_American_Free_Trade_Agreement, accessed on April 23, 2011.

http://www.en.wikipedia.org/wiki/South_Asian_Free_Trade_Area, accessed on April 23, 2011.

http://www.independent.co.uk/travel/news-and-advice/news-israeli-airline-to-fly-on-sabbath-731849.html, accessed on March 12, 2011.

http://www.indianexpress.com/ie/daily/19990305/ige05002.html, accessed on March 12, 2011.

http://www.itcportal.com, accessed on March 12, 2011.

http://www.nasscom.in/upload/68117/NASSCOM-Mercer-Gender-Inclusivity-Report.pdf, accessed on April 23, 2011.

http://www.planningcommission.nic.in/reports/sereport/ser/stdy_ict/4_e-choupal%20.pdf, accessed on March 12, 2011.

NCAER study, 1995.

Ray, Sandipan, "Structure of rural markets for achieving vertical coordination in the Indian food chain," *India Development Foundation.*

Sachs, Jeffrey and Woo, Wing Thye, "Structural factors in the economic reforms of China, Eastern Europe, and the former Soviet Union," *Economic Policy*, vol. 9, no. 18 (Apr), 1994, pp. 102–145.

Sethi, Ashok, "Asian Consumer Trends," TNS, December 2007.

Sheth, J.N. and Mittal, B., *Customer Behavior: A Managerial Perspective*, second edition, Thomson/South-Western, Ohio, 2004.

Sivakumar, S., Workshop on scaling up ICT for poverty alleviation in India, Indian Institute of Management, Ahmedabad, February 26–27, 2004.

Chapter 3

http://www.chillibreeze.com/articles/Indian-children.asp, accessed on March 30, 2011.

http://www.thehoot.org/web/home/searchdetail.php?sid=1268&bg=1, accessed on October 8, 2010.

Thorelli, Hans B., Performance audits: The MNC through the glasses of the LDC, *International Marketing Strategy*, third edition, Pergamon Press, Oxford, England, 1990, pp. 605–617.

Verma, D.P.S. and Nanda, Shashi, "Impact of consumerism on marketing practices: A study in national capital region," *Journal of Advances in Management Research*, vol. 4, no. 1, 2007.

Chapter 4

Fennell, G., "Consumers perception of product use situations," *Journal of Marketing*, April 1978

Greene, D. and Lepper, M.R., "How to turn play into work," *Psychology Today*, vol. 8, no. 4, 1974, pp. 49–54.

http://www.experiment-resources.com/overjustification-effect.html, accessed on February 25, 2011.

http://www.grin.com/en/e-book/17220/the-importance-to-marketers-to-understand-human-motivation, accessed on February 25, 2011.

http://www.learnmax.in/Psychology-Basics/Horney-s-Approach.html, accessed on February 25, 2011.

http://www.webspace.ship.edu/cgboer/adler.html, accessed on February 25, 2011.

Schiffman, J.B. and Kanuk, Lealie Lazar, *Consumer Behavior*, sixth edition, Prentice-Hall, 1997.

Sheth, J.N. and Mittal, B., *Customer Behavior: A Managerial Perspective*, second edition, Thomson/South-Western, Ohio, 2004.

Sheth, J.N., Newman, B.I., and Gross, B.L., "Why we buy what we buy: A theory of consumption values," *Journal of Business Research*, vol. 22, 1991, pp. 159–170.

Ward, Lorna A., Cain, Owen L., Mullally, Ryan A., Holliday, Kathryn S., Wernham, Aaron G.H., Baillie, Paul D., and Greenfield, Sheila M., "Health beliefs about bottled water: A qualitative study," *BMC Public Health*, vol. 9, no. 196, 2009.

Zeims, D., "The morphological approach for unconscious consumer motivation research," *Journal of Advertising Research*, June, 2004.

Chapter 5

http://www.graphicdesign.spokanefalls.edu/tutorials/process/gestaltprinciples/gestaltprinc.htm, accessed on March 25, 2011.

http://www.marketingpractice.blogspot.com/2006/11/ganga-soap-rip.html, accessed on October 24, 2010.

http://www.mouthshut.com, accessed on October 24, 2010.

http://www.nt.walletwatch.com/ascerc/History.asp?CompanyCode=12520018&companyname=Godrej+Industries+Ltd, accessed on October 24, 2010.

http://www.people.usd.edu/~schieber/coglab/WebersLaw.html, accessed on March 25, 2011.

http://www.tanishq.co.in/tanishq-story, accessed on October 24, 2010.

Schiffman, J.B. and Kanuk, Lealie Lazar, *Consumer Behavior*, sixth edition, Prentice-Hall, 1997.

Sheth, J.N. and Mittal, B., *Customer Behavior: A Managerial Perspective*, second edition, Thomson/South-Western, Ohio, 2004.

Solomon, Michael R., *Consumer Behavior*, eighth edition, Prentice-Hall, 2009.

Chapter 6

Aaker, J.L., "Dimensions of brand personality," *Journal of Marketing Research*, vol. 34, August, 1997, pp. 347–356.

Cattel, R.B., Eber, H.W., and Tasuaka, M.M., *Handbook of the Sixteen Personality Factors Questionnaire*, Institute for Personality and Ability Testing, Champaign, IL, 1970, pp.16–17.

Dolich, Ira J., "Congruence relationships between self images and product brands," *Journal of Marketing Research*, vol. 6, no. 1, 1969.

http://www.biggerindia.com/business/4420-do-celebrity-endorsements-work.html?print, accessed on May 23, 2011.

http://www.golf.about.com/b/2009/12/13/accenture-fires-tiger-woods.htm, accessed on November 6, 2010.

http://www.marketingpractice.blogspot.com/2006/04/reid-taylor-bond-with-best.html, accessed on April 2, 2011.

http://www.msnbc.msn.com/id/34406263/, accessed on November 6, 2010.

http://www.newsroom.accenture.com/article_display.cfm?article_id=4915, accessed on November 6, 2010.

http://www.oppapers.com/essays/Influence-Personality-Consumer-Behavior/180277, accessed on April 2, 2011.

Keller, K.L., "Conceptualizing, measuring and managing customer-based brand equity," *Journal of Marketing*, vol. 57, 1993, pp. 1–22.

McCracken, Grant, "Who is the celebrity endorser? Cultural foundations of the endorsement process," *Journal of Consumer Research*, vol. 16, no. 3, 1989, pp. 310–321.

Schiffman, J.B. and Kanuk, Lealie Lazar, *Consumer Behavior*, sixth edition, Prentice-Hall, 1997.

Sheth, J.N. and Mittal, B., *Customer Behavior: A Managerial Perspective*, second edition, Thomson/South-Western, Ohio, 2004.

Chapter 7

Domjan, M. and Burkhard, B., *The Principles of Learning and Behavior*, second edition, Brooks/Cole, Pacific Grove, CA, 1986.

Hoch, S.J. and Deighton, J., "Managing what consumers learn from experience," *Journal of Marketing*, vol. 53, 1989, pp. 1–20.

Holyoak, Keith J., Koh Kyunghee, and Nisbett, Richard E., "A theory of conditioning: Inductive learning within rule-based default hierarchies," *Psychological Review*, vol. 96, no. 2, 1989, pp. 315–340.

http://www.managementconsultingcourses.com/Lesson18Learning.pdf, accessed on February 3, 2011.

http://www.scribd.com/doc/20005638/Consumer-Behaviour-6-Learning, accessed on February 3, 2011.

http://www.steconomice.uoradea.ro/anale/volume/2008/v4-management-marketing/210.pdf, accessed on February 3, 2011.

Maggi noodles: A 25 year journey in the Indian market, rajeshaithal.blogspot.com/.../maggi-noodles-25-year-journey-in-indian.html, accessed on March 13, 2011.

Nicorette: for every cigarette, there is nicorette, http:// www.marketingpractice.blogspot.com/2011/01/nicorette-for-every-cigarette-there-is.html, accessed on March 13, 2011.

Chapter 8

Baron, Robert A., Branscombe, Nyla R., and Byrne, Donn R., *Social Psychology*, 12th edition, Pearson, 2008.

Chakrabarti, Asabari, "More or less," *The Times of India*, February 22, 2011.

Chhabra, Shruti Seth, "Candies take off," *The Times of India*, February 22, 2011.

Dennis, Everrete E. and Wartella, Ellan A. (Eds.), *American Communication Research: The Remembered History*, Lawrence Erlbaum Associates, Mahwah, NJ, 1996.

Engel, J.F., Blackwell, R.D., and Miniard, P.W., *Consumer Behaviour*, fifth edition, The Dryden Press, 1994.

http://www.en.wikipedia.org/wiki/Theory_of_reasoned_action, accessed on March 6, 2011.

Kotler, P., *Marketing Management: Planning, Implementation and Control*, sixth edition, Prentice Hall of India, 1994.

Lavidge, Robert J. and Steiner, Gary A., "A model for predictive measurement of advertising effectiveness," *Journal of Marketing*, vol. 25 (October), 1961, pp. 59–62.

Mower, J.C., *Consumer Behaviour*, McMillan Publishing Co., 1987.

Runyon, K.E. and Steward, D.E, *Consumer Behaviour*, third edition, Merill Publishing Co., 1987.

Schiffman, J.B. and Kanuk, Lealie Lazar, *Consumer Behaviour*, fifth edition, Prentice Hall of India, 1995.

Solomon, M.R., *Consumer Behaviour*, Allyn and Bacon, MA, 1994.

UNAIDS, Government of India and Clinton Foundation sign agreement to scale up HIV care and treatment, http://www.data.unaids.org/media/press-release02/pr_clinton_indiangovernment_29sept04_en.pdf, downloaded on October 12, 2011.

Wilkie, W.L., *Consumer Behaviour*, John Wiley & Sons Inc., 1986.

Chapter 9

Agarwal, Vishant V., "Nostalgia on speed," *The Times of India*, February 8, 2011.

Beatty, Sharon E., Kahle, Lynn R., Homer, Pamela, and Giltvedt, Anders, "A Cross-Cultural Exploration of the VALS Typology," in: Pitts, Robert E., Sheth, Jagdish, and Valencia, Umberto (Eds.), *Cultural and Subcultural Influences in Consumer Behavior*, in press.

Beatty, Sharon E., Kahle, Lynn R., Homer, Pamela, and Misra, Shekhar, "Alternative measurement approaches to consumer values: The list of values and the rokeach value survey," *Psychology and Marketing*, vol. 2, no. 3, 1986, pp. 181–200.

Becker, Boris W. and Conner, P.E., "Personal values and the heavy users of mass media," *Journal of Advertising Research*, vol. 21, 1981, pp. 37–43.

Berrien, F.K., "Japanese and American values," *International Journal of Psychology*, vol. 71, 1966, pp. 129–142.

Brand culture failures: Kellogg's in India, http://www.brandfailures.blogspot.com/2006/11/brand-culture-failures-kelloggs-in.html, accessed on November 15, 2006.

Burnett, Ken, *The Project Management Paradigm*, Springer Books, 1998.

Feather, Norman T., *Values in Education and Society*, Free Press, New York, 1975.

Holman, Rebecca, *A Values and Lifestyles Perspective on Human Behavior*, in: Pitts, Robert E., Jr. and Woodside, Arch G. (Eds.), *Personal Values and Consumer Psychology*, Lexington Books, Lexington, MA, 1984.

Homer, Pamela M. and Kahle, Lynn R., "A structural equation test of the value-attitude behavior hierarchy," *Journal of Personality and Social Psychology*, in press.

http://www.context.org/ICLIB/IC03/SRIVALS.htm, accessed on November 12, 2009.

http://www.strategicbusinessinsights.com/vals/academics/permission.shtml, accessed on November 12, 2009.

Kahle, Lynn R., *Attitudes and Social Adaptation: A Person-Situation Interaction Approach* Pergamon, Oxford, UK, 1984.

Kahle, Lynn R., Beatty, Sharon E., and Homer, Pamela M., "Alternative measurement approaches to consumer values: The list of values (LOV) and values and lifestyle segmentation (VALS)," *Journal of Consumer Research*, vol. 13 (December), 1986, pp. 405–409.

Kahle, Lynn R. and Eisert, Debra C., "Social values in the American workplace," in: Flamholtz, Eric, Randle, Yvonne and Sackmann, Sonja (Eds.), *Future Directions in Human Resource Management*, UCLA Publications, Los Angeles, 1986, pp. 203–223.

Kahle, Lynn R. (Ed.), *Social Values and Social Change: Adaptation to Life in America*, Praeger, New York, 1983.

Kahle, Lynn R., "Social values in the eighties: A special issue," *Psychology and Marketing*, vol. 2, Winter 1985, pp. 231–237.

Kahle, Lynn R., "The nine nations of North America and the value basis of geographic segmentation," *Journal of Marketing*, vol. 50 (April), 1986, pp. 37–47.

Kellogg's failure in India, http://www.suraen.wordpress.com/2010/09/13/kellogg%E2%80%99s-failure-in-india, accessed on September 13, 2010.

Kotler, P., *Marketing Management: Analysis, Planning, Implementation and Control*, Prentice Hall of India Pvt. Ltd., Delhi, 1987.

Kotler, P., *Principles of Marketing*, Prentice Hall of India Pvt. Ltd., Delhi, 1987.

Loudon, David L. and Della Bitta, Albert J., Consumer Behaviour, TMH Publications, 2002.

Maslow, Abraham H., *Motivation and Personality*, Harper, New York, 1954.

McQuarrie, Edward F. and Langmeyer, Daniel, "Using values to measure attitudes toward discontinuous innovations," *Psychology and Marketing*, vol. 2 (Winter), 1985, pp. 239–252.

Meheer, Thakare, Branding mishaps: Kellogg's India venture a failure, http://www.communications.webalue.com/2009/09/14/branding-mishaps-kelloggs-india-venture-a-failure, accessed on September 14, 2009.

Mitchell, Arnold, *The Nine American Life Styles*, Warner, New York, 1983.

Pitts, Robert E., Jr. and Woodside, Arch G. (Eds.), *Personal Values and Consumer Psychology*, Lexington Books, Lexington, MA, 1984.

Riesman, David, Nathan, Glazer, and Revil, Denney, *The Lonely Crowd*, Yale University Press, New Haven, CT, 1950.

Rokeach, Milton, *The Nature of Human Values*, Free Press, New York, 1973.

Schiffman, J.B. and Kanuk, Lealie Lazar, *Consumer Behavior*, Prentice Hall of India Pvt. Ltd., Delhi, 1988.

The memory market, *The Times of India* report, February 8, 2011.

Veroff, Joseph, Elizabeth, Douvan, and Kulka, Richard A., *The Inner American*, Basic Books, New York, 1981.

Wainer, Howard, "Estimating coefficients in linear models: It don't make no never mind," *Psychological Bulletin*, vol. 83 (March), 1976, pp. 213–217.

Wang, M.W. and Stanley, Julian C., "Differential weighing: A review of methods and empirical studies," *Review of Educational Research*, vol. 40, 1970, pp. 663–705.

Zavalloni, M., "Values," in: Triandis, Harry C. and Brislin, Richard W. (Eds.), *Handbook of Cross-Cultural Psychology*, vol. 5, Allyn and Bacon, Boston, 1980.

Ziman, John, *Public Knowledge: An Essay Concerning the Social Dimension of Science*, Cambridge University Press, Cambridge, UK, 1968.

Chapter 10

Bullis, D., Selling to India's consumer market, Quorum Books, Westport, CT, 1997.

Eckhardt, Giana M. and Mahi, Humaira, "India will survive: Understanding the role of consumer agency in the globalization process in emerging markets," *Journal of Macromarketing*, Sage Publications, 2004.

http://www.infosciencetoday.org/type/research-type/cross-cultural-issues-in-the-21st-century-marketing.html, accessed on October 22, 2010.

http://www.i18nguy.com/translations.html, accessed on April 20, 2011.

Joy, A. and Wallendorf, M., The development of consumer culture in the third world, in: Consumption and macromarketing, Belk, R.W., Dholakia, N. and Venkatesh, A. (Eds.), South-Western, Cincinnati, OH, 1996, pp. 104–142.

Khan, Habibullah, Facebook banned in Pakistan, http://www.abcnews.go.com/Technology/International/facebook-banned-pakistan-prophet-muhammad-sketch-competition/story?id=10688625, May 19, 2010.

Kluckhohn, Clyde, *Culture and Behavior*, Free Press of Glencoe, 1962.

Mintz, S.W., Swallowing modernity, in: Golden arches east: McDonald's in East Asia, Watson, J.L. (Ed.), Stanford University Press, Stanford, CA, 1997, pp. 183–200.

Tylor, Edward B., *Primitive Culture* (reissued by Cambridge University Press, 2010, ISBN 9781108017527), 1871.

Chapter 11

Bachmann, Gwen R., Deborah, R. John, and Rao, Akshay R., "Children's susceptibility to peer group influence: An exploratory investigation," *Advances in Consumer Research*, vol. 20, in: Leigh, McAlister and Michael L., Rothschild (Eds.), Provo, UT: Association for Consumer Research, 1993, pp. 463–468

Bearden, William O. and Etzel, Michael J., "Reference group influence on product and brand purchase decisions," *Journal of Consumer Research*, vol. 9 (September), 1982, pp. 183–194.

Boost is the secret of our energy, February 21, 2007, http://www.marketingpractice.blogspot.com/2007/01/boost-is-secret-of-our-energy.html, accessed on January 21, 2011.

Chapman, David and Theo, Cowdell, *New Public Sector Marketing*, FT Prentice Hall, Essex.

Childers, Terry L. and Rao Akshay R, "The influence of familial and peer-based reference groups on consumer decisions," *Journal of Consumer Research*, vol. 19 (September), 1992, pp. 198–211.

Guzmán, Francisco, (2005) "Brand building towards social values: Associating to public goods," Universitat Ramon Llull – ESADE, Barcelona, Spain, unpublished dissertation.

http://www.boost.com, accessed on August 21, 2010.

http://www.en.wikipedia.org/wiki/Boost_(health_food), accessed on August 21, 2010.

http://www.jeremywaite.wordpress.com/2010/04/27/top-10-negative-celebrity-role-models/, accessed on October 12, 2011.

Lovelock, Christopher H. and Weinberg, Charles, *Marketing for Public and Nonprofit Managers*, John Wiley & Sons, New York, NY, 1984.

Impact of celebrity endorsement on a brand, http://www.chillibreeze.com/articles/Celebrity-endorsement.asp, accessed on January 21, 2011.

Mayur suitings on expansion mode, February 13, 2007, http://www.thehindubusinessline.com/2007/02/14/stories/2007021403510500.htm, accessed on January 21, 2011.

Mayur suitings signs on Salman, February 14, 2007, exchange4media News Service.

Mayur suitings: Stars ki pasand, February 20, 2007, http://www.marketingpractice.blogspot.com/2007/02/mayur-suitings-stars-ki-pasand.html, accessed on January 21, 2011.

Park, C. Whan and Lessig, V. Parker, "Students and housewives: Differences in susceptibility to reference group influences," *Journal of Consumer Research*, vol. 4 (September), 1977, pp. 102–110.

Paul, Peter J. and Olson, Jerry C., *Consumer Behaviour and Marketing Strategy*, Tata Mcgraw Hill India Pvt. Ltd, 2005.

Scalas, Jennifer Edson and Bettman, James R., "You are what you eat: The influence of reference groups on consumers' connections to brands," *Journal of Consumer Psychology*, vol. 13, no. 3, 2003, pp. 339–348.

Solomon, Micheal R., *Consumer Behaviour: Buying, Having and Being*, Pearson Education, 2005.

Chapter 12

Bapna, Amit, "Code uncode," *The Economic Times*, October 12, 2011.

Engel, James F., Blackwell, Roger, and Kollatt, D., *Consumer Behavior*, CBS College Publishing, New York, 1986.

Loudon, D.L. and Della Bitta, A.J., *Consumer Behavior, Concepts and Applications*, McGraw Hill, 1984.

March, J.G. and Simon, H.A., *Organizations*, John Wiley, New York, 1959.

Scanzoni, John H., *Shaping Tomorrow's Family: Theory and Policy for the 21st Century*, Sage Publication, 1983

Schiffman, Leon G. and Kanuk, Leslie Lazar, *Consumer Behavior*, Prentice Hall Inc., Englewood Cliffs, 1987.

Sheth, Jagdish N., The theory of family buying decisions, http://www.jagsheth.net/docs/A%20Theory%20of%20Family%20Buying%20Decisions.pdf, accessed on January 1, 2011.

Chapter 13

Berkman, Harold W. and Gilson, Christopher, *Consumer Behaviour: Concepts and Strategies*, South-Western Educational Publishing, March 1986.

Chopra, Komal, Pidilite industries: Fevicol success story, http://www.ibscdc.org/Case_Studies/Marketing/Marketing%20Strategies/MKS0072P.htm, accessed on March 6, 2011.

http://www.gizmag.com/refrigerator-ruaral-india-chotukool/13680, accessed on March 16, 2011.

http://www.marketingpractice.blogspot.com/2007/02/scotch-brite-makes-cleaning-fast-and.html, accessed on March 4, 2011.

http://www.marketingpractice.blogspot.com/2007/09/fevistik-clean-sticking.html, accessed on March 6, 2011.

http://www.slideshare.net/amit_k102/product-branding-of-fevistik-and-komfo-by-amit-singh, accessed on March 6, 2011.

Mukherjee, Writankar and Mamgain, Pramugdha, "LG, Godrej, Panasonic, Mirc & Samsung roll out newer, tweaked products for professionals," *The Economic Times*, October 14, 2011.

Ray, Achintyarup and Maitra, Subhro, "Train of memories," *The Times of India*, March 6, 2011.

Robertson, Thomas S., "The process of innovation and the diffusion of innovation," *The Journal of Marketing*, vol. 31, no. 1 (Jan.), 1967, pp. 14–19.

Rogers, Everett M., *Diffusion of Innovations*, fifth edition, Free Press, New York, 2003.

Schiffman, Leon, G. and Kanuk, Leslie Lazar, *Consumer Behaviour*, Prentice Hall of India Pvt. Ltd., Delhi, 1988.

Chapter 14

Engel, J.F., Blackwell, R.D., and Miniard, P.W., *Consumer Behaviour*, fifth edition, The Dryden Press, 1993.

http://www.blackberry.com, accessed on January 22, 2011.

http://www.marketingpractice.blogspot.com/2007/02/blackberry-smallsmart-stylish.html, accessed on January 22, 2011.

http://www.uie.com/publications/whitepapers/ImpulseBuying.pdf, accessed on January 22, 2011.

http://www.wikipedia.com, accessed on January 22, 2011.

Indians search for the most cheap air ticket, *The Times of India*, March 16, 2011.

Kotler et al., *Consumer Behaviour* and *A Model of Consumer Behaviour*, Chapter 7, Pearson Education, 2004, pp. 242–244.

Loudon, D.L. and Della Bitta, A.J., *Consumer Behavior: Concepts and Applications*, McGraw-Hill, London, 2002.

Majumdar, Ramanuj, *Consumer Behaviour—Insights from Indian Market*, PHI India Pvt. Ltd., 2010.

Mower, J.C., *Consumer Behaviour*, MacMillan Publishing Co., 1987.

Redefining communication—A consumer connect initiative, *The Times of India*, March 13, 2011.

Runyon, K.E. and Steward, D.E., *Consumer Behaviour*, third edition, Merill Publishing Co., 1987.

Schiffman, Leon G. and Kanuk, Leslie Lazar, *Consumer Behaviour*, sixth edition, Prentice Hall India Pvt. Ltd., 2004.

Wilkie, W.L, *Consumer Behaviour*, John Wiley & Sons Inc., 1986.

Chapter 15

Andeason, A.R., *Attitudes and Consumer Behaviour: A Decision Model in New Research in Marketing*, Preston, 1965.

Bagozzi, Richard P., Gürhan-Canli, Zeynep, and Priester, Joseph R., *The Social Psychology of Consumer Behaviour*, in: Applying Social Psychology, Sutton, Stephen (Ed.), Open University Press, Buckingham, 2002.

Belch, G.E. and Landon, E.L, "Discriminate validity of a product-anchored self-concept measure," *Journal of Marketing Research*, vol. 14, 1977, pp. 252–256.

Berlyne, D.F, "Novelty, complexity and hedonic value perception," *Psychophysics*, vol. 8 (November), 1970, pp. 278–286.

Cooper, C.P., *Tourism: Principles and Practice*, Pitman, London, 1993.

Dusenberry, J.S., *Income, Saving and the Theory of Consumer Behaviors*, Harvard University Press, Cambridge, 1949.

Du Plessis, P.J., Rousseau, Deon, Rousseau, G.G., Blem, Norman, and Boshoff Christo, *Buyer Behaviour: A Multi-Cultural Approach*, International Thomson Publishing, South Africa, 1999.

El-Emam, Hesham El-Sayed, "Consumer behaviour models in tourism: Analysis study," *Journal of King Saud University* (Tourism and Archaeology), vol. 21, no. 1, 2009.

Engel, J., Kollat, D., and Miniard, P., *Consumer Behaviour*, Drydren Press, Hinsdale, IL, 2002.

Ferber, Robert, "Consumer economics: A survey," *Journal of Economics Literature*, December 1973, pp. 1303–1342.

Gilbert, D.C., *An Examination of the Consumer Behavior Process Related to Tourism*, in: Cooper, C.P. (Ed.), Progress in tourism, recreation and hospitality management, Belhaven Press, London, 1991, pp. 78–105.

Hirschman, Elizabeth C. and Mills, Michael K., "Shoppers use to pick store," *Journal of Advertising Research*, vol. 20, no. 1, 1980.

Horton, R.L., *Buyer Behaviour: A decision Making Approach*, Charles E. Merrill Publishing Company, Columbus, 1984.

Howard, J.A. and Sheth, J.N., *The Theory of Buyer Behavior*, John Wiley and Sons, New York, 1969, pp. 9–28.

http://www.brandbhai.com/relaunch-of-frooti-the-digen-verma-campaign, accessed on August 23, 2010.

http://www.churcher.com/FOSM/foundations-of-senior-management-10013.htm

http://www.ingrimayne.com/econ/FiscalDead/PermIncome.html, accessed on May 21, 2011.

http://www.marketingpractice.blogspot.com/2006/03/frooti-fresh-n-juicy.html, accessed on August 23, 2010.

Izard, C.E., Emotion—cognition relationship and human development, in: Izard, C.E., Kegan, J., Zajonc, R.B. (Eds.), *Emotions, Cognition, and Behaviour*, Cambridge University Press, Cambridge, England, 1984, pp. 229–263.

Izard, C.E., Human Emotions, Plenum Press, New York, 1977.

Katona, G., *Aspirations and Affluence Comparative Studies in the USA and Western Europe*, McGraw Hill, NY, 1971.

Katz, Danie, "The Functional Approach to the Study of Attitudes" *Public Opinion Q*, vol. 24 (summer), 1960, pp. 16–204.

Lunn, J.A., *Consumer Decision Process Models in Models of Buyer Behaviour*, in: Sheth, Jagdish N., (Ed.), Harper and Row, New York, 1974, pp. 34–69.

Loudon, D.L. and Della Bitta, A.J., *Consumer Behavior: Concepts and Applications*, McGraw-Hill, London, 1993.

Loudon, D.L. and Della Bitta, A.J., *Consumer Behavior: Concepts and Applications*, McGraw-Hill, London, 2002.

Majumdar, Ramanuj, *Consumer Behaviour: Insights from Indian Market*, PHI Pvt. Ltd., 2010.17.

Marshall, A., *Principle of Economics*, vol. 1, Macmillian, London, 1890.

Nicosia, F., *Consumer Decision Processes*, Prentice Hall, Englewood Cliffs, 1966.

Nicosia, F.M. and Robert, W., "Consumer behavior toward sociology of consumption," *Journal of Consumer Research*, 1976.

Oliver, Richard L., "A cognitive model of the antecedents and consequences of satisfaction decisions," *Journal of Marketing Research*, November, 1980, pp. 460–469.

Schiffman, J.B. and Kanuk, Lealie Lazar, *Consumer Behavior*, sixth edition, Prentice Hall, 1997, p. 446.

Sheth, J.N., Newman, B.I. and Gross, B.L., "Why we buy what we buy: A theory of consumer behavior," *Journal of Business Research*, vol. 22, 1991, pp. 159–170.

Solomon, Michael R., *Consumer Behaviour*, third edition, Prentice Hall, Englewood Cliffs, NJ, 1996.

Westbrook, Robert A. and Oliver, Richard L.O., "The dimensionality of consumption emotion pattern and consumer satisfaction," *Journal of Consumer Research*, vol. 18, 1991, pp. 84–91.

Chapter 16

Aggarwal, Manoj K., Burger, Philip C., and Reid, David A., *Readings in Industrial Marketing*, Prentice-Hall Inc., Englewood Cliffs, New Jersey, 1986.

Alexander, Ralph, Cross, James, and Hill, Richard M., *Industrial Marketing*, third edition, Homewood Irwin, Illinois, 1963.

Ames, Charles B. and Hlavaack, James D., *Managerial Marketing for Industrial Firms*, Random House Business Division, New York, 1984, pp. 247–265.

Choffray, Jean-Maris and Lilien, Gary L., *Market Planning for New Industrial Products*, John Wiley & Sons, New York, 1980.

Corey, Raymond E., *Industrial Marketing, Cases and Concepts,* third edition, Prentice Hall Inc., Englewood Cliffs, New Jersey, 1983.

Dodge, Robert H., *Industrial Marketing,* McGraw Hill, New York, 1970.

Hutt, Michael D. and Speh, Thomas W., *Industial Marketing Management*, Dryden Press, Chicago, 1981.

Kotler, Philip, *Marketing Management—Analysis, Planning, and Control,* fifth edition, Prentice-Hall Inc., Englewood Cliffs, New Jersey, 1984.

Robinson, Patrick J., Faris, Charles W., and Wind, Yoram, *Industrial Buying and Creative Marketing,* Allyn & Bacon, Boston, 1967.

Sen Gupta, Nandini and Doval, Pankaj, "Japanese Car and Electronics Makers Shut Plants, Assess Damage Auto cos may face parts shortage," *The Times of India*, March 15, 2011.

Sharma, Samidha, "Supply crunch to hit durables cos," *The Times of India*, March 15, 2011.

Sheth, Jagdish, *Journal of Marketing,* vol. 37, October 1973, pp. 50–56.

Webster, Frederick E., *Industrial Management,* second edition, Wiley, New York, 1984.

Webster, Frederick E., Jr. and Wind, Yoram, "A general model for understanding organizational buying behavior," *The Journal of Marketing,* vol. 36, no. 2 (Apr), 1972, pp. 12–19.

Chapter 17

Kotler, Philip, Keller, Kevin Lane, Koshy, Abraham, and Jha, Mithileshwar, *Marketing Management*, 13th edition, 2009, pp. 250–251.

Malhotra, Naresh K., *Marketing Research*: *An Applied Orientation*, fifth edition, pp. 32–660.

Margo: Lost in the neem trees!, http://www.marketingpractice.blogspot.com/2006/02/margolost-in-neem-trees.html, accessed on February 27, 2006.

Pearlpet: Har dil ka pet, http://www.marketingpractice.blogspot.com/2009/04/pearlpet-har-dil-ka-pet.html, accessed on April 30, 2009.

Raghubir, Priya, "Free gift with purchase: Promoting or discounting the brand," *Journal of Consumer Psychology*, vol. 14 (1and 2), 2004, pp. 181–186.

Rao, Venugopal, "Effect of sales promotions on consumer preferences—The moderating role of price perceptions and deal proneness (A study of FMCG products)," *Vilakshan, XIMB Journal of Management*, pp. 2–17.

Ravichandran, K. and Natarajan, S., "Factors determining the brand preference of TV: With special reference to Thoothukudi district in Tamil Nadu," *Indian Journal of Marketing*, vol. xxxiv, no. 4, 2004.

Research says video games are good for teenage girls when parents join the fun: It's caring by sharing, *The Times of India*, February 3, 2011.

Schiffman, Leon G. and Kanuk, Leslie Lazar, *Consumer Behavior*, Prentice Hall, 2007.

Name Index

T

V

W

Z

Subject Index

A

B

C

D

E

F

T

U

V

W